Discovering Christ in Revelation

DISCOVERING CHRIST
IN
REVELATION

Donald S. Fortner

EVANGELICAL PRESS

EVANGELICAL PRESS
Faverdale North Industrial Estate, Darlington, DL3 0PH, England

Evangelical Press USA
P. O. Box 84, Auburn, MA 01501, USA

e-mail: sales@evangelicalpress.org

web: http://www.evangelicalpress.org

First published 2002

British Library Cataloguing in Publication Data available

ISBN 0 85234 487 2

All Scripture quotations are taken from the Authorized / King James Version.

Printed and bound in Great Britain by Creative Print & Design Wales, Ebbw Vale

To my beloved children,
the crown and glory of this father (Prov. 17:6),
William Douglas Hacker
Katherine Faith (Fortner) Hacker
Audrey Grace Hacker
William Stewart Hacker

Contents

Foreword

I have known the author of this volume since we became high-school friends in 1966 in Winston-Salem, North Carolina, USA. He then evidenced great boldness in the things he held dear, and unflinching loyalty to his friends.

Our paths went in different directions afterwards. He commenced his Christian pilgrimage considerably earlier in life than I did. But I later followed him in attending the same Bible college, and in sitting under the pastoral ministry of my father, Ernest W. Parks.

I have been intimately familiar with his ministry since 1984, when I was blessed to have him become a supporter of my own ministry as a missionary in the Caribbean. This familiarity increased when the Lord was pleased to place me in a pastorate just a short distance from where he presently pastors.

I have observed throughout this relationship that he continues to manifest great boldness in the things he holds dear, and unflinching loyalty to his friends. It is granted that these attributes did not always serve him well in his unregenerate state. But they most certainly have served him well since the Lord and Saviour Jesus Christ became his dearest Friend. In the many times I have sat under his ministry, both in person and through the recorded and printed media, I have never heard him devote a message to any subject other than Christ. And never have I witnessed him lacking boldness in proclaiming his Friend, or compromising the truth regarding him.

The same is true in this latest volume from his pen, a commentary on the last book of the Bible entitled *Discovering Christ in Revelation*. The central theme of his exposition is taken from the opening lines of the book of Revelation: 'The Revelation of Jesus Christ, which God gave unto him, to show unto his servants things which must shortly come to pass; and he sent and signified it by his angel unto his servant John' (1:1).

The first chapter of this volume is but a microcosm of what is to follow. Christ is set forth as 'the faithful witness', 'the first begotten of the dead', 'the prince of the kings of the earth', 'him that loved us, and washed us from our sins in his own blood, and made us kings and priests unto God', 'he that liveth', 'he who holds the keys of hell and of death', 'he that holdeth the seven stars in his right hand, who walketh in the midst of the seven golden candlesticks', 'the Lion of the tribe of Judah', 'the Root of David', 'the Lamb slain from the foundation of the world', 'Faithful and True', 'the Word of God', 'King of Kings and Lord of Lords', 'that one who declares, 'Behold, I make all things new', 'Alpha and Omega', 'the Bright and Morning Star', and the one who declares, 'Surely, I come quickly.'

The author ably disproves the view that the book of Revelation is too deep and dark for us to understand. God has emphatically promised in the introduction to this book a blessing to the sincere reader and hearer of it, and to the sincere keeper of its words (1:3). Such are lovers of Christ. They will search for Christ in this book, and be blessed to understand what it teaches regarding him. This commentary should certainly aid them in their search. My only regret regarding this volume is that it was not available when I preached through the book of Revelation some months ago. William Hendriksen's *More Than Conquerors* remains my favourite summary of this book. But the present volume has become my favourite commentary on it.

Daniel E. Parks,
Pastor, Redeemer Baptist Church
Louisville, Kentucky

Introduction

The book of Revelation gives us seven visions of the person and work of Christ in this gospel age. In these seven visions the Lord revealed to John what he had done, is doing and will yet do for his church, in his church and with his church. The whole purpose of the book is to assure God's children in this world of their ultimate conquest over the world, the flesh and the devil. This blessed book is 'the Revelation of Jesus Christ'. By revealing to us who he is and what he does, our Lord calls us ever to look unto him with confident faith and assures us that we are 'more than conquerors through him that loved us'.

The seven visions which John saw and recorded by divine inspiration are set before us in consecutive order in the twenty-two chapters of this book. He saw:

1. Christ in the midst of his churches, the seven golden candlesticks, in this world (chs. 1-3).

2. Christ opening and fulfilling the seven-sealed book of God's sovereign, eternal purpose (chs. 4-7).

3. Christ answering the prayers of his people, protecting them from their enemies and vindicating them by executing the seven trumpets of judgement in his providential rule of the universe (chs. 8-11).

4. Christ and his church persecuted by Satan, world government and false religion (chs. 12-14).

5. Christ sending his angels to pour out the seven vials of his wrath upon the earth (chs. 15-16).

6. Christ's conquest over Babylon, the beast and the false prophet (chs. 17-19).

7. Christ's dominion over, and destruction of, Satan and the glory of the new Jerusalem (chs. 20-22).

These seven visions each cover the whole gospel age from the first to the second coming of Christ. They do not represent different ages, dispensations, or prophetic events. They all tell the same story. They all tell us what our Lord has done, is doing and will yet do for the salvation of his people. The use of the word 'seven' is striking. There are 'seven golden candlesticks', 'seven stars', 'seven seals', 'seven trumpets', 'seven angels' and 'seven vials'. Seven is the number of perfection, completion and satisfaction. And in each of these seven visions, the Holy Spirit assures us of the perfect rule of Christ as the Monarch of the universe for the complete victory and eternal salvation of his church.

1.

The Revelation of Jesus Christ

Revelation 1:1

'The Revelation of Jesus Christ, which God gave unto him, to show unto his servants things which must shortly come to pass; and he sent and signified it by his angel unto his servant John' (Rev. 1:1).

The singular subject, theme and message of the entire Bible, the Old Testament and the New, is the person, work and glory of the Lord Jesus Christ. As in creation, providence and redemption, so in the Holy Scriptures, it is the purpose of God 'that in all things he might have the pre-eminence' (Col. 1:18). The Book of God is a book all about Christ (Luke 24:27,44-48). All the promises and blessings of God given to sinful men and women are in Christ (Eph. 1:3). Apart from Christ, God promises nothing but wrath, and every supposed blessing will prove to be a curse. All the love, mercy and grace of God are found in Christ. All the revelation and knowledge of the triune God are in Christ. Christ is not only the central message of Holy Scripture, he is *the* message of Holy Scripture. To understand that is to have the key that opens the Word of God and reveals its treasures.

That which is true of the whole of Scripture is especially and gloriously true of the last, closing chapters of the volume, the book of Revelation. This last book of the Bible is Christ's revelation of himself to his servants. This book

is 'the Revelation of Jesus Christ' (1:1). It is not the revelation of St John, but 'the Revelation of Jesus Christ' given
to, and recorded by, John. It is not the book of 'revelations'
(plural). It does not contain many revelations; it contains
one revelation seen in many things. It is 'the Revelation of
Jesus Christ'.

In his book *More Than Conquerors*, William Hendriksen
makes two points that are crucial to a proper understanding of the book of Revelation. First, 'The theme of this book
is: the Victory of Christ and of his Church over the Dragon
[Satan] and his helpers. The Apocalypse intends to show
you, dear believer, that things are not what they seem!' God's
purpose is not in jeopardy. Christ, his church and his truth
will be triumphant at last.

The second point Hendriksen made is about the visions
John describes. Each vision, or section of this book, must
be interpreted as a vision covering the entire gospel age.
'Each section,' Hendriksen writes, 'gives us a description
of the entire Gospel Age, from the first to the second coming of Christ, and is rooted in Israel's history under the old
dispensation to which there are frequent references.' Confusion comes when men try to mix the visions together and
make them form a prophetic history of world events. Each
vision is a picture of the person and work of Christ in redemption, grace and judgement throughout the gospel age.

Follow that basic, simple guide and you will not greatly
err in interpreting the book of Revelation, and your heart
will be comforted and thrilled in reading what God has
determined to do for you and with you in Christ. A general
survey of these twenty-two chapters of God's inspired Word
will give the reader a clear understanding of the fact that
the revelation given to John and recorded in this book is
'the Revelation of Jesus Christ'.

What this book teaches us about Jesus Christ

He is 'the faithful witness' (Rev. 1:5)

This title refers to our Saviour's prophetic office. He is that Prophet of whom Moses spoke (Deut. 18:15; John 6:14), both faithful and true. He is the faithful witness of God to his people (John 1:14,18), and our faithful witness before the holy Lord God, as our advocate with the Father (1 John 2:1-2).

He is 'the first begotten of the dead' (Rev. 1:5)

This refers to our Redeemer's priestly office. If he is 'the first begotten of the dead', then he must once have died. He died for the sins of his people and rose again for their justification. When he arose as our head and representative, 'He entered in once into the holy place, having obtained eternal redemption for us' (Heb. 9:12). With his own precious blood, our great High Priest has opened for us a way of free access to God (Heb. 10:19-22).

He is 'the prince of the kings of the earth' (Rev. 1:5)

By virtue of his finished work of redemption, the God-man, our mediator, has been made the sovereign Monarch of the universe (John 17:2; Rom. 14:9; Phil. 2:9-11). He is Lord and King even over his enemies. The kings of the earth have their crowns and kingdoms from him; they rule by his decree, doing his will (Prov. 21:1), and one day soon they will all bow before his throne and glorify him as King.

He 'loved us, and washed us from our sins in his own blood, and hath made us kings and priests unto God' (Rev. 1:5-6)

He 'loved us' particularly and distinctively, with an everlasting, immutable love. Because he loved us, he chose us in eternal election, became our surety in the covenant of grace and, with his Father, predestinated us unto heavenly glory. Therefore, he 'washed us from our sins in his own blood'. By the shedding of his blood, the Lord Jesus Christ effectually washed away the sins of God's elect. He washed our sins from the record of heaven, from the memory of God, and washed us from our sins, making us holy and righteous in the sight of God! That is the work of Christ in redemption. All whom he loved he washed and, in the fulness of time, he makes them 'kings and priests unto God'. That speaks of regeneration and conversion. Christ, sending his Spirit to redeem sinners, gives us a new, holy nature by which we are made to reign over the lusts of our flesh, so that we are no longer under the dominion of sin. And as priests, consecrated to God, we have direct access to God through his blood.

He says, 'I am he that liveth' (Rev. 1:18)

He lives for ever because he is life! Apart from him there is no life. He lives for ever because he is the living God. But here he is talking about himself as the God-man, our mediator, who once was dead, having died as our substitute for the satisfaction of divine justice. He died! We thank God for that, but he is now alive for evermore. Christ Jesus lives for ever on behalf of his elect, those for whom he died. He lives to make intercession for us (Heb. 7:25). He lives to give eternal life to all his redeemed ones (John 17:2). Because he lives, we live also. We live in him, by the virtue of his death and by the power of his life.

He holds 'the keys of hell and of death' (Rev. 1:18)

'Hell', in this place, simply refers to the grave. The Lord Jesus Christ, by the virtue of his resurrection, has power, authority and dominion over death and the grave (Ps.

68:18-20; 1 Cor. 15:51-58). He conquered death, hell and the grave when he died for us and rose again. Therefore, these great terrors have no power over us to do us harm, and should cause us no fear (Heb. 2:14-15). Christ has delivered us from spiritual death in regeneration, the first resurrection (John 5:25), and will deliver us from death and the grave in the resurrection of our bodies at the last day. It is written: 'Blessed and holy is he that hath part in the first resurrection: on such the second death hath no power' (Rev. 20:6).

He 'holdeth the seven stars in his right hand, [and] walketh in the midst of the seven golden candlesticks' (Rev. 2:1)

The seven golden candlesticks are the churches of Christ in this world. How blessed are those people who are privileged to gather with God's saints in public worship! (Matt. 18:20). The Lord Jesus Christ, the Son of God, walks in the midst of his churches! The seven stars are gospel preachers, God's appointed pastors, who are the angels, messengers of God, to his churches. The Lord Jesus Christ holds them in his right hand, puts them where he wants them, gives them the messages they are responsible to deliver, uses them as he sees fit and protects them as they go about his business. Let every true gospel preacher be esteemed by God's saints as an angel of God sent with a message from God for their souls (1 Thess. 5:12-13).

He is 'the Lion of the tribe of Judah' (Rev. 5:5)

Our Saviour sprang from the tribe of Judah and is comparable to a lion. Like a lion, he is strong and courageous. Like a lion, he devours his enemies. Like a lion, he always prevails. He prevailed over our enemies. He prevailed with God as our surety and substitute. And he prevails over the hearts of chosen sinners in saving grace.

He is 'the Root of David' (Rev. 5:5)

Later, he is called 'the root and offspring of David' (22:16). He is both the God from whom David obtained his life and the man who came from the root of David's house. As a man, our Saviour arose 'as a root out of a dry ground' (Isa. 53:2). Yet he is the root from which all his people draw their life. The root of our family tree is Jesus Christ himself!

'In the midst of the throne ... stood a Lamb' (Rev. 5:6)

That Lamb standing in the midst of the throne of God is Christ our Saviour, who was slain for us. He is seen standing in the midst of the throne because he is the centre of God's decrees and works and the one who executes all God's purposes. He alone is worthy and able to open the book of divine predestination and fulfil it. Christ stands in the midst of the throne and of the twenty-four elders (the church of God) and the four living creatures (the preachers of the gospel) as the Saviour of all his people and the one of whom all his servants speak. The throne John saw represents the glory of God as well as the dominion of God, and Christ, as the Lamb of God, is the revelation and accomplishment of God's glory.

He is 'the Lamb slain from the foundation of the world' (Rev. 13:8)

In the purpose and decree of God, in anticipation of the Fall, for the fulfilling of God's covenant, Christ was looked upon by God the Father as our all-sufficient, sin-atoning sacrifice before ever the world was made. God's elect were looked upon in him as being saved from eternity (Rom. 8:28-31; Eph. 1:3-6; 2 Tim. 1:9). All that we experience in time of God's redeeming grace was done for us in eternity in God's decrees. Before the world was made, in the mind and purpose of Almighty God, Christ was the Lamb slain.

That means that in the mind of God, from all eternity, the covenant of grace was fulfilled, the ransom price was paid, the surety was exalted and God's elect were saved.

He is called 'Faithful and True' (Rev. 19:11)

What a name for the Son of God! He well deserves it for he is faithful and true in all things. He is faithful to his people, to his covenant, to his promises and to himself. He is true. He is both the truth and the true one. Jesus Christ is a true Friend and Brother (Prov. 17:17), a true Saviour (1 John 1:9; 2:1-2) and a true Husband (S. of S. 5:1-9). So true is this Husband to his bride that he will never leave her and will never let her leave him.

He is 'the Word of God' (Rev. 19:13)

'In the beginning was the Word, and the Word was with God, and the Word was God' (John 1:1). Christ is the Word by whom God reveals himself and through whom the triune God performs all his works. He is the eternal, creating Word, by whom all things were made (John 1:3; Heb. 1:2). He is the incarnate, revealing Word, by whom God is revealed to man (John 1:14,18). And he is the almighty, saving Word (Heb. 4:12-13), by whom God calls out and saves his people in regenerating grace.

He is the 'King of kings and Lord of lords' (Rev. 19:16)

As we saw in Revelation 1:5, the Lord Jesus Christ is the absolute, singular, rightful, sovereign Monarch of heaven and earth (Acts 2:32-36).

He declares, 'Behold, I make all things new' (Rev. 21:5-6)

In grace, he makes all things new. 'Therefore if any man be in Christ, he is a new creature: old things are passed away;

behold, all things are become new' (2 Cor. 5:17). In heavenly glory, he makes all things new, granting to his people a new name and a new life, without the possibility of sin, sorrow, or death. And in the last days, he will create 'a new heavens and a new earth, wherein dwelleth righteousness' (2 Peter 3:13).

He is the 'Alpha and Omega' (Rev. 22:13)

He is the 'a' and the 'z', the first and the last, the beginning and the end of all things. The covenant of grace begins and ends with Christ. The whole of creation has its origin in Christ and will find its consummation in Christ. Every event of providence comes from Christ and will glorify Christ. The entire volume of Holy Scripture, from beginning to end, speaks of Christ. And in the salvation of God's elect Jesus Christ is the beginning, the end and everything between (1 Cor. 1:30-31).

He is 'the bright and morning star' (Rev. 22:16)

He is the light that shines in darkness, that shines in our hearts to give the light of the knowledge of the glory of God. He is the Day Star of grace, the Sun of Righteousness, risen over this sin-cursed earth with healing in his wings. And he is the star of that great eternal day yet to come.

He declares, 'Surely, I come quickly' (Rev. 22:20)

Soon he will appear! Suddenly, without warning, the King of glory will come again to destroy his enemies, save his people, restore his creation and glorify his Father. 'Then cometh the end,' when the God-man mediator will perform his last mediatorial work. He will deliver up the kingdom, all the hosts of his elect, unto God the Father, saying, 'Behold I and the children which God hath given me!' And God will be 'all in all' (1 Cor. 15:24-28; Heb. 2:13).

2.

Who is Jesus Christ?

Revelation 1:4-6

'John to the seven churches which are in Asia: Grace be unto you, and peace, from him which is, and which was, and which is to come; and from the seven Spirits which are before his throne; and from Jesus Christ, who is the faithful witness, and the first begotten of the dead, and the prince of the kings of the earth. Unto him that loved us, and washed us from our sins in his own blood, and hath made us kings and priests unto God and his Father; to him be glory and dominion for ever and ever. Amen' (Rev. 1:4-6).

Salvation is to be had only by trusting the Christ of Holy Scripture. Any other Christ is a false Christ. As John Legg puts it, 'The one who is to be enshrined in our minds and hearts must be the true Christ of the Bible. Otherwise we have an idol at the centre of our faith.' We must know who Jesus Christ is and what he has done if we are to trust him and be saved by him. Faith in a false Christ is false faith.

Knowing that many false prophets had gone out into the world in the spirit of Antichrist (1 John 4:1-3), John identifies the Lord Jesus Christ in his salutation (Rev. 1:4-6). He shows us that all grace and peace come to fallen sinners from the eternal, triune God (Father, Son and Holy Spirit). These two things fulfil every need we have before God and satisfy the desires of every renewed heart — grace and peace! Grace is God's free, loving favour bestowed upon those who deserve his wrath. It includes all the bounty of

heaven: the pardon of sin, justification, eternal life, preservation, sanctification and glorification. 'Peace,' William
Hendriksen writes, is 'the reflection of the smile of God in
the heart of the believer who has been reconciled to God
through Jesus Christ.' Peace is always the result of revealed
grace. Those who know the grace of God enjoy the peace of
God.

Who is Jesus Christ?

That question may seem trite to some who read these pages,
but there is no more important question. 'Jesus' is the name
given to him by the angel. It means 'Deliverer', or 'Saviour'
(Matt. 1:21). This Jesus is the Christ, God's promised
Anointed One, the Messiah, the one set forth in the types
and prophecies of the Old Testament Scriptures, the long-
awaited Redeemer King of his people. He is the Son of God
and the Son of Man, Immanuel, the God-man, God and man
in one glorious person. He is as much God as though he
were not man and as much man as though he were not
God. This God-man is 'the Saviour of the world' (1 John
4:14).

1. 'The faithful witness' (John 1:1-5,14,18; Heb. 1:1-3; Col. 2:9)

In his prophetic office he is the revelation of God's being
and attributes (John 14:9). He is the one in whom and by
whom the love, mercy, grace and goodness of God to his
people are revealed (John 17:2,6,22-26). The truth and justice of God are revealed in his sin-atoning death (Rom.
3:24-26), which is our only way of access to God (John
3:14-16; 14:6). It is Christ who has revealed the sure and
certain hope of eternal glory and opened the way for sinners to inherit it (John 11:25; 14:1-3). Though the revelation
of God is complete in Christ (no other word from God is
needed or expected!), it is continually made known to

chosen sinners by his Spirit through the ministry of the Word (1 John 1:1).

2. 'The first begotten of the dead'

This speaks of his priestly office. He who died for our sins rose again as our great High Priest and opened for us the way of life, giving us acceptance with, and access to, the holy God (Heb. 10:19-22). This title, 'the first begotten of the dead', implies three things. First, Christ was the first to be raised from death to immortality. Secondly, Christ was the first and the only one to be raised from the dead by his own power (John 10:18). Thirdly, Christ was raised from the dead as the first-fruits of the resurrection (1 Cor. 15:23). He was raised as the representative of God's elect and his resurrection is the pledge of theirs.

3. 'The prince of the kings of the earth'

As the result of his death and resurrection as our substitute, the Lord Jesus Christ has been exalted and given dominion over all flesh (Phil. 2:9-11). He is King of kings and Lord of lords. All men, both small and great, are under the sovereign dominion of the Lord Jesus Christ. His mediatorial rule over all flesh is the reward of his redemptive work (John 17:2; Rom. 14:9; Isa. 53:10-12). Christ, who died to redeem his elect, now rules the universe to save them. All people are ruled by him, absolutely. All are accountable to him. And, sooner or later, all must acknowledge his rightful claims as Lord over them.

What has the Lord Jesus Christ done?

'Unto him that loved us, and washed us from our sins in his own blood, and hath made us kings and priests unto God and his Father.'

It was not John's purpose to tell us all that Christ has done for us, but to excite our hearts with gratitude and praise to our Saviour. He mentions just three things that our great God and Saviour has done for his own elect, but they include all other things.

1. The Lord Jesus Christ loved us

Let men talk all they will about God's 'universal love', 'universal love' is no love at all! It offers no hope, inspires no gratitude and brings no praise to God. Christ loved us. He loved us particularly (Isa. 43:4; Mal. 1:2; Rev. 3:9). He loved us eternally (Jer. 31:3). He loved us freely (Hosea 14:4). He loved us effectually (Deut. 7:8). He loved us, and loves us, perseveringly (John 13:1). Because he loved us, our Saviour would not allow us to perish under the wrath of God!

Without question, there is a providential blessedness enjoyed by all men because of the fact that God's elect are still on the earth. If the Lord sends rain upon the just, it is likely that some will fall upon his unjust neighbour as well. But to suggest that providential goodness is an indication of God's love towards the reprobate is without foundation in Holy Scripture. If that were the case, we would be forced to conclude that the opposite is also true, and that when God sends famine and plagues upon the reprobate in providential judgement, and the righteous, as well as the wicked, go hungry, fall ill and die, such judgement must indicate divine wrath upon God's elect.

2. He 'washed us from our sins in his own blood'

All who are loved by Christ with an everlasting love have been washed from all sin in the fountain of 'his own blood'. The word 'washed' has a double meaning — 'washed' and 'loosed'. Christ washed away our sins when he poured out his lifeblood unto death upon the cross. By his precious

blood, the Son of God made an atonement for our sins, justified us from all sin and removed all sin from us, past,
present and future! So thorough, complete and effectual is
his atoning sacrifice that all for whom he bled and died are
fair, pure, without spot and perfectly holy in the sight of
God. Christ has also loosed us from the guilt and dominion
of sin by the Spirit's application of his blood to our hearts
(Heb. 9:14). This is redemption both accomplished and
applied. It was accomplished at Calvary and is applied in
effectual calling. Christ's blood atonement was both particular and effectual. It is as broad as the love of God and as
narrow as the number of those who are actually loosed from
their sins by it.

3. He has 'made us kings and priests unto God and his Father'

All who believe on Christ are kings and priests unto God in
him. Every child of God in this world is a king. We have
received a kingdom of grace which cannot be taken away.
We reign as kings over our enemies — sin, Satan and the
world. We live and fare as kings, robed in the royal apparel
of Christ's righteousness, fed and provided for from the
treasury of heaven and attended to by the angels of God.
When this life is ended, we shall sit as kings with Christ
upon his throne.

Every believer is also a priest. The priesthood of the believer has been twisted by many to mean that everyone has
the right to believe and do whatever he sees fit. Ask the
sons of Aaron about that! (See Lev. 10:1-3). The priesthood
of the believer means that God's people neither need nor
desire any earthly 'priest'. Christ is our Priest, and we are
priests unto God in him. In him, we have constant access
to God. We personally confess our sins to God and obtain
forgiveness at the mercy-seat, Christ Jesus. And we offer
up spiritual sacrifices acceptable to God by him (1 Peter
2:5).

What is the result of our Saviour's work?

'To him be glory and dominion for ever and ever. Amen.'
As God the Father has given Christ all pre-eminence, glory
and dominion as the reward of his work, so sinners saved
by his grace gladly ascribe to him all pre-eminence, glory
and dominion. Throughout the book of Revelation, as
throughout the entire Bible, all glory is ascribed to God in
Christ. None is ascribed or given to any creature (4:8,11;
5:9,13; 19:10-12; 1 Cor. 1:26-31). Christ has all glory and
dominion. His glory and dominion must and will endure
for ever. 'He must reign!' And every believer bows to, trusts
and delights in Christ's glory and dominion. We say with
John, 'Amen! — So let it be! ' So indeed it shall be!

Do you see who Christ is? Do you realize what he has
done? Have you experienced his saving work? Then give
all glory to him. As God the Father has put all things into
the hands of his Son, so you must trust all things into his
hands. You may safely trust him in all things and for all
things. He is Jesus the Christ!

3.

Christ the coming King

Revelation 1:7

'Behold, he cometh with clouds; and every eye shall see him, and they also which pierced him: and all kindreds of the earth shall wail because of him. Even so, Amen' (Rev. 1:7).

Here is an announcement worthy of attention, admiration and investigation: 'Behold, he cometh with clouds; and every eye shall see him, and they also which pierced him: and all kindreds of the earth shall wail because of him. Even so. Amen.' John is not describing the pompous parade of some earthly despot. He is talking about the glorious appearance of the great God who is our Saviour. He is proclaiming the second advent of the King of kings in his glory. That same Jesus whom the disciples saw ascending into heaven will come again. The God-man who now rules all things from his lofty throne in heaven is coming to this world again.

'Behold' — pause, look, consider this great fact. The finger of inspiration points to this momentous event and says, 'Behold, he cometh!' These words should sound like a terrifying alarm in the heart of every unbeliever, but they are words of joy, comfort, hope and peace to every child of God. Your trials may be heavy. Your temptations may be many. Though your heart now aches, both with affliction and with sin, you have reason to be of good cheer. All your

troubles are temporary. Do not look upon them as though
they will last for ever. 'Behold, he cometh!' And, 'I reckon
that the sufferings of this present time are not worthy to be
compared with the glory which shall be revealed in us'
(Rom. 8:18).

Having shown us in verses 5 and 6 what Christ has done
for us, John here encourages us to live in expectation of the
fact that the Lord Jesus Christ is coming again in power
and great glory. Though Christ's second coming is not the
central theme of the book of Revelation, 'Yet,' as Hendriksen
notes, 'it constitutes a real source of comfort for afflicted
believers. It is the hope of believers and the consternation
of the enemies of the church.' Therefore, John gives us this
picture of Christ the coming King.

Who is coming?

The one who is coming is the one John has just described
— 'Jesus Christ, who is the faithful witness, and the first
begotten of the dead, and the prince of the kings of the
earth ... [the one] that loved us and washed us from our
sins in his own blood, and hath made us kings and priests
unto God and his Father'. He is the one who came in humiliation as the Son of Man. Two thousand years ago the Son of
God came into this world as a man. In order to redeem his
people, he took manhood into union with himself and dwelt
in human flesh. Everything associated with the earthly life
and ministry of the Lord Jesus Christ was humiliation (Phil.
2:5-8; 2 Cor. 8:9). He was born in Bethlehem in a cow stable.
He lived in poverty and sorrow. He was tempted in all points
like as we are. His disciples, his followers, were the despised riff-raff of society — tax-collectors, fishermen, harlots and beggars.

This one who is coming is the one who suffered and
died as the sinner's substitute at Calvary. In dark Geth-

semane, our Saviour's agony was so great that it caused him to sweat blood. His heart broke within him as he anticipated the shame he must suffer to redeem us. There he was arrested like a common thief in the dark of night. The Lord of glory was beaten, mocked and led through the streets of Jerusalem in a procession of humiliation and sorrow. Then he was stripped naked, nailed to a wooden cross and hung up to die by the hands of wicked men. All of this he voluntarily endured because he had come into this world to die in the place of chosen sinners (Rom. 5:6-8; Gal. 4:4-5).

As he hung upon the cursed tree, the Lord Jesus Christ was made to be sin for us (2 Cor. 5:21; 1 Peter 2:24). He suffered all the vengeance and wrath of Almighty God in our place (Gal. 3:13). He died under the curse of God's holy law, satisfying all the claims of the law's justice against us, so that God might be just and yet justify the ungodly (Rom. 3:24-26). Then he was buried in a borrowed tomb.

This one of whom John says, 'Behold, he cometh,' is the Christ of God who now reigns as King of kings and Lord of lords. Though he lived as the man of sorrows and died as the sinner's substitute under the wrath of God, he is yet alive! On the third day after his death he arose triumphant over death, hell and the grave. Forty days later the crucified Christ was exalted. He ascended back into heaven, took his seat upon the throne of universal monarchy and was crowned with glory and honour. There he reigns as King supreme for evermore (Acts 2:36). This one who is coming is Christ the King. He is not coming *to be* king. He is coming *as* King! Christ the King is coming to put an end to all rebellion in his empire. 'And all that are incensed against him shall be ashamed' (Isa. 45:24). The Lord Jesus Christ, who 'loved us and washed us from our sins in his own blood, and hath made us kings and priests unto God', is coming again. 'Behold, he cometh!'

What should be our attitude with regard to Christ's coming?

We should look upon the Second Coming of Christ as a matter of fact. John does not say, 'He will come some day,' or 'He will come soon,' or even, 'He may come at any time.' He says, 'Behold, he cometh!' His language is in the present tense. He seems to have caught a glimpse of Christ coming even as he was writing. He speaks of it as a matter of fact, a present reality, not as a distant hope. He who came in humiliation to suffer is coming in power to conquer. He who came to redeem is coming to gather his redeemed ones. This is not something to be embraced as a prophetic theory in the development of a sound eschatological creed. It is a fact to be seen with the eye of faith and anticipated in the believing heart.

The Word of God speaks plainly and constantly about Christ's glorious second advent (Jude 14; Job 19:25; Dan. 7:13-14; Acts 1:11; 1 Thess. 4:16; 1 Peter 5:4; 2 Peter 3:10; John 14:3). Our Saviour gave us perpetual reminders of his second coming in the ordinances of the gospel. Every time a believer confesses faith in Christ by believer's baptism, we are taught to look for Christ's second coming. The new convert goes down into the watery grave as one crucified with Christ and rises up out of the water as one risen with Christ in the new birth, living in hope of the resurrection at the Lord's coming (Rom. 6:4-6). As often as we sit around the Lord's Table with God's saints and take the bread and wine, we are vividly reminded that Christ is coming (1 Cor. 11:24-26). Though that is a blessed ordinance, it is only a temporary thing. We shall cease to celebrate the Lord's Supper when our Lord, who has gone away, returns.

We should always look upon Christ's return with immediate interest and anxious expectation. I fear that our thoughts about Christ's second coming are too much like the scoffers' words. Though we might never actually say,

'Where is the promise of his coming?', I am afraid we live too much as those who do not expect it to happen. That should not be! John says, 'Behold, he cometh!' He will be here so soon that John puts it in the present tense: 'He cometh!' He means us to understand that Christ is already on his way back to this world.

Do not imagine that our Lord delays his coming, or that he is simply waiting in heaven to return at the appointed hour. Everything he is doing in providence and grace he is doing in preparation for his glorious advent. We grow uneasy because he has been gone for two thousand years, but he does not calculate time as we do. To him one day is as a thousand years and a thousand years as one day (2 Peter 3:8). By that measurement he has only been away for two days! He went away on business for his beloved bride (John 14:1-3; 16:7). As soon as his business is done, as soon as everything that has to be done is done, he will return. His bride may fret and worry, but he knows what he is doing. He will not be moved with passion. He is faithful. He dwells in the leisure of eternity and in the serenity of sovereignty. He is not limited by time and space. He will accomplish his work. Then he will return.

From the very moment that he went away, the Lord Jesus has been coming back again. Everything is moving towards that end. 'Behold, he cometh!' He is on his way! Every hour brings him nearer. Soon he will appear the second time, without sin, unto salvation. 'Now is our salvation nearer than when we believed.' At the time appointed, Christ will appear. We should await our Saviour's coming with patience and anticipation. The grace of God teaches us to be always 'looking for that blessed hope, and the glorious appearing of the great God and our Saviour Jesus Christ' (Titus 2:13). Looking for the glorious appearing of Christ, be patient in trial (1 Peter 1:7), diligent in service (Acts 1:10-11), and always watchful. Be standing on tiptoe, looking in faith for Christ to appear.

How will the Lord Jesus Christ appear?

John says, 'Behold, he cometh with the clouds.' John Gill
tells us that this 'denotes the grand and magnificent manner in which he will come, making the clouds his chariots
... and the visibility of his coming'. When our Saviour
comes, he will make a glorious, climactic appearance. As
William Hendriksen says, ' "He comes with clouds," that is
with glory (Dan. 7:13; Mark 14:62; Rev. 14:14; Ezek. 1:4-28)
and with anger, wrath and judgement (Zeph. 1:15; Ps. 97:2).
The Bible knows nothing about an invisible or secret second coming. Nowhere is this taught. On the contrary, "Every
eye shall see him." ' When Christ comes, everyone will know
it!

In the wilderness, the presence of the Lord was known
by the visible pillar of a cloud by day and of fire by night.
The cloud was the sure token of God's presence. In the same
way, every eye 'shall see the Son of man coming in the
clouds of heaven with power and great glory' (Matt. 24:30).
Christ will come with great majesty. The King of glory will
descend from heaven with clouds of angels and of saints at
his side. All the forces of nature will announce his arrival.
The archangel will shout, the trump of God will sound, the
thunder will announce him, the lightning will dance before him and the clouds will be his chariot. As God came
down upon Sinai in clouds and thick darkness to give the
law, so shall the God-man descend in final judgement.

His coming with clouds also implies the power with
which he will appear: 'His strength is in the clouds.' He
once came as a tender plant, a root out of dry ground, robed
in swaddling clothes and laid in a manger; but now he
comes with clouds, robed with the tapestry of heaven's
throne, in power and great glory. Certainly, the clouds represent the terror of his judgement. All believers will be
caught up together with him in the clouds, to meet the Lord
in the air (1 Thess. 4:17). But, to those unbelieving rebels

who remain upon the earth, those clouds will be signs of horrifying wrath and judgement (Ps. 97:1-6), as clouds filled with justice, vengeance and anger. The Lord Jesus Christ is coming with clouds of unparalleled splendour. To his saints, this is glorious. To his enemies, this will be terrifying (1 Thess. 5:2-10; 2 Thess. 1:6-10).

What will happen when Christ comes again?

It is evident that Christ's coming will be a literal appearance. It is true, Christ comes to his people spiritually in grace, in providence and at death. But John is talking about the literal, bodily, visible coming of the Son of God to this earth the second time. Child of God, you will see your Saviour with the very same eyes with which you read these words, for at his glorious appearance there will be a general resurrection (John 5:28-29; 1 Cor. 15:51-58; Job 19:25-26).

At his coming, the Lord Jesus Christ will be seen by all men. 'Every eye shall see him.' Every child of Adam, both the living and the dead, will see the God-man face to face. Your eyes and mine will look upon him. In that day, we shall look upon him — on nothing and no one else but him. Nothing else will be of any significance. Every believer will look upon him with satisfaction and delight (1 John 3:2).

'They also which pierced him' will see him. Pilate and Judas, Herod and Caiaphas, the Jews and the soldiers — all will see him. Indeed, all who have pierced him by enmity, rebellion and unbelief will see him. When our Lord appears the second time, an overwhelming horror will engulf the world. 'All kindreds of the earth shall wail because of him.' In the last day, as in this present day, God's elect in the world will be few. However, in that great day, Christ will conquer his enemies. Every knee will bow before him and every tongue will confess that he is Lord (Isa. 45:23-24; Phil. 2:9-11). Then every unbeliever, every rebel, will wring his hands in fear and scream in terror, and his heart will convulse with horror before the wrath of the Lamb (Rev. 6:14-17).

What do God's people say to these things? 'Even so. Amen!' 'Zion heard, and was glad; and the daughters of Judah rejoiced because of thy judgements, O Lord' (Ps. 97:8). Our hearts rejoice at the prospect of Christ's coming, his triumph over all his enemies, our complete salvation and the ultimate, universal revelation of our Saviour's glory.

4.

Christ the Alpha and the Omega

Revelation 1:8

'I am Alpha and Omega, the beginning and the ending, saith the Lord, which is, and which was, and which is to come, the Almighty' (Rev. 1:8).

Four times in the book of Revelation our Lord Jesus Christ appears to John and identifies himself with these words: 'I am Alpha and Omega' (1:8,11; 21:6; 22:13). The words contain no deep, hidden mystery. They are simply the first and last letters of the Greek alphabet. In our language the equivalent would be, 'I am A and Z' — that is, 'I am the beginning and the ending.' As John Gill points out, 'These letters, "Alpha and Omega", being the first and the last of the alphabet, may stand for the whole.' The meaning of the text is this: 'I am the beginning of all things and the end of all things, and everything between the beginning and the end.'

With these words, 'I am Alpha and Omega, the beginning and the ending ... the first and the last,' our Saviour identifies himself as Jehovah (Isa. 41:4; 44:6; 48:10-12). Indeed, this is what he says by way of explanation: 'I am ... the Lord, which is, which was, and which is to come, the Almighty.' The Lord Jesus Christ, our Redeemer, is God over all, was God from eternity, and is to come as God to judge the world. He is now the Saviour of all who come to God by him, was the Saviour of all his saints in the Old Testament, being the Lamb slain from the foundation of the world, and is to come as the Saviour of God's elect, without sin unto salvation.

This text describes the *eternality* of Christ, who is, was and ever shall be. It also speaks of our Saviour's *immutability*. He is always the same, unchanging and unchangeable. What he is, he always was, and will be for ever. He is the same, yesterday, today and for ever (Heb. 13:8). His person, his love, his virtue and his purpose are all immutable. The text also sets forth the glorious *pre-eminence* of Christ (Col. 1:18). As it has pleased the Father to give his Son pre-eminence in all things, it is so. Christ is the beginning of all things, the substance of all things and the end of all things. Our Saviour is himself God, 'the Almighty'! He is the Creator, Sustainer and Ruler of all things. The one whose blood and righteousness we trust, to whose dominion we gladly submit and into whose hands we have committed our souls, is himself God, the Almighty. We have nothing to fear. Our Saviour is God, and we are safe in his hands (John 10:27-30).

We shall now consider various aspects of the truth that Christ is the Alpha and Omega.

Christ's glory and humiliation

Without question, these words, 'I am Alpha and Omega,' have reference to the glorious dignity of our Saviour's person and to the depths of his willing humiliation to save us. Christ Jesus is Alpha, the first-born, the chief, the one who is pre-eminent over every creature. As a man, his body was created in time in the womb of the virgin by the Holy Spirit (Matt. 1:20; Heb. 10:5). Yet he is the one who created all things. Therefore, he is above all things (Heb. 1:1-14).

The word 'Alpha' suggests that Christ is the best. He is better than all who came before him. If you put all others together, he stands head and shoulders above them all as the best. We use the same kind of language today. We say of a car, 'It is A1'. That means it is in first-class condition, the best of its kind. We say of a craftsman, 'He is A1.' That means he is a top-quality workman, the best in his trade. Our Lord Jesus Christ says of himself, 'I am Alpha. I am A1. I am the best there is.' And all his people gladly acknowledge that it is so.

Is he a son? He is the first-born Son, the only begotten Son, the eternal Son and the only perfectly obedient Son. All other sons are made to be sons by faith in him who is the Son (Eph. 1:5). Is he a prophet? All other prophets stand behind him by an infinite distance and point to him, bearing witness to him (Acts 10:43). Is he a priest? All other priests of the Aaronic and Levitical orders were only types of him. Their only purpose was to represent Christ until he came. He is the fulfilment of them. He is the great High Priest of our profession (Heb. 9:11-12). Is he a king? Indeed, Christ is a King like no other. He is King of kings and Lord of lords! (Dan. 4:34,35,37). Is he the builder of his church? Then he is the wise Master-Builder. Is he a shepherd? Then he is the Good Shepherd, the Chief Shepherd and the Great Shepherd. Is Christ a foundation? Then he is the tried and proven foundation, the only sure foundation. Those who build upon this foundation shall never fall. Is he a cornerstone? Then he is the chief cornerstone. Is he a rock? Then he is the only rock of safety and refuge, the Rock of our salvation. Is he water? Then he is the Water of life. Is Christ bread? Then he is the Bread of heaven. Is he light? Then he is the Light of the world. Is he a refuge? Then he is the sure, eternal, saving refuge for our souls.

It matters not what title our Lord takes to himself, or what character he assumes, he is in all respects Alpha, A1. He infinitely surpasses all that may be compared to him, as the sun excels the stars. When the sun rises, the stars fade in its light. And when Christ appears, all others pale into insignificance. He who is best is pre-eminent, and well

deserves the praise and glory of all. Christ is Alpha. Let no
flesh glory in his presence! All who know him glory only
in him and give glory to him alone (Jer. 9:23-24; 1 Cor.
1:30-31).

Christ, we know, is also Omega, the lowest and the last,
in his voluntary condescension and humiliation. In order
to save us, Christ Jesus became the very least among men!
This, I believe, is the meaning of our Lord's words in Matthew 11:11: 'He that is least in the kingdom of heaven is
the greatest of all.'

How can a man describe the depths of our Lord's voluntary humiliation? He who is God stooped to become a man!
(Phil. 2:7-8). In order to save us, the Son of God became
one of us! He became what we are, so that we might be
what he is. He stooped to become a man, stooped again to
become the lowest of men, stooped again to become the
servant of men and stooped again to be made sin and die in
the place of sinful men! Behold the depths of his humiliation! When Christ was made to be sin for us, he who is
God was forsaken by God as the object of God's horrible
wrath! He cried, 'My God, my God, why hast thou forsaken
me? Why art thou so far from helping me, and from the
words of my roaring?' Then he answered his own agoniz-
ing cry: 'Thou art holy.' A holy God cannot look upon sin.
'But I am a worm, and no man; a reproach of men, and
despised of the people. All they that see me laugh me to
scorn: they shoot out the lip, they shake the head, saying,
He trusted on the LORD, that he would deliver him: let him
deliver him [if] he delighted in him' (Ps. 22:1-8). At last,
the Son of God stooped to death, death under the infinite,
inflexible justice of God for *us*!

In Scripture, Christ is the Alpha and the Omega

Luke 24:27,44-47 and John 5:39 plainly teach us the meaning and message of God's holy Word. Christ is Alpha, the

beginning, for the first line of Genesis speaks of him: 'In
the beginning God' (Gen. 1:1; cf. John 1:1-3). And he is the
Omega, the ending, for the last line of Revelation speaks of
him: 'The grace of our Lord Jesus Christ be with you all'
(Rev. 22:21). And he is everything between the beginning
and the ending. Every book of the Bible, every chapter, every
verse, every sentence, every word speaks, directly or in-
directly, of Christ, pointing us in some way to him. If you
could squeeze the whole volume of inspired Scripture down
to its very essence and substance, you would find Christ,
only Christ and nothing but Christ. Christ is the living Word
of whom the written Word speaks. The purpose of the Holy
Spirit in moving men to write the Scriptures was to reveal
Christ. That is the only purpose of the inspired volume
(John 16:14). Our Lord said concerning the Scriptures as a
whole, 'They testify of me!'

The whole message of the Bible is Jesus Christ, and him
crucified. The Word of God is like an alabaster box full of
very precious spikenard. Break it open, and you smell
nothing but the sweet aroma of Jesus Christ, our dear Redeemer. The Old Testament, from Genesis to Malachi, proclaims one message: 'The Redeemer is coming!' The prophets and the kings, the priests and the judges, the preachers
and the singers, the laws and the sacrifices all look one
way. They all stand like cherubim over the ark, desiring to
see God's salvation.

The four Gospels and the book of Acts all declare one
thing: 'The Redeemer has come!' Matthew, Mark, Luke and
John record in meticulous detail the incarnation, earthly
life, ministry, death and resurrection of Christ as the sinner's substitute. They speak of nothing else. In the book of
Acts, Luke records the works of Christ, the ascended King.
As the book of Revelation is called 'the Revelation of Jesus
Christ', so the book of Acts might well be called 'the Acts
of Jesus Christ our King'.

The apostolic epistles and the book of Revelation all say
one thing: 'The Redeemer is coming again!' From Romans

through Revelation, the apostles expound to us the meaning of our Lord's doctrine and call for us to watch for his coming with expectant hearts. Soon, Christ will appear to gather his redeemed ones unto himself!

The law of God

Ransomed sinners rejoice to know that with regard to the holy law of God, Christ is Alpha and Omega. He is the lawgiver, and so he is Alpha, the beginning of the law. And Christ is the fulfilment of the law, so he is Omega, 'the end of the law for righteousness to everyone that believeth' (Rom. 10:4). You and I are neither Alpha nor Omega to the law. We have not met, nor can we ever meet, its demands. Who among the fallen sons of Adam would dare assert that he has met the first letter of the law: 'Thou shalt love the Lord thy God with all thy heart'? And none of us measures up to the second letter of the law: 'Thou shalt love thy neighbour as thyself.'

If you would see the law fulfilled, look not to man, but to Christ alone. He alone honoured, kept and fulfilled the law. Christ fulfilled the law's requirements perfectly as a man. He loved God with all his heart and loved his neighbour as himself. And in death, Christ satisfied the law's justice, removed the law's curse and penalty from us and put an end to the law's covenant. Our dear Saviour obeyed the law as the representative of God's elect, and died under the penalty of the law as our substitute. His obedience has been imputed to all who believe, for righteousness.

Because we are in Christ, we are not under the law, in any sense whatsoever, but under grace! The plain statements of Holy Scripture unquestionably assert the believer's entire freedom from the law (Rom. 6:14; 7:4; 8:1; 10:4; Gal. 3:13,24-25; Col. 2:10-23; 1 Tim. 1:8-10). Believers look to Christ alone for all holiness and righteousness before God. We have no righteousness of our own, with which to commend ourselves to God (Isa. 64:6). We trust Christ, 'the LORD our Righteousness' (Jer. 23:6), who is made of God unto us 'righteousness and sanctification and redemption' (1 Cor. 1:30).

We seek holiness, but we never trust our holiness. We seek to live in righteousness, but we never imagine that we have attained righteousness. We seek virtue, but we never look to our virtue for merit with God. Our only saving, sanctifying righteousness is the righteousness of Christ. As we were made sinners, not by what we have done, but by what our father Adam did, even so we are made righteous, not by what we do, but by what our representative and federal Head, the Lord Jesus Christ, has done for us (Rom. 5:18-19).

We trust Christ alone for acceptance with God. With his imputed righteousness, we are complete, perfect, holy and for ever accepted in the Beloved (Col. 2:10). The law demands perfection, but it cannot demand, nor can it have, greater perfection than we have by the imputation of Christ's righteousness. The law demands satisfaction, but it cannot require, nor can it find, greater satisfaction than we offer in the blood of our dear Substitute. Christ is the Alpha and the Omega of the law.

The whole of creation

He is the beginning of all things, and the Ruler and Sustainer of all things from the beginning to the ending (Rom. 11:36). Christ is the Alpha of creation, for all things were created by him (John 1:1-3). He brought this world into being by his divine power. No, this world did not evolve into being from some mystical 'cosmic boom' billions of

years ago. It would require incredible ignorance, or wilful
rebellion against God, to imagine such a thing. Jesus Christ
our Saviour created this universe.

Christ is the Omega of creation, for all things were created by him (Rev. 4:11). In the end, when our Lord's purpose has been accomplished, it will be plainly revealed
that every creature in God's universe, animate and inani-
mate, and every event of providence, both good and bad,
has served him and has been used by him for the glory of
his own great name (Rev. 5:11-14). Yes, all men and angels,
either willingly or unwillingly, serve the cause of the Creator's glory. He sees to it (Prov. 16:4). From the beginning to
the ending of creation, Christ rules and sustains all things
for the glory of his own great name (Col. 1:15-20).

The covenant purposes of the triune God

I realize that the thoughts of God, his eternal purposes, his
sovereign decrees and his everlasting covenant are things
about which we know only a little. But this much is revealed: Christ is the beginning of all and the ending of all,
the Alpha and the Omega. In Isaiah 45 we read of God's
purposes and decrees, and his sovereign rule of all things.
The chapter ends with Christ our God calling upon men to
bow to him in faith and obtain eternal life (v. 22), and declaring that in the end all men shall bow to him (v. 23).
God's purpose will certainly be accomplished, and his purpose always has to do with his Son.

Election is God's choice of some from Adam's fallen race
to eternal life in Christ, and his determination to save them
by Christ (Eph. 1:4). Predestination is God's eternal decree
to make all of his elect like his dear Son, the Lord Jesus
Christ (Rom. 8:29-30). Providence is his wise, sovereign,
orderly arrangement, rule and disposition of all things to
accomplish that end (Eph. 1:11). The covenant of grace is
God's eternal purpose to save certain people by the merits

of his Son and for the glory of his Son (Heb. 10:5-7,10-17). If you and I could be permitted to read the book of God's eternal decrees, we would see that it is a book written from eternity, sealed with immutability, dyed crimson in the blood of the sin-atoning Lamb slain from the foundation of the world, written from beginning to end with one object in mind — and that one object is the eternal glory of Christ, the Son of God.

Salvation

In the whole affair of salvation, Christ is Alpha and Omega. John certainly refers to this fact. In the preceding verses, he described the work of salvation, and he ascribed the whole of it to the Lord Jesus (vv. 5-8). Christ loved us in the beginning. Christ redeemed us in time. And Christ is coming for us in the end. In the work of salvation, Jesus Christ is Alpha and Omega, the beginning and the ending, the first and the last, and everything between.

Christ is the Alpha of salvation because he called us from death to life by the power of his Spirit (John 5:25). He will at the last day present all his elect holy, blameless and unreprovable to his Father by the merits of his own blood and righteousness; so he is the Omega of salvation too (Col. 1:22). And Christ is everything between because, from beginning to end, he holds us in life by the power of his grace. Christ held us in physical life until he saved us by his grace, and he will hold us in grace until he brings us to glory. We are in his hands. He cannot be induced, by any means, or for any reason, to let us go (John 10:27-30). This is our security! Child of God, lean upon Christ with all the weight of your soul. Cast yourself entirely upon him. He will not fail. He who began his work in you will finish his work in you (Phil. 1:6). He who called you will keep you. Christ was never yet Alpha without being Omega too.

In the eternal glory of heaven

In Revelation 22:13, our Lord announces his glorious appearance with these words: 'I am Alpha and Omega, the beginning and the end, the first and the last.' When all the promises and prophecies of Holy Scripture are fulfilled, when the mystery of God's eternal purpose has been accomplished, when the judgement is over, when the damned are cast for ever into hell and the righteous are for ever with the Lord, when the new heavens and the new earth have been created, when time shall be no more, when the eternal glory has begun, Christ will still be Alpha and Omega!

He is the door of entrance, by whose merit we shall enter heaven. He will be the first and foremost object of our vision in heaven. So Christ is the Alpha, the beginning of heaven's glory. He is also the fulness, the consummation and the cause of heaven's eternal, unending joy and reward. So he is the Omega too. From eternity to eternity, for ever and ever, Christ is the Alpha and the Omega, our unchanging and unchangeable God and Saviour!

5.

'In the Spirit on the Lord's day'

Revelation 1:9-11

'I John, who also am your brother, and companion in tribulation, and in the kingdom and patience of Jesus Christ, was in the isle that is called Patmos, for the word of God, and for the testimony of Jesus Christ. I was in the Spirit on the Lord's day, and heard behind me a great voice, as of a trumpet, saying, I am Alpha and Omega, the first and the last: and, What thou seest, write in a book, and send it unto the seven churches which are in Asia; unto Ephesus, and unto Smyrna, and unto Pergamos, and unto Thyatira, and unto Sardis, and unto Philadelphia, and unto Laodicea' (Rev. 1:9-11).

I once read a story about a group of men who met at a local high school every Saturday night to play basketball. While they played, the school janitor usually sat off in a corner reading his Bible, trying to prepare for the worship of God the next day. Normally, he read until they were done. Then he would lock up and go home. One night, one of the men asked, 'What are you reading?' The old man replied, 'The book of Revelation.' The younger man asked, with a bit of a snigger, 'Do you understand it?' The old man said, 'I sure do. It says, "Jesus is gonna win."'

That is just about as good an explanation of the book of Revelation as I have ever read, or heard. When you read this book, always remember that the message of this book is just that — the Lord Jesus Christ is going to win!

That message is delightful and comforting to all of God's people in all ages, but it was particularly so in the time of severe persecution in which the apostle John was inspired by God the Holy Spirit to write these twenty-two chapters, describing the sure triumph of Christ over all things.

Persecution

By the time John was given this revelation the church of God was suffering intense persecution throughout the Roman world. The fact is, the seed of the serpent has always hated the seed of the woman and sought to destroy it. As Cain slew Abel, as Ishmael persecuted Isaac, so the world has always set itself in opposition to Christ, his gospel and his church. That was the way it was in our Lord's day. That was the way it was in John's day, and that is the way it is today.

The world is not opposed to religion. The world loves religion. But the world is opposed to Christ and to the gospel of his grace. The offence of the cross has not diminished. For the most part, at least in the Western world, God providentially restrains the world from exercising the violent persecutions of days gone by, but we must never imagine that the persecutor's heart has changed. It has not.

By the time the first century was drawing to its close, persecution against the church and kingdom of God was rampant and severe. Believers were looked upon with utter contempt and accused of the most vile things imaginable.

Politically, the Romans viewed the followers of Christ as being disloyal to Rome because they refused to acknowledge Caesar as the supreme authority of the universe.

Religiously, believers were despised as atheists and divisive sectarians, because they refused to acknowledge the gods of their pagan neighbours.

Socially, God's elect were despised by those who considered themselves to belong to an élite for obvious reasons. First, the declaration of Holy Scripture that all believers are one in Christ (Gal. 3:28; Col. 3:11) destroys racial prejudice. Secondly, the assertion that all are sinners and must come to God and find acceptance with him upon the grounds of grace alone, through the merits of Christ's blood and righteousness alone, destroys man's proud sense of self-worth and self-righteousness. And, thirdly, the fact that God's elect are for the most part common people (1 Cor. 1:26-31) makes social distinction meaningless.

Economically, believers were considered a threat to everyone. The priests, craftsmen and makers of idols, those who made their living in religious tomfoolery, looked upon the message of Christ as a threat. You will recall that this fear was used to stir up a riot in Ephesus (Acts 19). In fact, things got so bad in that superstitious age of religious ignorance that almost all natural disasters were looked upon by the brilliant, highly educated Romans as retaliations from their pagan gods against Christianity.

Tertullian spoke of this mentality (still common in the third century) very sarcastically, saying, 'If the Tiber reaches the walls, if the Nile does not rise to the fields, if the sky does not move, or if the earth does, if there is famine, if there is plague, the immediate cry is, "Christians to the lions!"'

Persecution was the everyday experience of God's saints in this hostile world at the end of the first century. It is against this backdrop that John wrote the book of Revelation, asserting, without the least hesitancy, the sure triumph of Christ and his church.

The apostle John told us in verse 7 that the Lord Jesus is coming back to this earth. He is about to give us a marvellously detailed description of what the Lord Jesus Christ is now like in his exaltation and glory as the risen and

ascended Lord and King. But, first, he introduces himself
(v. 9), tells us what frame he was in when he received 'the
Revelation of Jesus Christ' (v. 10) and then declares the
message the Lord gave him (v. 11).

Here we are assured that he who is the Alpha and the
Omega, the first and the last, the beginning and the ending
of all things, will be triumphant over all things and in all
things.

The Lord's servant

'I John, who also am your brother, and companion in
tribulation, and in the kingdom and patience of Jesus Christ,
was in the isle that is called Patmos, for the word of God,
and for the testimony of Jesus Christ' (v. 9). John, who was
the only surviving apostle, by now almost a hundred years
old, describes himself as one who is our brother, our companion and an exile for the gospel's sake. This man is held
before us by the Holy Spirit as an exemplary servant of our
Lord.

1. John describes himself as our brother

So averse are God's servants to taking titles, seeking recog-
nition, or promoting their own honour, that they genuinely
count it an honour to be numbered among God's elect as
one of the brethren. God's servants are not men who are
impressed with themselves; they are men who are impressed
with God! First and foremost, those who are God's servants, those men who are sent forth to preach the gospel of
Christ, are brethren in Christ. Brethren care for one another. Brethren have common interests. Brethren look out
for each other. If we are Christ's we are brethren. We belong to that family named after Christ (Eph. 3:15). We are
members of the household of God and of the household of

faith. We have been adopted by the same Father. We have the same Elder Brother. We are all born of the same Spirit. Let all who are Christ's endeavour at all times to live together in this world as brethren. As John himself put it, 'Beloved, let us love one another, for love is of God' (1 John 4:7; Eph. 4:1-7; 4:32 – 5:2).

2. John describes himself as our companion

Brethren are companions, companions in joy and in sorrow, in laughter and in weeping, 'in tribulation, and in the kingdom, and in the patience of Jesus Christ'.

We are companions in *tribulation*. We must through much tribulation enter into the kingdom of God, and those who know what tribulation is find great comfort in having a companion in tribulation (John 16:33; Rom. 5:1-5; 2 Cor. 1:2-5).

We who believe are also companions in *the kingdom of Christ*. You will notice that the kingdom of Christ is not spoken of here as something future, but as something present. The kingdom of Christ and the church of Christ are the same thing. We are born into this kingdom when we are born again by the grace and power of God, 'who hath delivered us from the power of darkness, and hath translated us into the kingdom of his dear Son'. Christ is our King. He has set his throne in our hearts. His Word is our law, our only rule of faith and practice. His will is our rule. That kingdom of which we are made citizens is the sphere of God's grace. It is the community of the redeemed over which Christ reigns as Lord and King.

All true believers are also companions in *the patience, or perseverance, of faith*. The word translated here as 'patience' would be better rendered 'perseverance'. It means 'to remain under'. This was precisely the point John was making. We must patiently persevere in Christ and in faith, especially amidst the onslaught of persecution and tribulation heaped upon us by a world set against us. We must remain faithful under the pressure of great opposition (Matt. 10:16-22).

3. John describes the circumstances and conditions surrounding him

He could have said much about his banishment for the gospel's sake. I am sure I would have said much, much more than he did. But John, writing by inspiration of God the Holy Spirit, was not seeking the pity or the applause of his brethren. He sought to encourage them. Therefore, he writes about his circumstances in the lightest terms imaginable. He simply says, 'I … was in the isle that is called Patmos, for the word of God, and for the testimony of Jesus Christ.'

He was not on some exotic island on holiday. Patmos is a small island off the coast of Greece, covered with volcanic rocks and very little vegetation. John does not himself tell us how he came to Patmos, but it appears that he was sent there as a criminal to be punished. Ignatius said he was banished to Patmos by Domitian, the Roman emperor. This is confirmed by both Irenaeus and Tertullian.

Domitian came to power following the death of Nero. There was a brief lull in persecution after the barbaric Nero died, but when Domitian became emperor, he launched an unprecedented, all-out, empire-wide attack against all Christianity. Enforcing emperor worship rigidly, he insisted that all men acknowledge him as god — not as the only god, but as one god among many. Many were slaughtered by this little tyrant.

John was banished to Patmos because of his faithfulness to 'the word of God and for the testimony of Jesus Christ'. That was his crime. For that he was sentenced to exile on Patmos, under the watchful eye of a Roman guard. John had been the faithful pastor of the church at Ephesus for a long, long time. He was a meek, unassuming, quiet man, but he would not deny his Lord, regardless of cost. His perseverance in the faith was unwavering. So here he is, a ninety-year-old man, in exile, separated from other believers and forgotten by everyone but God.

Yet all he says about it is that he was 'in the isle that is called Patmos'. He speaks of it almost incidentally, as though it were no big deal, because in the overall scheme of things, what happened to him really was unimportant. Do not misunderstand me. John is to be highly esteemed. He was faithful under great pressure. But Christ was still on his throne. That is what John is teaching us here. The cause of Christ was not hindered. He is urging us to follow his example of patient perseverance 'for the Word of God, and for the testimony of Jesus Christ'.

John was banished to Patmos 'for [or because of] the Word of God'. He was not banished because he said the Bible is the Word of God. The Bible had not yet been compiled. It had not all been written. He was banished because of his faith in the Lord Jesus Christ, who is the eternal, living Word of God, for asserting that Christ is the eternal God, for declaring that Christ is the revelation of God, for preaching that Christ alone is the way, the truth and the life.

This faithful old man was banished to Patmos 'for [because of] the testimony of Jesus Christ'. He was imprisoned for preaching the gospel, for his faithful, unequivocal, uncompromising proclamation of God's free and sovereign grace in Christ, the sinner's substitute (Rev. 1:2; 1 John 1:1-3). In the teeth of powerful persecutors God's faithful servant did not hesitate to proclaim Christ's eternal deity as the Son of God, his effectual atonement as the sinner's only substitute, his exalted supremacy, solitariness and sovereignty as the Lord of the universe, and the glorious gospel of everlasting salvation in him alone.

'The Lord's day'

John declares: 'I was in the Spirit on the Lord's day, and heard behind me a great voice, as of a trumpet' (v. 10).

John first asserts, 'I was in the Spirit.' I am certain that he is here describing an experience beyond the bounds of normal human experience and understanding. He is describing a condition in which he was utterly under the control of God the Holy Spirit, in a state in which he was given supernatural revelation by God. This was not a worked-up state of religious, or spiritual frenzy. John was seized by God and caught up in the Spirit. This is the very same thing that Ezekiel, Peter and Paul experienced (Ezek. 2:2; 3:12-14; Acts 10; 2 Cor. 12:1-6).

Yet there is a sense in which John's experience here was not unusual at all, at least not for God's people. You see, believers are men and women who live and walk in the Spirit. Living under the dominion of Christ our King in the kingdom of God, we no longer live after the flesh to fulfil its lusts. We live in the Spirit. We live in the realm of the Spirit, under the control of the Spirit, walking by faith in Christ, consecrated to Christ, worshipping and serving Christ. Romans 8:1-9 tells us emphatically that these things are true of all who are born of God.

Next, John declares that he was in the Spirit 'on the Lord's day'. This is a very unusual expression, so unusual that this is the only place in the New Testament where it is used. Yet John uses it as though it were a common expression, as indeed it was. There is nothing mysterious about it. There is no hidden prophetic meaning to it. And, certainly, he did not mean to say, 'I was in the Spirit on the sabbath day.'

'The Lord's day' is Sunday. The early believers commonly called it 'the Lord's day', and set aside that day as the specific day in which they would gather for worship (Acts 20:7; 1 Cor. 16:2). There was nothing legal about it. The Lord's Day had entirely replaced the Old Testament sabbath. 'The Lord's day' simply became the customary way in which believers referred to Sunday, because this was the day on which our Lord Jesus arose from the dead and upon which he appeared to his disciples after the resurrection (Mark 16:9; John 20:19,26).

Though John was banished from the house of God and the people of God, he was not banished from God, or from his worship. When the sun rose on Sunday morning and he was compelled to go out to his pile of rocks with his sledgehammer, this faithful old man was in the Spirit, worshipping God, gathered with the general assembly and church of the first-born, whose names are written in heaven (Heb. 12:18-24). If we worship God at all, this is how we worship him — 'in the Spirit' (John 4:23-24; Phil. 3:3).

On this particular Lord's Day, John heard a voice behind him, 'a great voice, as of a trumpet'. It had been more than sixty years since he had heard that voice, but it was as familiar to him as it had been in his youth. It was the voice of his Beloved that came leaping and skipping across the mountains to him! While he was in the Spirit, on the Lord's Day, the Lord Jesus Christ, the Son of God, appeared to John and spoke to him.

The Lord's message

'... saying, I am Alpha and Omega, the first and the last: and, What thou seest, write in a book, and send it unto the seven churches which are in Asia; unto Ephesus, and unto Smyrna, and unto Pergamos, and unto Thyatira, and unto Sardis, and unto Philadelphia, and unto Laodicea' (Rev. 1:11).

I want to draw your attention particularly to the first line of this verse. Here the Lord Jesus declared to John, and declares to us, that all is well. As we saw in the previous chapter, when the Master declares, 'I am Alpha and Omega, the first and the last,' he is assuring us that he is the eternal, self-existent God (Isa. 41:4; 44:6; 48:12), that he is the fulness of all things and that he is pre-eminent, the exalted Lord and King of the universe, in total control of all things.

But why did the Lord Jesus tell John to send his message to the churches? Why not send it to the Roman Empire? Why not send it to Domitian, the emperor? What good does it do to communicate this message to a few, fairly small, local churches? The answer should be obvious. God Almighty does his work in this world by his church. His purpose is to assure us that our labour is not in vain in the Lord. The gospel will prevail. The gates of hell will fall before us. The Lion of the tribe of Judah has prevailed, is prevailing and will prevail! The old janitor was exactly right: Jesus is going to win!

6.

The Christ of Patmos

Revelation 1:12-20

'And I turned to see the voice that spake with me. And being turned, I saw seven golden candlesticks; and in the midst of the seven candlesticks one like unto the Son of man, clothed with a garment down to the foot, and girt about the paps with a golden girdle. His head and his hairs were white like wool, as white as snow; and his eyes were as a flame of fire; and his feet like unto fine brass, as if they burned in a furnace; and his voice as the sound of many waters. And he had in his right hand seven stars: and out of his mouth went a sharp two-edged sword: and his countenance was as the sun shineth in his strength' (Rev. 1:12-16).

The apostle John had seen the Lord Jesus prior to this, not only with his natural eyes, but also with the eyes of his soul. He had beheld his Saviour with the spiritual, discerning eye of faith. John saw the Lord Jesus in his life of obedience, in his agony in Gethsemane and in his ignominious death. He had been privileged to behold the miraculous power, glorious transfiguration and heavenly ascension of the God-man. Being taught by the Spirit of God, he knew what these things meant (1 John 1:1-3). Now, as he sat before his Saviour in worshipful meditation in the Spirit, he was given this blessed vision of that one whom he loved above all others.

Why is this vision important?

Why should this vision of Christ which John had so many years ago be of any importance to us today? It is important and meaningful to us because this vision of Christ is a symbolical representation of the one who suffered and died for our sins. John immediately recognized the one who spoke to him as the Son of Man, his Lord and Saviour. He was different, because he was now glorified. Still, he was the same, identical person, essentially unchanged (Heb. 13:8). There were no thorns on his brow, but John knew the brow. There were no nails in his hands, but John knew those hands. There was no agony in his voice, but John knew his Master's voice.

This vision represents what Christ is now. What Christ was when he was upon the earth is of vital importance to us, but what he is now is equally vital. Too often men and women get so wrapped up in thinking about how Christ will appear in the future that they fail to recognize and adore him as he now is. As we struggle with the pains, sorrows and trials of life in this world, we need to know what Christ is now, where he is now and what he is doing now. The future will be glorious, both for Christ and his people, but we need help now! John's vision of Christ is of immediate interest to God's saints because it declares what Christ is to his churches in this world. John saw the Lord Jesus Christ in the midst of his churches. The vision should therefore be of special interest to all who are members of the churches of Christ. Every pastor, elder, deacon, or teacher in every Christian church, every member of a local church, should be greatly interested in the vision John describes here. It has to do with us! We are personally involved in it!

What does this vision tell us about our Lord Jesus Christ?

This is not a vision given for curious, speculative eyes to dissect and investigate. It is a vision for reverent, believing hearts to adore. The words of verses 12-16 are symbolic. They are not to be taken literally. They do not represent the physical appearance of Christ in heaven. They represent his spiritual dignity, majesty and glory. The candlesticks are not literal candlesticks. The two-edged sword going out of our Lord's mouth is not a literal sword! The only way to interpret John's vision — indeed, the only way to interpret any part of God's holy Word — is with a God-given eye of spiritual discernment (1 Cor. 2:14-16).

'I saw seven golden candlesticks' (v. 12)

These candlesticks represent the seven churches of Asia Minor, which represented all the churches of God in this world throughout the ages of time (v. 20). There is, no doubt, a reference here to the candlesticks in the sanctuary of the Old Testament tabernacle and temple (Exod. 25:37; Zech. 4:2). The church of Christ may be compared to a candlestick because it holds forth the light of the gospel in a dark world. It does not produce light. It simply holds forth the light put into it by the Holy Spirit. This is the privilege and responsibility of the local church. She must hold forth the light of the glorious gospel of Christ.

'And in the midst of the seven candlesticks one like unto the Son of man' (v. 13)

John saw the Lord Jesus Christ standing in the midst of his churches. What a delightful picture! Christ our risen Lord is ever present with his church in this world. He graciously visits the assemblies of his saints and holds sweet

communion with his blood-bought people (Matt. 18:20).
He walks in the midst of his churches. He perpetually abides
with his own. Christ rules as King in the midst of Zion. He
is the head of the church universal and the head of every
local church (Eph. 1:22; 4:15; 5:23). He provides for and
protects his churches. Our King is also our Priest. Like the
sons of Aaron in the tabernacle, Christ trims the candles in
the candlesticks, causing the light of the gospel to burn
bright and clear in his church.

*'Clothed with a garment down to the foot, and girt about the
paps with a golden girdle' (v. 13)*

This robe is like the robe of Aaron, a holy garment. It is the
righteousness of Christ. Do you get the picture? Christ is
ever in the midst of his people as a sin-atoning High Priest.
His royal robe of righteousness is a robe of his own making. It covers his whole body. It covers every member of his
spiritual body, the church. The golden girdle that he wears
is not around his waist, but around his 'paps', his chest.
Christ wears the golden girdle of a King. It is a girdle of
righteousness, faithfulness and power. He wears the golden
girdle of a Prophet. It is a girdle of truth. And he wears the
golden girdle of a Priest. It is a girdle of love, with the names
of his people inscribed upon it. How worthy Christ is of all
our faith, worship and love! He who redeemed us is ever
with us. He is a King to rule over us and protect us, a Prophet
to teach us and guide us and a Priest to intercede for us.
And all that he does, he does in love for his own!

*'His head and his hairs were white like wool, as white as snow'
(v. 14)*

In the Song of Solomon, we are told that 'His locks are bushy,
and black as a raven' (5:11). Is there a discrepancy? Certainly not! In the Song of Solomon, the church, his bride,
is describing the perpetual youth and strength of her

Beloved. Here John is viewing his eternality, purity and
wisdom. He who ever has the dew of his youth is the
Ancient of Days (Dan. 7:9). In both passages, the picture of
Christ is symbolical, not literal!

'And his eyes were as a flame of fire' (v. 14)

This speaks of our Saviour's omniscience. He sees all and
knows all. And the all-knowing Saviour has flaming eyes
of love for his people. His love never dims or grows cold
and, being shed abroad in our hearts by his Spirit, it warms,
revives and refreshes us. His love, like a flame of fire, melts
the hearts of his people. Child of God, these eyes are ever
upon you. He who sees all and knows all can and will provide well for his own. Yet these very eyes burn with wrath
and vengeance against his enemies, and ours.

*'And his feet like unto fine brass, as if they burned in a fur-
nace'* (v. 15)

These feet of brass refer to the power of Christ to support
and defend his people. The reference to his feet being
burned in a furnace indicates that in all our afflictions he
is afflicted. When we pass through the refining furnace of
trials, afflictions and chastisements, as all who follow Christ
by faith must, our dear Lord is ever present with us (Isa.
43:2; Dan. 3:25). And these feet of brass will tread down all
our enemies before us (Isa. 41:10-11).

'And his voice as the sound of many waters' (v. 15)

His voice is the gospel of free grace preached by his servants in this world. It is sounded across the waters, proclaimed throughout all the world. When sounded out, when
preached in the power of the Holy Spirit, it is the effectual,
irresistible power of God unto salvation (Isa. 55:11; 1 Thess.
1:5).

'And he had in his right hand seven stars' (v. 16). These 'stars are the angels' of the churches (v. 20), God's appointed pastors, God's messengers and ambassadors to his people, those men who faithfully preach the gospel of his free and sovereign grace in Christ Jesus. Gospel preachers are compared to stars, because God has placed them where he wants them as guiding lights to point sinners to Christ, the way, the truth and the life, directing their steps in the way of salvation, and to give direction to his people in this world (Heb. 13:7,17). These stars, faithful gospel preachers, are the angels of God to his churches, and Christ holds them in his right hand. In the right hand of the Son of God, the pastor of the local church, God's messenger, is in the place of authority, power, approval and security. Those men who come to the churches with God's message come with God's authority, do their work by God's power, have God's approval and are kept and protected by God's mighty arm. They are 'in his right hand'! Behold God's messenger in Christ's right hand of sovereign power, and hear him say, 'Touch not mine anointed, and do my prophets no harm' (1 Chr. 16:22).

'And out of his mouth went a sharp two-edged sword' (v. 16)

This sword is the Word of God (Heb. 4:12). It is a weapon of both offence and defence. With it, Christ conquers his enemies and defends his church. It is a sword with two edges. It cuts both ways. With one side it slays our sin; with the other side our self-righteousness. It is the sword of the Spirit, the Word of God, that pricks the heart and brings sinners down in repentance before the sovereign Christ.

'And his countenance was as the sun shineth in his strength' (v. 16)

John had seen this before (Matt. 17:2). It speaks of the purity, dignity, majesty and glory of Christ, who is the Sun of

Righteousness (Mal. 4:2). In the spiritual realm, Christ is the Sun, the source, sustainer and strength of all spiritual life. If you look directly at the brilliant, noonday sun, it will burn your eyes, so that when you look away, no matter where you look, you will still see the sun. In the same way, those who look upon Christ by faith and see the glory of God in him, have 'Son-burnt' eyes. No matter where they look, they see Christ!

What was the result of this vision?

No one has ever had Christ revealed to him and walked away the same as he was before. When Christ reveals himself to a person, something happens. The results of such revelations are always pretty much the same. The flesh always withers before Christ, when he is pleased to reveal himself. John writes, 'And when I saw him, I fell at his feet as dead' (v. 17). The same thing happened to Manoah (Judg. 13:20), Ezekiel (Ezek. 1:28), Isaiah (Isa. 6:1-5) and Daniel (Dan. 10:8-9). How blessed it is to fall at his feet as one who has been slain in his glorious presence! We are never so much alive as when we are dead at his feet. We are never so truly living as when our flesh withers in death before our great and glorious Saviour. Every believer wants, more than anything else, the death of all that is sinful and rebellious in him.

Christ, who slays the flesh, will always raise and revive those he slays by the hand of his almighty grace. 'And he laid his right hand upon me' (v. 17). Life comes out of death. Revival comes out of withering. If you fall at his feet in the humiliation of broken-hearted repentance, he will raise you up by his grace.

Christ revealed in the heart always brings a word of comfort and assurance to the one to whom he reveals himself. 'Fear not; I am the first and the last: I am he that liveth and

was dead; and, behold, I am alive evermore, Amen; and
have the keys of hell and of death' (vv. 17-18). There is no
reason for any believer to fear anything. Christ Jesus lived
as our surety from eternity, died as our surety in time and
lives for evermore as our surety in heaven; and he who is
our surety has sovereign power over death and the grave
(Ps. 68:18-20). He will protect us in all our appointed ways
and keep us by his grace. Cast all your care upon him. 'He
careth for you' (1 Peter 5:7). And he will take care of you!

Once Christ reveals himself to a man, he gives that man
a message to declare. He said to John, 'Write the things which
thou hast seen, and the things which are, and the things
which shall be hereafter' (v. 19). Then he explained the
meaning of the vision John had: '... the mystery of the seven
stars which thou sawest in my right hand, and the seven
golden candlesticks. The seven stars are the angels of the
seven churches: and the seven candlesticks which thou
sawest are the seven churches' (v. 20). Everyone who has
Christ revealed to him receives a message to declare to his
fellow men. The message is always from Christ and about
Christ, and the one who receives it understands it. We who
have seen the Lord are his witnesses (Isa. 6:8; Acts 1:8). Let
all who know him, young and old, men and women, go
and tell the world what a great and glorious Saviour our
Lord Jesus Christ is!

7.

Jesus Christ is alive!

Revelation 1:18

'I am he that liveth, and was dead; and, behold, I am alive for evermore, Amen; and have the keys of hell and of death' (Rev. 1:18).

Always entertain great thoughts of Christ and you will have great delight in him. A great Saviour gives a great sense of security to those who trust him. That sense of security promotes, not licentiousness, but dedication. It produces joy and peace which keep the heart ever leaning upon Christ. If you would rise above the cares of the earth and the trivial things of time, you must set your affection on Christ and let your thoughts of him be elevated. Earth diminishes as Christ rises. The way to grow in grace is to let your thoughts of Christ grow.

As we look at Revelation 1:18, my sole object is to set before you the greatness of Christ, our ever-living God and Saviour. I want you to see him 'high and lifted up'. I want, by the Spirit of God, to inspire your heart to

Bring forth the royal diadem
And crown him Lord of all!

May God make Christ glorious in your heart! I have no other desire. I know of no better way to show you Christ's greatness and glory than to give you his own description of his own glorious being. This is how the glorified Christ described himself to John: 'I am he that liveth, and was dead; and, behold, I am alive for evermore. Amen.'

Our Saviour is alive

That great God who came into this world as a man, that God-man who lived as our representative to establish right-eousness for us and died as our substitute to put away our sins, that very same God-man is alive today! And Christ is exactly the same now in heaven as he was when he was here upon the earth. It is true that he has undergone the great change of glorification and exaltation, but he is es-sentially the same. His nature, his heart, his love, his will, his grace and his purpose are all unchanged (Heb. 13:8). He who is now the light of heaven is the same Christ who was born at Bethlehem. He who now sits upon the throne of glory is the very same Christ who stilled the troubled waters, healed the sick, fed the hungry and raised the dead. He who is now clothed with majesty is the very same Christ who bore our sins in his body on the cursed tree. Meditate upon the character of our Lord during those forty days be-tween his resurrection and his ascension. Those forty days of his glory on earth will serve as a picture of our Saviour's character today.

It seems that Christ made a point of showing us five spe-cific things about himself after his resurrection. By his gra-cious appearances to his disciples, he seems to have said, 'What I am now, I will for ever be.'

1. He was loving, tender and forgiving towards his sinful people

Remember, all had forsaken him. All were, for a time, over-come with sinful unbelief. The only one of our Lord's dis-ciples who seems to have understood and believed what he taught about his death and resurrection at the time was Mary, who anointed him for his burial. Yet his love towards his own was unquenched. His forgiveness was free. His tenderness was evident. The Lord first appeared to Mary Magdalene (John 20:11-17). Then, he sent special word to Peter to confirm his love to his fallen disciple (Mark 16:6-7). He stooped to remove Thomas' unbelief (John 20:26-29). Then he lovingly restored Peter to his fellowship and confirmed his place among the apostles (John 21:15-19). Believer, that is just the way Christ is today. Our Saviour's heart is full of love, tenderness and forgiveness towards his erring disciples.

2. He was constantly with his beloved church

The Gospel writers only tell us of specific appearances, but Christ appeared to his disciples whenever they met. When one searched for him, she found him. When two or three gathered to talk of him, he was present. When the twelve met, he was there. When five hundred brethren gathered in his name, immediately he was present with them. This is exactly the character of our Saviour today (Phil. 4:4).

3. He taught them about himself

He opened the Scriptures and taught his disciples things concerning himself (Luke 24:27,44-47). Is this not still true today? When the Son of God is our Teacher, our hearts burn within us as he talks to us about himself. Blessed is that assembly where Christ is taught and where Christ is himself the Teacher!

4. He was full of grace towards helpless, perishing sinners

For the sake of lost, justly condemned sinners, the Son of God sent his disciples into the world to proclaim the glorious gospel of his grace, telling them that 'repentance and remission of sins should be preached in his name among all nations'. And he told them to begin by preaching the gospel to the people of Jerusalem who had crucified him! Our Saviour is full of grace to sinners!

5. He promised them the enabling of his Spirit

The risen Christ, just before he ascended back into heaven, told his disciples that the success of their labour was entirely dependent upon the power of the Holy Spirit, whom he would send upon them (Luke 24:49). This is a blessed word of comfort and assurance. We need never fear failure. We need never look to ourselves for success. The Spirit of God works by us, and he cannot fail!

Do you understand these things? Christ in glory is exactly the same as he was when he was upon the earth. He is loving, tender and forgiving. He is constantly with us. He opens the Scriptures to us. He is gracious to sinners. And he promises the power of his Spirit to those who wait for him!

Christ's work of redemption as our substitute is finished

Our Saviour says, 'I am he that liveth, and was dead.' Though he is alive, he was dead, and his death was the death of death for all his people. By his death on the cross, Christ made a complete and final atonement for sin (Heb. 10:10-14). He did not merely make atonement possible, or merely provide a way by which men could have atonement for their sins. He actually satisfied divine justice and atoned for our sins. 'He is the propitiation for our sins' (1 John 2:2). He obtained eternal redemption for us (Heb. 9:12). So gloriously effectual is the death of our Lord Jesus Christ that there is no possibility of condemnation for those people for whom he died (Rom. 8:1,34).

His love for us is unchanging

The love which compelled our Lord to die for us is the love which rules the heart of that man who rules the world. What could be more comforting and assuring? 'If when we were enemies, we were reconciled to God by the death of his Son, much more, being reconciled, we shall be saved by his life' (Rom. 5:10). That God-man who rules the world is himself ruled by the love of his heart for us! What then shall we fear? His love is free and everlasting, without cause, without beginning, without limit and without end. If the God who rules the world loves me, all is well with me. Nothing shall harm me in time or eternity.

The purpose for which he died will certainly be accomplished

'He shall not fail' (Isa. 42:4). There will not be one lost soul in hell for whom Christ died. He has paid the debt for his elect. Therefore, his elect cannot be charged with sin. The law and justice of a righteous God will not allow it!

> Payment God cannot twice demand,
> First at my bleeding Surety's hand,
> And then again at mine.

It is nothing short of blasphemy to suggest that the Son of God was born into this world, lived and died for the purpose of saving any who are not saved by his grace. To say that Christ died for and endeavours to save those who perish in hell is to say that he died in vain for them, that he could not perform what he desired to perform. In other words, it is to deny that he is God! Our God and Saviour is no failure! He is mighty to save! 'The pleasure of the LORD shall prosper in his hand. He shall see of the travail of his soul, and shall be satisfied' (Isa. 53:10-11).

His sacrifice is eternally effectual

Because he was raised from the dead and ever lives in heaven, we are assured that the merit of Christ's sacrifice is eternally and perpetually effectual. Our Saviour died once, but he will never die again, because there is no need. That death of his, which took place two thousand years ago, is just as fresh and meritorious with God as if it had happened this morning.

> Dear dying Lamb, thy precious blood
> Shall never lose its power,
> Till all the ransomed church of God
> Be saved to sin no more!

Any sinner who comes to God upon the grounds of Christ's death as the sinner's substitute, God will not turn away. God himself cannot reject the merits of his dear Son!

Our Lord's mediatorial rule shall never fail

This, too, is implied in the text: 'I am he that liveth, and was dead; and, behold, I am alive for evermore. Amen.' That is to say, 'I shall never die again. I will reign for ever and ever, to accomplish my purpose as the covenant head and mediator of my people.' This great Christ, our ever-living Saviour, 'is able to save to the uttermost all who come to God by him' (Heb. 7:25). Because he died and lives for ever as the immutable Priest over the house of God, he has power to save for ever all who trust him. Our sovereign Lord will fulfil all his covenant engagements (Isa. 42:1-4; 53:10-12). In eternity, he assumed the responsibility of our salvation and, in the end, all for whom he is a surety will be with him in glory (John 10:16). This ever-living Christ

will subdue all his enemies beneath his feet (Isa. 45:20-25).
Either by the sceptre of his mercy or by the rod of his wrath,
all men and women will be brought in subjection to the
Son of God (Phil. 2:9-11). Our dear Saviour is alive! His
work of atonement is finished and complete. His mediatorial
rule shall never fail.

8.

Christ the ruler of death and hell

Revelation 1:18

'I am he that liveth, and was dead; and, behold, I am alive for evermore, Amen; and have the keys of hell and of death' (Rev. 1:18).

Death is the king of terrors. All men by nature are prisoners in bondage under the fear of death. How men strive against this enemy! People are willing to endure any misery if they might escape death. In our generation, we have seen human beings subjected to inhuman agonies as doctors practise their skills on them, trying to find a way to overcome, or at least postpone, death. Men seem ready enough to submit to almost any torture if they might only live a little longer. All men by nature fear death above all things. And this fear of death among men is a most reasonable thing. After death men must face the terror of hell!

What can be more horrifying than hell? Endless torment! Unceasing agony! Eternal torture! In hell, the worm of the awakened conscience, eating away at a man's soul, never dies. In hell, the fire of God's wrath, burning in a man's being, shall never be quenched. Who can describe the torments of the damned? Who would dare try? In hell, body and soul will suffer the unmitigated wrath of Almighty God for ever! This is the second death. It is an eternal awareness of, but an eternal separation from, all bliss, all comfort and all grace. Hell is to be for ever banished from heaven, with heaven in plain view! Hell is to be banished for ever from Christ, with Christ and his redeemed ones ever before your eyes! From that place of torment, none shall ever escape. Death and hell are the just rewards of sin. But sinners do not have to go to hell!

There is one who is sovereign over death and hell. There is one who has the power to deliver us from the fear of death and the torments of hell. He is Jesus Christ, the Son of God, the sinner's substitute. He says, 'I am he that liveth, and was dead; and, behold, I am alive for evermore. Amen.' Then, as the result of his life, death and resurrection as the God-man mediator, our Saviour declares, 'I … have the keys of hell and of death.' Death for us is an unsurveyed land of darkness before which we tremble, but Christ has explored and conquered that land. Now, as a sovereign King, he holds the key to the iron gates of death. Hell is a horrible region of terror, a kingdom of darkness and a habitation of evil, but the Lord Jesus Christ sits as King over hell just as fully as he sits King in Zion, and he will deliver all who trust him both from the fear of death and the power of hell. Nothing in heaven above, in the earth below, or in hell beneath the earth is out of his control (Ps. 115:3; 135:6). The sovereign dominion of the Lord Jesus Christ extends to the whole of his creation. No province is beyond his rule. No man is free of his dominion. No power threatens him. Let every believer rejoice in the fact that Christ sits King upon the throne of universal dominion and sovereignly rules everything everywhere. Nothing happens by chance. Nothing is free of Christ's dominion. The Lord our God has prepared his throne in the heavens and his kingdom rules over all. Our Saviour's sovereignty over all things should encourage us to trust him in all things and not be afraid. The Lord Jesus Christ, our Saviour, says, 'I have the keys of hell and of death.'

Who has these keys?

As you read Revelation 1, you cannot help noticing that it
lays particular stress upon the man Christ Jesus. He who
holds the keys of hell and of death is one of us. John describes him as 'one like unto the Son of man' (v. 13). He is
not quite the same, because he is now glorified, but Christ
in heaven is essentially the same as he was when John re-
clined next to him at the table. We must never try to separate our Saviour's manhood from his divinity, nor his
Godhood from his humanity. Christ in heaven is still a man.
This fact is full of hope and comfort to the fallen sons of
Adam. He who rules the universe is a man. He who has the
keys of hell and of death is a man. Yes, he is the God-man.
We rejoice in that fact. But still he is a man, a man like us,
bone of our bone and flesh of our flesh. God has entrusted
the dominion of the universe to the glorified man Christ
Jesus (Heb. 2:6-9; Phil. 2:9-11). This man established righteousness in the earth as the federal head and representative of God's elect by his holy obedience to the will of God
(Isa. 42:1-4, 21; Rom. 5:19). This man died under the penalty of God's law as the sinner's substitute, fully satisfying
divine justice for all his people (1 Peter 2:24; 3:18). He made
atonement for us. He is the propitiation for our sins. He
obtained eternal redemption for us. By his blood, God is
both just and the justifier of all who believe. This man
arose in triumph over the grave and reigns in glory as the
Mediator-King of his redeemed (Zech. 6:12-13). This man
is the hope of men (Isa. 32:1-2). Jesus Christ, the Son of
God, came into this world as a man to save men. He lived
for men. He died for men. He rose for men. He received
gifts for men. He intercedes for men. And he rules in heaven
for men. Immanuel, 'God with us,' is his name, and
'Immanuel' means 'God for us', too! God became a man,
that men might live by him (John 3:17), and now the God-
man holds the keys of hell and of death so that he might

surely accomplish his purpose (John 17:2). Not one of those shall perish whom he has undertaken to save!

What do these keys imply?

Keys represent ownership, dominion, authority and control. The man who carries the keys is in charge. The picture of Christ with the keys of death and hell is intended to show us that the Lord Jesus Christ has the rightful and actual dominion over death and hell. He actually rules the domain of death and hell. Unto him belong the issues of death (Ps. 68:20). And he rules even the dark chambers of hell. The rule of Christ is so thorough and absolute that even the devices of Satan are subject to him. They are either restrained by him, or they are overruled by him to serve his own glorious purpose. The keys of hell and of death in the hands of our Saviour say, 'Christ is supreme, Lord, King and Sovereign Ruler of all things.' His dominion extends to all the universe, even death and hell. Either willingly or unwillingly, all things serve him.[1]

The keys of death

Christ our Lord holds the keys of death (Ps. 68:18-20). As our Saviour is sovereign over the lives of men, he is also sovereign over the deaths of men. All live and all die by the will of Christ and by the hand of Christ (1 Sam. 2:6). Christ takes men and women out of this world when he pleases, as he demonstrated with Ananias and Sapphira (Acts 5:1-11). And he has already appointed the hour of

---

1. The word translated here as 'hell' is 'Hades'. It means the state of death and can therefore refer to the abode of departed spirits either in bliss or in torment. Our Lord Jesus Christ is King in heaven, King over hell and King over death.

every individual's departure from this world. None lives beyond his time, and none dies before his time. This fact is comforting to all who believe. Our hearts rejoice to sing:

> For now the future holds no fear,
> God guards the work begun:
> And mortals are immortal here,
> Until their work is done.

Yet let every rebel be warned. His day is marked. God has set a day and prepared the instrument by which he is to be slain!

If our Lord is pleased to do so, he has the power to deliver his own elect from death's grip, even when it appears that death will surely take them. The illustrations of Christ's power over physical death are numerous (Matt. 8:5-15; Luke 8:49-56; John 4:46-50; 11:43-44). What he did while he was upon the earth, our Lord can do today. Christ Jesus still has power to deliver his own from the jaws of death (James 5:14-15). I do not believe the charismatics' claims to gifts of healing. Those gifts ceased with the apostles. The so-called faith-healers of today are a mere sham! However, I do believe in the sovereign power of Christ. When it is according to his will, for the glory of his name and for the good of his people, he still delivers his own from the very jaws of death. The fact that I am writing these lines almost twenty years after my doctors thought I would be dead is proof of my Saviour's power over death!

The Lord Jesus Christ will raise the dead to life again at the last day. He raises those who are dead spiritually to life in the new birth, and he will raise the dead literally when he comes the second time (John 5:25-28). He said, 'I am the resurrection and the life: he that believeth in me, though he were dead, yet shall he live' (John 11:25).

The keys of heaven

As he holds the keys of death, our Lord Jesus Christ also holds the keys of heaven (John 14:1-6). Jesus is the Lord of heaven! Child of God, Christ has gone to prepare a place for you. When your place is ready, he will come for you, and call you home. Christ will open those gates of pearl, and lead you into the heavenly city. His key opens the gate. Once he has led you into the blessed city, he will shut you in, just as he shut Noah in the ark. His key locks the gate.

> Far from the world of grief and sin
> Christ will securely shut us in!

When Christ shuts us in, he will shut out all our sorrows, trials and troubles for ever (Rev. 21:4-6). There, in heaven's vast domain, Christ our Lord sovereignly rules as Lord and King. He rules among his redeemed ones. Those glorified spirits around the throne serve King Jesus perfectly. He rules among the angelic hosts. He rules all things from heaven, because he is determined to bring his ransomed ones to heaven.

The keys of hell

Our Lord Jesus Christ also holds the keys of hell (Rev. 20:1). It is Christ himself who will cast the wicked and unbelieving into hell (Matt. 25:31-34,41). Christ will shut every rebel up in the pit of the damned, from which there is no escape (Luke 16:26). Even now, our Lord Jesus Christ sovereignly rules over Satan and the demons of hell. The prince of darkness is under the dominion of King Jesus! (See Luke 8:28; John 12:31; Job 1:8,12; 2:6). Satan is a bound slave of King Jesus, an oarsman in the ship of providence, a beast which Christ has harnessed to accomplish his own purpose.

Do you see how these keys represent the sovereignty and dominion of our Lord Jesus Christ? He is King over death, King over heaven and King over hell! There is no province over which Christ does not totally rule. But how did our Saviour get this universal power?

How did Christ get the keys of death and hell?

It is certainly true that Christ holds these keys by divine right, because he is God over all. There can be no dispute about that fact. Since Christ is God, Creator and Sustainer of all things, he is owner of all things in heaven, earth and hell. God has the right to do with his own whatever he will, and he always does (Matt. 20:15; Ps. 135:6). But this man, Christ Jesus, holds the keys of death and of hell by right of his mighty conquests as our mediator and representative (John 17:1-5; Isa. 53:10-12; Ps. 89:19-27).

In order for Christ, the man, to ascend the throne of universal dominion, in order for him to be seated upon the throne of God, he had to make certain conquests as a man. At every point where the first Adam was defeated, Christ, the Last Adam, must be triumphant. This man, the Lord from heaven, had to endure and prevail over the temptations of the devil (Heb. 2:10,17,18; Matt. 4:1). He had to establish righteousness in the earth by obeying both the letter and the spirit of the law as our representative (Rom. 5:18-19). He had to overcome the weakness and frailty of the body of flesh, learning obedience by the things he suffered (Luke 22:42-44; Heb. 5:8). He had to be made sin for us and satisfy the demands of the law and justice of God against us, so that he might save us from our sins (Rom. 3:24-26; 2 Cor. 5:21; Gal. 3:13). And he had to rise from the dead in triumph as our victorious Saviour (Ps. 16:9-11). Thanks be to God, all that was required of our substitute, he has accomplished! He said to the Father, 'I have finished the work which thou gavest me to do' (John 17:4).

It is this man, Christ Jesus, who now reigns as King over death and hell to save his people (John 17:2). This man will reign sovereignly for ever until he has saved all his elect and put all things beneath his feet, even until all his enemies are completely vanquished (Isa. 45:20-25). He will save all his covenant people. He will subdue all his enemies. At last, he will make all things new! This man, Christ Jesus, holds the keys of hell and of death as the reward of all that he has done as the mediator and surety of the everlasting covenant.

What does our Lord's dominion say to us?

Our Lord says, 'I have the keys of hell and of death.' John Gill wrote, 'This is an expression of the sovereignty, power and authority of Christ; and is designed to encourage and support the believer in his present concern and anxiety of mind.' Our Saviour had laid his hands upon John, and said, 'Fear not.' This is what he said to calm John's fears: 'I have the keys of hell and of death.' Behold the sovereign Christ with the keys of death and hell in his hands, and do not be afraid! Do not fear the troubles and the trials which you must face in this world. Christ is on his throne. All is well! Do not fear the powers of hell itself. Jesus Christ rules all things. Satan cannot harm you! Do not fear the valley of the shadow of death. For the believer, death is only a shadow. You will not die, but live, and declare the wondrous works of the Lord. You must pass through the valley — but you will pass through it. Christ will see you through! Do not fear the unseen world of eternity. You are only going home! If you trust Christ, your sins are gone. You have all the righteousness God requires. You will live for ever. You have nothing to fear!

9.

Christ the faithful pastor warning his churches

Revelation 2:1 - 3:22

'Write the things which thou hast seen, and the things which are, and the things which shall be hereafter; the mystery of the seven stars which thou sawest in my right hand, and the seven golden candlesticks. The seven stars are the angels of the seven churches: and the seven candlesticks which thou sawest are the seven churches' (Rev. 1:19-20).

The Lord Jesus Christ himself is the Shepherd and Bishop of our souls (1 Peter 2:25). All earthly pastors are his under-shepherds. In Revelation chapters 2 and 3, we have seven letters which the Lord Jesus dictated to the apostle John, which were sent to the pastors of the seven churches in Asia Minor. Each letter was sent to a specific local church in the cities named: Ephesus, Smyrna, Pergamos, Thyatira, Sardis, Philadelphia and Laodicea. These were literal local churches in the apostolic era. However, these seven churches represent all the churches of Christ in this world throughout the gospel age. These are letters from Christ to us. They are just as pertinent to the life and ministry of the local church to which you belong as they were to the seven churches to which they were originally sent. 'He that hath an ear, let him hear what the Spirit saith unto the churches.' This admonition is given seven times in these two chapters because our Lord Jesus means every believer to pay particular attention to the warnings contained in these seven letters. In these letters, the Son of God himself warns us plainly of the most prominent dangers we must face in this world.

A fact we must never forget

The Lord Jesus Christ says, 'I know thy works' (2:2,9,13,19; 3:1,8,15). God has ordained that all who are saved by his grace walk in good works for the honour of his name (Eph. 2:8-10). And that which God has ordained, God will bring to pass. He will see that his people walk in good works. The indwelling presence of God the Holy Spirit makes all believers new creatures in Christ (2 Cor. 5:17). The bent of that new nature created in the heaven-born soul is towards Christ and holiness (2 Peter 1:4; Gal. 5:22-23). Those who profess faith in Christ but deny him by their works are reprobate (Titus 1:16). This is not a debatable issue. True believers glorify God before men by their good works.

For the religious hypocrite, these words are terrifying — 'I know thy works.' 'The eyes of the Lord are in every place, beholding the evil and the good' (Prov. 15:3). His eyes are a flaming fire and darkness is light before him. A man may deceive his pastor, his family and even himself, but the Son of God is not deceived. All things are naked and open before him (Heb. 4:13). That makes hypocrisy a losing game. 'The hypocrite's hope shall perish' (Job 8:13).

For the believer, these words are full of comfort and cheer — 'I know thy works.' What a delight! Our dear Saviour looks not at our works themselves, but at the motive behind them. He looks into the heart and sees why we do the things we do. And he is well pleased with the most feeble efforts of sincere, believing hearts. By the merits of his blood and righteousness, he makes our works a sweet-smelling sacrifice to God, acceptable and well-pleasing in his sight (1 Peter 2:5). Imagine that — God is well-pleased with the faltering steps of believing sinners for Christ's sake, because they are steps towards him! God will not forget your works of faith and labours of love (Heb. 6:10). The works of those who die in the Lord 'shall follow them' (Rev. 14:13). And they will be named by Christ himself in the Day of Judgement (Matt. 25:37-39). The Son of God, our Saviour, says, 'I know thy works.' What could be more comforting?

Warnings of dangers that must be overcome

In these two chapters, the Lord Jesus identifies six conditions which, if they are not resisted and overcome, will result in apostasy and eternal ruin. If these conditions are allowed to go unchecked in any local church, it will soon wither and die. It may continue to exist in name, but that is all. Christ will withdraw the light of the gospel from it. Instead of being a house of light, it will be a den of darkness.

Here are six dangerous conditions into which we are constantly tempted to fall. The world, the flesh and the devil all strive to pull us down into these pits. If you find yourself described in these letters, the Lord Jesus warns you to repent and turn to him.

1. Apostasy from our first love

The Lord Jesus Christ says, 'I have somewhat against thee, because thou hast left thy first love' (2:4). These Ephesians were zealous in good works, patient in trials and afflictions of life, and thoroughly orthodox in doctrine. But there was a dreadful decay in the matter of love to Christ! As William Hendriksen says, 'A wife may be very faithful to her husband and may give evidence of bustling assiduity in all matters pertaining to him — and yet, there may be a decay in love. Her sense of duty may cause her to remain faithful in all the details of attention she bestows upon him.'

In just the same way, you and I may be very faithful in all
the outward forms of godliness and remain perfectly orthodox in doctrine, while our hearts' love and devotion to Christ
declines and decays. Are you like the Ephesians? Does your
love for Christ decline? Do you find yourself more and more
concerned about the cares of this world and less and less
concerned about Christ? Repent! Turn anew to Christ! Re-
nounce all but him and set your affection on him alone
(Col. 3:1-3).[1]

2. Compromise with false doctrine

Next we are warned not to embrace the doctrine of Balaam
(2:14). When Balak called for Balaam to curse Israel, God
restrained him. Much to Balak's disgust, God forced Balaam
to bless his people (Num. 22-24). Yet Israel became involved
in the worship of Baal (Num. 25:1-3). Their sin, we are told,
was the result of Balaam's counsel (Num. 31:16). The doctrine of Balaam is the doctrine of compromise with the religion of the world. Balaam did not advise Israel to give up
the worship of Jehovah. He simply told them it would be
wise to accept the worship of Baal and go along with the
religious customs, traditions and practices of their pagan
neighbours.

Be warned! Compromise with false religion is damning
to the souls of men. Compromise is the way of least resist-
ance, the way approved of by the world, the way that is
easiest on the flesh. But any compromise of God's truth is
an outright denial of Christ (2 Cor. 6:14-18). The only way
to remove the offence of the gospel is to deny the gospel.
We must never give any credibility to the religion of this
world. Those who preach free will and the freedom of man

---

1. The correction for dead doctrine is not the absence of doctrine, emotionalism, or Pentecostalism, but steadfast commitment to Christ. Like
Mary, let us take our place at his feet and have our hearts ravished with
his love (Luke 10:39-42).

deny the sovereignty of God. Those who preach salvation by the will, works, or worth of the sinner deny salvation by grace. Those who preach universal atonement deny the efficacy of Christ's blood. Those who preach universal grace deny the efficacy of God's saving grace. God's people must never seek agreement with such men, even in the name of peace, unity and brotherly love. The only way those who believe the gospel can get along with those who do not is for us to deny the gospel. That we must not do!

3. Antinomianism

We are all, by nature, tempted to embrace the doctrine of the Nicolaitans (2:15). These were a group of heretics in John's day who taught that it was all right for believers to engage in the sexual immoralities of pagan religions. According to John Gill, they 'committed fornication, adultery, and all uncleanness, and had their wives in common, and also ate things offered to idols'. They were antinomians. They were opposed to the law of God. Their doctrine was: 'Let us sin that grace may abound. Since we are saved by grace, it does not matter how we live.' Without question, any man who preaches salvation by grace alone will be accused of antinomianism (Rom. 3:8). It is not possible to preach redemption, justification and sanctification by grace alone, through the merits of Christ alone, without some legalist crying, 'That is antinomianism! That will lead to licentiousness!' Having said that, this must also be declared: any man who is an antinomian is a lost man. God's elect seek holiness and righteousness. They are not self-willed, licentious rebels. Their hearts and lives are ruled by the love of Christ. And the love of Christ prevents lawlessness.

4. Tolerance of false prophets

The churches of Christ and individual believers are constantly under pressure from the world to be tolerant of false

prophets (2:20). The church at Thyatira was charitable, diligent in service, patient in trial and well established in the
faith of the gospel. But it was tolerant of 'that woman Jezebel'. There was a women in the church who claimed to be
called by God and gifted as a preacher, a prophetess. Our
Lord calls her 'Jezebel' after Ahab's wife, because she was a
deceiver. Though the Word of God clearly forbids the ordi-
nation of women and the tolerance of women as preachers
and teachers in the house of God (1 Tim. 2:11-12), this
church allowed this woman to teach and to seduce the
people with her doctrine. The flesh says, 'Do not make a
fuss about false prophets. It will only cause trouble.' The
world says, 'Do not judge others! To condemn the actions
of another is bigotry.' Satan tempts us to be silent, lest we
create strife and division. Yet the Bible warns us constantly
to 'beware of false prophets' (Matt. 7:15). If they are not
identified, exposed and denounced, they will soon devour
a congregation (Gal. 1:6-9; 2 Tim. 2:16-18).

5. Hypocrisy and formality

We must guard against the tendency of our flesh towards
hypocrisy, ritualism and lifeless orthodoxy (3:1). We are all
prone to hypocrisy. We are all by nature very skilled in the
art of pretending. Being natural born hypocrites, we have
in us an innate tendency to substitute ritualism for worship, a creed for Christ and orthodoxy for life. 'Beware ...
of the leaven of the Pharisees, which is hypocrisy' (Luke
12:1). We must take care that we live in the pursuit of true
godliness, not a mere form of godliness. We must carefully
observe the ordinances of Christ (baptism and the Lord's
Supper), but resist the mere outward practice of religious
ceremonies. We must tenaciously adhere to the doctrine of
Christ, but fear that form of doctrinal purity that has no
heart. All who have, practise and hold to a form of religion
without Christ are like the church at Sardis, to whom it
was said, 'Thou hast a name that thou livest, and art dead!'

6. Lukewarmness, apathy and indifference

Our Lord warns his churches of the most dangerous of all
fleshly tendencies — that of lukewarmness, apathy and
indifference (3:15-16). The Laodiceans were lukewarm.
Nothing is more disgusting to the palate than lukewarm
coffee, lukewarm stew, lukewarm gravy, or lukewarm milk.
And nothing is more disgusting to Christ than lukewarm,
half-hearted, apathetic, indifferent men and women. Yet
we are ever prone to become lukewarm about the things of
Christ. Every faithful pastor has seen many gradually sink
into disgusting apathy. Once the gospel of the grace of God
made the faces of men and women light up with joy who
now are unmoved by it. Once the story of redeeming love
filled them with rapturous gratitude and melted their hearts
to tears, but now nothing moves them. They are lukewarm.

How to avoid these dangers

If we would overcome these evil tendencies of the flesh,
we must obey the counsel of our compassionate Saviour.
There is no guesswork involved. The Lord Jesus tells us
exactly what must be done: 'Remember ... from whence
thou art fallen' (2:5). 'Repent ... and do the first works' (2:5).
'That which ye already have hold fast' (2:25). Tenaciously
adhere to the truth of God, the gospel of his free and sovereign grace in Christ. 'Be watchful, and strengthen the things
which remain' (3:2). 'Buy of me!' (3:18). Without money
and without price, by faith alone, we must buy from Christ
the gold of his grace and the white robe of his righteousness, as we did in the beginning, and anoint our eyes anew
with the eye-salve of the gospel.

Promises given to overcomers

Here are the promises the Son of God gives to those who heed his word, overcome these dangers and persevere unto the end. Let the wise make personal application to himself. Return to your first love, and Christ promises you the blessedness of eternal glory (2:7). Hold fast the doctrine of Christ and confess him in the midst of his enemies, and he promises to own you as his (2:17). Continue in the way of faith, and the Son of God will give you power over the world (2:26). Awake, arise from the dead, and he will give you the light of life (3:5; Eph. 5:14). Return to Christ with a true and fervent heart of faith, and he will cause you to reign with him for ever (3:21). The Son of God, the Lord Jesus Christ, leans hard against the door of his church, knocking to his beloved (3:20). If anyone in his house will open to him, he will come in and sup with him!

10.

Christ's letter to the church at Ephesus

Revelation 2:1-7

'Unto the angel of the church of Ephesus write: These things saith he that holdeth the seven stars in his right hand, who walketh in the midst of the seven golden candlesticks; I know thy works, and thy labour, and thy patience, and how thou canst not bear them which are evil: and thou hast tried them which say they are apostles, and are not, and hast found them liars: and hast borne, and hast patience, and for my name's sake hast laboured, and hast not fainted. Nevertheless I have somewhat against thee, because thou hast left thy first love. Remember therefore from whence thou art fallen, and repent, and do the first works; or else I will come unto thee quickly, and will remove thy candlestick out of his place, except thou repent. But this thou hast, that thou hatest the deeds of the Nicolaitans, which I also hate. He that hath an ear, let him hear what the Spirit saith unto the churches: To him that overcometh will I give to eat of the tree of life, which is in the midst of the paradise of God' (Rev. 2:1-7).

Ephesus was a wealthy, prosperous, magnificent city, famous for its extravagant temple for the pagan goddess Diana. For many years it was the centre of commerce in Asia. It was connected to all the major cities of Asia Minor by well-maintained roads. Its harbour accommodated the largest ships of the day. The temple of Diana in Ephesus was a museum, a treasure house and a place of refuge for criminals. That pagan temple provided employment for artisans and silversmiths, who made and sold little shrines, religious trinkets and idols to the worshippers and tourists who passed through the temple.

The apostle Paul came to this city of more than 225,000 people on his third missionary journey. He preached the gospel in Ephesus for over three years (Acts 18-20). Multitudes were converted by the grace of God. A gospel church was established, which quickly became a lighthouse for truth, from which the gospel of God's free and sovereign grace in Christ was preached. The church at Ephesus was devoted to Christ. It was known throughout the Christian world for its devotion to, and zeal for, Christ.

But now more than forty years had passed. Another generation had arisen. The church at Ephesus still walked in the truth. The gospel of Christ was still proclaimed from its pulpit. But something desperately evil had happened. The Lord Jesus Christ discovered a very sad fault in his church at Ephesus. The pastor, 'the angel of the church', did not discern the fault. The people were unaware of it. But Christ saw it. Therefore he sent this letter to the church, to be read publicly in the assembly of the saints. How their hearts must have sunk when they read these words from the Saviour: 'I have somewhat against thee, because thou hast left thy first love'!

This letter was not written to the church at Ephesus alone, but to all the churches of Christ in this world. 'He that hath an ear, let him hear what the Spirit saith unto the churches' (v. 7). It is written to you, and it is written to me. Let us each ask God to give us ears to hear and hearts to obey the word of Christ to his church.

Let us each ask ourselves this question: 'Is there in me a declension from my first love to Christ?' Painful as the question is to the heart of one who truly does love the Saviour, it must be asked and honestly answered.

A commendation

We must not fail to recognize that there was much in this Ephesian church which the Saviour commended (vv. 2-3,6). Our Saviour always deals with his people in love, kindness and tenderness. When there is a stern reproof to be given, he cushions it with a kind word of commendation and encouragement. Let no one imagine that the church at Ephesus was an apostate, or even indifferent, congregation. Nothing could be further from the truth! Few are the churches to whom such a laudable commendation could be given.

The Lord Jesus Christ, who is the faithful and true witness, said to these Ephesian believers, 'I know thy works, and thy labour, and thy patience, and how thou canst not bear them which are evil: and thou hast tried them which say they are apostles, and are not, and hast found them liars: and hast borne, and hast patience, and for my name's sake hast laboured, and hast not fainted... [And] this thou hast, that thou hatest the deeds of the Nicolaitans, which I also hate.' With these words, the Lord Jesus Christ commended his church at Ephesus for eight noble things. Blessed is that man, blessed is that local church, in which such commendable characteristics of grace are found!

1. 'I know thy works'

These were not idle believers. Their faith was practical. By works of obedience to God, works of charity to men and works of devotion to Christ, the saints of God at Ephesus demonstrated their faith. They did not merely *profess* faith. They *practised* faith. Their works were known, approved of and accepted by Christ.

2. 'I know thy labour'

These believers not only walked in good works before God, they put themselves wholeheartedly into the work God gave them to do for his glory. They zealously and anxiously went about serving the cause of Christ in their generation with all their might. These men and women were not lazy, loitering, listless people. They seized every opportunity to serve their Saviour. And they did it willingly.

3. 'I know thy patience'

There are many who labour, and labour well, but do so only for a while. They do not persevere in the work. Before long, they faint and fall by the wayside. Not these people! This congregation had laboured steadily, in the face of great opposition, in the midst of great trials and in a dark, pagan world of religious superstition and moral perversion. They had done so for more than forty years! This church threw all its energy and all its means into the cause of Christ, not in spurts and spasms, but in continual, unabated zeal for the glory of God!

4. 'I know how thou canst not bear them which are evil'

The Son of God also commended the church at Ephesus for its firm adherence to gospel truth. They had an intense loathing for that which is evil, both doctrinally and morally. They loved the truth. And their love for the truth made them 'hate every false way' (Ps. 119:104).

5. 'I know thou hast tried them which say they are apostles, and are not, and hast found them liars'

Few there are to whom these honourable words could be spoken! But the saints at Ephesus knew the difference between things that differ. They knew truth from error. When they heard Judaizers and proponents of free will (or, as we would say today, legalists and Arminians) preaching another gospel, another Jesus and another spirit, their blood

boiled. They boldly denounced all such pretentious preachers as liars, deceivers and wicked men.

**6. 'I know how thou hast borne, and hast patience, and for my
sake hast laboured'**

This church also bore reproach and persecution for Christ's
sake, and did so with patience. In the teeth of opposition,
they stood firm. In the midst of Christ's enemies, they boldly
confessed him. In the face of hardship, trial, persecution
and imprisonment, they confidently served their Master.
They were loyal to the core.

7. 'I know that thou hast not fainted'

The Saviour commended them for their rare faithfulness
and perseverance. They never failed. They never faltered.
They never quit. The saints of God at Ephesus were people
of a kind that is all too rare.

**8. 'I know that thou hatest the deeds of the Nicolaitans, which
I also hate'**

One other matter of commendation was their hatred of the
Nicolaitans. As we saw in the previous chapter, the
Nicolaitans were a sect of base antinomians which had
arisen in those early days of Christianity. They contended
that since God's elect are saved by grace and are free from
the law, nothing is evil. They made every excuse for lewd-
ness and licentiousness.

As we noted earlier, John Gill tells us that the Nicolaitans
'committed fornication, adultery, and all uncleanness, and
had their wives in common'. All this evil was practised
and promoted in the name of Christian liberty. All true believers, like these Ephesians, and like Christ himself, despise those who promote ungodliness in the name of grace.

A sad declension

These eight things the Lord commended. Commendable characteristics they are. Yet the church at Ephesus had one serious flaw, one dreadfully evil weakness, which, if it were not corrected, would end in utter ruin. The Lord Jesus said to this otherwise exemplary church, 'Nevertheless [though you are orthodox, zealous, patient, persevering, uncompromising and upright], I have somewhat against thee, because thou hast left thy first love.'

Does this charge apply to you? Does it apply to me? William Cowper took the charge personally. Should we not do the same?

> Where is the blessedness I knew
> When first I saw the Lord?
> Where is the soul-refreshing view
> Of Jesus in his Word?
>
> What peaceful hours I then enjoyed,
> How sweet their memory still!
> But now I find an aching void
> The world can never fill!

The sad fact is, love that is not fed with fellowship and communion soon decays into something worse than indifference. It decays into presumption and ingratitude.

What is this first love?

I am not sure that I can really define the term 'first love', but I am sure that it can be clearly identified. Do not imagine that this is merely an emotional or sentimental thing that has no real significance. This thing called 'first love' is very important to our God and Saviour (Jer. 2:1-2).

When our Saviour says, 'Thou hast left thy first love,' it is obvious that he is not talking about believers who once loved him, but have now ceased to love him. True love can never be quenched. Anyone who ceases to love Christ never truly loved Christ at all. Love for Christ is a gift of God's grace that can never be taken away, lost, or destroyed (Jer. 32:38-40; Hosea 2:19-20).

Yet God's people do sometimes leave their first love. Through indolence, neglect of duty and the care of this world, the heat and fervour of our love for Christ abates, and the exercise of love towards him diminishes.

Let me stir up your memory a little. Go back to the place where you first met the Saviour. Go back to Mt Calvary, where the Lord Jesus Christ first appeared to you, bleeding upon the cross as your substitute. Do you remember how he spoke to your heart and said, 'I am your salvation. I have redeemed you. All your sins are forgiven, washed away in this fountain of blood'?

Immediately, you fell in love with him. Had he asked you then to give everything you had to him, you would gladly have done so. In fact, he did ask it, and you gladly laid all at his feet. If you are a believer, I know that was your experience. Faith, in its very essence, involves a voluntary surrender of all to the dominion of Christ as Lord (Luke 14:25-33).

It was that first love which caused us to confess Christ before men, identifying ourselves with him in believer's baptism, and caused us to witness earnestly and zealously to men, telling all who would hear us what a wonderful Saviour he is. That first love inspired our hearts to almost unceasing prayer, praise and communion. That first love for Christ made his Word our most delightful treasure. That first love made the house of God, the ministry of the Word and the fellowship of God's saints the most important and most joyful things in the world to us. How delightfully we learned and sang the songs of Zion! How easily our hearts broke with joy, as we ate the bread and drank the wine at the Lord's Table, remembering our Saviour! How anxiously we read and studied the Word of God! How anxious our hearts were to hear the preaching of the gospel! You do remember, don't you?

That first love caused us to do the will of God with unquestioning faith and unhesitating obedience. We would give anything for the cause of Christ. We would do anything for the glory of Christ. We would go anywhere at the bidding of Christ. Like the apostle Paul, once the will of God was known in any matter, we 'conferred not with flesh and blood'.

> Those peaceful hours [we] once enjoyed,
> How sweet their memory still!

Do you remember how it was then, when your heart was still burning with those live coals from off the altar? But now we are more refined. Now we are more settled. Now we are more learned, more mature, more cold, more dead, more useless. Is that not so?

What happened?

Where did we go wrong? How did we leave our first love? Rarely, if ever, does such a decline in love begin with some climactic event. It gradually steals over our hearts and suffocates us by degrees. But the cause of the decline is not hard to find. If we will be honest with ourselves, we shall find, I am sure, that any decay from our first love comes from three sources.

1. Wilful neglect of Christ (S. of S. 5:2-6)

One of our most besetting sins is the neglect of Christ, the neglect of sweet communion with our Saviour. Give us something to do for Christ, for the good of his church, for the furtherance of the gospel, and we will immediately put ourselves into the work. But we are not, it must be shamefully confessed, nearly as quick to open our hearts to communion with Christ. Yet love to Christ very much depends upon nearness to Christ. If we live near Christ, in close, intimate communion, we cannot help loving him and being controlled by love for him. The heart that lives nearest Christ in sweet communion is most aflame with love for Christ.

2. The love of the world (Matt. 13:22)

There are few, very few, people who increase in riches and increase in grace at the same time. Of all the temptations to which God's people are exposed in this world, this is the most dangerous, because it is the most subtle. Too much of the world is an evil encumbrance to any man. None of us is sufficiently aware of what our Lord calls 'the care of this world and the deceitfulness of riches'.

3. Our innate tendency towards presumption, self-confidence and self-righteousness (Amos 6:1)

When we begin to think much of ourselves, we think little of Christ. Presumption destroys perseverance. Self-confidence destroys faith. And self-righteousness destroys love. He is wisest who walks before God always as a poor, needy sinner, trusting Christ alone for everything (Col. 2:6). He is strongest who knows his utter weakness and total insufficiency, finding Christ's grace and strength sufficient (2 Cor. 12:9-10).

What can be done to rekindle our first love?

If we belong to Christ, through we decline in love to him, his love towards us will never decline, and because he loves us he will chasten us and cause us to return to him (S. of S. 5:6-7). If we do not return to Christ, if our hearts do not again glow with love for him, if our decline is a permanent decline, it is because our love is a fake, a pretence, a sham profession and no more. Let us not be presumptuous. We might be wise to sing with John Newton:

> Help me to love thee more and more,
> If I love at all, I pray;
> If I have not loved before
> Help me to begin today.

If you would return to your Saviour and regain that first love, the Lord Jesus here gives you three words of instruction.

1. 'Remember!'

'Remember therefore from whence thou art fallen.' 'Remember' what a blessed condition your soul was in when you enjoyed that first love (S. of S. 2:4-6). 'Remember' where and what you were when the Saviour found you and saved you by his grace (Isa. 51:1). 'Remember' what you owe Christ (Ezek. 16:6-14).

2. 'Repent!'

'Repent' as you did at the first. Repent of the evil you have done to Christ in leaving your first love. 'Repent' of your shameful neglect of your Saviour. 'Repent' of your sinful love of the world (Col. 3:1-3). 'Repent' of your proud presumption, self-confidence and self-righteousness.

3. Return!

'Repent and do the first works.' That is just another way of saying, 'Return unto the Lord.' Many years ago, a young preacher went to visit an older preacher whom he admired, to seek his counsel about the work of the ministry. The young preacher asked the old man, whom he esteemed so highly, 'Can you give me one word of advice that I can remember, by which to direct my life and ministry for the glory of God?' Without hesitation, the old man replied, 'Take great care that you never lose your sweetheart love for the Lord Jesus Christ.'

Wiser counsel was never given. Yet when that love does decline, as it is ever inclined to do, return! Return to the place where you first met Christ. Return to the foot of the cross. Bathe your sin-sick soul again in the precious blood of Christ. As you did at the first, trust Christ. As it was in the beginning, let your soul be ravished with his love, and look on him until your heart breaks with love for him again (S. of S. 5:8).

In order to stir up our hearts to return to him and regain that first love, our Saviour gives us a warning and a promise. The warning is this: '[If you do not remember, repent, and return to me], I will come unto thee quickly, and will remove thy candlestick out of his place' (v. 5). That believer who goes on in indifference will be put away like a broken tool, in uselessness. That local church which goes on in indifference to Christ will have the light of his presence taken away, and their usefulness will cease.

The promise is this: 'To him that overcometh will I give to eat of the tree of life, which is in the midst of the paradise of God' (v. 7). Those who lose their first love fall, but those who regain their first love are made to stand. And that love is fed and nourished by Christ himself, both now upon this earth and for ever in heaven's glory. The Lord Jesus Christ will be, to all that love him sincerely, 'the tree of life' in heaven, 'the paradise of God'. The feeding of love upon Christ is heaven begun already in the soul!

If I could have anything on earth I might desire, I would choose to have nothing but love for the Lord Jesus Christ, and to do nothing but that which is for his sake and that which is done out of love for him. Oh, may God the Holy Spirit fill our hearts with love for Christ! Yet, I know that there will be no returning of our hearts to our first love, once it is in declension, unless Christ himself causes us by his Spirit to return. So this is my prayer: 'Turn us unto thee, O LORD, and we shall be turned: renew our days as of old. Amen.'

11.

Christ's letter to the church at Smyrna

Revelation 2:8-11

'And unto the angel of the church in Smyrna write: These things saith the first and the last, which was dead, and is alive; I know thy works, and tribulation, and poverty, (but thou art rich) and I know the blasphemy of them which say they are Jews, and are not, but are the synagogue of Satan. Fear none of those things which thou shalt suffer: behold, the devil shall cast some of you into prison, that ye may be tried; and ye shall have tribulation ten days: be thou faithful unto death, and I will give thee a crown of life. He that hath an ear, let him hear what the Spirit saith unto the churches: He that overcometh shall not be hurt of the second death' (Rev. 2:8-11).*

Smyrna, like Ephesus, was a rich coastal city. It was located about thirty-five miles north of Ephesus on the Aegean Sea. It was a loyal ally of Rome, even before Rome gained its greatness. Smyrna was also a place of emperor worship. The city built a temple for the worship of the Emperor Tiberius. In a word, Smyrna was a wealthy, powerful, pagan city, entirely given over to idolatry. But, in his merciful providence, God was pleased to send a gospel preacher to that city and establish a gospel church in her midst.

We have no way of knowing for certain how this church began, but in all likelihood it was established by Paul during his ministry at Ephesus (Acts 19:10). This church had remained faithful for many years in the midst of great trial.

It was sound in doctrine, strong in faith and in a spiritually healthy state. There was nothing in this church that needed to be corrected. The sole purpose of our Lord's letter to this church was to encourage his people to remain faithful, even unto death. Christ, who knows all things, knew what severe trials the church at Smyrna must face. In this letter he wisely prepares his people for their trials.

Our Lord Jesus Christ dictated this letter to John to comfort and strengthen his church in the midst of her earthly trials and to encourage her to persevere in the faith of the gospel. Though this letter was addressed particularly to the church at Smyrna, historically, it was intended by Christ to be a message to us today. Though those of us who live in free societies no longer fear the persecutions experienced by God's church in days gone by, because God providentially restrains the powers of wicked men, yet it is still true that 'All that will live godly in Christ Jesus shall suffer persecution' (2 Tim. 3:12). If we follow Christ and seek to live in this world for the glory of Christ, we shall suffer abuse at the hands of Christ's enemies. Our Saviour has told us plainly, 'In the world ye shall have tribulation' (John 16:33).

In this letter our Lord does four things to comfort and encourage his church in the midst of her troubles: first, our Lord Jesus Christ calls our attention away from our troubles to himself (v. 8); second, our Saviour assures us of his constant care (v. 9); third, the Lord graciously quietens our fears (v. 10); and, fourth, the Lord Jesus Christ encourages us to persevere (v. 11).

Look to Christ

As the letter opens, our Lord Jesus Christ calls our attention away from our troubles to himself: 'And unto the angel of the church in Smyrna write: These things saith the first and the last, which was dead, and is alive' (v. 8).

The church at Smyrna was a flock of harmless sheep in the midst of ferocious wolves. It was the object of malicious slander, reproach and persecution. Its troubles were many. And, like all of us in times of trouble, the people of God at Smyrna were in danger of falling into the pit of self-pity, which always leads to despondency, if not despair. In order to prevent this from happening, the Lord Jesus says, 'Do not look upon your troubles, but look to me.' That is the thrust of this salutation: 'These things saith the first and the last, which was dead, and is alive.'

If we could learn to meditate upon, and look to, Christ with believing hearts, rather than meditating upon our earthly woes, the problems and difficulties we face on this earth would give us far less trouble. Everything on this earth is temporary. Christ, who is the first and the last, is eternal, and he has secured for us an eternal inheritance in glory. Let every troubled believer look to Christ, our eternal, unchangeable Saviour, and his troubles will seem insignificant.

The Lord Jesus Christ, our Saviour, is the first and the last. He is the first, for by him all things were made. He is before all things, and by him all things consist. Christ is the first, for he is himself God, from everlasting to everlasting. And he is the last, for all things were made for him. All things will be brought to their final end by Christ. All things will be judged by Christ. And all things will show forth the praise of Christ. Christ is the first, for he is the foundation laid in Zion. And he is the last, for he is the top-stone, the chief-cornerstone, and the head-stone of the corner in his spiritual temple, the church.

Our Saviour particularly would have us dwell and meditate upon his most glorious work and most glorious character, as our all-sufficient, unchanging, exalted mediator and King. He is the one who 'was dead, and is alive'.

There is no cure for despondent hearts like the knowledge of redemption by Christ. The cross of Christ is like the tree Moses cast into Marah's bitter waters. Take the blessed gospel doctrine of blood atonement and cast it into the bitter waters of your earthly trouble, and it will make your bitter troubles sweet to your soul. Whenever you look for something to comfort your heart, encourage your faith, revive your soul and cause your spirit to leap with joy, meditate on these two facts: first, he was dead; second, he is alive.

1. The Lord Jesus Christ was dead

He died as our substitute, under the penalty of our sins. He died to satisfy the offended justice of God for us, to put away our sins. By his death, the Son of God purchased salvation for us. Christ died for us. What reason then do we have to fear?

2. He is alive

Having died under the penalty of sin as our substitute, the Lord Jesus rose again for our justification, and he is alive for evermore. Christ died to obtain salvation. And he lives to apply salvation. 'For if, when we were enemies, we were reconciled to God by the death of his Son, much more, being reconciled, we shall be saved by his life' (Rom. 5:10). Christ lives as our Priest and King for ever to save his elect (Isa. 53:9-11). He lives to intercede for his people (John 17:9,20; 1 John 2:1-2). He lives to protect his own (John 10:27-30). Surely, when we are aware of what Christ has done and is doing for us, we can smile at Satan's rage and face a frowning world (Rom. 8:28-39).

Assurance

In verse 9 our Lord assures us of his constant care: 'I know thy works, and tribulation, and poverty, (but thou art rich) and I know the blasphemy of them which say they are Jews, and are not, but are the synagogue of Satan.'

More tender, assuring, comforting words could not be spoken to troubled believers than the words of Christ to us in this verse. He says, 'I know.' It is enough for the child to know that his Father knows what is troubling him. It is enough for the wife to know that her loving husband knows her need. And it is enough for God's saints to know that Christ knows our peculiar circumstances. Here our Saviour gives us five words of assurance.

1. 'I know thy works'

Christ, who is the omniscient God, knows our works. For the unbelieving hypocrite this is terrifying. But for the believer it is comforting. He whose glory is our chief delight knows our works for him. He not only knows them, he accepts them, through his own merit, and delights in them. He knows the motive of our works, that they are done out of love for him (2 Cor. 5:14). He knows that the strength by which we perform our works for him is the strength which his own grace supplies. And he knows that our works are performed from a sincere heart that desires his glory. Peter's consolation, even in the teeth of his horrid sin, was the Master's knowledge of him (John 21:17). Let every believer find comfort here: 'Lord, thou knowest all things; thou knowest that I love thee.'

Believers never speak to God of their own works. We recognize that our best works are marred by sin and must be washed in the blood of Christ. But Christ will not fail to remember even a cup of cold water offered in his name (Matt. 10:41-42).

2. 'I know thy tribulation'

This is our Lord's legacy to his church: 'In the world ye shall have tribulation' (John 16:33). He told us plainly that we must through much tribulation enter into the kingdom of heaven (Acts 14:22). For the people of God, this world is a place of sorrow. Believers are soldiers in a hostile territory. Conversion is the beginning of conflict. To worship Christ is to enter into warfare with this world. No one can follow Christ without paying a price for doing so. In those early days of Christianity, believers suffered banishment, imprisonment and death by wild beasts or burning at the stake. Today, in many parts of the world, the conflict is perhaps more subtle, but it is just as real. If you and I follow Christ, we shall have to march contrary to the world at all times. It is the confession of Christ that causes the conflict. If we do not confess Christ in the teeth of his enemies, we shall face no conflict. But that lack of confession will be a proof that we do not truly know Christ (Matt. 10:32-34).

Believers are a confessing people. We confess our sin to our Saviour, and confess our Saviour before men. We confess Christ in the waters of baptism: being buried with him in the watery grave and rising with him from the grave, we identify ourselves with our Lord and publicly declare our allegiance to him (Rom. 6:3-6). We confess Christ when we defend his honour amidst his enemies. We confess our Lord when we press his claims upon his enemies. We confess the Lord Jesus Christ when we make his gospel and his glory the rule by which we live in this world.

3. 'I know thy poverty'

These believers at Smyrna were brought to extreme poverty because of their confession of Christ. It was not at all uncommon for a man to lose his job when he was baptized. In those days, to be a believer, from an earthly point of view, meant real sacrifice. Indeed, it is still true today, in measure. Believers frequently lose much by following Christ. If we are believers, anything that would keep us from worshipping Christ or honouring Christ must be forsaken, though it may cost us much in earthly goods. 'Ye cannot serve God and mammon.'

4. 'But thou art rich'

For the gospel's sake, these believers suffered tribulation and poverty. But there was no reason for them to begin to pity themselves. They may have seemed to be poor. Indeed, they were very poor in the matter of earthly goods. But they were rich towards God, rich in spiritual possessions and rich in grace (Matt. 6:20; 19:21; Luke 12:21).

Do not allow today's prophets of health, wealth and prosperity to deceive you. Earthly riches are no sign of divine approval. And earthly poverty is no sign of divine displeasure. If we are believers, if we are in Christ, we are rich (Eph. 1:3). All the riches of God's grace are ours in Christ. All the blessings of God's covenant are ours in Christ. We are heirs of God and joint-heirs with Christ (Rom. 8:17). It is written: 'All things are yours' (1 Cor. 3:21).

5. 'I know the blasphemy of them which say they are Jews, and are not, but are the synagogue of Satan'

Here our Lord assures us that he knows his true people from those who merely profess to be his people. There was a large population of Jews in Smyrna. They had settled there because Smyrna was a good place of business and built a synagogue. As always, these Jews were filled with hatred for the people of God. They both blasphemed Christ and accused his people of horrible crimes before the Romans. These physical descendants of Abraham thought they were the people of God. But our Lord calls them the synagogue of Satan.

'How anyone can say that the Jews of today are still, in a very special and glorious, and pre-eminent sense, God's people, is more than we can understand,' writes William Hendriksen. 'God himself calls those who reject the Saviour and persecute true believers "the synagogue of Satan". They are no longer his people.'

Yet this text has a wider application. Those assemblies which are set up in opposition to the truths of the gospel, though they call themselves Christian churches, are all synagogues of Satan. He presides over them. He works in them. And his interests are served by them. What are these synagogues of Satan? Any church that equates morality with righteousness (Rom. 10:1-4). Any church that promotes will-worship (Col. 2:23). Any church that puts salvation and redemption in the hands of man (Gal. 2:21). Any church that substitutes ceremonialism and ritualism for worship.

God's covenant people, the true Israel of God, is the church of God, Christ's spiritual seed. A man's family tree, outward religious exercises, profession of religion and doctrinal creed have nothing to do with his relationship to God. Christianity, faith in Christ, is a matter of the heart. It is altogether inward and spiritual. 'They are not all Israel, which are of Israel' (Rom. 9:6; 2:28-29; Phil. 3:3).

It is most comforting to believers, in the midst of their earthly trials, to hear the Son of God say, 'I know.' He who is our Saviour is the sovereign King of the universe, and he knows all about us. His eye is always upon us.

'Fear none of those things'

Our Lord graciously quietens our fears in verse 10: 'Fear none of those things which thou shalt suffer: behold, the devil shall cast some of you into prison, that ye may be tried; and ye shall have tribulation ten days: be thou faithful unto death, and I will give thee a crown of life.'

Again, I remind you that, as long as we live in this world, we are going to suffer. And our Lord here plainly warns us that the longer we live in this world, the more our sorrow will increase. He is talking in particular about the evil which

we must suffer at the hands of wicked men, who, unknow-
ingly, are the pawns of Satan himself. Yet our blessed Saviour says, 'Fear none of those things.' Though Satan roars
against us, he cannot devour God's elect. No matter how
great our sufferings on this earth may be, here are four facts
which should quieten our fears.

1. Our sufferings in this world are governed and regulated by our Saviour (1 Cor. 10:13)

It is true, we often suffer at the hands of wicked men. And,
like Job, we suffer much from Satan himself. But both
wicked men and Satan are under the rule of Christ. They
can do nothing without our Redeemer's permission (Job
1:12; 2:6). And whatever God permits our enemies to do
will be best for us (2 Sam. 16:10-12).

2. Those things that we suffer will not last long

Our sorrow will not be perpetual. It will last for a set time,
and that set time is really a very short time: 'Ye shall have
tribulation ten days,' that is to say, 'You will suffer for a
definite, but brief time.' Surely, we who live for eternity
and live in eternity should be able to bear our light afflictions patiently, realizing that they are but for a brief moment in time (Isa. 26:20; 54:8-10; Matt. 24:22; 2 Cor. 4:18;
1 Peter 1:6).

3. The purpose for our trials is to prove our faith

God allows the temptation, the trial and the tribulation,
'that ye may be tried'. God sovereignly uses Satan's vicious
attacks to prove his elect. Satan's intent is to destroy us.
But God graciously uses his wicked designs to prove us
(James 1:2,3,12). To put it in the words of John Gill, 'Suffering times are trying times, whether men are real Christians

or no; whether they have the true grace of God or not; and whether the principles they hold are right and true, and are worth and will bear suffering.' Sooner or later, God will prove our faith. It will be clearly demonstrated whether or not we really trust him.

4. All who endure temptations will receive a crown of life

Our Master says, 'Be thou faithful unto death, and I will give thee a crown of life.' This is not a promise of a special crown for martyrs. All who belong to Christ will receive a crown of life. God has promised this crown to all who love him (James 1:12). The crown is eternal life itself (1 Cor. 9:25). Faithfulness is the one thing God requires of his people. And faithfulness is the one thing all believers give. God's people are faithful. Once a sailor, sailing through a storm, made this statement: 'God, you may sink me if you will; you may save me if you will. But, whatever happens, I will keep my rudder true.' That is the believer's attitude. To those who are faithful unto death, Christ promises the crown of glory, eternal salvation (Matt. 10:22).

Perseverance encouraged

Here is a promise to those who persevere unto the end, to those who are conquerors and more than conquerors in Christ: 'He that hath an ear, let him hear what the Spirit saith unto the churches: He that overcometh shall not be hurt of the second death' (v. 11).

There is a second death. Death in itself is the result of sin, and physical death is tormenting to men; but there is a second, eternal, spiritual death, which is the death of the body and of the soul in hell (Rev. 20:14). This second death has no claim upon God's elect. Though we may be put to death physically, we shall never die (John 5:25; 11:25; Rev.

20:6). We have been ordained to eternal life (Acts 13:48). Christ purchased eternal life for us (Heb. 9:12). We have eternal life now (1 John 5:13). We shall soon obtain the glory of that eternal life. Christ himself will give it to us.

The greatest encouragement to faithfulness and perseverance is the assurance of our security and eternal life in Christ (Heb. 11:13-16; Col. 1:21-23).

12.

Christ's letter to the church at Pergamos

Revelation 2:12-17

'And to the angel of the church in Pergamos write: These things saith he which hath the sharp sword with two edges; I know thy works, and where thou dwellest, even where Satan's seat is: and thou holdest fast my name, and hast not denied my faith, even in those days wherein Antipas was my faithful martyr, who was slain among you, where Satan dwelleth. But I have a few things against thee, because thou hast there them that hold the doctrine of Balaam, who taught Balak to cast a stumbling-block before the children of Israel, to eat things sacrificed unto idols, and to commit fornication. So hast thou also them that hold the doctrine of the Nicolaitans, which thing I hate. Repent; or else I will come unto thee quickly, and will fight against them with the sword of my mouth. He that hath an ear, let him hear what the Spirit saith unto the churches: To him that overcometh will I give to eat of the hidden manna, and will give him a white stone, and in the stone a new name written, which no man knoweth saving he that receiveth it' (Rev. 2:12-17).

Pergamos means 'exalted, lofty, or elevated'. It was the name of a city in Asia Minor (also known as Pergamum), which was built on a huge rocky hill. The Romans made this city the capital of the province. In Pergamos Aesculapius, the pagan god of healing, was worshipped. The emblem of this god was a serpent, which to the people of God is the very emblem and symbol of Satan. Therefore, our Lord called

Pergamos the place 'where Satan's seat is'. The great altar to the Greek god Zeus was also in this city, as were many other altars to pagan gods.

In addition to these things, Pergamos was the centre of emperor-worship. Temples were dedicated to the worship of Caesar. All men, including the disciples of Christ, were expected to offer incense to the emperor's image and say, 'Caesar is Lord.' Those who refused to do so suffered great hardship and persecution for their fidelity to Christ. One example was a man named Antipas, a faithful believer who suffered martyrdom because he would not deny Christ.

The majority of those who were members of the church in Pergamos were faithful. They held fast the name of Christ and would not deny his faith. But there were a few, even there, who tried to straddle the fence. Though they claimed to be Christians, they were willing to compromise with the pagans. They followed the doctrine of Balaam. In order to avoid persecution they tried to remove the offence of the cross by incorporating the worship of pagans into the worship of Christ. They would offer incense to Caesar, eat meat in the temple of Aesculapius, pay homage to Zeus and then come to worship with the people of God on Sunday.

Others in the church went beyond the doctrine of Balaam. They followed the licentious practices of the Nicolaitans. As we have seen, these Nicolaitans were base antinomians, who openly taught and practised fornication and adultery and shared their wives with one another. In a word, they lived and acted like pagans, but called themselves Christians.

Notice the character under which our Lord Jesus Christ presents himself to the church at Pergamos: 'Those things saith he which hath the sharp sword with two edges' (v. 12). Christ stands before the door of his church with a sword drawn and ready to do battle. The sharp, double-edged sword with which the Son of God does battle is the Word of God. There are two reasons for this picture.

1. Christ will destroy those who defile his name

He speaks to those in the church who hold the doctrine of Balaam and the doctrine of the Nicolaitans and says, 'Repent; or else I will come unto thee quickly, and will fight against them with the sword of my mouth' (v. 16).

Notice he says, 'I will fight against *them*' — not against 'my church', but against those who are in his church but have forsaken him. There is a parallel passage in Matthew 3:12. John the Baptist tells us that Christ's 'fan is in his hand, and he will thoroughly purge his floor, and gather his wheat into the garner; but he will burn up the chaff with unquenchable fire'.

Christ's love for his church is manifest by his judgement against the traitors within her walls. The Word of God is a sword of judgement and destruction to hypocrites. By the preaching of the Word, our Lord disciplines his church, separates the wheat from the chaff and binds up the tares for the burning (Matt. 13:30). He turns his sword against those within the church who have no right to be there. Such a sight should make every hypocrite tremble — but nothing makes hypocrites tremble.

2. He will defend his church

Christ presents himself here as a man of war, with his sword drawn, to comfort and defend his church. He is saying to the faithful, 'I will defend you. I will fight off those who attack you. I will destroy your enemies and I will purge you of all those wicked men within who would defile you.' The Lord Jesus is our Joshua. He will chase the enemy before us and lead us onward, conquering and to conquer. Thus in this letter our Lord encourages us to persevere in the faith of the gospel.

The name of Christ and the faith of Christ

The passage shows us that the name of Christ and the faith of Christ are one. Our Lord says, 'Thou holdest fast my name, and hast not denied my faith' (v. 13). These two things are identical. They can never be separated. The faith of the gospel has Christ for its centre, Christ for its circumference and Christ for its substance. The name of Christ — that is his person, his character, his work and his teachings — is the faith of the gospel.

The great doctrines of the gospel are all intimately connected with the Lord Jesus Christ himself. They are the rays, and he is the sun. We never hold the faith of Christ, except as we hold Jesus Christ himself as the centre and object of that faith. In the faith of the gospel Jesus Christ is all and in all.

Election is God choosing us in Christ before the world was made. Redemption is God purchasing his elect out of the hands of his own law by the blood of Christ. Regeneration is God giving dead sinners life in Christ, and Christ living in us. Forgiveness is God pardoning our sins through the blood of Christ. Justification is God clothing us with, and imputing to us, the righteousness of Christ. Sanctification is God forming Christ in us, imparting his righteousness to us. Resurrection is God raising us up by the power of Christ. Glorification is God conforming us to the image of Christ, to which end we were predestinated in the eternal purpose of his grace.

To the Jews the law was never in its proper place until it was laid in the ark, and covered with the mercy seat. And this is still true with us. We never see the law properly until we see it fulfilled in Christ. The same is true of the gospel. The gospel is the golden ring of our faith, but Christ is the diamond set in the ring. Christ is the author and finisher of our faith. He is the sum and the substance, the top and the bottom, the Alpha and the Omega of the faith of the gospel. When we hold fast the name of Christ we have not denied the faith.

Denying the faith

Our Lord tells us that there are many who do deny the faith. In Pergamos there were some who held the doctrine of Balaam and others the doctrine of the Nicolaitans. In doing so they had both denied the name of Christ and the faith of the gospel. This is a painful fact, but it is a fact, and one that we have to face. In every local church there are some who will, for one reason or another, deny the faith. How do men and women deny Christ and his faith?

1. By refusing to confess it

Secret disciples are always suspect disciples. Those who confess Christ and the faith of the gospel only among his friends have, by their silence, denied him (Matt. 10:27, 32-33). Those who know the truth but refuse to confess it in the teeth of Christ's enemies, deny the truth.

Many, in this age of self-serving pragmatism, say, 'I do not think we should offend people, or try to force anything down their throats. We must try to get along.' Are you of that opinion? This is what the Son of God says about the matter: 'I came not to send peace, but a sword' (Matt. 10:34). 'He that is not with me is against me; and he that gathereth not with me scattereth abroad' (Matt. 12:30). 'And whosoever doth not bear his cross, and come after me, cannot be my disciple' (Luke 14:27). If we are Christ's disciples, sooner or later, he will see to it that we confess him before men, even before his enemies. The time will come when Nicodemus will identify himself with his Lord (John 7:50-51) and Joseph of Arimathea will openly own his Master (John 19:38).

2. By embracing false doctrine

In Pergamos some had embraced the doctrine of Balaam and others the doctrine of the Nicolaitans. Neither was an open denial of the gospel, but both were a practical denial of it. The doctrine of Balaam was the acceptance of, and compliance with, false religion. It was an attempt to say, 'We do not have to denounce the religions of men in order to hold to the truth of God' (Num. 25:1-2; 31:16). The doctrine of the Nicolaitans said, 'Faith in Christ does not require godliness and obedience to Christ.'

How does this apply to us today? If we embrace error regarding Christ's person, work, or doctrine, if we believe what our Lord did not teach, or refuse to believe what he did teach, then we have denied his name and his faith.

Let us ever focus our hearts and minds on Christ our Lord, and shun everything that would turn our thoughts away from him. Christ is the way we must follow. That is practical Christianity. Christ is the truth we must believe. That is doctrinal Christianity. Christ is the life we must live. That is experimental Christianity. It matters not whether you talk about practical godliness, doctrinal truth, or experimental religion, all must be found in Christ, all must come from Christ and all must direct us to Christ. We cannot be right in any area unless Christ is the sum and substance of all. Our religion is Christ. Apart from this there is no true religion. Any doctrine divorced from Christ is heresy. Any precept divorced from Christ is legalism. Any religious experience divorced from Christ is fanaticism.

3. By lives that are contrary to the gospel

Paul said to Timothy, 'If any provide not for his own, and especially for those of his own house, he hath denied the faith, and is worse than an infidel' (1 Tim. 5:8). Morality will never produce faith, but faith always produces morality. This was the error of the Nicolaitans. They held the truth in creed, but denied it in their lives. It matters not what I say I believe; if my manner of life is contrary to the gospel, I am an infidel, an unbeliever.

4. By forsaking Christ and the gospel (John 6:66; 1 John 2:19)

There are some who deliberately choose to forsake the gospel, while others are gradually overcome by the deceitful charms of the world, but all who forsake Christ, all who forsake the gospel of the grace of God, have denied the faith. And by their actions they prove that their faith was false.

Persevering faith

All true believers hold fast the name of Christ and will not deny the faith of the gospel. It is true that some, like Peter, fall at times and deny Christ for a season, but none of God's elect does so permanently and totally. In the tenor of their lives, God's people are faithful. All true believers will persevere in the faith to the end. This is clearly the teaching of Holy Scripture (Jer. 32:37-40; John 10:27-30).

How do we hold fast the name of Christ and the faith of the gospel? How is it that God's elect persevere in the faith? We must, in our hearts as well as in our heads, hold fast the faith of the gospel. The gospel is the message of God's free grace to sinners in Christ. It is the message of full atonement and free justification by the obedience of Christ as the sinner's substitute. It is the message of salvation by grace alone without the works of man. It includes electing grace, redeeming grace, regenerating grace and preserving grace. The grace of God in Christ is sovereign, free, irresistible, effectual and saving. This is the faith of the gospel (Eph. 1:3-14; 2 Tim. 1:9-12). Believing sinners hold it fast, knowing that we have no hope but the hope of free, sovereign grace in Christ.

We hold the faith by the full consent of our minds. God deals with the heart, but he does not bypass the mind. When Christ speaks, our minds assent to what he says and our hearts consent to his revelation. Our motto is: 'Let God be true, and every man a liar.'

Yet there is more. We not only agree to the truth of the gospel, we have received the love of the truth. We hold the faith of the gospel in the affections of our hearts (2 Thess. 2:10-12). Many acknowledge the truth, but few love the truth. God's people love the truth. Divine sovereignty, electing love, effectual atonement, imputed righteousness and almighty, infallible, irrevocable grace are matters of unceasing joy, thanksgiving and consolation to needy sinners who have been made to experience them.

We hold the faith when we hold forth the faith of the gospel in the teeth of all opposition. Those who believe the gospel do not hide their colours. They raise the banner high. If men resist, we hold it higher still. If they oppose, we hold it high and wave it in their faces. If I believe the gospel, I am not ashamed to confess the gospel. Men may count me a fool. Men may ridicule me as a fanatic. Men may denounce me as an instigator of strife, but I am honoured to be counted a fool, ridiculed and despised by men for Christ's sake.

If we would hold the faith of Christ, we must hold fast the name of Christ. We must, like those disciples to whom our Lord said, 'Will ye also go away?' reply, 'Lord, to whom shall we go? Thou hast the words of eternal life. And we believe and are sure that thou art that Christ, the Son of the living God' (John 6:67-69).

Always hold fast the deity of Christ's name. We rejoice to know that our Saviour is a man. But let us never forget that that man is 'the mighty God' (Isa. 9:6). He is Immanuel, God with us, God in human flesh. When you put the finger of faith into the nail print in his hand, always cry with the heart of faith, 'My Lord and my God' (John 20:28).

The royalty of Christ's name must never be forgotten (Rom. 14:9; Phil. 2:9-11). Our Saviour is the Lord Jesus Christ. He reigns as King over all things and must continue to reign as King of kings and Lord of lords until he has put all his enemies under his feet. Believing hearts bow in submission to Christ's kingly throne, trust his kingly power, submit to his kingly will and obey his kingly rule.

Never was there a name of such greatness and grandeur as Christ's name. 'His name is great in Israel' (Ps. 76:1). I will 'praise thy great and terrible name, for it is holy' (Ps. 99:3). 'There is none like unto thee, O Lord; thou art great, and thy name is great in might' (Jer. 10:6). 'I am a great King, saith the Lord of hosts, and my name is dreadful among the heathen' (Mal. 1:14).

It is impossible to speak too highly, or even highly enough, of Christ's name. It is impossible to make too much, or even enough, of him and his great name. His name is who he is. Surely, none can imagine that it is possible to make too much of him who is all. The Lord Jesus Christ is the Alpha and the Omega; he is all and in all. The whole Bible was written to set forth his name (Luke 24:27). The covenant of grace was ordered in his name. All the promises of God are 'Yea' and 'Amen' in his name. All the blessings of grace are received through his name. We are saved by faith in his name (Acts 4:12; Rom. 10:13). We prevail in prayer through his name. God's servants are sent to preach his name. We find all comfort in his name.

Jesus, the name that charms our fears,
That bids our sorrows cease,
'Tis music in the sinner's ears,
'Tis life, and health, and peace.

In the name of Christ — only in the name of Christ — we have a confident hope of victory (Rom. 7:24-25; 8:35-39). Constantine once had a dream in which he imagined that

God showed him the cross of Christ, and he took it as his emblem, with this motto: 'By the cross I conquer!' Believers care nothing for Constantine's superstitious idolizing of the sign of the cross, but we hold forth and hold fast the doctrine of the cross, the doctrine of the gospel and the name of Christ in it, and we say, 'By Christ we conquer!' If we persevere in the faith and hold fast the name of Christ firm unto the end we shall be saved (Matt. 10:22; Col. 1:21-23; Heb. 3:6,14; 10:35-39). And all who are born of God will persevere to the end, because God Almighty who has 'begun a good work in you will perform it until the day of Jesus Christ' (Phil. 1:6).

Hidden manna, a white stone, a new name

This is our Saviour's promise: 'To him that overcometh will I give to eat of the hidden manna, and will give him a white stone, and in the stone a new name written, which no man knoweth saving he that receiveth it' (v. 17). In other words he is saying, 'If in the midst of much opposition from the world, the flesh and the devil you hold fast my name and do not depart from the faith of the gospel, you will overcome your enemies and I will receive you into my heavenly kingdom.'

The hidden manna which Christ will give us to eat for ever is the very manna which we now eat by faith — it is Christ himself (John 6:32-35). As today we live by feasting upon the merits of Christ's righteousness and shed blood (John 6:54), so also in heaven our souls will live for ever, feasting upon him.

The white stone which Christ will give us is the stone of complete absolution in the Day of Judgement (Jer. 50:20). The allusion here is to the common practice of the Romans in judgement. After a man had been tried for a crime, if he was found guilty, the judges would cast a black stone into an urn, which meant condemnation. If he were found innocent, they would cast in a white stone, which signified that he had been acquitted and absolved of all guilt.

The new name which Christ will give us, which none can know but those who receive it, is 'The LORD our Righteousness' (Jer. 23:6; 33:16). We have been made so perfectly righteous and holy by the imputation to us of Christ's righteousness that our everlasting name will be 'Jehovah our Righteousness' (Isa. 56:5; 62:2).

13.

Christ's letter to the church at Thyatira

Revelation 2:18-29

'And unto the angel of the church in Thyatira write: These things saith the Son of God, who hath his eyes like unto a flame of fire, and his feet are like fine brass; I know thy works, and charity, and service, and faith, and thy patience, and thy works; and the last to be more than the first. Notwithstanding I have a few things against thee, because thou sufferest that woman Jezebel, which calleth herself a prophetess, to teach and to seduce my servants to commit fornication, and to eat things sacrificed unto idols. And I gave her space to repent of her fornication; and she repented not. Behold, I will cast her into a bed, and them that commit adultery with her into great tribulation, except they repent of their deeds. And I will kill her children with death; and all the churches shall know that I am he which searcheth the reins and hearts: and I will give unto every one of you according to your works. But unto you I say, and unto the rest in Thyatira, as many as have not this doctrine, and which have not known the depths of Satan, as they speak; I will put upon you none other burden. But that which ye have already hold fast till I come. And he that overcometh, and keepeth my works unto the end, to him will I give power over the nations: and he shall rule them with a rod of iron; as the vessels of a potter shall they be broken to shivers: even as I received of my Father. And I will give him the morning star. He that hath an ear, let him hear what the Spirit saith unto the churches' (Rev. 2:18-29).

Thyatira was the home of Lydia, whose heart the Lord opened. It was a place of great commerce, a city with many, many people passing through its streets every day. Thyatira was a place of wealth and power. In that place of great commerce, the guilds, which were the trade unions of the day, were well organized and powerful. Wool-workers, linen-workers, tailors, craftsmen in leather, tanners, potters, etc. were all associated in business, in one way or another, with pagan idolatry. Each guild had its own guardian god.

The situation there was such that if you wanted to get ahead in business, you had to belong to one of the trade guilds. If you belonged to the guild, your membership implied that you worshipped its god. You would be expected to eat the food offered to those gods at their pagan festivals. Joining in these festivities implied that you acknowledged that you had received the food from the gods. After the feasts, base orgies would begin. You could not dare insult your peers by walking out of their festivities!

What could a believer do in such circumstances? If he were to quit his guild, he would lose business. If he remained in the guild, attended the immoral festivities and joined in the idolatrous and licentious practices of pagan worship, he would be denying his Lord and sinning against his conscience. God's saints at Thyatira had to face problems of this kind everyday, in much the same way that many of God's people do, to varying degrees, in this degenerate age.

There was a prophetess in the church at Thyatira called Jezebel who claimed to have a solution to the problem. She reasoned that in order to conquer Satan, you must get to know him. 'You will never be able to influence the idolaters if you condemn them and refuse to go along with their religion. You do not have to deny Christ, but you cannot expect to get along in the world if you do not accept the world's religion, or at least accept it as an acceptable form of religion. After all, who are we to condemn another man's religion? You just cannot say that someone's religion is false!'

Does that sound familiar? By her cunning craftiness, this prophetess seduced many in the church and persuaded them to commit fornication, not only spiritual fornication, but literally to commit fornication in the name of religious unity! That was the condition of the church at Thyatira.

Almost all the old commentators suggest that this letter has reference to the rise of papacy and the heretical, immoral doctrines and practices of the Roman Catholic Church. I have no tolerance for papacy. I am always ready to denounce it as antichrist. Romanism is idolatry. It promotes immorality. Its doctrines are nothing but heretical superstitions. However, it is a grave mistake to limit this letter to the church at Thyatira to the rise of Romanism. Like the other six letters, this letter is addressed to God's people today. It warns us of certain dangers the church of Christ is sure to endure in any age: 'He that hath an ear, let him hear what the Spirit saith unto the churches.' In this letter our Lord warns every local church, every pastor and everyone who professes faith in his name of the subtle and damning influence of false religion.

An assuring revelation

As this letter opens, our Lord Jesus makes an assuring revelation of himself (v. 18). He who walks in the midst of his churches and holds her pastors in his right hand is himself 'the Son of God, who hath his eyes like unto a flame of fire, and his feet are like fine brass'. In times of trouble and danger, nothing is more assuring to God's saints than the comforting knowledge of Christ's presence. 'The Lord is at hand' both to observe and to protect his own.

The Son of God addresses himself to the angel of the church at Thyatira. As we have seen repeatedly, the angel of the local church is its pastor. He is God's messenger to the church. You will notice that in each church there is only one angel, one pastor, one messenger from God to his people. It is his responsibility, entrusted to him by God, to instruct the people of God and protect them from the many forms of false religion that arise. The means by which he does this is the faithful preaching of the gospel, expounding Holy Scripture (Eph. 4:11-14; Acts 20:28-30).

Identifying himself as the Son of God, our Saviour calls us both to trust him and to obey him. He who is the head of the church is no mere man, but the Son of God himself, our Saviour and our Lord. He calls himself the 'Son of Man' (1:13) to assure us of his love and sympathy towards us. He calls himself the 'Son of God' to assure us of his sovereign, almighty power. Our Saviour is God Almighty, and he is a man touched with the feeling of our infirmities.

His eyes are like a flame of fire. He has a piercing, penetrating, perfect knowledge and insight into all things and all people. He searches the hearts and knows the motives of all actions. He tries the reins and knows the principles of all people.

His feet are like fine brass. As he knows and judges all things with perfect wisdom, he rules all things and acts with absolute strength and perfect steadiness. His works of providence are deliberate and irrepressible. These two things ought to encourage every faithful pastor to remain loyal to Christ and the gospel of his grace: Christ knows all things, and he has all power. Whom or what shall we fear?

An acknowledged regard

Our Lord displays an acknowledged regard for the faithfulness of his people (v. 19). The Lord God promises to honour those who honour him (1 Sam. 2:30). Here he fulfils that promise. The Son of God here publicly commends the good works of faithful men and women: 'I know thy works, and charity, and service, and faith, and thy patience, and thy works; and the last to be more than the first.'

This commendation was not given by a stranger, or even by a casual observer. It was given by one who was well acquainted with them and with the principles upon which they acted.[1] In this nineteenth verse our Saviour names five specific works for which he commended his saints at Thyatira.

1. They were men and women of obvious charity

This is a clear evidence of real grace. Those who are born of God love Christ and love one another. Faith 'worketh by love' (Gal. 5:6; John 13:34-35; 1 Cor. 13:1-3; 1 John 4:20 – 5:1). Love is much more than mere sentiment or a sugary smile. Love is a thoughtful regard for and active pursuit of another person's happiness and well-being.

2. They were men and women of service to the gospel

No doubt they served one another in many ways. But the words, 'thy service', seem here to have a particular reference to the church's commitment to the ministry of the gospel. They were a missionary church, committed to the spread of the gospel. With great diligence, they sacrificed money, time and labour so that others might hear the gospel of the grace of God (1 Thess. 1:8).

---

1. While we must do nothing to honour the flesh and promote pride, it is always proper to recognize and commend faithfulness. To do so is but to follow the example of Christ himself. We should never neglect to commend, or show our appreciation for, the good things people do for Christ, his gospel, his church, or for us. Ingratitude is always inexcusable, especially when it hides behind the mask of spirituality!

3. They demonstrated great faithfulness to Christ

The Master commended their 'faith,' their faithfulness. They were not those who made a lukewarm, half-hearted religious profession, but faithful followers of Christ. Faithfulness is the one thing God requires of his people, and the one thing all his people give (1 Cor. 4:2).

4. They were patient

Those who are most charitable, most diligent in the cause of Christ, and most faithful in the things of God are likely to be the most tried. But in their many trials they display patience. 'Tribulation worketh patience' (Rom. 5:3). It cannot be learned any other way. Patience is simply the peaceful, believing resignation of one's heart to the will of God (Phil. 4:12).

5. Their last works were more than the first

In addition to all these things our Lord commended the saints at Thyatira for the fact that they grew steadily in devotion to him. Their last works were better and more numerous than their first. Others had left their first love and lost their first zeal; not these people! As they grew old, they grew wise. As they matured in years, they matured in grace. As they declined in physical strength, they grew in spiritual strength.

These five things ought to be matters of constant concern and prayer to every believer. Let us ever seek grace from our God to love our brethren, serve the cause of Christ, be faithful to our God, walk with patience before God and men, and grow in the grace and knowledge of our Lord Jesus Christ.

An alarming reproof

In verses 20-23, our Lord sounds an alarming reproof to those who embrace, or even show a tolerance for, false religion: 'Notwithstanding I have a few things against thee, because thou sufferest that woman Jezebel, which calleth herself a prophetess, to teach and to seduce my servants to commit fornication, and to eat things sacrificed unto idols. And I gave her space to repent of her fornication; and she repented not. Behold, I will cast her into a bed, and them that commit adultery with her into great tribulation, except they repent of their deeds. And I will kill her children with death; and all the churches shall know that I am he which searcheth the reins and hearts: and I will give unto every one of you according to your works.'

This reproof is not so much directed to the church itself as it is to the wicked seducers within its ranks. Yet the church itself was at fault. The members are reproved for their tolerance of false religion.

There was within the church a woman who claimed to be a prophetess, a female preacher. No one dared assert the teachings of Scripture and reprove the abominable practice. But our Lord calls this woman 'Jezebel'. He compares her to Ahab's wicked wife, Jezebel, because she encouraged the patronage of false religion, kindness to false prophets and the acceptance of idolatry. She seduced God's servants to engage in the pagan festivities connected with idol worship, including fornication! She did all this in the name of God, pretending all the while that she was promoting the worship of Christ. And people believed her!

The church in Thyatira was to be blamed in part for the spread of this wicked woman's heresy because they tolerated her and afforded her the opportunity to preach her damning doctrines. They allowed a woman not only to teach, but also to preach, in direct opposition to the Word of God (1 Cor. 14:34-35; 1 Tim. 2:11-12). By allowing her to spread her doctrine, and by embracing her as a believer, this church became a partaker with her in her evil deeds (2 John 10-11).

If we are to be faithful to the souls of men and to the glory of God, false religion and false prophets must be pointedly and plainly exposed by us. We preach a positive gospel and it is right that we should endeavour to avoid being negative. Yet we must never allow any room for the acceptance of any doctrine that is contrary to the gospel of God's free and sovereign grace in Christ. The popular, accepted, mainstream religion of our day is a religion of works. The vast majority of religious denominations, respected religious leaders and churches — local, national and international — are unified in the essence of their message. Virtually all preach salvation by man, either by his works or by his will. They are modern Jezebels, deceiving and seducing the souls of men. We have no point of agreement with them. If free grace is true, free will is false. If the gospel of grace is true, any and every mixture of works with grace is false. Two opposite messages cannot both be true. That means that there is no room in the house of God for free-will, works religion.

All who deny the totality of man's depravity deny the Word of God, which declares it plainly (Rom. 3:9-19). All who deny the sovereignty of God in salvation deny the Word of God, which declares it (Rom. 9:11-16). All who deny the efficacy of Christ's blood atonement deny the Scriptures, which proclaim it universally (Gal. 3:13). All who deny the effectual, irresistible power and grace of God the Holy Spirit in regeneration deny the gospel, which asserts it boldly. Such people — whether men, women, churches or denominations — must never be received, heard, embraced, or supported by the people of God as our brethren, as co-labourers with us in the cause of Christ (Gal. 1:6-8; 5:12).

God will destroy all false prophets and all who follow them, if they do not repent and receive the love of the truth (vv.22-23). There is nothing more damning to the souls of men than Arminian, free-will, works religion. Those who are deceived by it will be damned by it (2 Thess. 2:7-12; Matt. 7:15).

The purpose and design of Christ in destroying these wicked seducers is that his elect may be both made manifest and instructed (v. 23). When heresies come, God's elect are made manifest by their adherence to the truth (1 Cor. 11:19). When false prophets are destroyed by the hand of God in judgement, God gives instruction and reproof to all men.

God's judgement upon the seducers of men reveals his infallible knowledge of their hearts. God knows the deceitful principles by which they operate, the hypocrisy of their religion and the motives of their actions. And he will judge them accordingly. His justice is impartial. He will give every false prophet the exact reward of his works. In the Day of Judgement they will not be able to hide behind the name of Christ. Their popularity will provide them no sanctuary (Matt. 7:21-23).

An assigned responsibility

In these dark days of apostate religion our Lord lays before each of us an assigned responsibility: 'But unto you I say, and unto the rest in Thyatira, as many as have not this doctrine, and which have not known the depths of Satan, as they speak; I will put upon you none other burden. But that which ye have already hold fast till I come' (vv. 24-25).

These false prophets call their doctrines the *depths* of theology. They love to dazzle men with deep mysteries and persuade them that they have profound insight into the things of God. They love to talk about prophetic mysteries, the nature of angels, the work of demons and almost anything that intrigues the imagination.

Our Lord calls their deep things 'the depths of Satan'! (See 2 Cor. 11:3). False prophets will always draw your attention away from Christ and the gospel of his grace. Their mysteries are the mystery of iniquity, satanic delusions and diabolical doctrines. The gospel sets forth the mystery of godliness, which is Christ crucified. Let us never be turned from it. Christ crucified is the sole message of the Bible, the sole object of all true faith, the sole centre of all true worship, the sole theme of all true preaching and the sole motive of every believer's life.

It is our responsibility to hold fast the doctrine of Christ until he comes again. That is, first and foremost, above everything else, the business of every local church (2 Tim. 1:9-13; Titus 1:9).

That form of sound words, which we must hold fast, can be summed up and set forth in six brief statements:

1. God Almighty is absolutely sovereign over all things (Rom. 9:11-26).

2. All men and women, since the sin and fall of our father Adam, are spiritually dead and totally depraved (Rom. 5:12; 3:9-19).

3. God has an elect people in the world, chosen from eternity, who must and will be saved by his sovereign operations of grace (2 Thess. 2:13-14).

4. The Lord Jesus Christ died for and redeemed all God's elect, infallibly securing their everlasting salvation by the satisfaction of divine justice on their behalf (Isa. 53:8-11; Heb. 9:12).

5. God the Holy Spirit regenerates, calls to life and faith in Christ and preserves in grace all who were chosen by God the Father and redeemed by God the Son, by his almighty, effectual, irresistible grace (Ps. 65:4).

6. All who believe on the Lord Jesus Christ will persevere in faith, being preserved and kept unto

eternal glory by the grace and power of God (John 10:27-30).

When the Lord Jesus Christ comes again, he will put an end to all heresy, and truth will reign triumphantly for ever.

An assured reward

If we persevere in faith and hold fast the doctrine of Christ, our Saviour, the Son of God, promises us an assured reward: 'And he that overcometh, and keepeth my works unto the end, to him will I give power over the nations: and he shall rule them with a rod of iron; as the vessels of a potter shall they be broken to shivers: even as I received of my Father. And I will give him the morning star. He that hath an ear, let him hear what the Spirit saith unto the churches' (vv. 26-29).

Those who overcome are those who hold on to Christ's works, not their own. They will rule and reign with the Son of God for ever. We shall rule with Christ over all our enemies. All who persevere in the faith of the gospel will sit as kings with Christ upon his throne and rule over all things with him for ever (Matt. 19:28; Luke 22:29; Rev. 3:21; 20:4). All believers will sit with Christ in judgement over all his enemies. Fallen angels, false prophets, every rebel against Christ's throne and Satan himself will all be judged and condemned by our Lord, and we shall be his witnesses in the judgement (1 Cor. 6:3; Heb. 13:17; Ps. 2:8-9). The Lord Jesus Christ will give us himself (all of himself!) for ever (v. 28). He is our souls' eternal 'Morning Star' (2 Peter 1:19; Rev. 22:16). The Day Star that will introduce us into the glorious day of eternal bliss is Christ himself! He is our glory. He is our crown. He is our heaven (Ps. 73:25-26).

14.

Christ's letter to the church at Sardis

Revelation 3:1-6

'And unto the angel of the church in Sardis write: These things saith he that hath the seven Spirits of God, and the seven stars; I know thy works, that thou hast a name that thou livest, and art dead. Be watchful, and strengthen the things which remain, that are ready to die: for I have not found thy works perfect before God. Remember therefore how thou hast received and heard, and hold fast, and repent. If therefore thou shalt not watch, I will come on thee as a thief, and thou shalt not know what hour I will come upon thee. Thou hast a few names even in Sardis which have not defiled their garments; and they shall walk with me in white: for they are worthy. He that overcometh, the same shall be clothed in white raiment; and I will not blot out his name out of the book of life, but I will confess his name before my Father, and before his angels. He that hath an ear, let him hear what the Spirit saith unto the churches' (Rev. 3:1-6).

Sardis was a relatively small city, but it was rich and strong, situated on what was thought to be an inaccessible hill, and protected by what was considered to be an impregnable fortress. Its people were proud, arrogant, over-confident. But the city had one unobserved, unguarded weak point, a small crack in the rock wall that surrounded it. One night, in an unsuspecting hour, the enemy came as a thief in the night, and Sardis was conquered. Later the city was partially destroyed by an earthquake. By the time

John wrote the book of Revelation, Sardis was in decay, experiencing a slow but sure death.

The condition of the city was a vivid picture of the spiritual condition of the church in Sardis — proud, but decaying. The church at Sardis was proud, arrogant, overconfident. The enemy had come, and by degrees had silently destroyed the life of this once magnificent church. The church existed in peace. Neither the Jews nor the Gentiles bothered the church at Sardis, because the church at Sardis did not bother them. There was no persecution in Sardis. The church enjoyed great peace. But it was the peace of a cemetery. The church was dead.

Here our Lord calls for Sardis to remember the past, and recall their former vitality, faith, obedience and zeal. And he calls for them to return, to strengthen the things that remain, to hold fast that which they had and to repent. If they refused, he would come upon them as a thief in the night to destroy them.

How descriptive this letter is of the condition of Christ's church at this hour! In general, the church of Christ appears to be in a state of decay. Remember, this letter is not just addressed to the church in general. It is addressed specifically to each local church. Its message is to us.

The epistle to Sardis is a letter of reproof and warning. Let it be read with weeping eyes and received with broken, penitent hearts. 'He that hath an ear, let him hear what the Spirit saith unto the churches.' Spiritual decay is the forerunner of spiritual death, total apostasy and eternal ruin.

A prevailing reproach

Our Lord rebukes us and lays at our door the charge of a prevailing reproach. The corruption at Sardis was a general corruption. In Pergamos a few of the congregation had followed the doctrine of Balaam and the doctrine of the Nicolaitans. In Thyatira a few had followed Jezebel. But in

Sardis the congregation as a whole was corrupt, and only a few were faithful.

The church was sinking into a spiritual stupor. Therefore, Christ describes himself as 'he that hath the seven spirits of God, and the seven stars'. He is able to revive the dead church. He has the spirit of life and he can cause the angel of the church to preach the gospel with renewed power and fervency.

Christ charges this church with four faults:

1. They had a name that they lived, but they were dead (v. 1)

Sardis had a good reputation. They were admired and applauded by many. But it was a reputation they did not deserve: 'Thou hast a name that thou livest, and art dead.' They were big on profession, but little in possession. They were long on ceremony, but short on commitment. They were precise in doctrine, but negligent in devotion. They had great activity, but little worship.

Is this not the state of most who wear the name of Christ today? I seldom meet a man or woman who is not religious, who does not profess to be a Christian, but I seldom meet anyone who is committed to Christ! For the most part, even in our most orthodox churches, I see nothing but deadness. The meetings for worship are poorly attended. The people, it is obvious, seldom read, much less study, the Scriptures. Prayer appears, usually, to be the stating of words (accurate enough), but not the pleading of burdened hearts. The worship of Christ, for the vast majority of those who profess faith in him, is a convenience, not a necessity. I fear that 'Ichabod' might be written on the doors of most of our church buildings.

2. They were negligent in the most important matters (v. 2)

The Master says, 'Be watchful, and strengthen the things which remain, that are ready to die: for I have not found

thy works perfect before God.' Sardis should have been a
lighthouse. It should have been a beacon. It should have
been a pillar and ground of the truth. But it failed in the
most important matters. And those things that remained
were ready to die.

Like the others, this letter was addressed first and foremost to the pastor, the angel of the church. And usually —
not always, but usually — the church is merely a reflection
of its pastor. The pulpit is the greatest strength or the greatest weakness in the church. Here the pastor was negligent,
the elders were negligent, the deacons were negligent and
the people were negligent. No one was watchful for the
faith, earnestly contending for it, wrestling against the
wicked one, labouring for the souls of men and for the spread
of the gospel. Christ saw in this church nothing but slothfulness, coldness, lethargy and death.

Is it not so today? Where are those men who have
hazarded their lives for the gospel? Where is the man who
counts not his life dear unto himself, so that he may finish
his course with joy? Where is the man whose heart burns
with zeal for Christ? Truth had fallen in the streets, but
Sardis did not care. Christ's lambs were starving for lack of
bread, but Sardis did not care. I ask again, is it not so in
this day?

3. They were formalists, ritualists, ceremonialists, and no more (v. 2)

They had many works, but Christ says, 'I have not found
thy works perfect before God.' The forms were there. The
religious customs were there. The ceremonies were kept
up. The religious traditions were maintained. The services
were there. But the essence was lacking. There was no genuine, sincere love, faith and hope. There was an abundance
of activity, but no faith; plenty of parade, but no power. In
the sight of other people Sardis was a splendid, prosperous
church, but in the eyes of Christ it was an empty corpse.

4. They were careless about the things they had heard (v. 3)

'Remember therefore how thou hast received and heard, and hold fast, and repent. If therefore thou shalt not watch, I will come on thee as a thief, and thou shalt not know what hour I will come upon thee.'

The Lord called for them to remember how they had received and heard the gospel (v. 3). The greatest evil in the church today is the impurity and laxity of doctrine and commitment to the truth of God, the acceptance and approval of any religion as long as it is sincere. We are supposed to believe that everyone is right, no matter what they believe. If anyone dares to assert that there is a real difference between the truth of God and the lies of hell, he is branded a bigot, a fanatic and a narrow-minded, hardhearted instigator of strife.

The fact is that there can be no alliance between truth and error. Those who preach divine sovereignty and those who deny it are not brethren. Those who preach electing love and those who denounce it are not companions. Those who preach effectual redemption and those who despise it are not friends. Those who preach salvation by grace and those who preach salvation by works are not children of the same household and the same family.

A plain recommendation

In order for Sardis to recover from her terrible condition, our Lord gives a plain recommendation (vv. 2-3). He says, 'Be watchful' over your own souls. 'Strengthen the things which remain' — the people of God, the remnant of the faithful and the faith and grace that is in them. 'Remember' the past — the grace you have experienced, the faith you have professed and the blessedness you have enjoyed. 'Hold fast' the truth in which you have been established (Jer. 6:16). 'Repent.' Return unto the Lord. 'If therefore thou shalt not

watch, I will come on thee as a thief, and thou shalt not
know what hour I will come upon thee.' Apostasy will bring
judgement (Isa. 63:9-10).

A precious remnant

In verse 4 the Lord Jesus graciously calls our attention to a
precious remnant: 'Thou hast a few names even in Sardis
which have not defiled their garments.' Blessed be God,
there is always a remnant according to the election of grace.
They were few in number, but they were known to God.
They had not defiled their garments by departing from
Christ, by licentious behaviour, or by embracing false
doctrine.

A promised reward

To those few who persevere in the faith of the gospel, Christ
will give a promised reward (vv. 4-5). He says, 'They shall
walk with me in white.' What could be more blessed? Those
who continue in the faith, who devote themselves to Christ,
his will, his glory and his gospel, will walk with him in
sweet communion, justified before God, accepted in their
Saviour and rejoicing in him (Eccles. 9:7-8). They will walk
with Christ because 'they are worthy', made worthy by grace
(Col. 1:12).

And all who persevere and overcome at the last will live
for ever (v. 5). They 'shall be clothed in white raiment',
robed in the white robe of Christ's own righteousness,
wrapped in the garments of his salvation. To these the Son
of God promises, 'I will not blot out his name out of the
book of life.' They 'shall never perish' — no, not for any
reason, under any circumstances, or by any means. Rather,
the Saviour says, 'I will confess his name before my Father,
and before his angels.'

In the light of these things, 'knowing the time, that now it is high time to awake out of sleep: for now is our salvation nearer than when we believed' (Rom. 13:11), are you among the few who have not defiled their garments? Am I? If so, let us 'hold fast the form of sound words, which thou hast heard ... in faith and love which is in Christ Jesus' (2 Tim. 1:13). Are you yet without Christ? Then 'Seek ye the LORD while he may be found, call ye upon him while he is near' (Isa. 55:6).

15.

Christ's letter to the church at Philadelphia

Revelation 3:7-13

'And to the angel of the church in Philadelphia write: These things saith he that is holy, he that is true, he that hath the key of David, he that openeth, and no man shutteth; and shutteth, and no man openeth; I know thy works: behold, I have set before thee an open door, and no man can shut it: for thou hast a little strength, and hast kept my word, and hast not denied my name. Behold, I will make them of the synagogue of Satan, which say they are Jews, and are not, but do lie; behold, I will make them to come and worship before thy feet, and to know that I have loved thee. Because thou hast kept the word of my patience, I also will keep thee from the hour of temptation, which shall come upon all the world, to try them that dwell upon the earth. Behold, I come quickly: hold that fast which thou hast, that no man take thy crown. Him that overcometh will I make a pillar in the temple of my God, and he shall go no more out: and I will write upon him the name of my God, and the name of the city of my God, which is new Jerusalem, which cometh down out of heaven from my God: and I will write upon him my new name. He that hath an ear, let him hear what the Spirit saith unto the churches' (Rev. 3:7-13).

'That which is highly esteemed among men is an abomination in the sight of God' (Luke 16:15). I wonder if we will ever learn that fact. Those things which men value most, esteem most highly, and to which they attach the greatest honour, God despises. And that which men ridicule, belittle and despise, God honours. The wisdom of this world, the pride of this world, the moral righteousness of this world, the honour of this world and the religion of this world, God Almighty holds in utter contempt. We see this fact throughout the Scriptures. And we see it plainly in Christ's letters to the churches.

The church at Sardis was great in name and reputation. Men approved of her and honoured her. But Christ looked at that church and said, 'Thou art dead.' The church at Laodicea was rich and increased with goods. It appeared that she lacked nothing. But that church was so nauseating to the Son of God that he was ready to spew it out of his mouth. He said, 'Thou art wretched, and miserable, and poor, and blind, and naked.' You see, God looks on the heart. He is not in the least degree impressed by those things that impress and deceive men. 'That which is highly esteemed among men is an abomination in the sight of God.'

The church at Philadelphia was not like the ones in Sardis and Laodicea. C. H. Spurgeon wrote, 'The Philadelphia church was not great, but it was good; it was not powerful, but it was faithful.' The Lord Jesus commended this church for its faithfulness. Men might have looked at the little church in Philadelphia, as they do at many like it today, with contempt. It did not meet in an elaborately decorated, impressive building. So far as I have been able to discover, there were no men in this church of great political, economic, or academic power and influence. But it was a church known for its faithfulness.

Faithfulness honours God and is honoured by God. And faithfulness, like slothfulness, has a way of rubbing off on others. Hence we read of faithful men and women in the church at Philadelphia for many centuries. The pastors of this church were consistently influential (not in the world, but in the kingdom of God) for eight hundred years. We read in church history of their influence from the first through the eighth centuries. Let us ever be found faithful to our God. He alone knows what influence our faithfulness, or lack of it, will have upon the generations to come.

The Lord Jesus found nothing in this church to rebuke, or even to correct. He gave no word of reproof to the saints at Philadelphia. That is a remarkable testimony to these people whose names are known only in heaven. To this congregation the Son of God spoke nothing but words of praise and encouragement.

In Revelation 3:7-13 the Lord Jesus Christ holds the church at Philadelphia before us as an example of what every believer and every local church ought to be. A careful reading of the Saviour's letter to the church at Philadelphia ought to put a prayer in our hearts, crying, 'Lord, make me faithful.' Read the Saviour's words and learn this: God honours faithfulness.

A divine person

In verse 7, our Lord Jesus describes himself as a divine person. This letter was dictated to John by one who is himself God. This God is our Saviour. 'These things saith he that is holy, he that is true, he that hath the key of David, he that openeth, and no man shutteth; and shutteth, and no man openeth.' Here are three divine attributes, or characteristics, of our Lord Jesus Christ.

1. The Lord Jesus Christ is holy

He is the holy God. 'Holy and reverend is his name' (Ps. 111:9). He is the Holy One of Israel. Being God, he is 'glorious in holiness' (Exod. 15:11), in every way equal with the Father and the Holy Spirit. Specifically, this text has reference to Christ's holiness as the God-man, our Saviour. It is not our Saviour's divine, essential holiness that comforts and encourages his people. That terrifies any man who has any sense of it (Heb. 12:21; Judg. 13:22). It is our Redeemer's representative, mediatorial, vicarious holiness that gives us comfort and encourages us to trust him.

Our Saviour was himself 'holy, harmless, undefiled, separate from sinners' while he lived as a man in this world (Heb. 7:26). He had no sin — no original sin and no actual sin. Though he was made to be sin for us by divine imputation when he died as our substitute, Christ had no sin of his own. He knew no sin (2 Cor. 5:21). As our representative and substitute, the Son of God lived in this world as a man in perfect holiness.

This mediatorial holiness, this representative righteousness of Christ as our mediator, is the basis of our acceptance with God (Rom. 5:19). If you are a believer, if you trust Christ, his blood washed away your sins. His sacrifice paid your debt and satisfied the law and justice of God that demanded death. His death removed your guilt before God. But the righteousness of Christ is just as necessary for our salvation as his blood. His righteousness (his complete obedience to God as a man), being imputed to us, just as our sins were imputed to him, gives us merit with God. Therefore he is called *Jehovah-tsidkenu*, 'THE LORD OUR RIGHTEOUSNESS' (Jer. 23:6).

Christ is our righteousness, our holiness and our sanctification. He is that 'holiness without which no man shall see the Lord' (Heb. 12:14). He is that perfect righteousness, exceeding that of the scribes and Pharisees, without which we cannot enter into the kingdom of heaven (Matt. 5:20). Christ, who is holy, and who is our holiness, is our sanctification. His holiness was imputed to every chosen sinner in justification when he accomplished our redemption at Calvary. And his holy nature is imparted to every chosen, redeemed, justified sinner in the new birth. Salvation, in the experience of it, is 'Christ in you, the hope of glory'.

We have no holiness of our own. We have no ability to produce holiness, or do anything that is truly holy. All the holiness we have is what we get from Christ. As John Gill puts it, 'Christ is the Cause and Author of holiness to his people. We are sanctified in him. We have our sanctification from him. And we are sanctified by him.'

Those who talk about sanctification by degrees, or sanctification being accomplished by the works of a man, simply do not understand the doctrine of sanctification, or for that matter the totality of grace in salvation. Christ is our sanctification (1 Cor. 1:30; Heb. 10:10-14).

2. Christ is 'true'. He is truly God and truly man

Our Lord Jesus Christ is true and faithful in all his mediatorial offices and covenant engagements. He is true to God the Father and true to his people. In fact, Jesus Christ is truth itself (John 14:6). Apart from him there is no truth. Christ is the truth of which all the types and prophecies of the Old Testament were just pictures. Christ is the truth of God, the embodiment of truth, the sum and substance of all gospel truth. As the embodiment of truth, Christ is the revelation of the invisible God. He is the living Word of whom the written Word speaks (John 1:1-3, 14-16,18).

3. The Lord Jesus Christ is the sovereign King

He describes himself here as 'he that hath the key of David, he that openeth, and no man shutteth; and shutteth, and no man openeth'. With these words our blessed Saviour describes his sovereign power and absolute authority over all things as the Son of David, the Messiah, the King. He who is the Christ of God is Lord over all things. This dominion is not something that Christ will have some day. It is his right now! Our crucified, risen, exalted Saviour is now sitting as King upon the throne of David, which is the throne of God (Isa. 22:22; Matt. 28:18; John 17:2; Acts 2:34-36; Heb. 1:3; Rev. 5:5).

Here is one example of his absolute sovereignty: he opens, and no man shuts; he shuts, and no man opens. Christ opens the Scriptures to his elect, giving us the light and knowledge of gospel truth by the power of his Holy Spirit (John 14:26; 16:13). But he shuts the Scriptures to others, giving them blindness and hardness of heart (John 12:39-40). The Son of God opens a door of utterance for the gospel in one place, and shuts it in another, according to his own sovereign will (Acts 16:6-10). The Good Shepherd opens the door for his sheep and leads them in the way of life everlasting (John 10:3,9). And he shuts the door against those who will not obey his voice (Luke 13:23-30).

We worship 'him that is holy'. We trust 'him that is true'. We bow before the one who is sovereign. Our divine Saviour is the holy, true, sovereign Son of God.

A divine praise

When the Lord of glory spoke to the church at Philadelphia, as I said before, there is no word of reproof, warning, or correction, but only a divine praise: 'I know thy works: behold, I have set before thee an open door, and no man can shut it: for thou hast a little strength, and hast kept my word, and hast not denied my name' (v. 8).

Imagine that! The Son of God himself bends over from his lofty throne to speak a word of praise to a band of faithful believers on the earth! I would dearly like to be one of them. Wouldn't you?

Certainly, he is here giving us an example to follow. We are usually quick to point out one another's faults and failures. But love is always quick to forgive and quick to praise. A little praise is a great means of encouragement. Some people seem to think that kindness is blasphemy. But if the Son of God speaks an encouraging word of praise to his church, surely we shall be safe in giving a little praise to one another.

What was there about these Philadelphian believers that the Son of God saw fit to commend and praise? The matter of commendation and praise was their works, works of faith, love and patience.

1. 'I have set before thee an open door...'

The Lord God had set before this church an open door, which no man could shut. He does not tell us what this open door was, but generally this language is used to describe a door of utterance for the preaching of the gospel (2 Cor. 2:12). Apparently, the Lord gave these men and women an opportunity to serve him in the furtherance of the gospel, and they seized the opportunity he gave them. They faithfully performed the work God put into their hands. They did not talk about what they wanted to do, what they had done, what they used to do, or what they would do if they had more money and people. They simply did what they could for the glory of Christ and the furtherance of the gospel. It may be that their labour was insignificant in the eyes of men. But Christ looked upon it as an honourable thing. Nothing done for Christ is insignificant or meaningless to him (Mark 14:6-8).

The one thing God requires of his people is faithfulness (1 Cor. 4:2). The one thing God honours in his people is faithfulness (Matt. 25:23; Luke 19:17). When the Lord Jesus Christ opens a door for us, as we faithfully follow him, no man can shut the door, and he will not shut it.

2. 'Thou hast a little strength'

The faithfulness of these saints at Philadelphia was especially commendable because they had very little with which to work. The Master said, 'For thou hast a little strength.' This is not to be taken as a word of reproach, but as a word of praise. They had been faithful in their service to Christ, even though they had little strength. Many of the Lord's churches are like this church at Philadelphia: they have 'a little strength', but only a little.

They had little *numerical* strength. The church at Philadelphia was a small church. Therefore they had very little strength for taking on any great work. But their lack of numbers did not deter them. They just rallied together and did what they could. And Christ commends them for it. God thinks more of quality than of quantity. He has much greater regard for obedience than for tally sheets and numbers. Denominations, denominational representatives, religious businessmen and politically motivated preachers take polls and count heads. 'The Lord looketh on the heart!'

Because they were small in number, like most small churches, this church had little *monetary* strength. When money was required, they could do very little. This was, for the most part, a band of poor people. There were no men of means among them. But they were precious to Christ, who counts sincerity of greater value than all the gold in the world.

And, again like most small churches, this assembly had very little strength in the area of *talents and gifts*. At Corinth, the church had talents and gifts running out of their ears. They had an abundance of teachers, miracle workers and wealth. But very little was done. They were rich in ability, but poor in grace. Not this church. No one here seems to have had any great talent or ability. But the people were full of grace. Grace made them faithful. Much was done for the glory of Christ, the souls of men and the furtherance of the gospel. They had 'a little strength', but used every ounce of it for Christ.

'Thou hast a little strength.' Someone said, 'That was, perhaps, their misfortune, but not their fault.' Therefore they were not blamed for it. The Lord does not blame us for having little strength, but for having little faith, little love, little devotion, little zeal and little consecration. If our

strength is little, let us pray for grace, that our little strength
may be used entirely for Christ.

3. Thou ... hast kept my word, and hast not denied my name'

The saints of God at Philadelphia were faithful and persevering in the midst of great opposition. The Lord Jesus gave
them this word of praise and encouragement: 'Thou hast
kept my word, and hast not denied my name.' These men
and women simply could not be driven away from the word
of the gospel. They could not be persuaded to forsake the
gospel. They would not allow anything to come between
them and Christ. They had a little strength, but with all the
strength they had they kept God's Word and held fast to
Christ.

What is the word which they kept? We do not have to
guess. It was the word of the gospel. Our Lord says, 'Thou
hast kept the word of my patience' (v. 10). That is the gospel of Christ and him crucified, in which his patient
sufferings as our substitute are set forth (1 Peter 2:21-24).
The sinner's only hope before God is the gospel of
substitutionary redemption (2 Cor. 5:21). This is the word
we must hold fast.

How did these Philadelphian believers keep the word of
the gospel? They believed it (1 John 5:6-13). They loved it
(1 John 5:3). They obeyed it (Rom. 16:26). And they defended it (Jude 3; Phil. 1:7,17). Though they were weak,
few in number and a people of worldly insignificance, they
were ready at all times and against all odds to hold to and
defend the truth of God. Most men are like spiders, which
spin their webs out of their own entrails. They spin their
theology out of their own feelings, their own wisdom, or
their own experiences. These Philadelphian saints took
nothing to be truth but the truth of God revealed in sacred
Scripture. And, with regard to the truth of God, they val-
iantly refused to budge an inch. They had no regard for

current trends in theology and the wisdom of infidels. They walked in the old paths of everlasting truth (Jer. 6:16). May God give us grace, in these days when nearly the whole religious world teaches and embraces that which the apostle Paul calls 'will worship', to hold fast the gospel of his free and sovereign grace in Christ (2 Tim. 1:9-10).

Either God is totally, absolutely, universally sovereign, or he is not God (Ps. 135:6). Either man is totally depraved, guilty and helpless, or he needs no Saviour (Rom. 5:12; 3:9-19). Either God chose and determined to save his people in eternal, unconditional election, before the world began, or he has no people to save (Eph. 1:3-6; 2 Thess. 2:13). Either Christ effectually redeemed God's elect by his death on the cross, or he failed in his work and there is no such thing as blood atonement and substitutionary redemption (Matt. 1:21; Gal. 4:4-6). Either God the Holy Spirit regenerates and calls dead sinners to life and faith in Christ by effectual, irresistible power and grace, or man is saved by his own will, his own effort and his own work (Rom. 11:6; Eph. 2:1-10). Either all God's elect will persevere unto the end, or none of them will (John 10:27-30).

These are the truths by which we live and, if need be, God helping us, these are truths by which we shall die. But we will not, we cannot, give them up. This is more than mere doctrinal accuracy. This is the very fabric of our salvation. To deny these things would be to deny our only hope before God and to blaspheme the name of the one whom we most desire to honour. To deny these doctrines of the gospel is to deny Christ who taught them. Those who embrace these gospel truths are our brethren. Those who are enemies to these truths are the enemies of our God, and that makes them our enemies (Ps. 139:19-22; 2 Chr. 19:2).

Do you keep the word of the gospel? Do I? Perhaps we have no great talents, perhaps we have little strength, maybe we have little influence over other people, and we may always be numbered among a small group of people who are looked upon by the world as narrow-minded fanatics, but the simple fact is that the salvation of our souls depends upon our persevering adherence to the truth of the gospel (Col. 1:22-23).

The saints in the church at Philadelphia were commended and praised by Christ because they kept and did not deny the word of his grace and truth in the gospel. Blessed is that man, blessed is that woman, who cannot be induced by Satan to forsake the gospel for any reason.

A divine protection

Inasmuch as they were faithful to him, our Lord assured the saints at Philadelphia that he would be faithful to them and declared that he would keep them with a divine protection: 'Behold, I will make them of the synagogue of Satan, which say they are Jews, and are not, but do lie; behold, I will make them to come and worship before thy feet, and to know that I have loved thee. Because thou hast kept the word of my patience, I also will keep thee from the hour of temptation, which shall come upon all the world, to try them that dwell upon the earth. Behold, I come quickly: hold that fast which thou hast, that no man take thy crown' (vv.9-11).

Those who keep God's Word will be kept by God. Those who hold fast the truth of God will be held in truth by the grace of God. Those who persevere in faith will be preserved by grace.

Our Lord will always separate the wheat from the chaff and the precious from the vile (v. 9). He says, 'Behold, I will make them of the synagogue of Satan, which say they are Jews, and are not, but do lie; behold, I will make them to come and worship before thy feet, and to know that I have loved thee.'

The Jews, who are Abraham's physical descendants, claimed to be God's people exclusively, and many to this day regard them as the people of God's choice. But in this ninth verse our Lord calls those who still worship according to the customs of Judaism and the law of Moses 'the synagogue of Satan'. It is not Abraham's physical seed, but his spiritual seed who are the people of God, the Israel of God, for whom the promises and the covenant were made. The church of God is the Israel of God (Rom. 2:28-29; 11:25-26; Phil. 3:3). Abraham is the father of all who believe on the Lord Jesus Christ (Rom. 4:1,16,22-25; Gal. 3:6-7). Today Judaism is an apostate religion.

There are many who, like the Jews, claim to be God's people who are not. They say they are Jews (Christians, children of God), but they lie. All who hope for acceptance with God because of a decision they made for Jesus, because of their baptism, their church membership, their good works, their taking the sacraments, their experiences, or their personal holiness are hypocrites. They may be called a church. They may think they are the house of God. But our Lord here identifies all such as 'the synagogue of Satan'. God's elect, the true people of God, are circumcised in their hearts by the Spirit of God, not in their flesh (Col. 2:10-14). We worship God in the Spirit, rejoice in Christ alone and have no confidence in the flesh (Phil. 3:3).

In the end the despised people of God will be exalted over their enemies. Our Lord will make our enemies to bow before our feet and know that he loved us, chose us, redeemed us, called us and saved us by his grace (Matt. 25:31-34,41).

As long as we live in this world, Christ will keep his own in the hour of temptation: 'Because thou hast kept the word of my patience, I also will keep thee from the hour of temptation, which shall come upon all the world, to try them that dwell upon the earth' (v. 10; cf. John 10:27-30; 17:11-15; 1 Cor. 10:13). He will preserve all his own from apostasy. Though heresies come and abound, God's elect will not be deceived. The ever-increasing acceptance of legalism, free-will, works religion and sheer ritualism will

not affect the saints of God (1 Cor. 11:19; 2 Thess. 2:7-13;
1 John 2:19-20). The Lord Jesus Christ will graciously preserve his elect in the midst of their trials (Isa. 43:1-5). The
Son of God will preserve all his elect in the way of faith,
grace and obedience unto life everlasting (Ps. 37:23-24; Jer.
32:38-40). God's elect cannot and will not perish. Not even
one of the chosen shall be lost. We are kept by the power of
his grace in the hands of an omnipotent Saviour.

It is our Lord's promise of preservation that inspires us
to perseverance: 'Behold, I come quickly: hold that fast
which thou hast, that no man take thy crown' (v. 11). It is
upon the basis of his promise to preserve us from temptation that our Redeemer admonishes us to persevere. Contrary to popular religious opinion, the promise of absolute,
unconditional grace does not promote licentiousness, but
devotion and godliness. In fact, that is the very basis of
godliness and the motive for it (Titus 3:4-8).

These two things are facts so plainly revealed in Holy
Scripture that they simply cannot be denied: first, all God's
elect will be preserved unto eternal glory; but, second, only
those who persevere in faith, who go on in the way of grace
and righteousness, and who hold fast the gospel unto the
end will be saved (Matt. 10:22; Col. 1:22-23; Heb. 3:6,14;
10:26,38-39).

A divine promise

In verse 12, our Lord Jesus Christ gives a divine promise to
all who hold fast and persevere in the faith of the gospel:
'Him that overcometh will I make a pillar in the temple of
my God, and he shall go no more out: and I will write upon
him the name of my God, and the name of the city of my
God, which is new Jerusalem, which cometh down out of
heaven from my God: and I will write upon him my new
name.'

Those who persevere in the faith will conquer all their enemies in the end and be gloriously triumphant in Christ (Rom. 8:35-39). The Son of God says, 'Him that overcometh will I make a pillar in the temple of my God.' A pillar is a permanent structure in a permanent place. So Christ is here promising us a place of permanent, eternal residence in heaven itself. And while we live here below, while we go on persevering in the faith, holding fast the gospel, clinging to him as our only hope and our only Saviour, he gives us assurance of our interest in him. This is what he says: 'I will write upon him the name of my God, and the name of the city of my God, which is new Jerusalem, which cometh down out of heaven from my God: and I will write upon him my new name.' In a word, our Saviour is saying, 'I will make you to know that you belong to me. I will make it evident that you belong to God, to the New Jerusalem, and to me, and that all the blessings and privileges of the sons of God are yours for ever.'

Our Saviour's new name, his acquired name, which he promises to write upon his people is *Jehovah-tsidkenu*, 'THE LORD OUR RIGHTEOUSNESS' (cf. Jer. 23:6; 33:16). Let us give ourselves wholeheartedly to him who promises us such grace (Rom. 12:1-3). I urge you, hold fast the hope of the gospel. Let nothing and no one either drive you from it or entice you to forsake it (1 Cor. 15:1-3). The Son of God will hold us in his grace. Let us therefore cling to him. 'He that hath an ear, let him hear what the Spirit saith unto the churches.'

16.

Christ's letter to the church at Laodicea

Revelation 3:14-22

'And unto the angel of the church of the Laodiceans write: These things saith the Amen, the faithful and true witness, the beginning of the creation of God; I know thy works, that thou art neither cold nor hot: I would thou wert cold or hot. So then because thou art lukewarm, and neither cold nor hot, I will spew thee out of my mouth. Because thou sayest, I am rich, and increased with goods, and have need of nothing; and knowest not that thou art wretched, and miserable, and poor, and blind, and naked: I counsel thee to buy of me gold tried in the fire, that thou mayest be rich; and white raiment, that thou mayest be clothed, and that the shame of thy nakedness do not appear; and anoint thine eyes with eye-salve, that thou mayest see. As many as I love, I rebuke and chasten: be zealous therefore, and repent. Behold, I stand at the door, and knock: if any man hear my voice, and open the door, I will come in to him, and will sup with him, and he with me. To him that overcometh will I grant to sit with me in my throne, even as I also overcame, and am set down with my Father in his throne. He that hath an ear, let him hear what the Spirit saith unto the churches' (Rev. 3:14-22).

The Lord Jesus Christ ought to be loved ardently, with an all-consuming love. Behold, how he loved us! He ought to be served with an all-consuming zeal. Behold, how zealously he has served us! Yet there are many who, professing to know him, professing to trust him, professing to love him, are lukewarm, apathetic, indifferent towards him. And it must be acknowledged that even those who do truly know, trust and love him, because of the weakness of our flesh, because of our own sinfulness and the corruption of our hearts by nature, struggle incessantly with a horrid tendency towards lukewarmness. Our Lord's letter to the church at Laodicea was written specifically to deal with our dreadful liability to lukewarmness and indifference towards him.

Laodicea was a famous city of great wealth in Asia Minor. It was the commercial, financial centre of the region. Laodicea was the home of millionaires. It had three marble theatres, a great stadium and a huge gymnasium equipped with baths. There was a famous school of medicine at Laodicea, which, among other things, claimed to have produced a remedy for weak eyes. The city was also well known for its hot springs, which emitted lukewarm water continually.

The people of Laodicea were rich. They were the envy of the world — and they knew it. They were very proud of themselves. Really, they were unbearable snobs! This arrogant 'We are it' attitude was also found in the church at Laodicea. Perhaps they thought that their wealth was a sign of God's favour. But, in general, the church at Laodicea had gradually become a lukewarm, apostate, useless assembly of people who were outwardly religious but were without life before God. It was in danger of being entirely rejected by Christ.

Apparently this church was at one time a healthy, strong, spiritually vibrant congregation, a pillar of truth and a lighthouse in the midst of great darkness. Paul, at least once, wrote a letter to this Laodicean church. He talked about it with warmth, and never mentioned anything amiss concerning it (Col. 2:1-2; 4:13-16). Since the apostle Paul held this church in such high esteem, it is safe for us to assume that, at least during his ministry, it was a strong, vibrant congregation.

Something went wrong. In the process of time this great church, once on fire for God, degenerated into a sickening state of lukewarmness. It became careless, lax and indifferent. Perhaps the earlier generation had died out. Perhaps its wealth had seduced this assembly into worldliness. Perhaps its freedom from persecution had produced in the people a sense of worldly ease. Whatever the cause, the church was now in a state that was nauseating to the Son of God. It was neither cold nor hot, but lukewarm.

Nothing can be done with lukewarm people. There is hope for cold, hardened rebels. And it is a great joy to work with men and women whose hearts glow with love and zeal for Christ. But professing Christians who are lukewarm are sickening, nauseating, disgusting! Christ himself cannot stand them. He says, 'Because thou art lukewarm, and neither cold nor hot, I will spew thee out of my mouth.' Lukewarmness, apathy and indifference towards Christ betray the apostasy of the heart from Christ.

The charge of lukewarmness

In verses 14-17 the Lord Jesus Christ lays a solemn charge against the church at Laodicea. It is a charge that would most assuredly be followed by judgement, if they did not repent. The charge was one of lukewarmness, apathy, indifference and carelessness:

> And unto the angel of the church of the Laodiceans write: These things saith the Amen, the faithful and true witness, the beginning of the creation of God: I know thy works, that thou art neither cold nor hot: I would thou wert cold or hot. So then because thou art lukewarm, and neither cold nor hot, I will spew thee out of my mouth. Because thou sayest, I am rich, and increased with goods, and have need of nothing;

and knowest not that thou art wretched, and miserable, and poor, and blind, and naked...

Let us be warned. Lukewarmness is gradual apostasy,
lingering death and the forerunner of judgement. Stephen
Charnock wrote, 'If once we become listless, we shall
quickly become lifeless.' Complacency is at best a spiritual
sickness. It is usually a sign of spiritual death. May God
save us from this plague, which seems to have swept
through the church of this age.

This letter, like the other six, was addressed to the angel,
the pastor, of the church at Laodicea. It appears that there
were some in the church whose hearts were true, but, generally speaking, the whole congregation was insensitive to
Christ, the gospel of his grace, and the glory of his name.
There was no fire in the pulpit and no warmth in the pew.

This message of stern reproof came from Christ himself,
the righteous Judge. He calls himself 'the Amen, the faithful and true witness, the beginning of the creation of God'.
Our Saviour is 'the Amen'. He is steady, unchangeable,
immutable in all things. His purpose will stand. His promises are sure. His word is true (Mal. 3:6; Heb. 13:8; 2 Cor.
1:20).

Our Lord Jesus is 'the faithful and true witness'. He who
is our Judge is faithful and true in his judgement. What he
says is true, and what he does is just. Because he is both
faithful and true Christ's testimony of God to men is to be
received and believed, and his testimony to God about men
will be received. Those whose names Christ confesses to
the Father will be accepted. Those lukewarm, worldly ones
who merely profess faith in his name, whom Christ will
deny before his Father, will be rejected.

The Son of God also calls himself 'the beginning of the
creation of God'. That is just another way of saying that he
is himself God. He who is the parent, producer and first
cause of all things is himself God (John 1:1-3; Heb. 1:1-3).

Jesus Christ, our Saviour, the Son of God, is the one who
began everything that is, has been, or will be in the future.
He is the beginning of the old creation. He created all things
out of nothing. And he is the head and beginning of the
new creation, the church and kingdom of God. Jesus Christ,
our mediator, is 'the everlasting Father' (Isa. 9:6) from whom
all things have life. As he describes himself here, Christ is
saying to the Laodiceans, 'You are dead. You need life. You
need a new heart. Look to me. Turn to me. I can make you
new creatures.'

'The Lord reveals himself here,' wrote William Hendriksen, 'as the One whose eyes not only see exactly what is
going on in the hearts of these people of Laodicea but whose
lips also declare the exact truth of what is seen.'

In verses 15-17 the Son of God draws up a solemn in-
dictment against this church at Laodicea. He says to the
church as a whole, to the pastor, to the elders, to the deacons, to the teachers and to the people in general, 'Thou
art lukewarm.' They had been so secure. They thought they
were healthy and strong. But Christ knew their hearts. He
said, 'Thou art lukewarm.'

Christ, who is our life, charges this congregation of professed believers with spiritual death: 'I know thy works,
that thou art neither cold nor hot: I would thou wert cold
or hot' (v. 15). The Laodiceans were not hypocrites. They
were deceived. They were blind men who thought they
had perfect vision. They were dead men who thought they
were alive. They were lost people who were very sure they
were saved.

A state of lukewarmness, apathy and indifference regarding the Lord Jesus Christ is the very worst condition in
which a person can be in this world. If Jesus Christ is real,
then he is the unspeakable gift of God. We should earnestly
seek him, lovingly embrace him and zealously serve him.
If he is an impostor, then he is the most vile impostor the
world has ever known, and we should earnestly oppose

him. If Jesus Christ is worth anything, he is worth every-thing! 'Why halt ye between two opinions?' If Jesus Christ is God our Saviour, faithful and true, we should devote ourselves to him totally. If he is not, we should set our-selves against him totally. Concerning the Son of God and the gospel of his grace there is no room for neutrality! Matthew Henry wrote, 'Christ expects that men should de-clare themselves in earnest, either for him or against him.' With Joshua, I hope we can, each of us, declare, 'As for me and my house, we will serve the Lord.'

Indifference is an intolerable evil. Our Lord says, 'I would thou wert cold or hot.' It is better to be utterly ignorant of the gospel than to be a vain, worldly-minded, indifferent, lukewarm professor of faith. These Laodiceans professed faith in Christ, but had no interest in promoting it. They professed love for Christ, but had no real, heart attachment to him. They professed allegiance to the gospel, but had no zeal for the gospel. They were lukewarm.

This lukewarmness, this apathy and indifference towards the Son of God, is nauseating to him: 'So then because thou art lukewarm, and neither cold nor hot, I will spew thee out of my mouth' (v. 16). He threatens, 'I will spew thee out of my mouth.' As lukewarm water turns the stomach and induces vomiting, so lukewarm religion turns the stomach of the Son of God and sickens him. Those are not my words, but his! Men excuse their apathy, calling it moderation, charity and meekness. But Christ looks upon it as effemi-nacy. Quite literally, the Lord is saying, 'I am gagging on you. I am about to vomit you out of my mouth.' This is Christ's warning to all compromising fence-straddlers, who try to serve God and mammon. They will be rejected, com-pletely rejected, and rejected for ever!

One great cause of this Laodicean lukewarmness was their foolish pride: 'Because thou sayest, I am rich, and increased with goods, and have need of nothing; and knowest not that thou art wretched, and miserable, and poor, and blind, and naked' (v. 17).

Their pride deceived their hearts. These men and women had a very high opinion of themselves. Therefore they had a very low opinion of Christ. They flattered themselves with the delusion that all was well, when in fact nothing was well. They were doctrinally sound and morally pure, but they were spiritually dead. They had a great name to uphold, a sound creed to defend and religious ceremonies to maintain. All they lacked was life!

Look at the high opinion they had of themselves: 'Thou sayest, I am rich and increased with goods, and have need of nothing.' Without a doubt, this congregation was materially wealthy, rich and getting richer every day. They had no earthly needs. But riches seldom do any good for churches or for men who seek to serve Christ. The problem was that these rich men and women presumed that they were rich towards God, that their souls were rich in spiritual things.

They knew the way of life, so they presumed that they were in the way. They had the doctrines of Christ, so they presumed that they had the life of Christ. They had the gifts of the Spirit, so they presumed that they had the grace of the Spirit. They kept the ordinances of God, so they presumed that they had the power of God.

How careful we must be that we do not deceive our own souls! There are multitudes in hell today who once thought they were heirs of God and joint-heirs with Jesus Christ (Ps. 139:23-24). Be warned — there is nothing more dangerous, more deadly, or more damning to our souls than self-complacency, self-satisfaction and self-conceit. Complacency, satisfaction with yourself, is your soul's most deadly enemy.

Now look at the opinion Christ had of these proud, secure Laodiceans. Though they did not know it, Christ knew that they were 'wretched, and miserable, and poor, and blind, and naked' (v. 17). They were spiritually poor — not 'poor in spirit', but spiritually poor. Their souls were starving, though they lived in affluence. They were spiritually blind. Yet they thought they had perfect vision. The light that was in them was darkness. They could not see their own condition. And they could not see the things of God (John 3:3; 1 Cor. 2:14).

They were naked. Their righteousnesses were filthy rags. They had nothing but their rags of self-righteousness to cover them. And those rags were filthy. Not only were they naked before God, their filthy rags of self-righteousness increased their defilement.

Though they were very religious and moral, the Laodiceans were sinners, dead before God in trespasses and sins, and as such they were both wretched and miserable. They were 'wretched', deserving of the wrath of God, under the just sentence of death and in danger of hell. And there was nothing they could do to change their condition. They were 'miserable', or pitiable. Who is more to be pitied than a person who imagines he is a true believer and an object of Christ's favour, while in reality he is utterly disgusting and revolting to the Son of God?

Let us not be so foolish as to read this charge of lukewarmness as a mere historical narrative about a church that once existed in Laodicea. This is a message from Christ to you and me. Will you honestly examine yourself? Will I? Let us ask God to show us our true condition before him. Lukewarmness is indifference, apathy and complacency regarding the things of God. Lukewarmness is caused by self-satisfaction and a false sense of security. Lukewarmness will result in reprobation. Apostasy is always followed by reprobation.

God Almighty does reject men and women who reject his counsel (Hosea 4:17). Our Lord does stamp 'Ichabod' upon the doors of churches where once his glory was revealed and known (Jer. 7:12-16). Very often, if not always, those whom God has rejected are so far from knowing that judgement has fallen upon them that they vainly imagine that God is greatly blessing them.

The counsel of love

'I counsel thee to buy of me gold tried in the fire, that thou mayest be rich; and white raiment, that thou mayest be clothed, and that the shame of thy nakedness do not appear; and anoint thine eyes with eye-salve, that thou mayest see. As many as I love, I rebuke and chasten: be zealous therefore, and repent' (vv. 18-19).

What a tender, compassionate Saviour Christ is! He stoops to counsel and reason with sinful men (Isa. 1:18). He counsels sinners to buy salvation from him (Isa. 55:1-7), though we often cast his counsel behind our backs. There is hope for sinners so long as Christ, the sinners' Friend, speaks graciously by the gospel. 'Today, if ye will hear his voice, harden not your hearts' (Heb. 3:7-8).

Here is the counsel of love which the Son of God gives to wretched, miserable, poor, blind, naked sinners, even to proud, self-righteous sinners. Our Lord counsels the poor to buy of him gold tried in the fire. The exceeding riches of God's grace in Christ are like gold. But, as gold is refined by fire, so the grace of God comes to sinners only through the blood of the crucified Substitute, who endured the fire of God's wrath for us. Grace is gold that was refined in the oven of God's infinite wrath and justice at Calvary. Like gold, the grace of God in Christ makes poor sinners rich before God (2 Cor. 8:9).

The Son of God counsels naked souls to buy 'white raiment' from him. This, of course, refers to his perfect righteousness. It is white because it is pure. It is called 'raiment' because like a garment it warms, beautifies and adorns us, making us perfect, holy and blameless before the Lord God himself (Ezek. 16:6-14; S. of S. 4:1,7,9-11).

The Lord Jesus counsels spiritually blind sinners to anoint their eyes with eye-salve that they might see. The eye-salve in this text is the gospel of the grace of God. When applied to our hearts by the grace and power of God the

Holy Spirit, it illuminates our souls and brings us out of darkness into God's marvellous light. This blessed eye-salve gives us 'the light of the knowledge of the glory of God in the face of Jesus Christ' (2 Cor. 4:6).

Only in the gospel of substitutionary redemption can we see the glory of God revealed in saving sinners (Rom. 3:24-26). God's glory is his grace and righteousness in Christ (Exod. 33:18 – 34:7). Though this eye-salve can only be effectually applied to sinners by the irresistible grace and power of God the Holy Spirit, we must each personally apply it to ourselves by hearing it (Rom. 10:17), believing it (Acts 16:31), and seeking to understand it (Ps. 86:11; 119:26-27). This is the wise and gracious counsel of the Son of God, the Wonderful Counsellor. If we follow his counsel, he is honour-bound to make it effectual.

The Son of God graciously rebukes and chastens the people he loves, tenderly, but effectually, causing them to repent and come to him (v. 19; Ps. 65:4; Hosea 2:6-20). The Lord Jesus Christ will not lose the soul he loves. Every blood-bought child will be brought by his grace to repentance. He may lead them through great difficulties and terrifying troubles to cause them to come to him, but he will get their attention and fetch them to himself. If he has to set their barley fields on fire, he will set their barley fields on fire. If he has to send a swarm of bees, he will send a swarm of bees. If he has to destroy their idols, he will destroy their idols. But he will make them willing to come to him (Ps. 107:1-42).

He rebukes by his own gospel. He chastens by the terrors of his law and his providence. He calls to repentance by the almighty, irresistible power of his Spirit. And he inclines their hearts towards him by the chastening rod of his love. The chastening of the Lord, both that which brings us to Christ in the beginning and that which brings us to him day by day, is proof positive of his eternal love for us (Heb. 12:5-12).

The call to life

In verses 20-22 our Lord tenderly calls the dead to life: 'Behold, I stand at the door, and knock: if any man hear my voice, and open the door, I will come in to him, and will sup with him, and he with me. To him that overcometh will I grant to sit with me in my throne, even as I also overcame, and am set down with my Father in his throne. He that hath an ear, let him hear what the Spirit saith unto the churches' (vv. 20-22).

Picture him, if you can, leaning, as it were, upon the door of this church, a door that had been bolted against him by complacency and self-sufficiency. But, thanks be to God, he is not willing to be turned away! He knocks by the word of the gospel. He speaks by the voice of his Spirit. And he calls to all who hear his voice, saying, 'Open the door.' If we are his, he will not take 'No' for an answer. Instead, he puts his hand of grace into our hearts, opening the bolted door, and causes our hearts to burn with love for him. Thus, he effectually draws us with cords of love and graciously causes us to run after him (S. of S. 5:2-6).

Yes, our Lord sovereignly opens the door and lets himself into the hearts of his people. Yet he only comes in where he is wanted. He opens the door in regeneration and in the reviving of our languishing souls, pouring in his grace. We open the door in conversion, earnestly desiring and seeking him. We must not confuse the two (John 3:3-8; Acts 16:14; John 1:11-13).

If we will open our hearts to, and receive, the Lord Jesus Christ, he will graciously come in to abide with us for ever (v. 20; John 14:23). I fully realize that dead men have no ability in themselves to do anything. Yet I know that if any will awake and rise from the dead, Christ will give them light (Eph. 5:14). If any do rise up from their tomb of death and come to Christ, the fact that they do so is evidence that he awakened them and raised them from the dead. If any open to him and receive him into their hearts by faith, it is because he has already entered their hearts in life-giving power. Yet we must open to him. Otherwise, we shall perish for ever without him. Let us ever open our hearts to the Son of God!

That fellowship and communion which begins on earth in conversion will continue in heaven in everlasting glorification (v. 21). All who overcome the terrible temptations and natural tendencies of the heart to lukewarmness, worldly indifference and proud complacency will sit with Christ in his throne for ever. And this is the victory by which we overcome the world: faith in Christ (1 John 5:4). 'He that hath an ear, let him hear what the Spirit saith unto the churches' (v. 22).

If the Son of God has spoken to you by his Spirit, open to him, believe on him, come to him. He will save you. Indeed, if you believe on him, he has saved you by his grace. If you are a believer, but one who has become somewhat indifferent to Christ, flee away to him now, cast yourself down at his feet, open to him. He will come in again to you. He will forgive you.

Child of God, fear worldly-minded presumption like you would fear the most deadly plague. The thought of lukewarmness and indifference terrifies me. Yet it is ever with me. Only Christ can keep me in life and grace. Let us ever beware of our danger and hold fast to our dear Saviour, trusting his grace alone to sustain us, preserve us and bring us to glory (Jude 24-25).

17.

Christ the door

Revelation 4:1-11

'After this I looked, and, behold, a door was opened in heaven' (Rev. 4:1).

With wide-eyed wonder, John saw a door standing open in heaven. He knew the significance of that door. He was about to see visions of God (Ezek. 1:1). While he was looking at the door in astonishment, he heard the voice of his dear Saviour, like the sound of a trumpet, speaking clearly to him: 'Come up hither.' The Son of God called John up to heaven!

There is a way of access to God! There is a door opened into the Most Holy Place, by which sinners may approach and find acceptance with the Most High God. That way is Christ. That door is Christ (John 10:9; 14:6; Eph. 2:18; Heb. 10:19-20). We draw near to God by faith in the blood and righteousness of Christ. Salvation is ours when we come to God by faith in his dear Son (Heb. 7:25). When the believer leaves this world, he is immediately with the Lord in heaven (2 Cor. 5:1-9). And on the Last Day, we shall, in resurrection glory, enter into the presence of the divine majesty, there to abide for ever (1 Thess. 4:13-18). But the only door by which sinful man can enter in is the Lord Jesus Christ.

He said to John, 'Come up hither, and I will show thee things which must be hereafter.' That is to say, 'I will show you things which must happen in the future.' But remember, this took place nearly two thousand years ago! These words do not imply that there is another dispensation of time yet to come. John himself tells us that this present gospel age, the time in which we are now living, is 'the last time' (1 John 2:18). These future things 'must' come to pass because they were appointed and decreed by God in his eternal purpose of predestination.

'And immediately I was in the spirit.' Again, John's soul was drawn away from his earthly surroundings and the cares of this life. His heart was fixed on God. He ceased to see with his physical eyes and hear with his physical ears. He was 'in the spirit'. With the eyes of his soul, he looked, 'and behold, a throne'. John's thoughts were focused on a throne. This throne is the theme of John's second vision. All of chapters 4 and 5 are taken up with, and consumed by, this throne and its occupant. The word 'throne' is mentioned seventeen times in these two chapters. Remember, this is a spiritual vision. The throne is a symbol of sovereign power, authority and dominion.

The message of this chapter is as clear as the noonday sun: all things are under the control of our God who sits upon the throne of universal dominion. This fourth chapter of Revelation does not merely give us a picture of heaven. It gives a picture of the entire universe from heaven's viewpoint. And from heaven's viewpoint, the only matters of importance are the throne of God and the people of God. In beautifully symbolic language, John shows us that all things are absolutely and totally governed by our God and Saviour. In chapter 6, John will tell us about the many trials God's people must endure upon the earth. But first we are assured that God is in control: 'Behold, a throne!' No trial will be unbearable to a believer if he can but realize with assurance that our God is on his throne.

What did John see when he entered by the door?

The throne and the one who sits upon it (vv. 2-3,5-6; Ps. 93:1-5; 97:1)

God's throne is set, fixed and permanently established in heaven: 'Behold, a throne was set in heaven, and one sat on the throne' (v. 2). This throne is a symbol of power, dominion and judgement. It is set, permanently fixed in heaven. This means that God has ruled, is ruling and will rule for ever. His throne is immutably secure (Ps. 93:2). The power and dominion of God's throne reach to all the ends of the earth. His dominion is everlasting and universal. It extends to all things (Dan. 4:34-35,37; Isa. 45:7; 46:9-11).

The one who sits upon the throne is God. Tell me who is in control of the universe, and I will worship him, because the one who is in control of all things is God. Notice John's words: 'One sat on the throne.' He sat in the perfect ease and serenity of total sovereignty, because he is God. He will never give up his right to rule. None can ever overthrow, or even temporarily impede, his rule (Ps. 115:3; 135:6).

He 'was to look upon like a jasper and a sardine stone'. John is not describing God himself, for God cannot be described by anything physical (Exod. 20:4). He is describing the majesty and glory which he saw radiating from the one who sat upon the throne. John does not give us an image of God. He does not use any human feature to describe the Almighty. He simply says that God is glorious to look upon. According to Matthew Henry, 'The jasper is a transparent stone, which offers to the eye a variety of the most vivid colours, signifying the glorious perfections of God.' It is crystal clear (Rev. 21:11), representing the perfect holiness of God. The sardine stone is blood-red, representing the justice of God. God will never give up his holiness, justice and truth. He is gloriously just in his government of the world, both in his saving grace and in his fearful judgements. God is just, both in pardoning sin and in punishing sin, both in the salvation of his elect and in the damnation of the unbelieving. He is 'a just God and a Saviour' (Isa. 45:20-25).

'And there was a rainbow round about the throne, in sight like unto an emerald.' What glorious comfort! Round about the throne of this august God, there is a rainbow. The rainbow is a symbol to us that God, for Christ's sake, will remember his covenant and be merciful to his people. He will never lift his omnipotent arm in anger against his covenant people, but only in mercy (Gen. 9:13; Ps. 89:28-34; Isa. 54:7-10). 'And out of the throne proceeded lightnings and thunderings and voices' (v. 5). Proceeding from the throne of the great God, we see the lightning bolts of divine wrath, hear the thunderous terror of his holy law and hear the sweet, tender voices of love, mercy and grace in the gospel. The 'seven lamps of fire burning before the throne, which are the seven Spirits of God', symbolize the eternal, wise, all-seeing Spirit of God. The number seven represents perfection. The Spirit of God, full of wisdom, light and holiness, constantly burns like fire to consume his enemies and to refine his people. 'Our God is a consuming fire' (Heb. 12:29). And John saw before the throne 'a sea of glass like unto crystal' (v. 6). In the tabernacle and temple of the Old Testament there was a brazen laver filled with water in which the priests were required to wash themselves when they came to minister before the Lord (Exod. 30:18; 38:8; 1 Kings 7:23). Symbolically, this 'sea of glass' represents the blood of Christ, which is a fountain opened in which we must be washed before we can approach the throne of God.

Twenty-four elders and four living creatures around the throne (vv. 4,6-8)

Around the throne of God he saw twenty-four seats, smaller, subordinate thrones, and these seats were all occupied by the twenty-four elders, sitting before God. These elders were all clothed with white garments, and they all wore crowns of pure gold on their heads. And round about the throne, between the throne of God and the twenty-four elders, John saw four 'beasts', or living creatures. Who were these people? The twenty-four elders represent the whole church of God. As the twelve patriarchs represent the whole church of the Old Testament and the twelve apostles represent the whole church of the New Testament, these twenty-four elders represent all of God's elect, the whole church of God, the Israel of God (Rev. 21:12-14). Several things need to be observed about these twenty-four elders.

1. Every seat around the throne is filled. Not one of God's elect will be missing in that great day when Christ presents his redeemed ones in glory.

2. All of these redeemed ones seated around the throne are wearing the garments of salvation. They are all clothed in the white robes of Christ's righteousness.

3. And every one of these twenty-four elders is wearing a crown of victory. The white garments represent our purity and priesthood in Christ. The crowns of pure gold represent our kingship, signifying that we are made kings as well as priests in Christ. John Gill says of these twenty-four elders, 'They now reign as kings over sin, Satan, and the world, and have a kingdom of grace which shall never be removed; and they shall reign with Christ ... to all eternity in heaven.'

4. These redeemed ones from every corner of the earth do but enhance the glory of God their Saviour. His throne represents his sovereignty. These twenty-four elders constantly render homage to him.

The four beasts, or living creatures, represent those men who preach the gospel of Christ to his church in all the successive ages of history (vv. 6-8). It is commonly assumed that these four living creatures are angelic, spirit beings. But that is a mistake. These four living creatures are said to be redeemed by the blood of Christ (Rev. 5:8-11). The heavenly angels were not redeemed from sin, for they never sinned. These four living creatures represent all faithful gospel preachers throughout the ages. John tells us ten things about these living creatures as he saw them symbolically representing God's servants.

1. There are *four* of them (v. 6). God's servants are sent into the four corners of the earth to preach the gospel for the gathering of his elect out of every nation, kindred, tribe and tongue.

2. They are *living* creatures. They have been made alive by the regenerating power and grace of the Holy Spirit, and go about their work of preaching the gospel with liveliness and fervency.

3. They *stand between God and his people*, not as priests, but as ambassadors. They receive their message from God and deliver it to his people, leading them in the worship of God.

4. These living creatures are *full of eyes*, before and behind. They are gifted with spiritual insight into the mysteries of the gospel, possessing that God-given evangelical knowledge and wisdom necessary to minister to the needs of immortal souls. They have eyes before them to look into the Word of God and discern

its meaning. And they have eyes behind them to observe how that all the sacrifices, types, prophecies
and promises of the Old Testament have their accomplishment in Christ.

5. The first beast had *the features of a lion* (v. 7).
God's servants are not timid wimps. They are bold
men.

6. The second living creature was *like a calf*. As
the ox is an animal of labour, faithful gospel preachers labour diligently in the work of the ministry.

7. The third beast which John saw had *the face of a
man*. God's servants are men like those to whom they
preach. They are tender-hearted and sympathetic with
their fellow creatures. Like the Lord Jesus himself,
they are touched with the feelings and infirmities of
God's saints in this world.

8. The fourth living creature was *like a flying eagle*.
As the eagle is both wise and swift, that man who is
called of God to the work of preaching the gospel is
given wisdom in the Word and wisdom with men,
and he is given a heart of readiness to do the will of
God in publishing the everlasting gospel (Rom.
1:15-17).

9. Like the seraphim Isaiah saw (Isa. 6:2), each of
these gospel messengers had *six wings* (v. 8). With two,
they might cover their faces in reverence before God.
With two, they might cover their feet with humility,
knowing themselves to be nothing else but sinners
saved by grace. With two, they might swiftly fly to do
the will of God.

10. And these four heralds of the gospel are constantly engaged in their glorious work (v. 8). '*They
are full of eyes within.*' They are ever looking within
themselves, acknowledging their own sin and corruption by nature. And they have within themselves the
testimony of the truth of God. That is to say, they

preach to men only what they have proved to be true by experience. *'And they rest not day and night.'* Faithful gospel preachers give themselves entirely to the work of the ministry. They are wholly and wholeheartedly given to the work of preaching the gospel, crying, 'Holy, holy, holy, Lord God Almighty, which was, and is, and is to come.'

The church in heaven worshipping before the throne of God (vv. 9-11)

Observing this blessed scene, we learn how to worship the living God: 'Those beasts give glory and honour and thanks to [God].' It is the responsibility of gospel preachers to ascribe all glory, honour and praise to the Lord our God, and to him alone (v. 9). The first message of evangelism is: 'Behold, your God.' The second part of the message God has sent his servants to preach is: 'All flesh is grass' (see Isa. 40:1-11). Man is nothing and Christ is everything. We ascribe all glory to the Father, our covenant-keeping God, to the Son, our divine Redeemer, and to the Spirit, our blessed Comforter. We give God the glory because he is God, because of his covenant mercy and grace bestowed upon us (Eph. 1:3-14), and because of the salvation he has accomplished for poor sinners in Christ. The twenty-four elders fell down before him that sat on the throne. That is the posture of faith. It humbles itself before the throne of God's august majesty and worships him.

These glorified saints, as they worshipped God, 'cast their crowns before the throne'. It is not possible for a bowed head to wear a crown. All God's people cast their crowns at the foot of his throne. This symbolic gesture is very instructive. Taking the crown of honour off our heads and casting it before the throne of God our Saviour, we declare, in the first place, that we are what we are by the grace of God (1 Cor. 15:10). Any crown we have, now or in heaven, we have received as the free gift of God's grace. Secondly, we admit that we are not worthy of the least honour before God. In all that we endeavour to do for our God, we recognize that we are only unprofitable servants. We have not begun to do even that which is our most reasonable duty. Thirdly, we cast our crowns at the feet of Christ our King acknowledging our subjection to him as our only and our rightful Lord. It is not possible to worship Christ, it is not possible to trust him, until he is acknowledged as Lord. The beginning of faith is voluntary submission to his sovereign dominion. All who bow before God's throne worship him and cast their crowns before his throne; they delight to give him the glory and honour due unto his name, saying, 'Thou art worthy, O Lord, to receive glory and honour and power: for thou hast created all things, and for thy pleasure they are and were created.' The everlasting praise of the triune God is a well-deserved praise. He is the Creator of all things and the end of all things (Prov. 16:4; Rom. 11:36). This great God, the Creator, Sustainer and the one who disposes of all things, to whom all worship is due, is none other than Jesus Christ, our Saviour (Col. 1:16-17).

18.

Christ the Lamb of God

Revelation 5:1-14

'And when he had taken the book, the four beasts and four and twenty elders fell down before the Lamb, having every one of them harps, and golden vials full of odours, which are the prayers of saints' (Rev. 5:8).

In Revelation 5, the vision that John relates to us conveys one message: everything God has for men is in the Lamb, provided by the Lamb, revealed through the Lamb and designed to bring praise to the Lamb of God. All that God gives to sinners, he gives through Christ. And all that God receives from sinners, he receives through Christ. In chapter 4, John saw the sovereign majesty of the triune God in creation. In chapter 5, he tells us how he was made to see the sovereign majesty of the triune God in the redemption of sinners by Christ Jesus. John saw and heard five things which are described in these fourteen verses.

1. The throne of God

The central object in the vision which John sets before us in chapters 4 and 5 is the throne of God. His gaze was constantly focused on 'him that sat on the throne' (v. 1). In these two chapters, he calls our attention to God's throne seventeen times! In chapter 4, John describes the incomparably glorious splendour of the triune God, Father, Son and Holy Spirit, in his sovereignty. In chapter 5, he describes the mediator, the Lamb, whom he 'beheld ... in the midst of the throne' and by whom the triune God makes himself known to men. And that Lamb is himself God the Son.

As always, the throne of God is a symbol of his *sovereignty*. It is a symbol of God's supreme majesty and universal power, authority and dominion. Let it never be forgotten that our God is God upon a throne. He rules all things in total sovereignty. A god without a throne is a worthless god, for such a god is no god at all! 'But our God is in the heavens: he hath done whatsoever he hath pleased' (Ps. 115:3). 'Whatsoever the LORD pleased, that did he in heaven, and in earth, in the seas, and all deep places' (Ps. 135:6). The Lord our God, the one true and living God, is a God of absolute sovereignty. He always does exactly what he wills in creation (Rev. 4:11), in providence (Rom. 8:28; 11:36) and in grace (Rom. 9:11-24). Every believer has learned, and rejoices to know, 'that the heavens do rule' (Dan. 4:26).

And we rejoice to know that God's sovereign throne is a throne of *grace* (Heb. 4:16). Grace originates at God's throne, grace is dispensed from God's throne and grace brings sinners to God's throne. Our God is sovereign and he is gracious. He is great and he is good. He is almighty and he is merciful. 'He delighteth in mercy!' God always exercises his sovereign power and dominion to accomplish his everlasting purpose of grace towards his elect.

2. The book of God

In the right hand of the eternal God, John saw a book — a book written within and without, bound shut and sealed with seven seals (vv. 1-4). This book is the book of God's eternal decrees. It represents God's eternal plan and purpose of grace, his purpose of predestination, which includes all things. It is to this book that our great Surety referred when he said, 'Lo, I come: in the volume of the book it is written of me, I delight to do thy will, O my God' (Ps. 40:7-8; Heb. 10:5-10). William Hendriksen said of this book, 'It symbolizes God's purpose with respect to the entire universe throughout history, and concerning all creatures in all ages and unto all eternity.'

Our God is a God of purpose — eternal, unalterable purpose (Isa. 46:9-11). God's purpose of predestination includes all things (Eph. 1:11). The object of God's eternal purpose of predestination is the salvation of his elect (Rom. 8:28-30). Everything that comes to pass in time was purposed by God in eternity (Rom. 11:36). And the object of God in all that he does is the effectual accomplishment of the everlasting salvation of his elect. In election, God chose a people whom he would save. In predestination, he sovereignly ordained all things that come to pass to secure the salvation of his chosen. And in providence, he accomplishes in time what he purposed from eternity.

As John saw it, the book of God was closed, a mystery sealed with seven seals. These seven seals do not represent, as it is sometimes claimed, seven 'dispensations' of time. The writing, within and on the back, and the seven seals simply mean that God's purpose is full, complete, perfect and unalterable. Nothing can be added to it. Nothing can be taken from it. The seven seals also tell us that God's purpose of grace is unknown, unrevealed, a secret known only to God until Christ revealed it. He revealed it at first in the types, shadows and prophecies of the Old Testament. Then, in these last days, he has revealed it to us more fully in the gospel. And in the last day, when the restitution of all things is made, our Lord will perfectly reveal God's purpose in all things.

The closed book indicates that God's plan was both unrevealed and unexecuted. If the book were to remain closed, God's eternal purpose would not be realized. His

plan would not be executed. The thought of God's purpose
being shut up, unrevealed and unfulfilled caused John great
lamentation and grief, and he began to weep. If God's book
is opened, if the seals are broken, then the universe is ruled
and governed in the interest of God's elect, according to
the purpose of his grace. Then God's glorious purpose of
redemption would be accomplished. But if it is not opened
and fulfilled, then the purpose of God himself would be
thwarted. The grace of God would be frustrated. The plan
of God would go unfulfilled. God himself would lose his
glory. But there is no cause to weep, as we see from the
next thing John describes.

3. The Lamb of God took the book to open it (vv. 5-7)

'One of the elders,' one of those chosen by God, redeemed
by the blood of the Lamb and saved by grace, 'saith unto
me, Weep not.' Why should John stop weeping? 'Behold,
the Lion of the tribe of Judah ... hath prevailed to open the
book, and to loose the seven seals thereof.' In other words,
Christ has conquered all his enemies, and ours (John
12:30-32). By the shedding of his blood, by his death upon
the cross, this Lion of Judah, the Root of David, has prevailed. He has removed the sins of his people, satisfied the
law, crushed the serpent's head and conquered death. By
virtue of his sacrifice, Christ has earned the right to open
the book and to rule the universe in accordance with God's
eternal purpose of grace (Rev. 10:1-3). God has given him
power over all flesh that he might give eternal life to his
elect (John 17:2).

John beheld the Lord Jesus Christ, not only as a conquering Lion, but also as a sin-atoning, mediating Lamb.
He saw the Lamb in the midst of the four living creatures
and the twenty-four elders as a Lamb that had been
slaughtered. This means that the virtue and merit of his

sacrifice are abiding, perpetual and efficacious (1 John 1:9; 2:1-2). This Lamb, symbolically, has 'seven horns'. Horns are emblems of power. Christ is the horn of salvation. As such, he has plenty of power. He is able to save his people (Heb. 7:25), keep them in his grace (John 10:27-29) and do for them all that they need. He also has 'seven eyes', abundant wisdom. These seven eyes represent the gifts, power and wisdom of the Holy Spirit which are dispensed to God's elect upon the earth by virtue of Christ's death, resurrection and exaltation as our substitute (Ps. 68:18-20).

Then, as John looked on, Christ the Lamb took the book out of the right hand of him that sat upon the throne (v. 7). John Trapp said, 'As a Mediator he took it, as God he gave it.' Our Saviour did not ask for the book. He took it, because it is his right to do so. This is the significance of what John saw: the Lord Jesus Christ, our mediator, received authority to rule the universe according to the will of God by virtue of his sin-atoning sacrifice (John 17:2). This is a picture of the coronation of King Jesus (Heb. 2:8-9). As the Father's reward to him for his mediatorial accomplishments at his ascension, Christ received for himself a kingdom (Luke 19:12; Phil. 2:6-11; Ps. 2; 110; Dan. 7:9-14). God has turned the world over to the rule of the God-man, the Lamb, our mediator! God governs the universe, according to his own eternal decrees, through the Lamb. This is Christ's reward and every believer's comfort.

4. The song of the redeemed (vv. 8-12)

As soon as the Lamb took the book in his hands, and accepted the sceptre of universal monarchy, a song of praise broke out in heaven. This song began with the church, the redeemed ones, and was taken up by the heavenly angels. This song is a celebration of Christ's worthiness to rule the universe according to God's purpose (Rev. 10:1-3), and to receive all praise, honour and glory for ever. The basis of both his worthiness of such honour and the praise given to him by saints and angels is his effectual redemption. Praise is not given to him simply because he was slain (many have been slain!), but because his slaughter was the accomplishment of our redemption. The death of Christ as the sin-atoning Lamb was the accomplishment of a particular and effectual redemption. The song does not say, 'Thou hast redeemed every kindred, tongue, people, and nation.' That would mean either that his blood was shed in vain for the multitudes who are lost, or that all the universe is saved, neither of which is true. This song says, 'Thou hast redeemed us ... *out of* every kindred, tongue, people, and nation!'

5. The consummate purpose of God (vv. 13-14)

It is God's ultimate purpose that everything and everyone in his creation should bow before, and bring honour to, his dear Son. And God will see to it that his purpose is accomplished in the end (Ps. 76:10; Isa. 45:20-25; Col. 1:18). He who made all things, sustains all things and rules all things will ultimately have the eternal praise of all things. 'O the depth of the riches both of the wisdom and knowledge of God! How unsearchable are his judgements, and his ways past finding out! ... For of him, and through him, and to him, are all things: to whom be glory for ever. Amen' (Rom. 11:33,36).

These are the things John saw when he was in the Spirit. He saw that the entire universe is governed by the throne of Almighty God, and that God rules the universe through the Mediator Christ Jesus, the Lamb of God. Having accomplished the redemption of his people by the sacrifice of himself, our Lord Jesus ascended back into heaven and sat down at the right hand of the Majesty on high, exalted above all principality, power and dominion. God the Father put all things in subjection to Christ, under his feet, and made him to be head over all things to his church, which is his body, 'the fulness of him that filleth all in all' (Eph. 1:22-23). Ultimately, all things will glorify Christ, our God and Saviour. God's purpose will be carried out in his creation. The throne of God is secure. The Lamb of God reigns supreme, without rival, by incontestable right. The kingdom of God is safe and secure. The glory of the eternal God is sure. Blessed is that person to whom these things have been revealed!

19.

Christ the Lamb in the midst
of the throne

Revelation 5:1-14

'And I beheld, and, lo, in the midst of the throne and of the four beasts, and in the midst of the elders, stood a Lamb as it had been slain, having seven horns and seven eyes, which are the seven Spirits of God sent forth into all the earth' (Rev. 5:6).

Everything in the Bible is built upon, centres in and points to a lamb. In the Old Testament, the hope of Israel and the centre of worship was a lamb. All the symbolism of Old Testament worship focused the attention of the people upon a lamb. All the promises and prophecies of the Old Testament Scriptures find their fulfilment in a lamb. In a word, all the blessings of mercy and grace from God symbolically flowed to the people through the blood of a lamb. The Lamb that was pointed to and represented by the typical worship of the Old Testament is Jesus Christ, the Son of God, our substitute. When John the Baptist saw Christ coming towards him, he pointed his disciples to him and said, 'Look, here he comes, the one promised, typified and hoped for, the one upon whom we trust, the one I have been telling you about — "Behold, the Lamb of God, which taketh away the sin of the world!"'

From the beginning, the only way sinful men could approach the holy God was through the blood of a slain lamb. They had to bring the blood of an innocent victim, offered as a sacrifice to God. That innocent lamb was a picture of

Christ, the Lamb of God, who died, the just for the unjust, that he might bring us to God (Gen. 4:4; Exod. 29:38-39; Lev. 1-8; 16:5-10). Yet all the blood of those innocent victims offered upon Jewish altars, day after day and year after year, could never take away sin. They did nothing to appease the wrath of God. They did nothing to change the sinner. Those sacrifices simply taught one lesson which God always kept before men: sinful men cannot approach God in his holiness without a blood sacrifice. They pointed men to Christ, the Lamb of God.

As fallen man cannot approach the holy God without a blood sacrifice, so also the holy Lord God will not approach fallen man except through the blood of a sin-atoning lamb. God always deals with men through the Lamb. Judgement comes upon those who despise the Lamb, and mercy is bestowed upon those who trust the Lamb. This was clearly set forth in the sacrifice of the Passover lamb, which was a type of Christ (Exod. 12:13; 1 Cor. 5:7). Even before the world was made, God's covenant mercy was bestowed upon his elect through the merits of the Lord Jesus Christ, the Lamb of God, slain from the foundation of the world (Rev. 13:8).

Everything in the Word of God points to and finds its consummation in the Lamb. The same thing is true with regard to eternity. In heaven's eternal glory, the central figure is the Lamb of God. When John was called up into heaven to behold things from heaven's vantage-point, he said, 'I beheld, and, lo, in the midst of the throne and of the four beasts, and in the midst of the elders stood a Lamb as it had been slain.' Then he saw all the hosts of God's elect, both of men and of angels, falling down before the Lamb, crying in unison, 'Worthy is the Lamb!' Jesus Christ, in his sacrificial character as the Lamb of God, is the centre of all things, the ruler of all things and the pre-eminent object of all true faith and worship. He is not the *only* object of faith and worship: we worship the Father and the Spirit, as well as the Son (1 John 5:7). But the triune God has given all pre-eminence to Christ, the Son, so that we worship the Father, the Son and the Spirit only *through Christ*, the mediatorial Lamb.

The perception of the Lamb

How did John see Christ? What condition was he in when he looked and beheld the Lamb of God in his glory? If you read verses 1-4, you will notice that before the Lamb appeared, when there was no one found who was worthy to open the book that was held in the hand of him that sat upon the throne, John said, 'I wept much.' Commenting on this fact, C. H. Spurgeon said, 'By weeping eyes the Lamb of God is best seen... Eyes washed by repentance are best able to see those blessed truths which shine forth from our incarnate God, the bearer of our sins. Free grace and dying love are most appreciated by the mourners in Zion.' David said much the same thing: 'I sought the LORD, and he heard me, and delivered me from all my fears. They looked unto him, and were lightened: and their faces were not ashamed' (Ps. 34:4-5). The Lamb of God must be revealed before he can be seen, but he is revealed to all who look to him. So look to him that he may be revealed. Seeing him, you will weep over your sins (Zech. 12:10). And seeing him through the watery eyes of repentance, ask for grace that you may, by the Spirit of God, see him clearly, perceiving by faith who he is and what he has done for you.

The personality of the Lamb

Christ's worthiness to receive all honour, worship and praise is to be seen primarily in the greatness and glory of his person and work. He is worthy, because of who he is and what he has done. 'We love him, because he first loved us' (1 John 4:19). Had he not loved us and redeemed us, we would never have loved him at all. Yet, above all else, we love him for himself: 'Unto you therefore which believe he is precious' (1 Peter 2:7). Who is the Lord Jesus Christ? He is God our Saviour, and a man like us. He is God and man in one glorious person. Notice how the elder in verse 5 describes him to John.

The Lamb of God is 'the Lion of the tribe of Judah'. This speaks of the dignity of Christ's office as our King and the majesty of his person as our Lord. According to the flesh, Christ came from the tribe of Judah (Gen. 49:9-10). Like a lion, he is great in strength. He is the mighty God, the able Saviour, the strong Deliverer. He is an effectual redeemer, an almighty protector, a powerful avenger. There is no lack of power and strength in our Saviour. We may trust him with implicit confidence. Like a lion, he is also bold and courageous. He engaged Satan, the enemy of our souls, with lion-like boldness, defeating him and the powers of darkness with unflinching courage. Christ our Saviour is full of irresistible power! He has a lion's heart and a lion's strength. He comes forth conquering and to conquer. Yet — and here is a great wonder — to redeem us from the curse of the law, this lion became a lamb led forth to the slaughter!

The Lamb is also 'the Root of David'. In his humanity, Christ is the Son of David (Isa. 11:10; Rev. 22:16); he is David's offspring. Yet he is David's Lord (Matt. 22:41-45). He is the root out of whom David came and to whom David owes his existence. In the same sense, Christ is the root from whom all God's elect spring. We derive our life from him. We live by virtue of his life (John 15:1-8). Christ, the Lamb of God, is a mighty conqueror. He has 'prevailed to open the book, and to loose the ... seals thereof'. On the cross, the Lion of Judah, the Root of David, conquered Satan, death and hell. Prevailing over his enemies and ours, Christ Jesus earned the right to rule the universe according to the

purpose of God (John 17:2). This book (vv. 1-5) is the book
of God's eternal decrees. It represents God's eternal plan
and purpose of grace, his purpose of predestination, which
includes all things. As a prophet, Christ opens, reveals and
fulfils all the decrees of God. He explains everything. The
Lamb is the key to every secret. Apart from faith in Christ,
the Lamb of God, nothing can be known of God's purposes,
but to those who believe everything is as plain as day.
Nothing is hidden from them that believe (John 15:15; 11:40;
Eph. 1:9-10). Just in proportion as we trust the Lord Jesus
Christ, we shall see the will of God and the glory of God in
all things.

The position of the Lamb

'And I beheld, and, lo, in the midst of the throne and of the
four beasts, and in the midst of the elders, stood a Lamb as
it had been slain, having seven horns and seven eyes, which
are the seven spirits of God sent forth into all the earth'
(v. 6). The Lamb is in the midst of the throne. He is perfectly at home in the midst of God's dazzling, unapproach-
able glory, because he is himself God. The glory of God,
radiating from that throne, is his very own. Jesus is God!
The Lamb who was slain for our sins is himself the almighty
God! The Lamb that was slain is the mediator between God
and men. As stated before, it is only through Christ as our
mediator that God comes to man and man comes to God.
Were it not for the Lamb in the midst of the throne, no
creature could ever draw near to that throne, but because
of him, the saints in heaven are as much at home there as
he is! Even while upon the earth, we can and should approach the throne of God with confidence, if Christ is our
mediator (Heb. 4:16). The Lamb in the midst of the throne
is the centre of all. The Lamb, the Lord Jesus Christ, is the
centre of that blessed circle of holy fellowship between God,

his people and the holy angels. As in the church below, so in the church above, 'Christ is all!'

In heaven's glory, we see all things meeting in Christ the Lamb. Christ is the summing up of all existence. In him, God and man, angels and men, the spiritual and the material are united. All things find fulfilment in Christ. The Lamb in the midst of the throne is the centre of all. In the picture before us, it appears that everyone in heaven looks to him. The Father's eyes are always upon the Lamb. The eyes of the four living creatures, God's preachers, are always on the Lamb. The elders, the angels and all the forces of nature are turned towards the Lamb. Jesus Christ as the Lamb of God is the centre of all love, thought, action and praise in the glory-land! Everything revolves around, and rallies to, the Lamb.

The performance of the Lamb

Around the throne of God in heaven they never cease to speak of the wonderful works of Christ, the Lamb of God (vv. 7-10). It is in his character as a Lamb, our mediator and substitute, that Christ takes the book of God's eternal decrees and makes it known. He took the book in the covenant of grace into his hands. He fulfils all that is written in the book by his obedience and death as our substitute, and by his providential rule and disposition of all things. He opens and reveals the contents of the book by his Spirit through the gospel. This spotless Lamb was slain as a sin-atoning sacrifice for God's elect. He was slain by the sword of divine justice under the wrath of Almighty God. Thus he effectually redeemed his people from the curse of the law.

It is important not to miss the doctrine of verse 9: the death of Christ was an effectual atonement for sin — 'Thou ... hast redeemed *us*' (cf. Heb. 9:12). This atonement was

made and this redemption was accomplished for a particular people — '... *us ... out of* [not along with] every kindred,
and tongue, and people, and nation' (cf. Isa. 53:8).

Sending forth his Spirit in almighty, saving grace, by
virtue of his redeeming work, the Lamb of God has made
us (all believers) kings and priests unto God. As kings, believers rule themselves and their circumstances by the grace
of God. Neither the passions of the flesh, nor the circumstances of life have dominion over God's saints. As priests,
God's people draw near to him, confessing sin, worshipping and serving him by the blood of Christ. We do business directly with God in the holy place through the mediation of Christ (Heb. 10:19-22). We need no other priest
but Christ! As kings and priests unto God, we shall reign
with Christ for ever when he makes all things new.

The praise of the Lamb

Jesus Christ is the Lamb of God. He appeared in that character in the covenant of grace. He lived and died in that
character in time. He reigns in that character for ever. And
he is universally adored in that character. The praise of the
Lamb begins with the church of God's elect (vv. 8-10). The
angels of God unite with the redeemed in the praise and
adoration of the Lamb (vv. 11-12). They worship the Lamb
as the sin-atoning Saviour of men, because they have
learned the wonders of redemption from redeemed sinners
(Eph. 3:8-11). At last, the entire universe will praise, honour and extol the Lamb of God for his glorious work of
redemption (vv. 13-14; Ps. 76:10; Prov. 16:4). He who made
all things will one day receive the praise of all things (Phil.
2:9-11). All things will, in the end, be found to be to the
praise, honour and glory of our God, the Lamb (Rom. 11:36).

20.

Christ the mighty Conqueror

Revelation 6:1-17

'And I saw, and behold a white horse: and he that sat on him had a bow; and a crown was given unto him: and he went forth conquering, and to conquer' (Rev. 6:2).

Everything we have seen thus far in the book of Revelation has been leading up to, and preparing us for, the opening of the sealed book in chapter 6. In chapter 1, we saw Christ in his majestic power and glory as our exalted God and Saviour. There we were assured of his constant presence with his church. The Son of God constantly walks in the midst of his churches. He cares for, protects and provides for his own. He holds his messengers, his preachers, his ordained pastors in his own right hand. Whom, or what, shall we fear? Christ Jesus, the Son of God, is with us! He holds us in his omnipotent hand!

In chapters 2 and 3, we read the letters of Christ to the seven churches which reveal the various stages of spiritual declension and revival to which the church of Christ and individual believers are subjected in this world. So long as we are in this body of flesh we must struggle against sin, even the terribly evil sins of apathy and indifference. That which is true of individual believers is true of the church collectively. Therefore, we constantly need discipline, correction, instruction, encouragement, reviving and grace. These things our Lord faithfully supplies by the gospel and

Spirit of his grace. Were it not for his all-sufficient grace keeping us, we would soon wither away and die. But our dear Saviour always preserves his own!

In chapter 4, we are allowed to ascend with John into heaven itself. There we are shown the throne, the symbol of God's sovereign power and dominion; the twenty-four elders, the representatives of the church, the whole body of God's elect; and the four living creatures who represent God's faithful gospel preachers in all ages. In that chapter we are shown the representations of God's wisdom, power, glory and greatness. We are plainly taught that God's ultimate purpose in all things is the glory of his own great being. When we read chapter 4, we can almost hear the Lord saying to John, and to us by him, 'No matter what you read, see, hear, or experience, you have no cause to fear. My throne is secure. My people are safe. My purpose is unalterable. There is never any cause for alarm or fear' (see Isa. 46:9-10).

In chapter 5, we are given a vision of the throne, the book and the Lamb. The throne, as stated earlier, symbolizes God's total sovereignty over all things. The book, 'written within and on the backside, and sealed with seven seals', represents the plan of God for the ages, his eternal purpose and decrees of predestination. But God is unknown and his purpose is secret, a mystery, until the Lamb of God, the Lord Jesus Christ, appears in the midst of the throne. By virtue of his effectual, sin-atoning sacrifice, he is able and worthy to open the book of God. He both reveals and fulfils all that is written in the book of divine predestination. The entire universe is ruled by the sovereign throne of God through the mediation of the Lamb, our Redeemer, according to the book of God's eternal, unalterable purpose. Ultimately, in the end, all of God's elect will be saved. There will be no vacant seats around the throne. And all things will render praise to our God. Essentially, the vision of chapter 5 teaches us one thing: the Lord our God is carrying out his will and purpose for the good of his people and the glory of his own great name. That is to say, 'The Lord God omnipotent reigneth!' Therefore, we who believe have no reason to fear in times of trial, trouble, affliction, sorrow and persecution. God our Saviour will protect us, sustain us and make us triumphant!

As we come to chapter 6, we see Christ, the Lamb of God, opening the seals of the book, unfolding to us the mysteries of God's purpose and fulfilling his decrees. In this chapter, he opens six of the seven seals. The seventh seal is opened in chapter 8. In my opinion, it is a mistake to make the seals and the horsemen mentioned in this chapter representative of specific times. Rather, they refer to the many trials and difficulties through which God's people must pass as they make their pilgrimage through this world to their glorious inheritance in heaven. They have reference to the condition and experience of God's church and kingdom in this world in all ages and once more give assurance of the fact that ultimately the church of Christ will be triumphant. The purpose of this sixth chapter of Revelation is to assure us that, though we must suffer trials, afflictions and persecutions, Christ our Saviour is always in control. He is a mighty conqueror and we are more than conquerors in him.

Christ is a mighty, triumphant conqueror (vv. 1-2)

With the opening of the first seal, we see a rider upon a white horse. We do not have to guess who he is. This is Christ, our triumphant King, our victorious Captain, our conquering man of war (Rev. 19:11-16). The first thing revealed here is Christ's glorious sovereignty, his constant triumph over all things and his sure and certain conquest over all his enemies, and ours. We can safely trust the sovereign Christ.

Our Saviour is seen as one riding upon a white horse. White is always used as a symbol of holiness, purity and righteousness. It refers to that which is holy and heavenly. Our Lord's garments are white. He sits upon a great white throne. He gives his people a white stone of acquittal (2:17). And he will come again upon the white clouds of heaven. White is the colour of the horse ridden by a commanding officer when he returns from the battlefield victorious, with all the spoils of victory. Our Saviour's conquest is so certain that even as he goes out to battle he rides upon a white stallion!

There is a bow in his hand. This is his only weapon. The Son of God conquers his enemies with that one weapon. What does that bow symbolize? It is the everlasting gospel of grace preached by his servants (Rom. 1:16; 1 Cor. 1:21-24; 2 Cor. 10:3-5). When his servants preach the gospel in the power of the Holy Spirit, its precious truths are like pointed arrows flung from the bow of Christ himself, piercing the hearts of chosen sinners. His arrows never miss their mark!

'And a crown was given unto him.' This man of war is the King of glory, the Messiah, the Christ. By virtue of his obedience to his Father, as the reward of his travail, he was given the right to rule all things, so that he might sovereignly secure the salvation of his people (John 17:2; Rom. 14:9; Acts 2:29-36).

'And he went forth conquering, and to conquer.' His 'goings forth have been from old, from everlasting' (Micah 5:2). The Son of God came forth in the covenant of grace, before the world began, and stood as our mighty Captain, agreeing to conquer all our enemies and his, and thereby to save all his people. This he will do. 'He shall not fail'! (Isa. 42:4). When he died upon the cross, Christ conquered Satan and conquered sin, and by the power of the cross he conquers the hearts of chosen sinners (John 12:30-32). Wherever the gospel is preached by faithful men, in the power of his Spirit, he still conquers. And he will yet conquer (Ps. 2:1-8). Every knee shall bow before him. Every tongue shall confess him.

All his foes shall become his footstool (Isa. 45:20-25; Phil. 2:9-11; Heb. 10:10-13). Child of God, as you face your enemies in this world and the many trials and tribulations that beset you, keep the eye of faith fixed constantly upon this mighty Conqueror (Heb. 12:1-2). Trust him. You have nothing to fear. The Lion of the tribe of Judah has prevailed, is prevailing and will yet prevail!

We must endure trouble in this world (vv. 3-8)

Yet it is through much tribulation that we must enter into the kingdom of God. Sorrow is the common lot of God's people in this world (John 16:33). Not only must we suffer all the sorrows common to others, we also must endure those which are heaped upon us by wicked, persecuting men. These are the things represented by the red, black and pale horses.

The red horse is a symbol of war and slaughter. 'For thy sake we are killed all the day long; we are accounted as sheep for the slaughter' (Rom. 8:36).

The black horse is the symbol of economic hardship, poverty and injustice. If there is widespread poverty, famine, or injustice in a land, God's people are not exempted from the hardships they cause. And we are never exempted from persecution of one form or another (Matt. 10:22-36). Yet two things are certain:

1. When we do not have plenty, we shall still have enough. A loaf of bread may cost a day's wages, but if we have bread enough for today we have what we need. Christ provides for his own (Matt. 6:33).

2. All the poverty, famine and persecution in the world can never take away, or even diminish, the oil of his Spirit and the wine of his love and grace. Christ protects his own (Zech. 2:8; Ps. 34:7).

The pale horse is the symbol of death and the grave. These, too, are the common woes of humanity. Death comes by many means — the sword, famine, pestilence, war, wild beasts, etc. — but it is sure to come. Our bodies must return to the earth. However, the rider of the pale horse will be a welcome visitor to the children of God (Ps. 23; 2 Cor. 5:1-9).

Here are five things that will help us if we can hold on to them as we face the sorrows and difficulties of this life:

1. As long as we are in this world, pain, sorrow, affliction and persecution will be our constant companions (Isa. 43:2).

2. Whatever we suffer in this world, even at the hands of Satan and wicked men, we suffer from the hands of our gracious God and Saviour. Notice that 'Power was given to him' (v. 4). Satan can do nothing without divine permission! And when our trials come, they are always regulated by our Father's decree: 'Hurt not the oil and wine' (v. 6).

3. God uses these sorrows and afflictions to refine, purify and strengthen his people (Heb. 12:5-11).

4. In the midst of all our trials, our Saviour is with us (Isa. 41:10; 43:1-5).

5. Our trials will soon be over! Either by the intervention of providence or by calling us home, our God will soon put an end to our sorrow (Rom. 8:35-39).

God will not destroy this world until all his elect are saved

With the opening of the fifth seal, John sees the souls of Christ's martyrs, men and women who offered their lives as sacrifices upon the altar to Christ. They believed him, confessed him and followed him, even unto death, sealing their faith with their blood (vv. 9-11).

These martyrs cry for God's just retribution upon their enemies — not for their own sake, but for Christ's sake. These are people who have been slain, slaughtered as wild beasts and common criminals, because of their faith in Christ. Those who persecuted them to death were, in reality, persecuting Christ (Acts 9:5). Their blood cries out for justice. Christ is honour-bound both to avenge their blood and to destroy all who oppose his throne. Persecutors beware! The blood of God's saints cries for vengeance upon the vessels of wrath for the glory of Christ, that he might make known to all his power and justice (Gen. 4:10; Heb. 11:4; Matt. 23:34-35).

All God's saints in heaven are robed in the perfect white righteousness of Christ and are resting. None can enter heaven except those to whom God has given a 'white robe'. That represents the perfect righteousness of Christ imputed to every redeemed sinner (2 Cor. 5:21). And those who have entered into heaven have entered into rest (Heb. 4:9). Their trials are over. Their sorrows are ended. Their temptations have ceased. They have finished their work. Now they keep an eternal sabbath in glory! It is a sabbath rest that was typified in the law, was begun when they trusted Christ (Matt. 11:28-30) and is now consummated in his presence (Heb. 4:10-11).

The number of the martyrs is not yet complete. All God's elect are here referred to as martyrs — that is, as 'witnesses'. A martyr is one who witnesses for Christ and voluntarily lays down his life in his cause. In that sense, every believer is a martyr (Mark 8:35; Luke 14:26-27). God knows the number of his elect. Christ knows the number of his sheep. It has been fixed from eternity by divine decree. Until that number is reached, until all the elect are saved, judgement will not come. Christ will uphold and sustain this sin-cursed earth until he has gathered out of it all his sheep (2 Peter 3:9). But let no one foolishly imagine that judgement will not come.

God will at last avenge himself and his elect (vv. 12-17)

The sixth seal is opened to introduce the great and terrible Day of Judgement. In that day, there will be a total dissolution of the physical universe (vv. 12-15). It will be a climactic, not a gradual, thing (2 Peter 3:10-12). The entire world of reprobate rebels will be seized with sudden terror (vv. 15-17). In the words of Ron Lewis, 'In that great and terrible day, there will be a strange prayer meeting. Men will pray, but the men praying will not be saved men, but unsaved men. They will pray not to God, but to the mountains and rocks. They will pray not for life, but for death. And they will pray not that they may see Christ, but that they may be hidden from him!' When that day comes, the door of grace will be shut for ever! Christ will conquer all his enemies, either by the power of his grace or by the power of his wrath — but conquer he surely will (Isa. 45:20-25).

21.
Salvation to God and to the Lamb!

Revelation 7:1-17

'For the Lamb which is in the midst of the throne shall feed them, and shall lead them unto living fountains of waters: and God shall wipe away all tears from their eyes' (Rev. 7:17).

The subject of this chapter is the salvation of God's elect. Long ago, the prophet Jonah declared, 'Salvation is of the LORD' (Jonah 2:9). All God's saints on the earth learn the sweet words of David's song and rejoice to sing, 'The salvation of the righteous is of the LORD' (Ps. 37:39). 'Salvation is of the Lord' — in its planning, in its purchase, in its performance, in its preservation and in its perfection! From beginning to end, salvation is God's work and God's gift, and he gives it to whom he will (Rom. 9:16). When at last all the elect are gathered together around the throne of God, perfectly glorified in Christ, they will proclaim, 'Salvation to our God which sitteth upon the throne, and unto the Lamb' (v. 10). In these seventeen verses John teaches us four facts about the salvation of God's elect.

1. God preserves this world in order to save his elect in it (vv. 1-3)

No one should mistake God's longsuffering for lack of will or ability in the Almighty to punish his enemies. The entire sixth chapter of Revelation is a warning to men of the certainty and finality of God's judgement. The Lord's patience and longsuffering with men and women in this world is an unquestionable fact. He causes the sunshine and the rain to fall upon both the righteous and the wicked (Matt. 5:45). 'The Lord is good to all; and his tender mercies are over all his works' (Ps. 145:9). But temporal mercies are not an indication of God's favour (Ps. 92:5-7). Far from it! God has set the wicked in slippery places. Their feet will slide down to hell in due season (Ps. 73:18-20; Deut. 32:35). God has already prepared the instruments by which he will free himself of his adversaries and destroy all his enemies (vv. 1-2). The angels of destruction are armed with the winds of woe and are ready to execute judgement. These four angels control the instruments of destruction throughout the whole earth — north, south, east and west. They are prepared for their work of hurting, or destroying, the earth. But, suddenly, John sees 'another angel ascending from the east'. He cries with a loud voice to the four angels in verse 1 and commands them to withhold their judgement (v. 2).

This angel ascending up out of the east is the Lord Jesus Christ, the Angel of the covenant. Who but the Angel of the covenant (the Messenger of the covenant — Mal. 3:1), could have the seal of the covenant? Who but Christ, who holds his people in his hands and keeps them by the power of his grace, could seal his servants? He is the Day Star and the Sun of Righteousness who rose in the east, from Judah, out of Zion. When he arose to seal his people, he brought light, life, salvation and joy to us. There is healing beneath his wings (2 Peter 1:19; Mal. 4:2; Ps. 14:7). Christ has the seal of the covenant, which is the Spirit of God. As circumcision was the physical sign and seal of God's covenant with Abraham, so the Holy Spirit, given to God's elect in regeneration, is the seal of the covenant of grace (Eph. 1:13-14; 4:30).

It is Christ, our mediator, the Angel of the covenant, who preserves this world from destruction in order to accomplish the salvation of God's elect (v. 3). The only thing holding back the judgement of God from this world is the mediatorial work of Christ. God's patience, longsuffering and forbearance with this world are 'to us-ward', and are for the salvation of his elect (2 Peter 3:9,15). As God set his seal upon the houses of Israel when the destroying angel passed through Egypt (Exod. 12:23), so Christ has set his seal upon all the elect. As Aaron wore a signet upon his forehead which read, 'Holiness to the LORD' (Exod. 28:36,38), so Christ has set his sanctifying seal upon his people.

If you are a believer, the seal of God is upon you. Judgement will surely come, but you have nothing to fear! The woes of this book are against the wicked, persecuting world. No punishment from God will fall upon his chosen ones (1 Thess. 5:9). God punished the sins of his people in Christ, their substitute, to the full satisfaction of his justice. Since Christ has redeemed us from the curse of the law, we cannot be condemned (Gal. 3:13; Rom. 8:1,33-34). This sealing is one of the most precious things under heaven. The seal of God protects, preserves and keeps us. It is the mark of God's ownership upon us. It cannot be broken. Well might we pray, 'Set me as a seal upon thine heart' (S. of S. 8:6). God the Father sealed us with his decree of election (Jude 1). God the Son sealed us with his atoning blood (Heb. 10:10-14). God the Holy Spirit sealed us with his regenerating grace (Eph. 1:13-14).

2. All God's elect will be saved (vv. 4-12)

Many far-fetched and groundless speculations have been made and opinions voiced concerning the identity of these 144,000. This number, like all the rest of the vision, is symbolical. It is a definite number used to describe an indefinite multitude. How are we to discover who they are? Simply look at the context. The 144,000 represent all of God's sealed ones throughout the whole earth (vv. 3-4), the whole 'Israel of God', a great multitude of elect Jews and Gentiles that no man can number, who will be saved (v. 9). The twelve tribes of Israel which are named and the twelve thousand out of each tribe represent spiritual Israel, the church, the whole body of God's elect (Rom. 11:26). To suggest, as many do, that Jews will obtain God's mercy and grace because they are Jews, physical descendants of Abraham, is to fly in the face of Holy Scripture. Grace does not come to men as a matter of physical inheritance, but by spiritual heritage (John 1:12-13; Rom. 9:8).

John tells us five things about this 144,000 — that is, five things about God's elect:

1. They are a great multitude (vv. 4,9).

2. God's elect — and only God's elect — were redeemed by the blood of Christ (14:3).

3. The elect are known in time by their conversion to Christ (14:4; John 10:3-4,27-28; 1 Thess. 1:4-10).

4. All the elect are sealed in grace, preserved and kept by God the Holy Spirit (vv. 3-4). 'They shall never perish!'

5. All God's elect, the entire 144,000, will definitely be saved (vv. 9-12). John saw them all, the whole, great, innumerable multitude, standing before the throne of God and before the Lamb, clothed with white robes, holding palm branches in their hands, giving praise to God. What God has purposed, he will bring to pass!

3. They will all be saved through faith in Christ (vv. 13-14)

Election is not salvation; it is *unto* salvation (2 Thess. 2:13). Redemption guarantees salvation, but redemption is not salvation. Salvation comes to sinners only through faith in Christ. This faith is as much a work of grace and gift of God as election and redemption (Col. 2:12; Eph. 2:8). And it is just as necessary. No one can be saved without personal faith in Christ. We are told two things about all who enter into heaven. First, they all come out of great tribulation. That refers to the temptations, trials and persecutions of God's elect in this world (John 16:33; Acts 14:22). And, secondly, they have all 'washed their robes, and made them white in the blood of the Lamb'. They have placed their trust in the blood of Christ and have by faith obtained perfect righteousness in him (1 John 1:7,9).

4. Their salvation will be perfect, complete and eternal

This is seen in verses 15-17. 'Therefore,' because they have been redeemed and justified through the blood of Christ, the Lamb of God sacrificed in their place, 'are they before the throne.' There they worship and serve him in spontaneous, glad, unceasing devotion of heart, and these redeemed ones in glory enjoy sweet, full, intimate communion and fellowship with God through Christ. That is the essence of heaven's glory and bliss. All these things apply to all of God's elect. In heaven, we shall be in the immediate, eternal presence of our God and Saviour (v. 15). Everything we want, need or desire will be supplied with unlimited fulness (v. 16). We shall be completely delivered from all sin, sorrow, hardship and care (v. 17). Who could wish for anything more? (Ps. 27:4; 17:15). God's salvation is perfect salvation!

22.

Christ opens the seventh seal

Revelation 8:1-13

'And when he had opened the seventh seal, there was silence in heaven about the space of half an hour' (Rev. 8:1).

In Revelation 6:10 we hear the cries of God's saints: 'How long, O Lord, holy and true, dost thou not judge and avenge our blood on them that dwell on the earth?' In this eighth chapter, with the opening of the seventh seal, we are shown the trumpets of judgement. These seven trumpets of judgement which are described in chapters 8-11 show God's retribution upon those who are the persecuting enemies of his church. The final, complete retribution is reserved for the great Day of Judgement. Yet, as Hendriksen says, 'Even now the seals of persecution are followed by the trumpets of judgement.'

These trumpets of judgement do not symbolize single, isolated events, or specific periods of time. Rather, they are symbolic pictures of God's providential judgements which fall upon the wicked again and again throughout history. They are God's warnings of wrath to come. These are the things which God brings upon men and women, cities and nations, because of their opposition to Christ and their persecution of his church. And every act of divine judgement in time is a warning of eternal judgement to come, calling for God's enemies to bow to Christ in repentance and faith.

In chapters 8-11, God sends seven angels to 'blow the trumpet and warn the people' (Ezek. 33:3). In this eighth chapter of Revelation, we shall look at the first four trumpets of judgement as they are set before us. There are four things which stand out as prominent lessons to be gleaned from these thirteen verses.

1. Judgement is God's strange work

When the Lord Jesus opened the seventh seal of the book, John says, 'There was silence in heaven about the space of half an hour' (v. 1). For thirty minutes all songs, all praises, all movement stopped. Heaven was completely silenced when the Son of God began to open this seal of judgement.

This silence was an indication of *sober reflection*. The calm before the storm is always a time of sobriety and thoughtfulness. The triune God, the Lamb, the four living creatures, the twenty-four elders, the seraphs, cherubs and all the multiplied millions of angels and all the church of God were silent. God was thinking about what he was about to do. The angels were thinking about their mission. And the redeemed of the Lord were thinking about God's great mercy to them.

This half-hour of silence in heaven was also an indication of *great anticipation*. As Matthew Henry put it, 'Great things were upon the wheel of providence. And the church of God, both in heaven and earth, stood silent, as became them, to see what God was doing.' Throughout the Old Testament the goings forth of the Almighty to judgement were introduced by reverent silence (Hab. 2:20; Zeph. 1:7; Zech. 2:13).

Above all else, this silence in heaven indicated *something strange and terrible*. Someone said, 'The steps of God from mercy to judgement are always slow, reluctant and measured.' Judgement is God's 'strange work'. He 'delighteth in mercy' (Micah 7:18), but God is slow to anger and slow to wrath. The Almighty has no pleasure in the death of the wicked. 'God is love' (1 John 4:16). Judgement is 'his strange act' (Isa. 28:21). Yet his judgement is sure! Justice demands judgement. God will punish every transgression, either in the person of the one who commits it or in that of the substitute, Christ Jesus (Heb. 2:2; Isa. 53:8; Gal. 3:13).

2. The twofold ministry of the angels

The same angels of God who minister to his elect also execute judgement upon their enemies (v. 2). To God's elect these angels are ministering spirits sent forth to minister to those who will be the heirs of eternal salvation (Heb. 1:14). They are messengers of mercy to the people of God. They watch over and protect them in this world. But those very same angels are messengers of wrath and judgement to all who oppose and persecute the church of God (2 Sam. 14:15-17; 2 Kings 19:34-35).

3. God will avenge the cause of his people

There is a direct correlation between the prayers of God's people and his judgement upon their enemies (vv. 3-5). This angel of intercession is the Lord Jesus Christ himself, the only intercessor and mediator between God and men (1 Tim. 2:5-6; Heb. 7:24-27; 1 John 2:1-2). And as surely as he makes intercession for his elect, so also he will avenge them (v. 5). As a king is honour-bound to avenge the blood of his loyal subjects, so the Lord God is honour-bound to avenge the blood of his people upon their enemies who have persecuted, abused, tormented and killed them. The Lord Jesus Christ, our mediator, who offered up the prayers of his saints by his own merit, took fire from off the altar 'and cast it into the earth'. This fire caused many strange disturbances in the earth: voices, thunder and lightning, and earthquakes. These all came about as God's answer to the prayers of his saints (Rev. 6:10). God is our defender. God is our refuge. God is our avenger. Our cause is safe in his hands! (Luke 18:7; Rom. 12:19). 'And', after Christ gave the command of judgement, 'the seven angels which had the seven trumpets prepared themselves to sound' (v. 6).

4. Warnings of the judgement to come

Every providential act of judgement is a warning of the greater, eternal judgement that is to come (vv. 7-13). As we read the description of these trumpet judgements, we cannot fail to see a similarity between them and the judgements of God upon the Egyptians in the book of Exodus. As, then, the plagues were all poured out upon Egypt and Israel was unharmed, so here in Revelation, these judgements fall upon the wicked. They do not harm God's elect! God punished his elect in Christ for their sins. God's judgement against us fell upon our substitute. Though the wicked must be punished, 'There shall no evil happen to the just' (Prov. 12:21; Rom. 8:1).

The first trumpet sounds and brings a terrible storm, leaving destruction in its path (v. 7). It is a terrible mistake to limit the judgement to a strictly literal interpretation, though that is certainly included. Usually when divine judgement is dealt with in Holy Scripture, highly figurative language is used simply because it is such a horrible thing that nothing can properly describe it (Joel 2:28-32). Here is a terrible storm of hail, fire and blood. Perhaps it refers to a violent hailstorm that causes fire and death. It may refer to storms of pestilence, war and economic/political upheavals falling upon society in general. Perhaps it refers to a spiritual storm and has reference to the heresies by which God's elect are proved and those who rebel against his truth are destroyed (1 Cor. 11:19; 2 Thess. 2:10-12). But

even in wrath God remembers mercy! The storm of judgement is limited to only a third part of the earth.

The second angel sounds his trumpet and 'As it were a
great mountain burning with fire was cast into the sea' (vv.
8-9). The words 'as it were' are significant. They specifically tell us that the picture is symbolical, not literal. Most
likely this refers to idolized spiritual leaders, famous evangelists or pastors who appeared to burn with zeal for Christ
and his truth, falling publicly into sin and disgrace. These
self-appointed false prophets are not God's servants, though
multitudes follow them. When they fall, many are destroyed. Yet, 'The foundation of God standeth sure' (2 Tim.
2:15-19). God's elect are not deceived by such men.

The third angel sounds his trumpet and a star falls from
heaven, polluting the waters of the earth (vv. 10-11). Unlike the mountain that fell, this star was not a heretic of the
earth. Rather, he is one who is by profession in the kingdom of heaven, a preacher of the gospel, one who shines as
a brilliant lamp in God's church. But at last he falls into
heresy and with his heresy pollutes the Word of God and
the souls of men.

The fourth angel sounded his trumpet and brought great
darkness into the world (v. 12). In the Scriptures, the sun
represents Christ and the light of the gospel shining from
him (Mal. 4:2; Luke 1:78; John 8:12; 2 Peter 1:19). The
smiting of the sun represents the abundance of heresy in
this world, engulfing the churches (represented by the
moon) and preachers (represented by the stars) in thick
darkness. But even this thick darkness is limited to one
third. God always has his elect remnant! I will leave it to
others to debate about the meanings of these symbols, but
of this much I am certain: all temporal, providential judgements are merely warnings of the infinitely greater, everlasting judgement that is yet to come (see v. 13). Are you
ready for that great and terrible day?

23.

Christ our intercessor

Revelation 8:3-4

'And another angel came and stood at the altar, having a golden censer; and there was given unto him much incense, that he should offer it with the prayers of all saints upon the golden altar which was before the throne. And the smoke of the incense, which came with the prayers of the saints, ascended up before God out of the angel's hand' (Rev. 8:3-4).

The angel here is not one of the creatures of God, but the Son of God, our Saviour, in his mediatorial, priestly office. Here we see the Lord Jesus Christ performing his work as our great High Priest and intercessor before God (Exod. 30:1-10). At this moment, he stands before God as our representative. He has in his hand a golden censer full of incense (the merits of his blood and righteousness). The fragrance of that sweet incense makes the prayers which we offer up to God acceptable and well-pleasing in his sight. This symbolic picture is intended to teach us that our prayers and sacrifices are acceptable to God only through the merits of Christ. God's saints, those who have been redeemed and regenerated, even those who are already in heaven, are accepted by God only through the blood and righteousness of Christ (Eph. 1:6; John 14:6). Yet this is the believer's confidence and encouragement: we are accepted by God for Christ's sake (Eph. 2:13-18).

The Lord Jesus Christ is our only intercessor

All believers are priests unto God. We do business with
God ourselves in the person of Christ. We do not need Aaron,
Levi, or their sons; we have Christ. 'There is one God, and
one mediator between God and men, the man Christ Jesus'
(1 Tim. 2:5). We know that the angel mentioned in Revelation 8:3 is Christ, because he is the only mediator between God and men: 'Another angel came and stood at the
altar having a golden censer.' Of course, the picture here is
symbolical. There are no literal, material altars in heaven!
But the picture is most instructive. On the Day of Atonement in the Old Testament, burning coals of fire were taken
from the altar of burnt offering and placed in a censer. They
were brought to the golden altar of incense. When the incense was put upon the fire in the censer, a cloud of sweet-
smelling incense arose before the Lord (Lev. 16:12-13).
Those burning coals of fire and the sweet incense beaten
small represented the sufferings of Christ in the place of
his people. The wrath of God, like fire, was poured out
upon our dear Saviour. The agonies of his soul were the
fires of God's wrath burning in him. His body, crushed under
the wrath of God, was typified by the incense beaten small.
The altar represented our Lord's divine nature. As the altar
sanctified the gift offered upon it (Matt. 23:19), so it is
Christ's divine nature that gives virtue, merit and efficacy
to his sacrifice. The work which John saw, described in
verses 3-4, takes place within the veil before the presence
of God. As the burning coals were carried by Aaron within
the veil along with the blood of the lamb, so the Lord Jesus
entered into heaven as our great High Priest with the merits of his own blood, 'having obtained eternal redemption
for us' (Heb. 9:11-12). Usually, our Lord is pictured as one
who is seated at the right hand of the Majesty on high (Heb.
1:3; 10:12). This tells us that his work of redemption is finished and complete. But John saw him standing before the

altar. From this we learn that the merits of his sacrifice are perpetually fresh and effectual.

'And there was given unto him much incense.' The incense was given to him. All the work of Christ as our mediator was given to him by the appointment of God the Father in the covenant of grace (Heb. 5:4-5). God gave his elect to his Son to redeem and save them (John 6:39). The world was given to him to rule for the salvation of his people (John 17:2). His seed, God's elect, are given to him as the reward of his atonement (Isa. 53:10-12). As God, everything belongs to Christ by right of his own divinity. As our mediator, everything has been given to him as the rightful reward of his obedience (John 3:35). This incense was given to Christ, 'that he should offer it with the prayers of all saints upon the golden altar which was before the throne'. The incense sprinkled upon the burning coals from off the altar formed a sweet-smelling smoke, which rose up to God in heaven. This smoke of incense was a picture of Christ's intercession to God for his elect (Rom. 8:34; Heb. 7:25; 9:24). In the Old Testament, the incense was specifically described. If anyone offered a strange incense, mixed anything with the incense, or tried to imitate it, he was put to death (Exod. 30:7-8,34-38; Lev. 10:1-2). So also, any who attempt to add anything to the finished work of Christ for their acceptance with God cannot be saved (Gal. 5:2,4). Salvation and eternal life can be obtained only by faith in Christ.

As the incense was sprinkled upon the coals, our Lord's intercession to God for us is based upon, and arises from, his sufferings and death as our substitute. The prayers of Christ for his people are always effectual, because they are enforced by his precious blood (1 John 2:1-2). Notice the word 'much' in verse 3: 'There was given unto him much incense.' What a blessed word! There is a plentiful abundance and fulness of intercession arising from Christ for us, even as he accomplished a 'plenteous redemption' for

us (Ps. 130:7). Christ in heaven constantly makes intercession for transgressors, for his elect, covenant people, who
have no merit in themselves. We are all transgressors. We
all deserve God's wrath. But he makes intercession for us
according to the will of God. 'All saints,' all who have been,
all who are, and all who ever will be saints, are the objects
of his intercessory ministry at the throne of God. Our Lord's
intercessions are his prayers that all the needs of his elect
will be supplied and that all the blessings of grace will be
brought to them by the Spirit of God. He prays for the conversion of his elect, redeemed people (John 17:9,20), for
the non-imputation of sin to his people (1 John 2:1-2), for
the preservation of all believers in grace (John 17:15) and
for the ultimate glorification of all whom he has redeemed
(John 17:22-24).

The intercession of the Lord Jesus Christ is always pleasing and acceptable with the Father and always effectual.
What Christ seeks from his Father, he always obtains. His
prayers cannot fall to the ground! His intercession is according to the will of God, for the people of God's choice
and made effectual by the merit of his blood (Rom. 8:34).
Those sinners cannot perish for whom Christ makes intercession! He does not plead the goodness of his people, the
works of his people, the sincerity of his people, or even the
weaknesses of his people. He pleads the merits of his own
blood and righteousness on behalf of his people. God himself cannot resist the intercession of his Son! The Lord Jesus
Christ is our only intercessor with God, but we need no
other. He is an all-sufficient, accepted, perpetual, effectual
intercessor!

All God's saints are praying people

The dominant theme of John's vision in this passage is Christ
our intercessor, but he also speaks of 'the prayers of the

saints'. Prayers are the spiritual sacrifices which God's saints offer up to him (Heb. 13:15) and are accepted by him through the blood of Christ (1 Peter 2:5). We offer many things to our God as we seek to serve him, but the essence of all is prayer. Unless we offer the prayer of faith, we offer nothing! Christ our High Priest takes our prayers into his hands, perfumes them with the incense of his blood and right-eousness and offers them up to God our Father.

John describes God's people as 'saints'. All of them are saints. They are saints now and for ever. They are made saints by the work of God alone. All who believe on the Lord Jesus Christ are saints, holy and sanctified, by virtue of their union with Christ. Our sanctification is threefold:

1. We were sanctified, set apart as God's, for holy purposes in eternal election by God the Father (Jude 1).

2. We were sanctified, declared to be holy, by God the Son in redemption (Heb. 10:10-14).

3. We have been sanctified, given a holy nature, by God the Holy Spirit in regeneration (2 Thess. 2:13-14; 2 Peter 1:4).

All who are saints, sanctified by grace, are people of prayer. 'Every one that is godly,' David said, shall 'pray unto [the Lord]' (Ps. 32:6). John's description of God's saints and their prayers in the hands of Christ is very suggestive. First, prayer brings all the saints of God into communion with one another. All the prayers of all the saints are put into one golden censer. All the truest desires of all believers are the same (Matt. 6:9-13). Second, our Lord graciously re-ceives and accepts all the prayers of his saints. Even our groans and sighs are sweet to the ears of our heavenly Father through the mediation of Christ.

Our prayers are acceptable through Christ

Our gifts, prayers, worship and service to God are accepted by him because of Christ's intercession. It is Christ who offers up 'the prayers of the saints'. And it is by Christ's merit alone that we are accepted (1 Peter 2:5). Our text indicates three things that make our prayers acceptable to God:

1. They are offered by a fit *person* — the Lord Jesus Christ (1 John 2:1-2);
2. in a fit *place* — standing before the altar with the merits of his sacrifice (Rom. 8:34; Heb. 9:12; 10:10-14);
3. in a fit *manner* — 'with much incense'.

Our great Advocate and High Priest graciously mixes the perfume of his sacrifice with our prayers and wisely corrects our petitions. We do not know what to pray for as we ought. So our Saviour makes up for our ignorance (Rom. 8:26-28).

24.

Christ brings judgement

Revelation 9:1-22

'And in those days shall men seek death, and shall not find it; and shall desire to die, and death shall flee from them' (Rev. 9:6).

The Lord God declares, 'I make peace, and create evil' (Isa. 45:7). In this chapter, we see the Lord Jesus Christ, as he continues opening the seventh seal, bringing the evils of providential judgement upon the earth. Because of his mediatorial obedience as our Saviour, the Father has 'committed all judgement unto the Son' (John 5:22), and has 'given him power over all flesh' to execute judgement in the earth for the saving of his elect (John 17:2). John is describing the seven trumpet judgements which he saw with the opening of the seventh seal (8:2). These are divine, providential acts by which the Lord God both vindicates himself and avenges his own elect. Four of the angels blew their trumpets in chapter 8. Then, John writes, 'I beheld, and heard an angel flying through the midst of heaven, saying with a loud voice, Woe, woe, woe, to the inhabiters of the earth by reason of the other voices of the trumpet of the three angels, which are yet to sound!' (8:13). The voice was loud and clear. Its message was unmistakable. The three trumpet judgements that were yet to be revealed would be far worse than the four described in chapter eight. Two of the remaining three woes are described in chapter 9. In this chapter, we are clearly taught four important lessons.

1. Great tribulation for God's people

'We must through much tribulation enter into the kingdom of God' (Acts 14:22). Without question, Revelation 9 speaks of a time of great tribulation in this world. As long as time shall stand, God's people in this world must endure great tribulation. Sometimes the tribulation is greater and more evident than at other times. But in this world, tribulation is our lot (John 16:33). And, frequently, the tribulations through which we pass are the direct result of God's judgements upon the wicked. Yet the message of Revelation 9 is not one of gloom and doom. Tribulation must come, but God's elect will not be hurt. That is the meaning of verse 4. Those who trust the Lord Jesus Christ have the seal of God upon them. Having been chosen by God the Father, redeemed by the blood of Christ and regenerated by the Holy Spirit, the saints of God are always safe and secure. They will endure to the end. Even these times of great tribulation will prove to be for their spiritual and eternal good (Rom. 8:28). Even in his acts of judgement, God is for us, and he will do us good (Ps. 23:6).

2. Great apostasy in the world

There will be seasons of great apostasy in the world until Christ comes again (vv. 1-12). This first 'woe' is, perhaps, the greatest of all woes in this world, though few realize it. Because they 'receive not the love of the truth', because they will not believe the gospel, God leaves impenitent sinners to themselves, under the power of satanic delusion! Apostasy, falling away from the truth of God, has been the curse of multitudes throughout the history of the church, both in the Old Testament and in the New. Yet, as the end of the age approaches, the Scriptures warn of a general, universal apostasy. It will be a deception so great that, were such a thing possible, even God's elect would be deceived by it (Matt. 24:22-24; 2 Thess. 2:1-12; 1 Tim. 4:1-2; 2 Tim. 3:1-5; 2 Peter 2:1-3; 1 John 4:1-6; Jude 4,12-19). In these verses, John shows us how and why these times of great apostasy come.

John 'saw a star fall from heaven unto the earth' (vv. 1-2). This star is Satan (Luke 10:18). These verses describe the devil's present condition. Having rebelled against God, he lost his original position of holiness and splendour (Isa. 14:12-14). The key to the bottomless pit symbolizes authority and power over hell. But notice that Satan had this key given to him. Satan has great power, but he has absolutely no power except that which has been given to him by Christ, who bound him with the mighty chain of omnipotent sovereignty at Calvary (John 12:31; Rev. 20:1-3).

It is Satan who opens the pit of hell and fills the world with demonic influence (v. 2). John sees hell belching forth the filthy, black smoke of a great furnace, polluting the earth. That black smoke represents the deception and delusion of heresy. Free-will, works religion is the religion of hell. It so blinds men with ignorance, superstition and moral degradation that it blots out the light of the gospel (2 Cor. 4:3-4). Let none be mistaken. These times of satanic delusion are acts of divine judgement by which God warns men of his wrath and calls them to repentance (Prov. 1:23-33).

The locusts coming up out of the pit represent all false prophets, the messengers of Satan, who promote the religion of Antichrist (vv. 3-6). A plague more terrible than the plague of locusts is hard to imagine (Exod. 10:4-15; Joel 2:1-12). Locusts leave destruction and desolation in their wake. But these hellish locusts do not feed upon vegetation, but upon the souls of men! (See 2 Cor. 11:1-4,13-15). They are 'given power' by God (v. 3). Notice again that their power is given to them. Like scorpions, they poison the men and women of the earth with heresy. But they have no power to hurt God's elect (v. 4). Christ, who has absolute dominion even over false prophets (2 Peter 2:1), commands them not to hurt God's sealed ones. God's elect cannot be hurt (i.e., deceived) by the heresies of men, because the seal of God is in their foreheads (1 Cor. 11:19; 1 John 2:20). Verse 5 tells us that these distressing times of prevailing heresy are limited by divine decree to specific periods of time. As God raised up men like Luther and Calvin to break the arms of the papacy, so he will raise up chosen men to break the back of Arminianism at his appointed time.

Though the power of the locusts is limited, they do great harm to the souls of men (v. 6). False religion never gives real freedom and peace. It thrives on, controls and motivates by guilt. Those who have a religion of works, constantly reminding them of their guilt, are poisoned in their souls. Having no true sense of pardon, they soon grow weary of life. Their religion is a constant source of torment to them. Nothing but the truth, salvation by grace alone through the merits of Christ's blood and righteousness, makes sinners free and takes away their guilt (John 8:32; Heb. 9:14; Jer. 6:16).

In verses 7-11, John gives us the characteristics of these hellish locusts. God's servants preach one thing — 'Christ crucified' (1 Cor. 1:23; 2:2; 2 Cor. 4:5). The messengers of Satan preach many things, but their message always makes salvation to be ultimately dependent upon, and determined by, the will, works and worth of man. False prophets always have certain identifying characteristics too. They march through the world like horses prepared for battle (v. 7), presenting themselves as valiant warriors for truth and righteousness. They love the honour of men, wearing crowns like gold (v. 7), loving the praises of men. They are flatterers of human flesh. Having 'the faces of men' (v. 7), they have a show of compassion. Having 'hair as the hair of women' (v. 8), they are alluring, charming and impressive. Like harlots in gaudy clothes (Prov. 7), these religious hucksters attract simple souls by the gaudy ornaments of religious ritualism, emotionalism and sentimentalism, pretending to love them. They are spineless, effeminate men, soft and luxurious. But they are cruel, devouring beasts with teeth 'as the teeth of lions' (v. 8). False prophets have 'breastplates of iron' (v. 9). They carefully defend and protect themselves, and their hearts are as hard as steel. Like locusts beating the air, they make tremendous noise (v. 9). When John says, 'They had tails like scorpions' with the sting of death (v. 10), he is telling us that their doctrines are damning. In verse 11, we are told that the king of this hellish squadron is Satan, the Destroyer (Apollyon). With that statement, he tells us plainly that he is describing men, not a literal swarm of locusts, because locusts have no king (Prov. 30:27).

This first woe has to do with spiritual matters, false religion and false prophets. There will be seasons of apostasy in the world until Christ comes again. The second woe speaks of physical judgements and earthly trials.

Wars and coming judgement

The apostle shows us that times of sorrow, destruction and death are divine judgements by which God warns us of wrath to come (vv. 13-19). The sixth trumpet describes war — not one particular war, but all wars, past, present and future. Like everything else, the ravages of war are under the direct rule of our exalted God and Saviour, the Lord Jesus Christ. If we look at the picture, not in isolated parts, but as a whole, we learn four things:

1. The powers of evil in this world are graciously restrained until God turns them loose to accomplish his purpose (vv. 13-14; Ps. 76:10).

2. When sinners are ripe for punishment, the instruments of God's wrath will be turned loose upon them (v. 14). These angels of destruction are bound until the time of judgement comes. Then they are turned loose, but only to do God's bidding.

3. The duration of wars and the damage inflicted by them is determined, not by men, but by God (vv. 15-19). The horsemen and the horses, equipped with all the machinery of war (guns, cannons, bombs, etc.), belching fire, smoke and brimstone, have only one purpose — to kill and to destroy.

4. The purpose of God in wars, as in all temporal, providential judgements, is to warn men and women of wrath and judgement to come (Jer. 5:3-4; Ps. 78:22-33; Amos 4:6-13).

No repentance without God's mercy

Fourthly, verses 20 and 21 show us that all men are so obstinately sinful and rebellious that judgement alone will never bring them to repentance. It is 'the goodness of God [that] leadeth thee to repentance' (Rom. 2:4). Neither the threats of the law nor the terrors of wrath will produce true repentance, but the goodness of God revealed in the crucified Christ will (Zech. 12:10).

25.

The providential rule of Christ

Revelation 10:1-2

'And I saw another mighty angel come down from heaven, clothed with a cloud: and a rainbow was upon his head, and his face was as it were the sun, and his feet as pillars of fire: and he had in his hand a little book open: and he set his right foot upon the sea, and his left foot on the earth' (Rev. 10:1-2).

As we come to Revelation 10, six trumpets have sounded and the seventh, final trumpet is about to sound. Just before John sees the final, consummate judgement of God fall upon the earth, the Lord Jesus Christ appears with one last word of warning. He stood 'upon the sea and upon the earth [and] lifted up his hand to heaven, and swore by him that liveth for ever and ever' (Because he could swear by no greater, he swore by himself!) 'that there should be time no longer.' It is as though the Lord is saying, 'No more delay! Prepare to meet your God!'

If you read chapters 8-11 at one sitting, you cannot fail to see that chapter 10 is an abrupt interruption of events. It is almost parenthetical. It stands as both a word of warning to God's enemies of the certainty of divine judgement and a word of comfort to God's elect, for it portrays and assures us of the providential rule of Christ. What could be more comforting than the fact that he who loved us from eternity, died to redeem us at Calvary, and saves us by his almighty grace, sovereignly rules all things according to

God's eternal purpose for us? This is the picture we have before us in these verses.

John's representation of Christ (v. 1)

'I saw another mighty angel come down from heaven, clothed with a cloud: and a rainbow was upon his head, and his face was as it were the sun, and his feet as pillars of fire.' Here the Lord Jesus appears in the form of an angel: 'I saw another mighty angel.'

There is really nothing at all unusual about this. Our Saviour constantly appeared to his children in the Old Testament as the Angel of the LORD. Those angelic appearances recorded in the Old Testament Scriptures were pre-incarnate manifestations of Christ to his chosen ones. When Paul was in the storm at sea he said, 'There stood by me this night the angel of God, whose I am, and whom I serve' (Acts 27:23). Paul did not belong to, or serve, any ordinary angel. But he belonged to and served this angel of God, for this angel is himself the Son of God, our Saviour. And frequently in the book of Revelation, the Lord Jesus reveals himself in angelic form. In chapter 8:3, he appeared as the Angel of intercession, and here he again appears as an angel. To the wicked and unbelieving, he is the Angel of judgement. But on behalf of his covenant people, he is seen as the Angel of providence. The word 'angel', remember, simply means 'messenger'. And Christ, as the mediator between God and men, is God's messenger to men. Isaiah calls him 'the angel of [God's] presence' by whom we are saved (Isa. 63:9). And Malachi describes him as 'the messenger [or "angel"] of the covenant' in whom we delight (Mal. 3:1). He is the messenger sent by God to reveal his will, accomplish his purpose and redeem his people.

John sees him as 'a mighty angel'

Our Lord Jesus Christ is the mighty God, our Saviour, the mighty Mediator and the mighty King. He is able to protect, defend and save his own. Chapter 9 describes the terrible woe that must come upon the earth. Then, Christ, the 'mighty angel', appears. This appearance seems to say, 'Let not your heart be troubled. The ark of God is safe.' This 'mighty angel' is Christ our Saviour, who sovereignly rules all things.

John sees Christ 'come down from heaven'

This does not refer to our Lord's incarnation, or to his coming down to judge the world in the last day. These words refer to our Lord's appearance in providence to protect, defend and comfort his people. Though the Lord Jesus is in heaven, seated upon the throne of glory, he has not forsaken his church. His body has been taken from us, but not his heart. Christ is always with his people. As often as we need him, he comes to us in special grace, revealing his presence and power to us (Dan. 3:25).

John sees Christ 'clothed with a cloud'

Remember, John has just seen days of terrible spiritual darkness, apostasy and false religion which devour men's souls as locusts devour vegetation (9:3-4). In such times, the Lord Jesus hides himself from men. They cannot see his glory. It is as though he has hidden himself in a cloud. They know his name, but not his power. They know the facts of his death, burial and resurrection, but not the accomplishments of his redemptive work. They know that Christ is in heaven, but know nothing of the majesty of his heavenly throne. They know that he makes intercession, but know nothing of the efficacy of his intercession. They know that Jesus saves, but not how he saves. They know the words 'redeeming blood', 'saving grace' and 'matchless love', but they know

nothing of the blood's atonement, grace's power, or love's
immutability. This world is in a fog in so far as the things
of Christ are concerned. If you see the glory of his person
and the efficacy of his saving grace, you have great reason
to pause and give thanks. 'Flesh and blood hath not revealed it unto thee, but my Father which is in heaven' (see
Matt. 11:25-27).

The eye of faith sees in Christ what others cannot see.
The believer clearly sees the glory of his person and of his
work: 'Blessed are your eyes, for they see.' The eye of faith
sees the Lord Jesus as John saw him. 'A rainbow [is] upon
his head, and his face [is] as it were the sun, and his feet as
pillars of fire.' The rainbow upon his head is a token of the
everlasting covenant of grace (Gen. 9:15-16; Isa. 54:7-10).
In Revelation 4:3 we saw this rainbow of the covenant en-
circling the throne of God. Here we see it upon the Saviour's
brow. The rainbow, with all its glorious colours, represents
all the promises and blessings of God in the covenant. It is
an emblem of mercy, peace and reconciliation with God.
The rainbow tells us of the security of the world until God
has fulfilled every promise of the covenant and saved all
his elect.

Here we see that rainbow of the covenant upon our Saviour's head as he comes down to visit his afflicted people.
This tells us that the covenant of grace is fulfilled in and by
our Redeemer. He is ever mindful of his covenant. Even in
the worst of times, our dear Saviour rules this world according to the stipulations of the covenant. He will not allow his people to be overwhelmed by the flood of Antichrist's religion. The gates of hell shall not prevail against
his church. The Messenger of the covenant appears to bring
us peace, to let us know that better days are coming. Soon
we shall have times of refreshing, either from the presence
of the Lord or in the presence of the Lord. No matter how
dark the storms of life may be, if you can see that rainbow
upon that head, your heart will find peace and satisfaction
(2 Sam. 23:5).

John sees his face 'as it were the sun'

This is how the disciples saw him on the Mount of Trans-figuration (Matt. 17:1-8). This expression speaks of the purity and glory of Christ, both as God and as man. Being God, Jesus Christ our Saviour is the brightness of the Father's glory and the express image of his person. He lived as a man in this world in perfect righteousness. In all things he was, and is, holy, harmless, undefiled and separate from sinners. And the God-man in heaven is clothed with all the ineffable glory of the eternal God, for he is God. As God, he is light (1 John 1:5). As the mediator between God and men, he imparts the light of grace and glory to the sons of men.

John saw his feet 'as pillars of fire'

Our Lord's feet are like fire. In all his ways of providence, he is a consuming fire to his enemies. He will destroy them in a moment, as raging fire consumes dried grass. But he is a wall of fire about his church to defend and protect us. His feet are also pillars, unshaken, immovable pillars to up-hold all who trust him. Lean upon him. Christ is a mighty Saviour. All his ways of grace, providence, mercy and judgement are righteous altogether. He is too wise to err and too good to do wrong. His throne, his work and his purposes are both righteous and sure. His feet are 'as pillars of fire'.

John's picture of the sovereign rule of Christ (v. 2)

'And he had in his hand a little book open: and he set his right foot upon the sea, and his left foot on the earth.' There is nothing in all the world more comforting and cheering to the hearts of God's elect than the knowledge of our Saviour's sovereign rule of the universe. This rule of the world is the reward which was given to Christ by his Father for his obedience as our mediator. As God the Son, he always had the right to rule the world, because he created the world. But as the man Christ Jesus, our Lord was given the reigns of universal monarchy. Because of the death he accomplished at Jerusalem, by which he redeemed and justified all his elect, the triune God has turned the world over to the sovereign rule of the man Christ Jesus (Isa. 53:10-12; John 17:2). The God-man who loved us and gave himself for us rules the universe! What thought could be more delightful?

'He had in his hand a little book open'

This little book is the same book which he took from the right hand of him that sat upon the throne (5:1). We never read that he laid this book down, or gave it to someone else. This book is the book of God's eternal purpose of predestination. It is 'a little book' because now most of the things written in it have been accomplished. It is 'a little book open' because Christ, the Lion of Judah, the Lamb that was slain, has prevailed to open it.

All the purposes of God are fulfilled in Christ and by Christ. He reveals the will of God, and he accomplishes the will of God. Only Christ opens the book of God's secret decrees. This little book open is 'in his hand'. Our dear Saviour holds the book of God's purpose and grace in his hand. He took it before the foundation of the world, in the covenant of grace. Everything he has done, is doing, or will yet do, is carried out exactly according to that which is written in the book. Do you see him? The book of God's purpose is still in his hand.

'He set his right foot upon the sea, and his left foot on the earth'

What does this tell us? It simply tells us that Jesus Christ our Lord rules the world. The government of the universe is upon the shoulders of Emmanuel! The Lord Jesus Christ, our loved and loving Redeemer, stands as sovereign Monarch over the entire world. All things are put under his feet. His right foot is upon the sea. His left foot is upon the earth. He stands as triumphant Victor and reigning King over all the power of the world. And he holds the book of God's eternal decree in his hand. Christ rules all the inhabitants of the world (angels, demons, men and animals) and all the events of the world, upon every continent, on every island and in the depths of the sea, according to that which is written in the book of God's eternal predestination!

The whole picture speaks of the sovereign serenity of our Saviour's rule. All things, even the terrible woes of judgement that fall upon the earth, were ordained by God in eternal predestination. And they are all executed by Christ in time. No part of the universe is in chaos. Nothing is out of order. No corner of God's creation is governed by man. Nothing is ruled by Satan or the demons of hell. And nothing is left to mere chance, blind fate, or the fickle will of man. Our dear Saviour rules over all things, with absolute power, according to the eternal, unalterable purpose of God.

Christ will not put that book down until he has perfectly accomplished everything written upon its pages. In the end every rebel against God's throne will be locked away in the prison house of eternal torment so that they can no longer hurt or defile God's creation. There they will be punished with everlasting destruction from the presence of the Lord (Rev. 20:15). All of God's elect will be perfectly, completely and eternally saved, according to that which he has written in the book of his eternal purpose of grace (Rom. 8:28-39). And our great and glorious God and Saviour will for ever be glorified, praised and honoured in all things and by all things (Rev. 5:9-14). 'All thy works shall praise thee, O Lord.'

26.

Christ's two witnesses

Revelation 11:1-14

'And I will give power unto my two witnesses, and they shall prophesy a thousand two hundred and threescore days, clothed in sackcloth' (Rev. 11:3).

Throughout the book of Revelation, we are repeatedly assured of three facts: first, our Redeemer is in total control of the universe; second, the church and kingdom of God are safe; and, third, the people of God will be triumphant in the end. There is a reason for these repeated assurances. It often appears that we are losing ground and that our defeat is inevitable. Revelation 11:1-14 assures the believer of the safety and ultimate triumph of Christ's church, though at times may look as if her defeat is certain. In these verses, we are told what will happen during those days just before Christ's second coming.

The measuring of the temple (vv. 1-2)

Of course, this is a symbolical picture. To seek, as many do, a literal interpretation of the things written in this chapter is to miss its message altogether. John was commanded to measure the temple of God (v. 1). Specifically, he was commanded to measure the sanctuary, containing the Holy Place and the Holy of Holies, 'the altar, and them that worship therein'. This temple represents the church and people of God, all those in whom Christ dwells by his Spirit. All true believers, worshipping God in spirit and truth, are measured, protected and sealed.

The Lord did not command John to measure the size of the temple, as though he needed information, but simply to measure, or mark out for protection, the people of God. That is what this measuring means. Though God will inflict his judgements of wrath upon the wicked, persecuting world, his church is safe. Though God's saints suffer with the world, they will not perish with the world. God's elect are protected against eternal doom.

How do we know that this is the meaning of John's vision? First, the temple of God in the Old Testament was a type of the church, which is frequently called the temple of God in the New Testament (1 Cor. 3:16-17; 2 Cor. 6:16-17; Eph. 3:21). Second, the temple of God is here defined as the Holy Place and Holy of Holies, the inner sanctuary, where only the priests of God were allowed — 'the altar, and them that worship therein'. We who believe are God's 'royal priesthood', worshippers in the Holy Place, offering up sacrifices of prayer and praise to him through Christ Jesus (1 Peter 2:5,9). Third, the measuring of the temple in Ezekiel's vision was for the same purpose as in this vision — the protection of God's sanctuary, to separate the precious from the vile (Ezek. 40:3-5; 22:25-26).

The outer court of the temple was not to be measured (v. 2). God's special care and protection do not extend to those who are believers in name only. This 'court which is without the temple' represents all false religion and all who make a false profession of religion. This outer court is to be trampled under the feet of the heathen precisely because God is determined to destroy all false religion. The world invades the false church and possesses it. Followers of worldly, man-centred religion welcome the ideas and principles of the world. They feel perfectly at home in the world.

They are of the world, and the world loves its own. Even in the New Testament era, the true people of God were plagued with men and women in their midst who were governed and motivated by the principles and religion of the world. This condition of worldliness in the church will continue throughout the gospel age, represented by the time of forty-two months.

The Lord's two witnesses and their testimony (vv. 3-6)

Many conjectures have been made as to who these two witnesses are. But the context appears to indicate that they are another representation of the church of God. Throughout the gospel age, the church has been represented in the world by her two witnesses — pastors (elders) and evangelists (missionaries). The church functions as an organization through its pastors and missionaries, those who preach the gospel. These witnesses carry out their work for 1,260 days. That is another symbolic figure. It represents a definite, long period of time, but one the extent of which is unknown (to men) This period of 1,260 days, like the forty-two months of verse 2, represents the whole gospel age, from Christ's ascension to his second coming.

Notice the characteristics of these two witnesses, as they are represented in John's vision.

First, those men who preach the gospel are, in God's providence, the means by which his grace is bestowed upon his elect (v. 4). Like olive trees, they bring forth the oil of grace, the blessings of the Spirit and the light of the gospel (Rom. 10:13-17; 1 Peter 1:23-25).

Second, God's servants are under his special care and protection (v. 5). It is written: 'Touch not mine anointed, and do my prophets no harm' (1 Chr. 16:22). That which is done to Christ's church and his witnesses is done to him

(Matt. 10:40; Acts 9:4). And, just as Jeremiah's enemies were condemned by his word, those who oppose God's kingdom today will be condemned by the gospel we preach (2 Cor. 2:14-16).

Third, those who preach the gospel, as spokesmen for Christ and his church, have power with God and power over men (v. 6; 1 Kings 17:1; Exod. 7:20). This power is not absolute, but it is real (Luke 10:3-12). Not only does God judge men according to the prayers of his afflicted people (Rev. 8:3-5), but he also judges them according to the gospel we preach (Matt. 16:19; John 20:21-23; Rom. 2:16).

Fourth, they shall finish their testimony (v. 7). God's church and his servants will fulfil their mission in this world. The gospel shall be preached throughout the world. All the elect, having been redeemed by Christ, will be brought to Christ. But this present gospel age will come to an end. God's church and his witnesses will finish their testimony (Matt. 24:14).

Their death and the world's joy because of it (vv. 7-10)

The beast, the Antichrist and his religion, all those whose religion is represented by the outer court, will arise with hellish, worldwide power and kill the two witnesses. That does not mean that all God's saints and all true preachers will be killed, though many may be tortured and put to death by men who think they are doing God service (John 16:2). There will be true believers and true witnesses upon the earth when Christ comes again (Luke 18:8). The gates of hell shall not prevail against Christ's church (Matt. 16:18). It must be remembered that the picture before us is symbolical, not literal. It simply means that there is a time coming when the true church of God and true gospel preachers will appear to be almost totally eradicated from the earth.

Religion will thrive, but the church of God will appear to be a dead corpse in the earth, altogether without life and power (Amos 8:11-12).

That is precisely what will happen just before our Lord's glorious second advent. The voice of God's church will be smothered by the religion of Antichrist. It will lie like a dead corpse on Main Street in the world. Sodom and Egypt, which crucified Christ, will again join forces to silence his church. For three and a half days, a brief but definite period of time, the church in this world will appear to be dead. It will cease to have power and influence. The faithful will be so few that they will cause no disturbance in the world. This will be a time of terrible trial and religious deception (Matt. 24:22-25; Rev. 20:7-9). This time of heresy and religious deception must come. God has ordained it (2 Thess. 2:1-12; 1 Cor. 11:19). And in this reprobate age, God's elect are safe and have great reason for thanksgiving and praise (2 Thess. 2:13-16). While the corpses of God's two witnesses lie in the street, the world will throw a party (vv. 9-10). But their joy is premature. God has not finished yet. The end has not yet come. Christ has not yet turned the last page of the little book in his hand. Something else must take place.

Their revival and final triumph (vv. 11-14)

There is a day coming when the church of God will be revived, when the servants of God will once more be heard, when the gospel of God's free and sovereign grace in Christ will again be declared with heavenly power. The enemies of the truth will not party for ever! God will send the Spirit of life into his church again (v. 11). Just before Christ's second coming, right in the midst of wholesale apostasy, God will raise up his witnesses again! The church of God will again be triumphant (vv. 11-12). When God's church is revived again, as in the days of the Reformation and the Great

Awakening, the religious world and the political world will be frozen with fear.

Then the end will come. A voice will be heard, as the voice of the archangel, saying, 'Come up hither!' As the saints of God, both the living and the dead, ascend in a cloud of glory to meet the Lord in the air, their enemies will see them! (v. 12). There is no secret, mysterious rapture here. This is talking about the glorious resurrection of the sons of God (1 Thess. 4:13-18).

In that same hour, God's judgement will begin to fall upon the earth (v. 13). It appears that immediately preceding Christ's appearing in judgement, there will be a great earthquake, perhaps a great series of earthquakes. Multitudes will be slain. Those who remain will be terror-struck. Though they will not repent, they will give 'glory to the God of heaven'. Now the stage is set. This is the beginning of the end. 'The second woe is past; and, behold, the third woe cometh quickly' (v. 14). Are you ready?

27.

Christ's second coming:
the glory and the woe that follows

Revelation 11:14-19

'And the seventh angel sounded; and there were great voices in heaven, saying, The kingdoms of this world are become the kingdoms of our Lord, and of his Christ; and he shall reign for ever and ever' (Rev. 11:15).

It is impossible for us to know whether we are living in the times described as the first woe, where false religion engulfs the world (9:1-12), or in those times described as the second woe, when the worship of God appears to disappear from the earth (9:13-21; 11:7-10). It is impossible for us to know, because God does not intend that we should know (Acts 1:7). He simply warns us of what we must expect in this world, so that we may not be surprised when it happens. Believers experience enough of heresy, apostasy, violence and war in every age to keep them on tiptoe looking with expectant faith for Christ's glorious second advent, which John describes in Revelation 11:14-19 as 'the third woe'. For the ungodly and unbelieving, Christ's second coming and the judgement that follows it will be a time of great woe. But for Christ and his people, it will be a time of great glory. In these verses, John shows us the significance of the Day of Judgement as it relates to the triune God, to the Lord Jesus Christ, to believers and to unbelievers.

Christ the Judge of all

There is a day of judgement coming in which God will judge all men by Christ Jesus (Acts 17:31). Everyone will be judged according to exact righteousness and justice. The standard of judgement will be God's holy law, his entire revealed will. We shall be judged out of the books of God, in which all our earthly thoughts, words and deeds are recorded (Heb. 9:27; 2 Cor. 5:10-11; Rev. 20:11-12; Matt. 25:31-46). In that great and terrible Day of the Lord, every man will receive exactly what is due to him. None will be punished who does not deserve to be punished. And none will be received into heaven's bliss and glory who does not deserve it. All who are found guilty of any sin, of any infraction of God's holy law, will be cast for ever into hell. Those who are perfectly holy will enter into heaven (Ps. 24:3-4; Rev. 21:27; 22:11). The only hope any sinner has of eternal salvation and acceptance with the holy Lord God is that he might be saved through the merits of our almighty, all-sufficient Substitute. And the only substitute there is for guilty sinners is the Lord Jesus Christ, the Son of God!

Christ, by his own precious blood, has washed away the sins of his people. Their transgressions are no longer recorded against them in the book of God's law and justice (Isa. 43:25; 44:22). In that great day when God opens the books, he will find no sins recorded against those for whom Christ died (Jer. 50:20). Their sins were imputed to Christ. He was punished in their stead. By his blood, he fully satisfied the penalty required by God's law for their sins. Christ paid their debt to God's law. Now they have no debt to pay. Moreover, the Lord Jesus Christ is 'THE LORD OUR RIGHTEOUSNESS' (Jer. 23:6). His righteous obedience to God is imputed to all who trust him. In the sight of God's law, according to God's own record books, every believer is perfectly righteous.

The joy and praise of God's people

The Day of Judgement will be a day of great glory, joy and
praise for God's elect (vv. 15-17). If we are in Christ, united
to him by faith, washed in his blood and robed in his righteousness, the Day of Judgement will not be for us a dreaded
day of doom, or even of sorrow, but a day of victory, triumph and glory. We are to look upon the Day of Judgement
with sobriety, but not with dread and fear. In the Scriptures, God's saints are described as a people who looked
upon the glorious Day of the Lord with hope, expectation
and desire (1 Thess. 4:13-18; 2 Thess. 1:7-10; 2 Tim. 1:12;
4:6-8; Titus 2:13; Rev. 1:7). They did so because they trusted
the merits of Christ and the promises of God. Today, multitudes who profess to trust Christ live in fear and dread of
that day. Why? There can only be one reason: they expect
God to deal with them in that day, not according to the
merits of Christ, but according to their own merits.

The vision John gives here of that great day portrays all
the elect, angels and men, gathered around the throne of
God. No tears of sorrow are found in their eyes. No punishment is inflicted upon them. No reward is withheld from
them. No heads are hanging in shame. No reminder is made
of their sins, because Christ put away their sins for ever
when he died! There is nothing in the picture given here
but joy, glory and exultation among the elect at the bar of
God. Nothing but bliss and glory awaits God's saints on the
other side of the grave. John describes three things in particular for which elect angels and men give praise to God.

1. It is Christ's right to rule

They give praise to God and Christ because it is his right to
rule sovereignly over all things, both by creation and by
redemption. This world belongs to Christ, because he is

God who created it (John 1:1-3; Matt. 20:15), and because as the God-man mediator he purchased it (Isa. 53:10-12; Heb. 10:10-14). Jesus Christ is the absolute Monarch of the universe (John 17:2). He always does his will in all things.

2. He will be seen to rule over all

They praise the triune God for the evident display of Christ's sovereign power and dominion in that day. When the Day of the Lord is fully come, the royal sovereignty of King Jesus will be universally evident. In that day, Christ will assert his royal rights, exert his royal power and visibly take possession of his universe. Then all opposition to him will be completely abolished. All creation will see and acknowledge that God has put all things under his feet (Isa. 45:22-25; Phil. 2:9-11).

3. His reign will never end

This elect multitude rejoices, gives thanks and praises Christ for the fact that his glorious reign will never end. 'He shall reign for ever and ever!' The rule of Christ will not continue for a thousand years and then cease, as many suppose. He will reign for ever! His dominion is an everlasting dominion. When the end comes, Christ the mediator will deliver up his kingdom to God the Father. He will present his church before the throne of the triune God in all its glorious perfection and completion. But he will never relinquish his dominion as our mediatorial King. In that glorious day, our King will fully receive the reward of his labour as our mediator (Ps. 2:7-11; Dan. 7:13-14; Isa. 9:6-7; Luke 1:31-33; 1 Cor. 15:24-28; Eph. 5:25-27; Jude 24-25). As Matthew Henry says, 'None shall ever wrest the sceptre out of his hand.' 'He must reign!'

God's vengeance on his enemies

The Day of Judgement will be a day of just vengeance upon
God's enemies (v. 18). Let every rebel be warned! Let every
unbeliever tremble! Let every persecutor and abuser of
God's elect shake with fear! God will avenge his own elect.
Christ will punish his enemies with everlasting destruction. But even the manifest wrath of the Almighty will not
change the hearts of sinners. Even in that day, we read that
'The nations were angry' with God! Only grace brings repentance (Rom. 2:4). Those who live as rebels and die as
rebels will be rebels for ever. And every rebel will get exactly what he deserves from God. The eternal misery of the
damned will be a matter of strict justice. And the glorious,
eternal reward of the righteous will also be a matter of strict
justice (Ps. 11:5-7).

God will dwell with his people

The Day of Judgement will be the beginning of perfect, everlasting communion between God and his people (v. 19).
John sees the sanctuary of God in heaven standing wide
open. Even the Holy of Holies is open and perfectly accessible. Nothing is veiled. Nothing is hidden. The ark of the
covenant, so long concealed from men, is now in open view.
What does this mean?

That ark, with its mercy-seat, was the symbol of God's
presence and glory in the Old Testament. The fact that it is
now open declares that God will dwell for ever with his
people in intimate, glorious, uninterrupted fellowship
(Exod. 25:22). Through the sin-atoning sacrifice of our Lord
Jesus Christ, and in his glorious person, we shall for ever
be accepted by God. This opening of the temple of God and
the appearance of the ark of the covenant mean that the

covenant of grace, with all its promises and blessings, is ours for ever in Christ. But for the wicked and unbelieving, these things mean wrath, banishment and death. They mark the outpouring upon the lost of nothing but wrath, flashes of lightning, peals of thunder, earthquakes and destructive hail to beat them down into hell for ever! Let all who are wise heed the words of God's prophet: 'Prepare to meet thy God!'

28.

The incarnation of Christ

Revelation 12:1-17

'And she brought forth a man child, who was to rule all nations with a rod of iron: and her child was caught up unto God, and to his throne' (Rev. 12:5).

Revelation 12 gives us a panoramic view of the incarnation of our Lord Jesus Christ and its results. These seventeen verses span the entire gospel age, from the first to the second advents of our Saviour.

The vision opens with a statement of astonishment: 'And there appeared a great wonder in heaven.' That is exactly what the incarnation is. The 'man child' described in this chapter is the incarnate God. God the eternal Son assumed a real human soul and body and came into the world through the womb of a virgin. Divinity took humanity into permanent union with itself in the person of Jesus Christ (1 Tim. 3:16). In order to redeem his elect and save them by his grace, the Son of God became one of them (Isa. 7:14; 9:6-7; Matt. 1:18-25; John 1:14).

The wonder of the incarnation (vv. 1-4)

In these first four verses, John describes three things which were revealed to him in vivid, symbolic language.

The woman in this chapter symbolizes and represents the church (Isa. 50:1; 54:1; Hosea 2:19; Eph. 5:32). The church, which is the body, bride and kingdom of our Lord Jesus Christ, is made up and consists of all God's elect in every age, the people loved, redeemed and saved by Christ (Eph. 5:25-27), all true believers, past, present and future. The church of the Old Testament and the church of the New Testament are one and the same church. To the people of this world, God's church seems to be insignificant and worthy of ridicule and scorn. But in the eyes of God, she is glorious. All the beauty, glory and splendour of heaven are lavished upon her (v. 1). She is 'clothed with the sun' because she is exalted and glorious in God's eyes above all the nations and people of the earth (Isa. 43:3-4). 'The moon [is] under her feet' because she has dominion as the Bride of Christ; she is 'a royal priesthood', a generation of priests and kings (1 Peter 2:9; Rev. 1:6). She wears 'a crown of twelve stars' because she is always victorious (Rom. 8:37; 2 Cor. 2:14). She is described as a woman 'with child, travailing in birth, and pained to be delivered' (v. 2) because she must bring forth the Christ, God's Messiah (Rom. 9: 5).[1]

The 'man child' is the promised seed of the woman, the Lord Jesus Christ who came to save his people from their sins (v. 5; Gen. 3:15; Gal. 4:4-5; Matt. 1:21; Heb. 10:5-10). This is indeed the great wonder of heaven. God himself came into the world as a man to redeem and save fallen men!

The dragon is Satan, Lucifer, the fallen son of the morning, whose constant aim is the destruction of Christ (vv. 3-4). Satan's seven crowned heads represent his usurped dominion over the sin-cursed earth (Eph. 2:2; 6:12). The stars that fall from heaven are all the rebelling, reprobate

---

1. As Christ was brought forth into the world physically through his chosen people, so he must be brought forth into the world spiritually by the faithful witness of his church (Matt. 28:18-20).

angels, who followed Satan in his rebellion (Isa. 14:12-16; Job 38:7; 2 Peter 2:4; Jude 6). The 'ten horns' symbolize the old dragon's destructive power.

Christ's victory over Satan (vv. 5-6)

The Lord Jesus Christ ascended to heaven after he had finished his work upon the earth. Though Satan tried to destroy Christ as soon as he was born into the world, the old serpent's efforts were foiled. Herod slew multitudes of infants, but not the man child (Matt. 2:13-20). Satan was foiled again in the wilderness of temptation (Matt. 4:1-11), thwarted again in Gethsemane (Matt. 26:47-56) and again at Calvary (John 12:31-32; Rev. 20:1-3). Calvary was not Satan's defeat of Christ, but Christ's conquest of Satan! At last, when his earthly work was done, King Jesus was snatched up to heaven, out of the reach of the dragon's hands, to rule as King over all things (John 17:2; Phil. 2:5-11). Once Christ was caught up to heaven, for ever out of Satan's reach, the dragon turned upon the woman in a rage of anger because of her relationship to the man child (more about this when we get to verses 12-17).

As the result of our Saviour's obedience, death, resurrection and ascension as our substitute, the serpent's head was crushed. His power was broken. His usurped dominion over the nations of the world was overthrown.

The defeat of Satan (vv. 7-9)

John Gill suggests that Michael the archangel is Christ himself. The name 'Michael' signifies 'one who is God'. Without question, the work described in these verses is the work of Christ himself (John 12:31-32; Rev. 20:1-3). Notice the reproachful names given to our adversary in verse 9.

Because he is furious with rage, he is called 'the great dragon'. Because he is the deceiver of the whole world (2 Cor. 4:4), he is called 'that old serpent', the one who deceived Eve in the garden (Gen. 3:1-6). Because he ever accuses God's saints and seeks to turn God against us and us against our God, he is called 'the devil and Satan', who as a roaring lion goes about seeking whom he may devour (1 Peter 5:8). But the accuser who was cast out of heaven has also been cast out of his power over the nations. He who held the Gentile world in bondage, idolatry and ignorance throughout the Old Testament era was cast out by Christ, so that he could no longer deceive the nations. Thus, by his death on the cross, the Son of God opened the way for the gospel to be preached to the whole world, so that he might gather in his elect from the four corners of the earth (John 12:32; Rom. 11:25-26).

The salvation of God's elect by Christ (vv. 10-11)

Salvation is never presented in the Scriptures as a mere possibility, an opportunity, or an offer. Salvation is declared to be a thing already accomplished by our God (Rom. 8:29-30; 2 Tim. 1:9-10). God's servants are men who come preaching salvation finished (Isa. 40:1-2; 52:7). When the Lord Jesus Christ, the incarnate God, left this world and ascended back into heaven, he had finished the work of salvation for his elect, and said so. He brought in everlasting righteousness by his active obedience to God as our representative (John 17:4). And he made an end of sin by his sacrificial, sin-atoning death as our substitute (Dan. 9:24; John 19:30). Christ's ascension and exaltation proclaim his finished work of redemption (Rom. 8:34-39; Heb. 10:10-14). And the fact that Christ is seated upon the throne of God, exalted as head and Lord over all things, guarantees that all whom he came to save will be saved. All God's elect, all

redeemed sinners, overcome Satan and his accusations 'by
the blood of the Lamb, and by the word of their testimony'.
The blood of Christ, the Lamb of God, by which sin has
been put away and salvation has been accomplished, is the
message of the gospel (the word of testimony) by which
faith is given to God's elect (Rom. 10:13-17; 1 Cor. 1:21-24).
And every believer will persevere in faith because he is
preserved and kept by grace. 'They loved not their lives
unto the death.' All true believers continue in the faith all
their days (John 10:27-28). They live in faith and die in
faith (Heb. 11:13).

Satan's persecution of the church (vv. 11-17)

Though he is defeated, the devil's rage has not diminished.
He can do no harm to God's cause or his people. Therefore,
there is cause for all heaven to rejoice. But, like a mad dog
in a cage or a roaring lion on a chain, Satan demonstrates
his hatred of Christ in his growlings and roarings against
his church and people. He knows he has only a short time.
Therefore, 'He persecuted the woman' (v. 13). But God protects her (v. 14). Satan spews out floods of heresy to destroy
God's church, but they do no harm (v. 15; 1 Cor. 11:19;
Matt. 16:18). The reprobate of the earth swallow up the
floods of heresy (v. 16). And God, by the wise arrangement
of providence, sees to it that all things done in the earth
help the woman (his church) and never do her any harm
(v. 16; Hosea 2:18; Rom. 8:28).

The remnant of the woman's seed, the saints of God, are
described as those who 'keep the commandments of and
have the testimony of Jesus Christ'. They have the gospel.
They believe the gospel. They cannot be turned away from
the gospel. Though the dragon makes war with them, he
cannot harm them, for Christ makes intercession for them
(Luke 22:31-32).

29.

Christ — 'the Lamb slain from the foundation of the world'

Revelation 13:1-18

'And all that dwell upon the earth shall worship him, whose names are not written in the book of life of the Lamb slain from the foundation of the world' (Rev. 13:8).

Rather than focusing our attention on the beasts described in this chapter and the mark of the beast, we should concentrate upon him who saves his people from the power and influence of the beast — Christ, 'the Lamb slain from the foundation of the world'. Because of him, God's elect have nothing to fear from Antichrist and his religion.

William Hendriksen gives this clear, concise description of the beasts: 'The first [beast] is a monster of indescribable horror. The second has a harmless appearance and for that very reason is more dangerous than the first. The first beast comes out of the sea. The second arises from the land. The first is Satan's hand. The second is the devil's mind. The first represents the persecuting power of Satan operating in and through the nations of the world and their governments. The second symbolizes the false religions and philosophies of this world. Both of these beasts oppose the church throughout this dispensation.'

In this vision, we are assured of two facts: first, Satan's warfare against the church of Christ will never end as long as time shall stand; second, Satan's wrath against God's elect will never be successful. His number is the number of failure. As we read through these eighteen verses, five things are clearly revealed to us:

1. The beast rising up from the sea (the sea stands for the nations and governments of the world — Isa. 17:12; Rev. 17:15) represents all the civil, political powers of the world bent upon the destruction of Christ's church (vv. 1-7).

2. Though relentlessly persecuted, God's church is always safe and secure, preserved and protected in Christ by divine grace (vv. 8-10).

3. The beast coming up out of the earth represents all the false religion of the world, by which multitudes are deceived and damned (vv. 11-17).

4. The number of the beast is the number of failure, frustration and defeat (v. 18). There is no cause for alarm or despair. The number of the beast is the number of man. It is 666. Man was created on the sixth day. Six is not seven, and never will be. Seven is the number of perfection, victory and triumph. Seven is the number of completion, conquest and joy. Six is one short of seven. Six misses the mark. Six never comes to completion. Six is always failure! Let all who worship the Lamb and do not receive the mark of the beast (all who refuse to be identified with false, man-centred religion of any kind) rejoice. Victory is ours! The number of the beast is 666, which means failure upon failure upon failure! It is the number of man, because the religion of the beast glories in man. Therefore, it must fail. Once more, we are assured that though we must endure much tribulation, 'We are more than conquerors through him that loved us' (Rom. 8:37).

5. It is not possible for God's elect to be deceived, because their names are written 'in the book of life of the Lamb slain from the foundation of the world' (v. 8).

The strong delusion of false religion, the religion of this present age (decisionism, free-will, works salvation), is such a strong delusion, such a great counterfeit, that our Lord tells us plainly, 'If it were possible,' the false prophets, with all their signs and wonders, would 'deceive the very elect'. But, thanks be to God, it is not possible for God's elect to be deceived. The seal of God is upon them (Rev. 7:3). Those who are born of God have an anointing, an 'unction from the Holy One', and they know (by the inner witness of the Holy Spirit and the testimony of Holy Scripture) the difference between the truth and a lie (1 John 2:20-27). God's elect know the difference between free will and free grace. The multitudes will go after the stranger and follow him to destruction. But Christ's sheep 'hear his voice' and 'follow him'. 'And a stranger will they not follow, but will flee from him: for they know not the voice of strangers' (John 10:3-5).

Without question, we are living in days of darkness, deception and delusion. 'Many false prophets are gone out into the world' in the 'spirit of antichrist' (1 John 4:1-3). Before this age is finished, we are told, the influence of the beast (Antichrist) will be so great that 'All that dwell upon the earth shall worship him,' worship under his influence (v. 8). There is great cause for concern. Immortal souls are at stake. Multitudes are being damned by the religion by which they hope to be saved (2 Thess. 2:8-12). But there is no cause for concern regarding God's elect. They cannot be deceived. God will not allow it! In the midst of this vision of woe, we are reminded of three comforting, soul-cheering truths taught throughout the Word of God. Read verse 8 again. Here are three bright, shining lights of assurance which are the basis of our confidence.

The eternal election of grace

John speaks of 'the book of life' and those whose names are written in it, as well as those whose names are not written in it. There is a book in which the names of God's elect are registered, and have been registered 'from the foundation of the world'. This book is called 'the Lamb's book of life' (Rev. 21:27). It does not matter whether the book literally exists or is merely symbolical of God's immutable purpose. It teaches us that there is yet a remnant according to the election of grace (Rom. 11:5). Even in the darkest days of apostasy, though all the world seems to be engulfed in the religion of Antichrist, God has an elect people whom he will save, a people who cannot and will not perish with the world.

Let me remind you once more of this wonderful gospel doctrine. The election of grace took place, and the names of God's elect were inscribed in the Lamb's book of life, from the foundation of the world (Eph. 1:3-6; 2 Thess. 2:13-14). Divine election is altogether the work of God's eternal, sovereign grace, which was given to chosen sinners in Christ before the world began (Eph. 1:3; 2 Tim. 1:9; Jer. 31:3). And all those whose names have been inscribed in the book of life from eternity shall, most assuredly, attain eternal life in this world and eternal glory in the world to come (Titus 1:2; 2 Tim. 2:19). We trace the promise of life back to its original source in the sovereign purpose of God's free grace. And we find that the veracity of God, his very truth and faithfulness, is pledged in an oath taken by God himself, by which he bound the honour of his name to the salvation of his people (Heb. 6:14-20). All God's elect will certainly be saved (Rom. 8:28-30).

The eternal redemption of God's elect by Christ

Our Saviour is described as 'the Lamb slain from the foundation of the world'. In those words the Holy Spirit tells us that redemption was virtually accomplished for all the chosen before the world began. In the mind and purpose of God, Christ was slain from eternity as our covenant surety.

Just as Abraham, having purposed in his heart to slay his son, is said to have actually done so (Gen. 22:10-12; Heb. 11:17; James 2:21), so God the Father is said to have sacrificed his Son for the redemption of his people before the world began. Had it not been for the eternal accomplishments of grace in the covenant (Rom. 8:29-30; Eph. 1:3-6; 2 Tim. 1:9), God would have immediately destroyed the human race when Adam sinned. God's benevolence and longsuffering with reprobate men are the result of his eternal purpose of grace towards his elect (2 Peter 3:9). The reason God allows the world to exist, the reason he tolerates the wickedness of the reprobate, is just this: the Lamb of God was slain for his people before the world began, and those people for whom he was slain must be saved.

Everything in the Word of God points to Christ, the Lamb of God slain from the foundation of the world. In virtually all the prophecies of the Old Testament, Christ was presented as one already sacrificed (Ps. 22; 40; 69; 85; 89; Isa. 53). All the types portraying our Saviour's sacrifice bear testimony to him as the Lamb that had been slain. In every generation, from Abel to Malachi, the same sacrifices were offered in faith. And that faith was based upon the divine revelation that the only way of acceptance with God is by the blood of 'the Lamb slain'. God Almighty regarded Christ as the Lamb slain from eternity and looked upon his elect in Christ as redeemed, forgiven, justified and 'accepted in the Beloved' (Rom. 8:29-30; Eph. 1:3-6). And when the Son of God actually died at Calvary, he died according to the eternal purpose of God, which can never be frustrated, defeated, or overturned (Acts 2:23; 4:27-28; 1 Peter 1:18-20).

The eternal security of God's elect

The whole point of John's giving us this word about Christ is to assure us that those for whom this Lamb was slain, whose names were written in the book of life from eternity, can never perish. Christ's atonement for sin is an effectual atonement, made for a particular people, by which he obtained their eternal redemption (Gal. 3:13; Isa. 53:8; Heb. 9:12). Those chosen sinners for whom the Lamb of God was slain 'shall never perish' (John 10:27-30) for the following reasons: the purpose of God cannot be frustrated (2 Tim. 1:9); the blood of Christ cannot be nullified, made of non-effect, or shed in vain (Isa. 53:9-11); the seal of the Spirit cannot be broken (Eph. 1:13-14; 4:30); the grace of God cannot be defeated (Rom. 9:11-18); the gifts of God cannot be taken away (Rom. 11:29); and the promise of God cannot be broken (Titus 1:2).

30.

Christ our satisfied Saviour

Revelation 14:1-5

'And I looked, and, lo, a Lamb stood on the mount Sion, and with him an hundred forty and four thousand, having his Father's name written in their foreheads' (Rev. 14:1).

Isaiah declared that the Lord Jesus Christ 'shall see of the travail of his soul, and shall be satisfied' (Isa. 53:11). That simply means that, in the end, the Son of God will have with him in glory all those who were given to him from eternity (John 17:24) and that they will be made perfect, holy, unblameable and unreprovable, without fault before God himself (John 17:23). This is what it will take for Christ to be satisfied (Eph. 5:25-27). Nothing short of the eternal blessedness of God's elect will satisfy the one who met the demands of the wrath and justice of God in their place upon the cursed tree. In Revelation 14:1-5, the apostle John describes that eternal blessedness of God's elect in their ultimate glorification which is the satisfaction of Christ as the Lamb of God, their Redeemer.

Turning his eyes from the terrible scene of woe in chapter 13, John looked up to heaven, 'And, lo, a Lamb stood on the mount Sion.' This is that 'mount Zion, which cannot be moved, but abideth for ever' (Ps. 125:1). This Mount Zion is heaven, the city of our God, the final abode of God's saints (Heb. 12:22-23). John is still talking about the same place when he says in verse 2, 'And I heard a voice from

heaven.' In verses 6-20 he describes the events immediately preceding and leading up to the ultimate blessedness
of God's elect, but he appears to have been so overjoyed by
what he saw in store for God's saints that he had to describe their glorious end first.

Try to fix the picture in your mind's eye as John sees it.
There stands the Lord Jesus Christ, the Lamb of God, pre-
eminent in heaven. With him there are 144,000 who have
'his Father's name written in their foreheads'. This is the
same sealed multitude described in chapter 7:3-4. There
the saints were still living upon the earth, surrounded by
numerous enemies. Here they are seen standing in heaven
with the Lamb, enjoying the bliss and glory of their predestined inheritance after the final judgement. 'Although the
dragon has done his utmost to make them unfaithful to their
Lord, and although he has employed two beasts to assist
him, not a single one of the hundred and forty-four thousand is missing,' comments William Hendriksen. The scene
before us is both magnificent and inspiring! Child of God,
lift up your eyes to behold it. This will be your final end!
Let heart and soul rejoice! In the end, when all things are
finished, you will stand without fault before the throne of
God. In that glorious, perpetual day, you will worship and
serve the Lord Jesus Christ, who loved you and gave himself for you, and you will do so perfectly!

The worship of the Lamb

The singular object of adoration and worship in heaven is
the Lamb of God. Though John saw and described many
things, nothing so arrested his heart and mind as the person of that all-glorious Lamb, who is the Lord Jesus Christ,
our God and Saviour. That Lamb is the reward, glory and
delight of heaven. Indeed, Christ the Lamb is heaven! In
the words of Samuel Rutherford, 'Heaven and Christ are

the same things; to be with Christ is to be in heaven, and to be in heaven is to be with Christ.'

Notice the figure under which Christ is represented in heaven: 'I looked, and lo, a Lamb!' Twenty-six times in the book of Revelation, Christ is referred to as a Lamb. Why is the Lamb always in the forefront?

1. No one can approach God, but by the Lamb (Heb. 9:7).

2. We cannot know, serve, praise and honour God in true worship, but by the Lamb (John 1:18; 1 Peter 2:5).

3. Christ is worshipped as the Lamb in heaven, because it was as a lamb that he died and accomplished the redemption of his people (John 1:29; 1 Peter 1:18-20).

4. He who sits upon the throne of God in our nature is seen as the Lamb to encourage us to come to him. Christ is a lion to his enemies, but a lamb for his people. What child fears a lamb? We need never fear coming to the Lamb of God upon the throne of grace (Heb. 4:16).

Notice also the posture of the Lamb in heaven: 'A Lamb *stood* in heaven.' Standing is the posture of triumph. The Father said to the Son, 'Sit thou on my right hand, until I make thy foes thy footstool' (Acts 2:34-35). Now it is done! All his enemies have been made to bow before his throne. Like a mighty victor, he stands erect in the last day, gloriously triumphant. He stooped to be merciful to a sinner (John 8:6,8). He knelt to pray (Luke 22:41-42). Once he hung upon the cursed tree to put away the sins of his people (1 Peter 2:24). Today, he sits in sovereign dominion upon the throne of God (Heb. 10:12-13). But in the end we see him standing to receive eternal praise for all his accomplishments (Isa. 45:20-25; Phil. 2:9-11).

The followers of the Lamb

Those who will be found in heaven worshipping the Lamb
are God's elect multitude (v. 1). The 144,000 are, of course,
the same ones who were sealed in chapter 7. They are an
elect multitude, marked out from eternity with the Father's
name written upon their foreheads. The number 144,000
indicates two things.

1. God's elect are a very great multitude

At any given time and in any given place in history, they
appear to be few. But when all the elect are gathered in
heaven, they will be 'many brethren' (Rom. 8:29), a multitude which no man can number (Rev. 7:9).

2. The number of the elect is a certain number

We do not know who they are, but God does. We do not
know how many there are, but God does. The elect are a
multitude known by God from eternity whom he will gather
from the four corners. Thank God for his electing love! Were
it not for God's election, no one would ever have been saved
(John 15:16; Ps. 65:4). Election guaranteed that a great multitude, 'ten thousand times ten thousand', would be saved
(Rom. 8:29-30).

The song of the redeemed

The saints of God in heaven sing a new song, but it is a
song learned upon the earth (vv. 2-3). It is a song born of
experience, inspired by gratitude and intended solely for
the praise of the Lamb. It is a song sung by many, from
many places — 'many waters'. It is a song of majestic wonder, indicated by 'great thunders'. It is a song of great joy,

inspired by electing grace, indicated by the 'harpers harping'. it is a song of particular, special, accomplished redemption. The ones singing are all those who 'were redeemed from the earth', not redeemed with, but *from* the rest of the people of the earth. It is called a 'new song' because it is about the blessings and privileges of the new covenant (Heb. 8:8-12) and a new experience of grace — the resurrection of the body!

Who will stand before the throne?

Those who will be found in heaven worshipping the Lamb in eternity are those who experienced his saving grace upon the earth (vv. 4-5). None shall enter heaven but those who have been chosen by God the Father (2 Thess. 2:13), redeemed by God the Son (Gal. 3:13) and made to experience grace by the call of God the Holy Spirit (Ps. 65:4). And not one of the chosen, redeemed and called ones will fail to reach this blessed estate (Rom. 8:29-30). Grace is glory begun, and glory is grace completed. Grace does not merely offer glory; grace makes sinners worthy of glory and brings them into glory (Col. 1:12; Phil. 1:6). Though we are by nature corrupt and defiled, in Christ we are virgins (1 Cor. 6:9-11). Though we have all gone astray from God (Isa. 53:6), grace has made us followers of the Lamb (John 10:3-5). Though we were lost and ruined with Adam's fallen race, God's elect have been effectually 'redeemed from among men' (Gal. 3:13).

We observe that, throughout the book of Revelation, redemption is always presented to us as an effectually accomplished, particular work of grace specifically for those who are God's elect. It is never spoken of as a vague, general atonement for all people. Though we are by nature full of deceit (Mark 7:21-23), grace has made the believer guiltless, without hypocrisy and sincere (Phil. 3:3). And every child of God stands without fault before the throne of God! We are so now, judicially, through the blood of Christ and the imputation of his righteousness to us. And we shall be, in eternity, personally without fault as we stand before our God (Eph. 1:4; 5:25-27; Heb. 12:14). Will you be in that number?

31.

Look what Christ has done!

Revelation 14:4-5

'And in their mouth was found no guile: for they are without fault before the throne of God' (Rev. 14:5).

The apostle Paul tells us that God's reason for saving us by his grace in Christ Jesus is 'that in the ages to come he might show the exceeding riches of his grace in his kindness toward us through Christ Jesus' (Eph. 2:7). Just as the rich man saw Lazarus in Abraham's bosom and knew the blessedness he enjoyed, so, by some means or other, those who are damned for ever in hell will be able to see clearly the blessedness of God's elect in heaven. Those who despise God's grace will be tormented for ever by the realization of what grace has done for God's elect.

In Revelation 14 John sees the whole company of God's elect multitude, 144,000, gathered around the throne of God in glory. He describes them for us in verses 4 and 5. These are the characteristics of those men and women John saw around the throne of God. They describe all who are, or will be, the heirs of eternal life. It is as though the apostle John, by inspiration, anticipates that glorious day when God will show to wondering worlds the exceeding riches of his grace in his kindness towards us through Christ Jesus. Here the Holy Spirit, by John's pen, holds up all the hosts of God's elect as they will be in glory, and says, 'Look what Christ has done!' In heaven everybody ascribes the whole

work of salvation to the free and sovereign grace of God in
Christ. Nothing is said to the praise and honour of man,
because no praise or honour is due to man.

In these two verses, the apostle John describes five distinct works of grace experienced and enjoyed by all who
are found in heaven's glory and bliss around the throne.

1. They stand in God's presence as chaste virgins

'These are they which were not defiled with women; for
they are virgins.' This description of the Lord's people reveals two things about the character of God's saints in
heaven.

'They were not defiled with women'

These words do not speak of sexual purity or celibacy, as
opposed to impurity and marriage. John is describing the
spiritual purity and chastity of God's elect. He is in fact
telling us that all who enter heaven have been preserved
by the grace of God from the damning corruptions of false
religion. They have been preserved from defilement by the
great whore and her daughters (Rev. 17:1).

While the people of the earth have been made drunk
with the wine of Babylon's fornications, committing gross
acts of idolatry, superstition and will-worship, God's elect
are not. Idolatry is spiritual fornication, but God's elect are
preserved from it by his grace (2 Thess. 2:10-14; 1 John
2:19-20). Though they were persecuted by the beast and
surrounded by the delusions of the false prophet, though
all others embraced the religion of Antichrist and persecuted those who did not, these men and women remained
faithful to Christ. They were not turned away from the sim-
plicity that is in Christ (2 Cor. 11:3). Being preserved by
the grace of God, they would not drink of the wine of free

will, the liquor of works religion, or the champagne of ritualism (read Proverbs 7 and heed its warning to avoid the strange woman). God's saints cannot, and do not, defile themselves with false religion (2 Cor. 6:14 – 7:1; Rev. 18:4).

'They are virgins'

Grace has made them chaste, pure and undefiled in the sight of God. They are naturally as vile and corrupt as any other children of Adam. But God has, by his free grace, through the sin-atoning blood of Christ, removed all their sins and all the consequences of sin from them, so that in Christ he looks upon them as chaste virgins (1 Cor. 6:9-11; Hosea 2:18-20; S. of S. 2:10; 5:1-2; 6:4,9; Ezek. 16:8-14). God's church, all his saints, are compared to virgins (2 Cor. 11:2) for many reasons. First, they are betrothed and espoused to Christ as their Husband by their own voluntary profession. Second, like chaste virgins, all believers love Christ and cleave only to him. Third, like virgins adorned for their wedding, God's saints are clothed with the righteousness of Christ. Fourth, like virgins, they are chaste and pure in character, in doctrine and in worship. Grace has made them so.

2. They are followers of the Lamb

'These are they which follow the Lamb whithersoever he goeth.' It appears as if John saw in the glorified saints the character of God's people upon the earth. All Christ's sheep follow the Lamb wherever he goes (John 10:4-5,27). God's elect are not followers of men, but followers of Christ. They do not follow their feelings, but follow Christ. Hearing his voice, they follow him.

They follow the example of his life as the rule of their lives (John 13:15). They do not live under the yoke of Moses, which is hard and rigorous, but under the yoke of Christ, which is easy and light (Matt. 11:28-30; Eph. 4:32 – 5:1).

They follow Christ in all the duties, privileges and responsibilities of worship. With willing hearts and eager spirits, those who are born of God follow their Saviour in the worship of God. We cannot follow him perfectly, but, with sincere hearts, we strive to worship God as he did while he lived on this earth as a man. Like their Redeemer, all God's saints live by faith, call upon God in prayer and find their place in the house of worship. Like Christ, they seek to glorify God in all things (Eph. 4:17-21). And, like Christ, believers submit to the ordinances of God in public worship. In baptism, in the Lord's Supper, in songs of praise, in hearing the Word, in all matters of worship, those who know God worship in the Spirit (John 4:24; Phil. 3:3).

All who are born of God follow Christ, the Lamb of God, all the way to glory. Not one draws back to perdition. They all persevere to the end. Through water and through fire, through burning desert and freezing night, up the Hill of Difficulty and through the Slough of Despond, every believer follows Christ all the way home. We all went astray from the womb, speaking lies. All we, like sheep, wandered far, following our own wicked wills. But Christ bought us, Christ sought us and caught us, and Christ will carry us home. Christ is the way, Christ put us in the way and Christ will keep us in the way (John 10:27-29; Phil. 3:13-14).

3. They are redeemed

All who are in heaven are there because they were redeemed by the precious blood of Christ, the Lamb of God. 'These were redeemed [bought] from among men, being the first-fruits unto God and to the Lamb.' They were bought by an act of special, particular, effectual redemption. The text does not say, 'These were redeemed along with those who are in hell.' Of course not! That would be blasphemy! The text says, 'These were redeemed [effectually bought] from *among* men.' All who were redeemed are seen in heaven at last. None of those who are not with the Lamb in glory were bought by the blood of the Lamb at Calvary. Christ redeemed us by paying the price of our ransom from the hands of God's offended justice. And that ransom price was his own precious blood (1 Peter 1:18-20; 3:18). His work of redemption effectually ransomed all for whom he died from the penalty of the law by the satisfaction of divine justice (Rom. 3:24-26; Gal. 3:13; Heb. 9:12).

And the ransom price was paid for a particular people (Rev: 5:9; Isa. 53:8). The matter of particular, effectual redemption is not a minor point of strict doctrine. It is a major issue, vital to the faith of the gospel. Universal redemption denies the power and efficacy of Christ's blood. It is a doctrine that teaches that the Lord Jesus did not really accomplish anything by his death on the cross, but only made it possible for sinners to be redeemed, justified and saved. Universal redemption makes the Son of God a failure, declaring that he tries to save all men, but in most cases fails (Isa. 42:4; Matt. 1:21). And it makes man his own saviour, declaring that it is each man's faith that makes the blood of Christ effectual for his own salvation. That is nothing short of blasphemy!

John specifically tells us that this redeemed multitude in heaven was bought from among men because they are God's elect: 'Those were redeemed from among men, being [or because they were] the first-fruits unto God and to the Lamb.' There was a separation made. The first-fruits were for the Lord. They were set apart from the rest. God chose the first-fruits for himself. These 144,000 are not the first-fruits as opposed to other believers, a group of special supersaints. They are the first-fruits 'redeemed from among men'. In the Old Testament, Israel brought the first-fruits to the Lord. That belonged to him. He had no interest in the

rest. The Jews could do what they pleased with that (Exod.
23:19; Num. 15:20; 18:12; Deut. 26:2; Neh. 10:35,37). In
this chapter God's elect are the first-fruits. They are redeemed. They are called. They are gathered around the
throne. The rest are cast into the winepress of the wrath of
God as useless things (vv. 14-20). That which is not redeemed must be destroyed (Exod. 13:13).

4. They are without guile

'And in their mouth was found *no guile.*' God's rich grace,
freely bestowed upon them in Christ, has made them honest, sincere worshippers of God. They are not liars, deceivers, hypocrites (Phil. 3:3). Among these saints was found
no idolatry, superstition, false doctrine, or will-worship (Jer.
16:19; Amos 2:4; Jonah 2:8; Rom. 1:25). They did not speak
lies in hypocrisy, following Antichrist, pretending to be
what they were not. They were not given up with the reprobate to believe a lie (2 Thess. 2:11). These words, 'no
guile', declare the openness, sincerity and truthfulness of
God's saints. They are not pretentious deceivers. Like
Nathaniel, they are Israelites indeed (John 1:47). Christ has
made them so. They draw near to God, not in word only,
but in sincerity and truth, with believing hearts.

5. They are without fault before the throne of God

In themselves by nature, God's saints have many faults.
They have nothing but faults, wrinkles and blemishes! But
'They are without fault before the throne of God.' Not so
much as one fault or blemish is found upon even one of
God's saints — not even by God! (see Jer. 50:20). We were
chosen in eternal election that we might be holy and without blame before him (Eph. 1:3-4). We were redeemed by

the blood of Christ so that all our guilt, sin, fault and blame might be removed from us for ever (Eph. 5:25-27). And we shall be presented at last by the Lord Jesus Christ as trophies of God's almighty, saving grace, holy, unblameable, unreprovable and without fault before the presence of God's glory (Col. 1:22; Jude 24-25).

If you believe on the Lord Jesus Christ, you are among these 'first-fruits unto God and to the Lamb'. What Christ has done for them he has done and will do for you. Be sure you give him the glory for the great things he has done! (1 Cor. 1:26-31).

32.
Christ the Judge

Revelation 14:6-20

'And I saw another angel fly in the midst of heaven, having the everlasting gospel to preach unto them that dwell on the earth, and to every nation, and kindred, and tongue, and people, saying with a loud voice, Fear God, and give glory to him; for the hour of his judgement is come: and worship him that made heaven, and earth, and the sea, and the fountains of waters' (Rev. 14:6-7).

I do not pretend to understand all the prophecies of the book of Revelation, but I do know that everything in this world is moving to a foreordained, predestined end. I have made no attempt to explain those things that are hidden and shrouded in mystery. Many of the events described in this book, I am sure, will not be explained or fully understood until they occur. It has been my desire from the beginning of this exposition simply to show 'the Revelation of Jesus Christ' as it was given to and recorded by John. However, there are some things plainly revealed in this book which even the most casual reader cannot fail to see.

The worldwide proclamation of the gospel

The everlasting gospel of God's free grace in Christ will be preached throughout the entire world. Though false religion spreads through and permeates the entire world, deceiving the multitudes, until it appears that the truth of God is entirely expunged from the earth (11:1-11), there is to be a time of great revival. Just before the end of the world, God will once again stretch out his mighty arm and reveal his saving goodness, grace and glory in Christ by the gospel. The Spirit of life from God will again enter into his church and his witnesses will stand up on their feet and confound their enemies.

The overthrow of Antichrist and false religion

The power of Antichrist will be utterly destroyed, Babylon will at last fall and the abomination of false religion will be thoroughly defeated (v. 8). The superstitions of papacy, ritualism and free-will, works religion of every kind (whether Islam, Judaism, mysticism, or pseudo-Christianity) will be exposed, brought to utter confusion and destroyed by the power and grace of God through the preaching of the gospel. Bad as things may appear at present, the truth of God will prevail at last. The gates of hell shall not prevail against the church of the living God.

The return of Christ in glory

The Lord Jesus Christ will come again to this earth to reign gloriously and for ever in peace and righteousness (11:15). He who loved us with an everlasting love, washed away our sins in his precious blood, called us from death to life by the power of his Spirit and robed us with his own perfect righteousness, will come again in power and in great glory. He will destroy this present, sin-cursed earth with the brightness of his coming and create a new heavens and a new earth, 'wherein dwelleth righteousness'. In this new creation, Christ will reign as King for ever. With Job of old, we shall see our Redeemer, who 'shall stand at the latter day upon the earth' (Job 19:25-27).

The resurrection and final judgement

When Christ comes again, there will be a great, general resurrection and judgement of all who have ever lived upon the earth (Rev. 20:11-15; John 5:28-29; Matt. 25:31-46). I do not know how these events are to be chronologically arranged. But it is evidently revealed in Holy Scripture that there is to come, some time — we do not know when, but at the hour ordained by God from eternity — a solemn winding up of all the events of the world's history. God 'hath appointed a day, in the which he will judge the world by that man whom he hath ordained; whereof he hath given assurance unto all men, in that he hath raised him from the dead' (Acts 17:31). 'It is appointed unto men once to die, but after this the judgement' (Heb. 9:27). 'We must all appear before the judgement seat of Christ; that everyone may receive the things done in his body, according to that he hath done, whether it be good or bad. Knowing therefore the terror of the Lord, we persuade men' (2 Cor. 5:10-11). It is that great and terrible day of the Lord which John sees and records for us in Revelation 14:6-20. In this passage, the final judgement has arrived. It is described under the symbolism of a twofold harvest.

Christ will be the Judge

The Lord Jesus Christ is coming to judge the earth (v. 14). On that great and terrible Day of Judgement, Christ will come sitting upon a cloud to judge the inhabitants of the earth (2 Thess. 1:8-10). He says, 'Behold, I come quickly; and my reward is with me, to give every man according as his work shall be' (Rev. 22:12). The Judge of all men in that great day will be the Son of Man, our Lord Jesus Christ, to whom all authority has been given (John 5:21-22; Dan. 7:13-14; Rev. 1:7). Christ is the Judge by divine right, because he is God. And he is the Judge by right of his mediatorial accomplishments, having earned the place of highest authority and the right to judge all things by his obedience to God as a man (Ps. 2:6-8; John 17: 4; Rom. 14:9; Phil. 2:9-11).

The throne of judgement

The throne is described as 'a white cloud'. Our Lord does not borrow a throne from man. He sits upon a throne of his own making. No doubt the figure is symbolical, implying both supremacy and purity. Our Lord will never again come in humiliation. He will not stoop to assume an earthly throne, neither in Rome nor in Jerusalem. His throne will be a cloud in the heavens, so highly exalted and elevated that at one time all the inhabitants of the earth will be able to see him distinctly and hear his voice. All who have ever lived will be gathered in the presence of his august majesty!

The throne of judgement will be a throne of greatness, majesty and power, and it will be a throne of white purity (Rev. 20:11). Here John calls it 'a white cloud'. That word, 'white', does not so much express the colour of whiteness as it does the dazzling brilliance of light, holiness and purity (1 John 1:5). This throne will be without spot or blemish. It will be a throne of strict, inflexible justice, brilliant, dazzling purity, absolute truth and perfect righteousness. Before this august, holy throne, from the lips of this great Judge, everyone will receive precisely his just, righteous and true reward. All whose works are perfectly righteous and without any sin will receive the reward of eternal life. All whose works are evil will justly be condemned. All who believe on Christ will be accepted for ever on the basis of his blood atonement and imputed righteousness. All who do not believe will be damned for ever on the basis of their own sin. The judgement will not determine or alter anyone's condition or eternal estate. It will only reveal the grounds of man's acceptance or banishment, execute the just sentence of the law and vindicate the justice of God in both the salvation of his elect and the eternal ruin of the wicked.

A picture of the Judge

He is the Son of Man

John says, 'And upon the cloud one sat like unto the Son of man.' This one whom John saw was, and is, the Son of Man, our Saviour, who is also the Son of God. He is called 'the Son of Man' because he is the truest man who ever lived. He is the man after whose image man was created. He is the only man in whom manhood ever reached perfection. In that day, every eye will see that this man is himself God over all, blessed for ever. Yet he is a man. Though he is exalted to heaven's lofty throne, our Saviour is still a man. And when he comes to judge the earth, he will still be a man, the perfect man. The despised Nazarene is now Lord of all. The man who was stripped naked, beaten, spat upon, mocked and crucified by men at Calvary is now the exalted King. The man who bears in his hands, his feet, his head and his side the scars of his death will be our Judge. And those very scars will be either our plea for mercy or his plea for wrath.

He has on his head 'a golden crown'

That crown signifies both victory and sovereignty. The word used for 'crown' means 'a crown won in conflict'. It is the victor's crown. When Christ comes to judge the world, he will wear the crown which he won in the great battle which he has fought as our substitute. What joy it will be for the believing heart to see him wearing the crown of victory when he comes! That crown indicates that he is coming to claim the spoils of his victory. The crown also signifies sovereign dominion. His will is irreversible. His power is irresistible. His judgements are irrevocable.

He holds 'a sharp sickle' in his hand

The sceptre of his throne is a great reaping hook. It suggests that he has come to finish his last great work, to reap the harvest of the earth. And his work of reaping will be sharp, swift and decisive. He comes, not to sow but to reap, not to water but to mow down, not to show mercy but to execute justice. What a sight that will be! The day of harvest will come suddenly, the work will be done swiftly and, when it is over, the Lord of the harvest will reign gloriously (Rom. 9:28).

Christ comes to gather his people

When Christ comes again he will harvest his elect out of the earth (vv. 15-16). These verses speak of the harvest of wheat. The first order of business will be to gather his own people unto himself. He will gather his wheat into his garner before he mows down and burns up the tares (Matt. 3:12). The wheat which he sowed in the earth, watered with his own blood and raised up by his Holy Spirit, that precious grain will be Christ's first, primary concern when he comes again (see John 12:24).

The reaping of the wheat is the matter of first importance

Our Lord looks forward to the day when he will gather his redeemed ones unto himself. This is his delightful work.

His strange work of judgement must be done, but it is the work of his left hand. He puts it off to the very last. On the other hand, 'He delighteth in mercy'!

The reaping of the wheat is the first in order of time, too. Paul tells us plainly that the dead in Christ will rise first (1 Thess. 4:13-18). There will be a general resurrection and a general judgement. There will not be two resurrections and two judgements, one for the righteous and one for the wicked, separated by a long period of time. When Christ comes again, the order of events appears to be: first, the dead in Christ will rise (1 Thess. 4:14-16); second, living believers will be raptured, translated (1 Thess. 4:17); third, Christ will destroy the earth with the brightness of his coming and create all things new (2 Thess. 1:8-10; 2 Peter 3:11-13; Rev. 21:5); fourth, the unrighteous, unbelieving will be raised to the bar of judgement (Rev. 20:11-13).

Until Christ comes, the wheat and the tares grow together in his field

No man can tell the tares from the wheat until the harvest time. Should we try to uproot the tares, we would surely uproot some of the wheat. But in the harvest time, the wheat will be 'ripe'. The word 'ripe' might be translated 'dried'. The meaning is twofold. First, the wheat is dried in the field and must be gathered because the field has nothing more to offer it. There is nothing in the world for the believer, just as there is nothing in the ground for the dried wheat. Second, the wheat, at Christ's coming, will be ripe for heaven. How is a man made ripe for heaven? Not by works, but by grace alone (Col. 1:12). Christ has put away his sins. Christ has given him perfect righteousness and a new nature. Christ causes that new man to grow in the grace and knowledge of the Lord unto the full maturity of faith. He needs only to drop his robe of flesh!

It is Christ himself who comes to personally gather his wheat

'He that sat on the cloud thrust in his sickle on the earth; and the earth was reaped' (v. 16). He alone knows the value of the wheat. He chose us, redeemed us and called us. And he will gather us. When he comes to gather his own, every precious grain of wheat will be gathered into his heavenly garner. What a joyful, blessed hope! But there is another scene in this picture.

The judgement of unbelievers

After he has gathered his elect out of the earth, the Son of Man, our Lord Jesus Christ, will send his angel to gather out of the earth every wicked unbeliever who ever lived and destroy them all for ever in the winepress of the wrath of God (vv. 17-20).

After the wheat is harvested the grapes of wrath must be gathered as well (Matt. 13:41-43). In that day, the wicked will be clearly distinguished from the righteous. No one will make a mistake about them then. Here they are often confused. They go to the same place of worship. They sing the same hymns. They believe the same doctrines. We often mistake tares for wheat and wheat for tares now, but then there will be no mistake. The cluster of unregenerate men will fall like grapes from the vine when the angel of judgement thrusts in his sickle. Notice, it is not Christ, but an angel of Christ, that is sent to execute justice upon the wicked. Christ Jesus personally gathers his elect. But he will not even execute the wicked by his own hand. He has an angel appointed for the work of judgement. They would not have anything to do with him, and now he will have nothing to do with them, except to deliver them over to the hands of an angel for execution. They despised him; now he despises them. They mocked him; now he mocks them. They would not have him; now he will not have them.

These ungodly souls will be justly condemned for ever, because they are fully ripe for judgement (v. 18). Like ripe grapes ready for the winepress, they have filled up the measure of iniquity. They have reached the highest point of sin. They have added evil upon evil until they are fully ripe for wrath. All who persist in their sin, rebellion and unbelief will surely be trodden in the winepress of the wrath of God outside the city (vv. 19-20). These verses describe the terrible sufferings of lost men and women in eternity! But there is something far more terrible about the doom of the lost than language can ever express: endless banishment from God and all that is good; endless wrath without mercy; endless torment without relief; justice without mercy!

33.

The glorious triumph of Christ and his church by the gospel

Revelation 15:1-8

'And I saw as it were a sea of glass mingled with fire: and them that had gotten the victory over the beast, and over his image, and over his mark, and over the number of his name, stand on the sea of glass, having the harps of God' (Rev. 15:2).

Things look very bad now. False religion abounds on every side. Papacy has risen again to a position of prominence and acceptability throughout the world. The idolatrous superstitions of Rome have become acceptable and pleasing, even in those churches which were born in the great Reformation under the leadership of Luther, Calvin and Knox. The poisonous errors of Pentecostalism have spread throughout the world, to the ruin of millions of unsuspecting souls. The doctrines of easy-believism, decisionism, free will and salvation by works, parading through the world under nearly every denominational name, have spread darkness throughout the world. And liberalism, in its many pompous forms, continues to sway the minds of multitudes who are ready to embrace anything other than the Word of the living God. Add to these heresies the increased acceptability of Islam, Judaism and the mystic religions of the world, and one might almost sink in utter despair. The world today is more religious than it has ever been in history. But the world today is more godless than at any time in history.

As it has always proved down the centuries, the more popular false religion is, the more perverted society is. The more
men preach up the free will of man, good works and law,
the more man exercises his free will to do evil and live in
lawlessness. It appears that we are living in that day when
God's true witnesses lie as dead men on Main Street in the
City of False Religion, which is called Sodom and Egypt
(11:7-8). The religion of the world appears to have trodden
down the holy city of our God. It seems that Satan has been
loosed out of his prison for a little season to once again
deceive the nations of the world (20:7). The time of apostasy has come (2 Thess. 2:1-12). But there is no cause for
despair.

There is a better day coming! The Spirit of life from God
will once again enter into his church. His faithful witnesses
will once again stand up on their feet. And by the power of
the gospel that we preach fear will fall upon our enemies
(11:11). The gates of hell shall not prevail against the church
of God. Truth will prevail at last. Without political force,
without legislative power, without worldly weapons of any
kind, the cross of Christ, the simple preaching of free grace
through God's appointed, all-sufficient Substitute, will destroy the religion of Antichrist. Babylon and all her daughters will fall like dominoes before Zion, by the mighty arm
of the Lord, when the everlasting gospel is preached 'unto
them that dwell on the earth, and to every nation, and kindred, and tongue, and people' (14:6). This is the great and
marvellous sign that John saw in heaven and describes for
us in Revelation 15:1-8. This vision, like the ones before it,
runs throughout this entire age. It gradually builds up to,
and culminates in, the last days immediately preceding our
Lord's glorious second advent. Throughout the vision John
is telling us, 'There is a better day coming!' In the end,
Christ and his church will triumph and be victorious over
Antichrist and all false religion by the gospel.

The preparation of God's wrath (v. 1)

God's acts of judgement are not sudden outbursts of passionate fury. Judgement is always the just and righteous retribution of God upon men and women who, by their sinful rebellion and unbelief, have 'filled up the wrath of God'. These seven last plagues which John saw poured out upon the world were, in his mind's eye, acts of astonishing wrath and justice. This sign in heaven is the sign of our Lord's approaching advent and of the destruction of Antichrist (2 Thess. 2:8-10). It is called a 'great' sign because it speaks of great things: the fall of Babylon; the glory of Christ's church and kingdom and the ultimate triumph of Christ and his church. It is 'marvellous' indeed when we realize that the means by which all this will be accomplished is the very thing which the world most despises — the preaching of the gospel! As the walls of Jericho fell by the sounding of rams' horns, Antichrist and the empire of false religion will fall by the preaching of Jesus Christ and him crucified.

The 'seven angels having the seven last plagues' are gospel preachers, representatives and spokesmen for the church of God. They come out of the church, the temple of God (v. 6). Antichrist will be destroyed by the preaching of the gospel — not by political power, not by civil legislation, but by the preaching of the gospel. The 'seven last plagues' are the judgements of God upon the wicked and unbelieving, by which their eternal ruin is sealed for ever. They are called the 'last plagues' because they are God's last dealings with the wicked and impenitent upon the earth, and they will result in the final, eternal ruin of all who refuse to repent. God Almighty will not trifle with those who trifle with his Son and the gospel of his grace. When sinners harden their hearts against Christ, God responds by hardening their hearts to the gospel. And gospel-hardened sinners cannot repent (Prov. 1:22-33; Rom. 1:24; 2 Cor. 2:14-16;

1 John 5:16). Once a person has filled up the measure of the wrath of God by wilfully rejecting and despising the gospel of his grace, he is past all hope. The door is shut! His doom is certain. For such reprobate souls, the wrath of God is prepared!

The victory of God's church (vv. 2-4)

Without question, these verses may be applied to the glory and triumph of Christ's church in heaven. But in the context, they speak directly about the triumph and victory of God's church in this world by faith in Christ and by the preaching of the gospel. Notice the description the apostle gives of God's saints in this world.

1. 'A sea of glass mingled with fire'

There is an allusion here to the brazen sea in the temple and the laver of brass in the tabernacle (2 Kings 25:13; Exod. 30:18), in which the priests were required to wash before entering upon the service of God in his house. This 'sea of glass' represents the precious blood of our Lord Jesus Christ. All of God's people stand before him upon the basis of Christ's blood atonement. It is compared to a 'sea' because of its abundance and efficacy. It is called a 'sea of glass' because in it we are able to see clearly the fulness of free justification, the pardon of our sins and the basis upon which God can be both just and the justifier of all who trust his Son (Rom. 3:24-26). It is called a sea of glass 'mingled with fire' because of the fires of God's wrath which Christ endured as our substitute. When he was made to be sin for us (2 Cor. 5:21), the Son of God endured all the vehement fire of God's wrath against our sin and drowned the sins of his people in the depth of the sea of his own precious blood! This, and this alone, is the basis of our acceptance with God!

2. Victors over Antichrist

John saw 'them that had gotten the victory over the beast, and over his image, and over his mark, and over the number of his name'. They gained the victory over the beast by standing 'on the sea of glass', that is, by the blood of the Lamb, by their close, constant, persevering adherence to the gospel of Christ. Antichrist could not deceive them or destroy them because:

1. They were chosen by God the Father, whose purpose of grace cannot be frustrated (2 Thess. 2:13-14).

2. They were redeemed by God the Son, whose blood cannot be shed in vain (Gal. 3:13).

3. They were called and sealed by God the Holy Spirit, whose grace is irresistible and effectual (Eph. 1:13-14). Hence it is written: 'We are more than conquerors through him that loved us' (Rom. 8:37; see 8:32-39).

3. They had 'the harps of God'

Even in the midst of trials, troubles and persecutions, all God's saints are full of praise in their hearts, which are in an excellent frame, tuned and inclined by God to sing his praise and show forth his glory. Believers are people who in their hearts celebrate the praises of God with joy and gratitude, giving thanks always and for all things (Eph. 5:20; 1 Thess. 5:16-18; Phil. 3:3). The obvious allusion is to the children of Israel, led by Moses, singing and dancing beside the Red Sea as Pharaoh and the Egyptians were drowned (Exod. 15:1-21). Like them, we do, and shall, give praise to our God for the defeat of all our spiritual enemies (the world, the flesh and the devil), the redemption of our souls by the blood of Christ, God's Passover Lamb sacrificed for us (1 Cor. 5:7; Rev. 5:9-10), all his great and mighty

works of providence and grace, and as our sovereign,
mediatorial King. He is the 'King of saints'. And, as the
word implies, he is also the King of all nations and the
King of all ages. Our Saviour is the almighty Sovereign of
the universe (John 17:2). We give praise to him by ascrib-
ing to him alone all reverence, glory, holiness, righteousness and worship (v. 4).

Our Lord's instruments of judgement (vv. 5-8)

The basis of judgement is twofold: the law of God and the
gospel of his grace. It proceeds from the very throne of God,
the mercy-seat (v. 5). Those who have violated God's law
and despised the blood of his dear Son shall not be spared
his wrath. The instruments of judgement are gospel preachers (v. 6). God will use the gospel to judge those who hear it
and refuse to believe it (Rom. 2:16; Heb. 13:17). Indeed, as
the gospel is preached, sinners are judged by it (2 Cor.
2:14-16), and the messengers of God are binding up the
tares for the burning (Matt. 13:30). The pure, white linen
garments with which these messengers are clothed represent the righteousness of Christ by which they are accepted
by God and which they proclaim to, and wear before, men.

The golden girdle with which they are girded and
strengthened is the love of Christ and the grace of God bestowed upon them in him. The vials of wrath are the judgements of God upon those who refuse to repent and believe
the gospel (v. 7). They are vials, that is, measured bowls of
wrath. The wrath of God will be in exact proportion to the
sins of men, measured by divine justice. They are golden
vials, symbolic of righteousness and truth. They are full of
wrath. They are temporal judgements which result in eternal judgement. Those against whom judgement is passed
in this world in judicial reprobation will suffer the wrath
and judgement of God for ever in the world to come (Luke
13:24-25).

It is vital not to miss the lesson of verse 8: though judgement falls upon the wicked, in the last day the church of God will be filled with the power and glory of God. In that day, our God will reveal himself gloriously. His glory will be our defence, which will keep our enemies from entering into and destroying the church. The wicked shall not intrude into heaven's kingdom (Rev. 21:27). The saints of God will make no intercession for the damned, once judgement has been passed (Jer. 7:16; Rev. 19:1-6). And when John tells us that the seven last plagues will be fulfilled, he is assuring us that God's judgement upon Antichrist will be fully accomplished by the gospel of his grace.

The gates of hell shall not prevail against the church and kingdom of our God. The gospel will be triumphant at last. When Christ, the King of saints, is revealed in his ultimate glory, when he has at last conquered all his enemies, all nations and people will bow before him and acknowledge that he is Lord, to the glory of God the Father (Phil. 2:9-11). Every knee shall bow to the Son of God. If we bow to him now in humble faith, we are saved by his grace. But if you bow only when you are forced to do so, in the terror of his wrath, you will be damned for ever!

34.

The coming of Christ and the vials of God's wrath

Revelation 16:1-21

'And I heard a great voice out of the temple saying to the seven angels, Go your ways, and pour out the vials of the wrath of God upon the earth' (Rev. 16:1).

Throughout history there is a definite, constantly repeated order of events. From the Garden of Eden to the final Day of Judgement, this order of events in providence is evident. The book of Revelation deals with it throughout the gospel age.

A repeated sequence of events

The preaching of the gospel brings light

As it is effectually applied to the hearts of men and women by the Holy Spirit, gospel churches are established in the world. These churches are candlesticks holding forth the light of the gospel in a world of spiritual darkness. As these churches hold forth the light, they are blessed with the constant presence of Christ in their midst. That is the message of Revelation chapters 1-3. The only purpose for the existence of these churches, the only mission they have in this world, is to hold forth the light, to preach the gospel of Christ.

Preaching the gospel leads to persecution

God's people hold forth the light of the gospel before men and women who despise it, and are persecuted by the world. They are constantly subjected to trials and afflictions for the gospel's sake. This is seen in chapters 4-7. The offence of the cross has not ceased. Any pastor, evangelist, missionary, or any church, who faithfully preaches the gospel of God's free and sovereign grace in Christ will have to endure persecution from the world, because the religion of the world is man-centred and exalts 'free will'.

God's judgements fall upon those who persecute his people

By these acts of providential judgement, God is both defending his people and warning his enemies of judgement to come. But acts of judgement, no matter how severe and plain they are, will never lead sinners to repentance. We see this in chapters 8-11. It is the goodness of God that leads men to repentance. Judgement only hardens the hearts of the unbelieving. No one will ever repent until Christ is revealed in his heart by the Holy Spirit. Nothing will melt the heart of stone but a saving knowledge of God's goodness and grace in Christ, the sinner's substitute (Rom. 2:4; Zech. 12:10).

Warnings of judgement to come on the reprobate

To those who have eyes to see, this order of events is an evident fact: the gospel is preached, persecution arises and judgement falls. But this conflict between the church and the world points to a deeper, far more important warfare between Christ and Satan, between 'the seed of the woman' and 'the dragon'. This warfare is portrayed in chapters 12-14.

Whenever the wicked fail to repent, refuse to obey the gospel and harden their hearts against God's evident

warnings of wrath to come, he pours out the vials of his
wrath upon them. These vials of wrath are acts of judicial
reprobation. They are God's last plagues upon men, by
which they are sealed unto the judgement of the Great Day,
leaving them no more opportunity for repentance. As
William Hendriksen says, 'When the wicked, often warned
by trumpets of judgement, continue to harden their hearts,
death finally plunges them into the hands of an angry God.
But even before they die they may have crossed the dead-
line, the line between God's patience and his wrath.'

There is a line drawn by God, and known only to God,
between mercy and wrath, between hope and reprobation;
and any man who crosses that line by obstinate, wilful
unbelief cannot be saved, though he may yet live many
years upon the earth. He is as surely the object of God's
eternal wrath as if he were already in hell. The Scripture
repeatedly warns men and women to repent and turn to
Christ in faith, confessing their sins, lest they harden their
hearts and cross the line into hopeless reprobation (Exod.
10:27; Prov. 1:23-33; Jer. 7:13-16; Hosea 4:17; Matt. 12:31-32;
Rom. 1:24; 1 John 5:16; Isa. 63:8-10).

This is the link between chapters 15 and 16 and the chapters preceding them, between the trumpets of judgement
and the vials of wrath. The trumpets warn of wrath to come.
The vials are wrath poured out upon men, even while they
live. In chapters 8-11 men and women are warned of God's
wrath by the trumpets of judgement. In chapters 12-14 impenitent sinners so despise Christ and the gospel of his
grace that they choose false religion over the truth of God
and willingly wear the mark of the beast. In chapters 15-16
these same people have 'the vials of the wrath of God' poured
out upon them, sealing them up in doom until the judgement of the Great Day.

Once more, before the vials of wrath are poured out upon
the wicked, we see the people of God standing before him
secure upon the grounds of Christ's atonement. They have

gained the victory over their enemies, and are singing the praises of God even as he pours out his wrath upon those who refuse to worship the Lamb. We saw in chapter 15 how that God's saints are securely preserved from harm. These vials of wrath are not poured out against them, but against those who do not believe the gospel.

'The vials of the wrath of God' (v. 1)

These are the seven last plagues by which God smites those who despise the gospel of Christ. They are 'golden vials full of the wrath of God' (15:7) — 'golden' because they are acts of righteousness, justice and truth, and 'vials' (rather than 'bowls') because the vial is an instrument of measurement. These golden vials are full of God's wrath against men and women who have filled up the measure of wrath. By their wilful rebellion and obstinate unbelief, they have earned, and justly deserve, God's holy wrath.

Seven angels pour out the seven last plagues of God's burning wrath, which ultimately result in the final judgement of the Great Day. The point is this: once God withdraws the influence of his Spirit by the gospel from men, they become hardened to the gospel and their damnation is both just and irreversible. These seven last plagues are not merely future, prophetic events. They are taking place right now. They took place in John's day. And they will continue to take place until the Day of Judgement.

As we read of these plagues, we cannot avoid noticing a striking resemblance to some of the plagues in Egypt (Exod. 7-10), which foreshadowed all of God's acts of judgement upon unbelieving, impenitent men in the world (Deut. 28:20). God uses every element of his creation to punish those who oppose his Son and persecute his people. Those who refuse to be warned by the trumpets of judgement will be destroyed by the vials of wrath. And the same event

may be to one person a trumpet to warn and to another a
vial of wrath to destroy. For example, the worms which ate
Herod alive were a vial of wrath poured out upon him for
his obstinate pride, by which he was plunged into hell. But
those same worms were a trumpet to warn others of wrath
to come (Acts 12:23). Those who refuse to obey God's voice
are cursed in all they do (Deut. 28:15-16). John says, 'And I
heard a great voice out of the temple saying to the seven
angels, Go your ways, and pour out the vials of the wrath
of God upon the earth.' This is God speaking in wrath against
men who fully deserve his wrath.

1. Incurable disease (v. 2)

At times our Lord pours out upon men horrible, incurable
diseases, by which he brings down into hell those who will
not repent (Exod. 9:10; Deut. 28:27; Acts 12:23). Sickness
and disease are not the works of Satan, but the works of
God. The Lord may use Satan to inflict these things upon
men, but it is the Lord's work (compare Job 2:7 with 2:10).
Insofar as the unbeliever is concerned, every sickness is
either a warning of, or a prelude to, eternal wrath. Every
sickness is a warning from God of judgement to come. And
fatal disease is one means by which God brings the wicked
down into eternal ruin. Seldom, if ever, does a man find
repentance on his deathbed. The dying thief was the ex-
ception, not the rule, and he was not on a deathbed, but on
a cross! But for the believer the afflictions of the flesh are
acts of God's mercy, love and grace (Rom. 8:28). Sickness,
troubles, even fatal diseases are never vials of wrath for
God's elect. We often suffer the same things that the ungodly suffer, but not for the same reasons, and not in the
same way. Our diseases are acts of divine chastisement (Heb.
12:5-12). Our sicknesses help to wean us from the world
and prepare us for eternity. Our fatal diseases are blessings
of God to bring us home to glory (2 Cor. 5:1-9).

2. The sea (v. 3)

Sometimes God uses oceans and rivers as instruments of wrath against men (Exod. 7:17-21; 15:1; Ps. 78:53). All maritime calamities, all hurricanes, tidal waves, floods, etc., are warnings to the ungodly of judgement to come. By these disasters, the unbelieving are swept into hell. But believers are also drowned in the raging sea. Is this an act of judgement upon them? No. It is God's great mercy, bringing his elect safely home to heaven.

3. The rivers and fountains of water (vv. 5-7)

The rivers of water and fountains of life are made, by the hand of God, to be rivers of blood and fountains of destruction (Exod. 7:24; 1 Kings 17:1; 18:5,40). The angel who executes this act of wrath vindicates God's justice and declares his righteousness in all that he does to his enemies (v. 5). God's judgement upon the wicked is a matter of divine retribution, for which the blood of all the martyrs pleads (vv. 6-7; cf. 6:9-10; 8:3-5). None will perish under the wrath of God but those who fully deserve his wrath. 'The wages of sin is death.' And God's saints will praise him for his righteous dealings with the wicked as well as for his righteous dealings with them.

4. Terrible, scorching heat poured upon the earth (vv. 8-9)

God frequently uses the sun to punish ungodly men and nations (Deut. 28:22-24). But wicked men will never be brought to repentance by God's acts of judgement. They only become harder and more brazen in their blasphemy. They may appear to change for a while. But judgement never changes the heart. Only grace can change the heart of a man (cf. Num. 16:31-35,41).

5. Judgements on false religion (vv. 10-11)

The seat of the beast is the centre of all that is opposed to God (Nahum 3:1; Hab. 3:12-14). When God, by some great act of judgement, shakes the kingdom of Antichrist, even as they gnash their teeth and gnaw their tongues with pain, they are hardened in darkness, confusion and hatred for God. They blaspheme him and remain unrepentant.

6. Preparations for the battle of Armageddon (vv. 12-16)

Armageddon is not a great nuclear holocaust. It is not a terrible world war. I do not deny that fearful wars may well come upon the earth, causing widespread suffering and destruction. But Armageddon is a spiritual warfare, with consequences far more severe than any war between nations could ever be. It is the final conquest of Christ over Satan at his glorious advent. We will deal more with this later. For now, in this context, we see that Armageddon is the conquest of Christ over all evil. Armageddon is the place of God's victory! (Judg. 5:19).

The River Euphrates represents the wicked, unbelieving world (v. 12). When the great river dries up, when the economy and resources of the world are dried up by the hand of God, the way is prepared for the kings and people of the earth to move against the people of God in persecution. As it has been in the past, so it will be in the future. In the last day, the kings of the earth will be moved by hell-inspired religious leaders against Christ and his church (vv. 13-14).

John sees proceeding out of the mouth of the dragon (Satan) and the beast (pagan world government) and the false prophet (false religion) three unclean spirits. He compares these spirits to frogs to indicate the abominable, repulsive, loathsome character of world government and world religion in that last little season when Satan is loosed upon the earth. They represent all hell-born philosophy and religion. Are these things not applicable to our day and our society?

Then, just when all the forces of the world, political, philosophical and religious, are gathered against God, the Lord Jesus Christ will suddenly appear (v. 15). He comes as a thief in the night upon his enemies, suddenly, unexpectedly (Matt. 24:29; Judg. 5:4; Hab. 3:13; 2 Thess. 1:7-10). Because of this coming Day of the Lord, let all who believe watch over their souls and keep the garments of salvation, lest we be found naked and put to shame in the end (2 Peter 3:14). The Lord is here admonishing us to perseverance in the faith. The motive for this perseverance is the sure hope of Christ's coming.

7. The final judgement of God upon the world at Christ's second advent (vv. 17-21)

These verses describe the terror of that great and terrible Day of the Lord. It will come to pass when God says, regarding his own eternal purpose in the world, 'It is done!' In that day, there will be a total destruction of the earth, all evil, all false religion and all who oppose our God. God's judgement will be final and complete.

35.
No repentance without Christ

Revelation 16:8-11,21

'And men were scorched with great heat, and blasphemed the name of God, which hath power over these plagues: and they repented not to give him glory. And the fifth angel poured out his vial upon the seat of the beast; and his kingdom was full of darkness; and they gnawed their tongues for pain, and blasphemed the God of heaven because of their pains and their sores, and repented not of their deeds' (Rev. 16:9-11).

These verses describe the terrible judgements of God upon men and women, by which he warns all of judgement to come. Here we see men and women scorched with great heat, gnawing their tongues for pain, suffering the consequences of a drought more severe than tongue can describe, and at last being beaten to death with hailstones weighing over 100 pounds each! Surely, men and women suffering such terrible acts of judgement from God's almighty hand will be humbled, broken, submissive and seeking mercy. Surely, no heart can remain hard and unmoved by such evident acts of God! That would seem reasonable, wouldn't it? But that is not the case. When those men were scorched with fire from heaven, they 'blasphemed the name of God, which hath power over these plagues'. As they gnawed their tongues with pain, they 'blasphemed the God of heaven because of their pains and their sores'. When great hailstones fell out of heaven, crushing them to death, 'Men blasphemed God because of the plague of the hail.' And though God so plainly displays his power and wrath, warning men and women of the judgement to come, they 'repented not of their deeds' (v. 11). 'They repented not to give him glory' (v. 9). What will it take to break a sinner's heart? What will it take to make a rebel surrender to Christ? What will it take to produce true repentance in the heart of a stubborn, hardened, self-willed sinner?

Divine judgement alone will never produce true repentance

We must be careful here and not make hasty generalizations that are contrary to Holy Scripture. I do not say that God does not use acts of providential judgement to arouse, impress, subdue and humble his elect and bring them to repentance. Indeed, he sometimes does graciously use these things (Ps. 107:1-31; Luke 15:11-20). But I am saying this: divine judgement, in and of itself, will never produce repentance in the heart. Satan, after being under the wrath of God for thousands of years, has not mellowed or repented in any way. Many who live in poverty, with sickness and disease, and suffer earthly hardships of every kind, are hardened against God rather than helped by the judgements of providence. The heart of man is so obstinate, proud and hard that even in the torments of hell the damned will never repent.

There is no repentance in hell. They are scorched with heat and tormented with fire. Yet they still blaspheme God's name and will not repent to give him the glory. They curse him for their pain, but do not repent of their deeds. True repentance arises from faith and hope. But in hell there is no faith and no hope, but only endless torment, so there is no repentance. In hell there is much sorrow for pain, but no sorrow for sin. None can be saved except by the blood of the Lamb, but there is no blood to be found in hell. In that awful place of torment, the worm of conscience will gnaw away at men for ever, constantly bringing to mind the cause of hell's torment — wilful unbelief and obstinate impenitence. How often they were invited to heaven! How easily they might have escaped hell! But they would not. They will weep for ever over the loss of heaven's bliss and over the portion of their cup. They will weep for pain. But they will not shed a single tear over the cause of their pain. The damned in hell suffer and blaspheme, but they do not repent.

And, if there is no repentance in hell, where God's greatest judgements are executed, the lesser judgements of providence certainly will not change the sinner's heart and produce repentance. Someone said, 'Afflictions will make good men better, and bad men worse!' But afflictions will never make good men bad, or bad men good. Wrath converts no one. It is grace that saves. Judgement does not soften the sinner's heart; it hardens it. The men and women in this text were led by judgement to blaspheme. But 'They repented not.' The consequence of often-neglected warnings is irreversible hardness of heart.

Let those who are not yet hardened by the judgements of God and the terror of his wrath repent now, while God grants space for repentance: 'Today, if ye will hear his voice, harden not your hearts.' You may not be able to repent tomorrow. The long-suffering, goodness and forbearance of God should lead people to repentance and salvation (Rom. 2:4-5; 2 Peter 3:15). But if they despise his goodness, and harden their hearts in the day of his goodness, they will find it impossible to repent in the day of his wrath and judgement (Heb. 12:17; Prov. 1:22-33).

A false repentance

That repentance which is sometimes produced by acts of judgement is a false repentance which itself needs to be repented of (Ps. 78:31-37). Many, by providential acts of judgement, sickness, narrow escapes from death, bereavements, economic hardship, domestic trials and personal tragedies, repent after a fashion. They turn to God, perhaps even change their lives, and hope to ease their consciences. But repentance that is caused only by judgement and legal fear is always false repentance. You can mark it down as a matter of certainty: 'That which is born in the storm will die in the calm.'

Such repentance, caused by the fear of punishment, is a false repentance (Gen. 4:13). Temporary repentance, which subsides when the judgement is over, is false repentance (Exod. 9:27). Fearful sorrow, that does not change the heart or affect the life of a man, is false repentance (Matt. 14:9-10). Despairing remorse, that does not convert, is false repentance (Matt. 27:4-5).

Cain, Pharaoh, Herod and Judas all repented of the evil they had done, because they saw the judgement of God upon them, but they were not saved. They all repented, but their repentance was false. They all repented, but they did not repent to give God the glory. Such repentance as this only hardens the heart and usually keeps men from true repentance. False repentance mocks God, seeks to deceive him and gives the sinner a false refuge, a refuge of lies, in which he seeks and finds a false, but assured sense of, security from the wrath of God. Thomas Boston wrote, 'Trees may blossom fairly in the spring, on which no fruit is to be found in the harvest; and some have sharp soul exercises which are nothing but foretastes of hell.'

The nature of true repentance

Only the revelation of Christ in the heart can produce it

No one will ever truly repent of his sins and turn to God in genuine conversion until he sees Christ crucified as his

all-sufficient, sin-atoning substitute (Zech. 12:10). Repentance is the tear that drops from faith's eye (Job 40:4-5;
42:5-6). It is the gift of God the Holy Spirit (John 16:8-11).
Repentance is the result of converting grace and gospel instruction (Jer. 31:19). It is the response of faith to the promises of God in the gospel (Isa. 55:7; Jer. 3:11-13). Repentance arises not from the fear of punishment and the dread
of wrath, but from the love, mercy and grace of God in Christ
(Luke 7:37-38,47; 22:61-62). Judgement hardens the heart.
The law of God terrifies the heart. But one look at Christ,
crucified in his place, melts the sinner's hard heart in repentance towards God.

True gospel repentance glorifies God

The men and women spoken of in these verses 'repented
not to give him glory'. But those who truly repent do, by
their repentance, give God the glory (Ps. 32:1-5; 51:1-5).
True repentance recognizes, reverences and adores God's
omniscience (Ps. 139:1-6). It acknowledges the righteousness of God's law and the evil of sin (Rom. 7:9). Genuine
repentance glorifies the justice of God in the punishment
of sin (Ps. 51:4). Repentance that God has wrought glorifies
his sovereignty in the exercise of his mercy (Matt. 8:2;
15:21-28). It sees and acknowledges that there is only one
way by which God can be just and yet justify the ungodly
— by substitutionary redemption (Rom. 3:24-26). True repentance glorifies God by constantly pleading the blood
and righteousness of Christ alone, taking God at his word
and receiving the atonement by faith in Christ (Rom. 5:11).
Have you repented?

36.

Waiting for the Saviour

Revelation 16:15

'Behold, I come as a thief. Blessed is he that watcheth, and keepeth his garments, lest he walk naked, and they see his shame' (Rev. 16:15).

Would it surprise you if the Lord Jesus were to come again before you finish reading this sentence? It probably would. But that is a real pity. Believers should always be waiting for the Saviour, expecting his glorious appearing at any moment. The world does not expect his return. It goes on with its mundane pleasures, eating and drinking, marrying and giving in marriage, without the least thought of Christ's coming, judgement and eternity. But his family should ever be 'looking for that blessed hope, and the glorious appearing of the great God and our Saviour Jesus Christ' (Titus 2:13; cf. Matt. 24:36 – 25:13; Luke 12:22-40; 1 Thess. 4:13-5:6; 2 Peter 3:1-14). The promise of Christ's coming should fill our hearts with hope, expectation, joy and devotion.

There are three things in these words, which John heard fall from the lips of the Son of God, which demand our utmost attention.

1. A fact proclaimed

'Behold, I come as a thief.' Our Lord Jesus Christ will come
again in glory. We have his own word for it. One of the last
things he said to his disciples, before he left the earth, was:
'If I go and prepare a place for you, I will come again, and
receive you unto myself; that where I am, there ye may be
also' (John 14:3). And the very last thing he says to us in
the inspired volume of Scripture is: 'Surely I come quickly'
(Rev. 22:20). Those words might be translated, 'Most certainly, I am coming quickly.' Our Lord is now on the road
back to this earth. He is travelling as fast as wisdom permits. He is not waiting to come; he is coming now. With
every movement of providence, with every tick of the clock,
he draws nearer. He is coming now. And he will suddenly
appear in power and great glory.

Our Lord has promised to come, and to come in person

Some try to explain away the bodily, personal coming of
Christ by saying that he comes to his people in the hour of
death. No doubt that is true. When the believer dies, Christ
comes for him and takes him home to heaven. But there is
a great day appointed by God when the Lord Jesus Christ
will personally return to this earth (Acts 1:11; 1 Thess. 4:16;
2 Thess. 1:7-10; Rev. 1:7). The one who went up to heaven
will come again from heaven to earth. Our Lord will as
certainly be here again in a body of glory as he was once
here in a body of shame. He has promised it. Every redeemed
sinner may confidently say with Job, 'I know that my Redeemer liveth, and that he shall stand at the latter day upon
the earth; and though after my skin worms destroy this body,
yet in my flesh shall I see God; whom I shall see for myself,
and mine eyes shall behold, and not another; though my
reins be consumed within me' (Job 19:25-27).

The great plan and purpose of God in redemption requires Christ's second advent

It is part of God's purpose that, as Christ came once to put away sin by the sacrifice of himself, he must come a second time without sin unto salvation. As he came once to purchase his elect from the curse of the law, he must come a second time to gather the people he has so dearly bought. As he came once to have his heel bruised by the serpent, he must come again to crush the serpent's head and dash his enemies to pieces. As he came once to wear a crown of thorns, he must come again to wear the crown of universal praise. As he came once to be crucified by men, he must come again to be glorified among men. The purpose of God in redemption cannot be complete until Christ comes again for the redemption of his purchased possession (Rom. 8:21-23; 13:11). God's purpose of redemption will not be fulfilled until the church, the New Jerusalem, comes down from God out of heaven, having been prepared as a bride adorned for her husband. The heavenly Bridegroom comes forth riding upon a white stallion, conquering and to conquer, King of kings and Lord of lords. The man of Nazareth will come again. None shall spit in his face, deride him, or mock him then. In that day every knee shall bow before him and every tongue shall confess that he is Lord. The one whom they crucified will come again. With those hands which were once nailed to the cursed tree, he will hold the sceptre of total dominion and reign gloriously for ever. Hallelujah!

Our Lord will come in his own appointed time

Many ask the question, 'When will Christ come?' And multitudes, through the centuries, have tried to figure out the time. They point to signs, and say, 'After these things happen, the Lord will come.' All the curious speculations about prophecy are tricks of the devil, by which he endeavours

294   Discovering Christ in Revelation

to turn our hearts away from Christ. Our Lord tells us
plainly, 'Of that day and hour knoweth no man, no, not the
angels of heaven, but my Father only' (Matt. 24:36). The
Word of God gives us absolutely no light by which we may
determine the time of our Lord's coming. And this is
according to God's wise purpose, so that we may always be
expecting Christ to come at any moment. 'In such an hour
as ye think not the Son of man cometh' (Matt. 24:44).

Our Lord never told us to look for the signs of his coming, but always to look for him coming. We are not to look
for the gathering of the Jews to their homeland, the rebuilding of a temple in Jerusalem, or some earthly, millennial
kingdom, but for the coming of Christ the King himself. It
is always harmful to look for, or anticipate, any signs or
prophecies that must be fulfilled before Christ comes. Such
an understanding of any prophecy is wrong. It would cause
us to imagine that our Lord will delay his coming until
certain things are accomplished (Luke 12:45-46). Christ will
come as a thief, suddenly, unexpectedly. Therefore, we must
watch for him constantly. A thief gives no warning. He
makes no announcement of his coming. Only the foolish
sleep. Those who are wise will watch for Christ's coming.
It is a fact proclaimed: 'Behold, I come as a thief.'

2. A blessedness promised

'Blessed is he that watcheth, and keepeth his garments.'
With these words, our coming King promises blessedness
to those men and women who, in anticipation of his coming, are watchful and keep their garments. What is this
watching?

Throughout the Scriptures, whenever we read about
Christ's coming, the end of the world, judgement and eternity, we are exhorted to be watchful. What does that mean?

We must watch against sin, the lusts of our flesh and the cares of this world, lest they bring a sleepiness and slothfulness upon us and turn our hearts away from Christ (Matt. 13:22). We must watch against Satan and his temptations and devices, by which he seeks whom he may devour. And we must watch against those ministers of Satan who lie in wait to deceive and would by their false doctrine turn us away from the hope of the gospel. We must not be overly concerned with the things of this world (Luke 12:29-34; 2 Cor. 4:18).

'Blessed is he that watcheth.' To be watchful is to be engaged in our Master's business (Luke 12:37), waiting for his return with our lights burning (Luke 12:35). To be watchful is to live and act in the immediate expectation of Christ's return, with the sense that his eye is upon us. May God give us grace to live in constant expectation of our Lord's appearing! It is our responsibility to keep the watch appointed to us until our Lord sends other watchmen, or the Lord himself comes (Luke 12:38). We are to watch for our Lord's return with the anxious thought of opening the door to greet him (Luke 12:36). Let us ever watch over our souls and watch for our Lord, with expectant hearts.

But there is more: 'Blessed is he that watcheth, and keepeth his garments.'

What is this keeping of our garments?

As we watch for Christ's glorious advent, we must keep our garments. This involves two things.

First, we must keep our garments of life unspotted from the world (James 1:27). We must seek grace from the God of grace that we may keep ourselves clear of the corruption of this world — greed, ambition, selfishness, meanness and lasciviousness. We must keep our hearts, tongues, hands and feet from that which is evil. It is our responsibility to keep our garments. We must deny ungodliness and worldly lusts (Titus 2:10-14), and when we have defiled ourselves, we must wash again in the blood of the Lamb (Zech. 13:1).

Second, the text is admonishing us to perseverance in the faith. Our Lord is telling us to keep, cling to and hold fast the garments of our salvation, which are the doctrine of effectual, blood atonement and the robe of his imputed righteousness. We must never allow anything, any doctrine, any experience, any trial, or any temptation, no, not even any fall, to move us away from the hope of the gospel (Col. 1:23; Heb. 3:14). Ever keep the doctrine of blood atonement. Cling at all times to the robe of imputed righteousness.

What is the blessedness promised to those who watch and keep their garments? They will be blessed in the watching and keeping itself (1 John 3:2-3). This detaches them from the world! And they will be blessed with eternal salvation.

A warning posted

'Lest he walk naked, and they see his shame.' Those who cling to Christ, persevering in the faith, will be saved. When the Bridegroom comes, they will have on the wedding garments he has provided. But this is the warning: if you do not hold fast Christ alone as your only hope, your only righteousness, your only acceptance with God, you will be found naked when he comes and put to an open shame (Matt. 22:11-14). Christ is coming again. Soon, he will appear and summon us to stand before the bar of his great white throne. How will you appear before him? Are you washed in his blood? Do you have on the wedding garments of his imputed righteousness?

37.

Christ and Babylon

Revelation 17:1-18

'And upon her forehead was a name written, MYSTERY, BABYLON THE GREAT, THE MOTHER OF HARLOTS AND ABOMINATIONS OF THE EARTH' (Rev. 17:5).

When John was carried away to see 'the judgement of the great whore' (v. 1), he was carried away 'in the spirit into the wilderness' (v. 3). Wherever false religion occupies the place of the true worship of God there is desolation and emptiness (Amos 8:11-12). There may be great worldly wealth and glory; there may be a fulness of power, influence and approval; there may be purple and scarlet, gems and gold, pomp and luxury, and everything to gratify the sensual desires of the heart; there may even be worldwide acceptance and dominion; yet, where the Word of God, the gospel of his grace and the worship of Christ in all the fulness of his redemptive glory are despised and trampled under foot, there is a bleak, barren, empty, desolate wilderness.

This great harlot, false religion, is called by the name 'Babylon the Great'. We have seen this name twice already (14:8; 16:19). In both places the name is mentioned as the object of God's great judgement. In Revelation 17, 18 and 19 John describes that judgement, assuring us of the fact that all false religion, here represented by Babylon, will be destroyed and the truth of God will prevail to the glory of Christ.

Who is this woman?

Without question, there is in this vision a representation of Rome, its pagan culture, government and worship. Certainly, Roman Catholicism, the superstitious, idolatrous religion of papacy, is also involved in the picture before us. But it would be a serious mistake to limit the picture to Rome and Romanism. This woman is called 'the great whore that sitteth upon many waters... And upon her forehead was a name written, MYSTERY, BABYLON THE GREAT, THE MOTHER OF HARLOTS AND ABOMINATIONS OF THE EARTH' (vv. 1,5). This woman, Babylon, the great harlot, represents all false religion in this world, no matter what name that religion bears.

There are basically only two religions in this world. All religions, when reduced to their essential elements, must be categorized under one of these two: free grace or free will; the religion of God or the religion of man; the church of God or the synagogue of Satan. These two religions are represented to us in the book of Revelation by two women. In chapter 12 we saw the church of God, the religion of free grace, which proclaims salvation by the blood and righteousness of Christ alone, who is the man child, represented by 'a woman clothed with the sun'. Here, in Revelation 17, we see the religion of Satan, free-will, man-centred, works religion, represented by 'the great whore ... Babylon'. The character of all false religion is described in John's vision of the great harlot. Remember the picture is a symbol of false religion. Do not try to get a literal picture in your mind; try instead to grasp the spiritual meaning of the whole picture. Notice the features of this woman, by which we are instructed and warned, lest we be deceived by the great harlot, who 'with her much fair speech' and 'the flattering of her lips', has caused so many to follow her 'as an ox goeth to the slaughter' (Prov. 7:21-22). The angel calls her 'the great whore'.

She represents false religion

She is a harlot, and the mother of all spiritual harlots and abominations in the world. This is the standing symbol in the Word of God for false religion (see Jer. 3:6-9; Ezek. 16:28-37; Hosea 1-2; Rev. 2:22). This woman is called the great whore and the mother of harlots, because she is the embodiment and representative of all idolatry, false worship and false doctrine in the world. To give an indication of her age and her vileness, she is called Babylon the Great (v. 5). This is not a prophecy that the ancient city of Babylon will be resurrected and rebuilt. God destroyed that ancient city in his wrath, and swore that it would never again be inhabited (Isa. 13:19-20). This Babylon is any and all religious systems that are opposed to God. Babylon is the religion of man. It is that religion which teaches salvation by the works of man's hands and the power of man's will. Though it is seen in the sacrifice of Cain, it began as an organized religion, an organized system of worship in opposition to God, in the fourth generation after Noah, with Nimrod, the grandson of Noah's cursed son, Ham (Gen. 10:8-11). The Bible tells us that Nimrod was 'a mighty hunter before the LORD'. That is a very poor translation of the text. Literally, it means, 'Nimrod was a mighty rebel before the LORD, the mightiest rebel before the LORD in the earth.' His name, Nimrod, means 'a rebellious panther'. It was this 're-bellious panther', Nimrod, who built the city of Babel, or Babylon, and began the religion of confusion (Gen. 11:1-9).

Idolatry is not a gradual decline from truth by well-meaning, but unenlightened men. It began at Babel in intentional rebellion. It was the invention of a proud race who refused to come to God by faith in a substitute and refused to trust God's grace alone. Babylon was born in defiance of God and his Word. The men of Babel despised God's sovereignty, blood atonement and salvation by grace. They attempted to build a tower to heaven by the works of their hands, with no regard for the glory of God. God scattered those men and brought their religion to confusion. Yet, wherever these idolaters spread through the earth, their religion is essentially the same. All the pagan mythologies, idolatrous images and religious rituals of the world, no matter how much they differ, have an underlying sameness, which proves that they are all from one original source. That source is Babel, or Babylon, Nimrod's plan to defeat the purposes of the God of Noah. The one foundational tenet that is always the same in the worldwide religions of Babylon is this: man's salvation ultimately depends upon, and is determined by, man himself!

The appeal of false religion

She has made the inhabitants of the earth drunk with the wine of her fornication (v. 2). The religion of old Babylon is not limited to one race, one time, one place, or even one religious order. It encompasses all. The kings and inhabitants of the earth, from one generation to another, commit fornication with her and drink from her cup until they are thoroughly drunk, beyond the reach of reason. The cup which she holds out is a golden cup (v. 4). To the carnal, sensual heart, the world's religion is very appealing. It is bright, glittering, full of blessings, promising happiness, health, peace and prosperity to all who drink from its cup. But the cup is full of abominations, filthiness and fornication. This is a fact that cannot be disputed: wherever false religion gains popularity and acceptance, moral corruption follows. The doctrines of self-righteousness, free will and salvation by works always produce moral degradation. The cup is always the same. The old harlot has only one cup. It is always filled with the same, head-spinning wine of free will, self-righteousness and good works.

Persecution of God's people (v. 6)

She is drunk 'with the blood of the saints, and with the blood of the martyrs of Jesus'. 'In her was found the blood of prophets, and of saints, and of all that were slain upon the earth' (18:24). Throughout history, persecution and the murder of God's saints and prophets have been the work of this great harlot. It is old Nimrod trying still to destroy the kingdom of God. Persecution is not the work of God's church. It is the work of Babylon.

This woman sits upon many waters (v. 1). The angel tells us plainly that these waters are not literal bodies of water. They are 'peoples, and multitudes, and nations, and tongues' (v. 15). That is to say, 'The false religion signified by this great harlot is universal in its acceptance.' The prostitution of divine truth is supported and accepted by the fallen sons of Adam wherever they are found upon the earth. While the false religions of the world may at times fight among themselves, they will always be found united in their opposition to the Lord Jesus Christ and the gospel of the grace of God revealed in him.

The scarlet-coloured beast

She is depicted as sitting upon a scarlet beast, full of the names of blasphemy, having seven heads and ten horns (v. 3). The beast is the same one we saw in chapter 13. It tells us that this woman, the religion of this world, is inspired and empowered by Satan himself (v. 8; cf. 2 Cor. 11:1-5,13-15).

The seven heads of the beast are the kingdoms and empires of this world, by which false religion is both protected and advanced (vv. 9-10). The number seven may be merely a symbolical, figurative number, implying the complete, universal acceptance of false religion, all under the demonic influence of the beast (v. 11). William Hendriksen suggests that the seventh head might be the collective title for all anti-Christian governments from the fall of Rome unto the Second Coming of Christ, existing in that short space of time we call 'the gospel age' (Rev. 11:2-3; 12:6,14; 13:5).

The ten horns of the beast are kings, rulers of the world, raised up by Satan for brief periods of time to make war with Christ and his church (vv. 12-14). They are not mighty emperors, just little presidents, senators, congressmen, governors, legislators, prime ministers, etc., to whom Satan gives a brief time of power to oppose the cause of Christ. This woman, the great harlot, is the religion of this world, which reigns over the kings, people and nations of the earth in opposition to Christ and his church (vv. 14,18).

What is to become of the woman?

When John saw this great harlot, this great anti-Christian religious system, ruling over the people and nations of the earth, making the kings of the earth drunk with her idolatry and will-worship, he was astonished. He says, 'When I saw her, I wondered with great admiration' (v. 6). A better reading would be, 'I was astonished with great terror.' And well he might be! But he was also comforted and encouraged by the realization that this great harlot will be brought to destruction by the will of God, and that even she is under the dominion of our great God and Saviour, and will be made to serve his purpose (vv. 16-17). Take courage, Christ will prevail! And in him we shall prevail too. We are, in Christ Jesus, more than conquerors.

This great harlot, with all her hellish power, will have no influence over the church of God's elect (vv. 8,14). Though all the world is deceived by the charms of false religion, the mother of harlots cannot deceive or destroy any of God's elect. Our names were written, immutably, in the book of life before the world began (Rev. 13:8). We are called by God, and the gifts and callings of God are without repentance (Rom. 11:29). We have been chosen as the objects of God's mercy, love and grace, and the purpose of God in election must stand. God makes his elect faithful to Christ by the power of his grace, and faithful men and women cannot be turned away from their Master. Our Redeemer and Saviour is Jesus Christ, the Lamb of God, who is the almighty Lord of lords and King of kings (1 Tim. 1:17).

In the end, by the will of God, this woman will be destroyed (vv. 16-17). It seems at times that Antichrist will prevail. But as our God sent confusion to the people of Babel and turned them against one another, as he overthrew Egypt, Babylon, Assyria and Rome, so he will utterly destroy all false religion and make the great harlot desolate in the end, so that even those who once carried her upon their shoulders will despise her and devour her. In God's time, Babylon will fall. And even Babylon will prove, in the last Great Day, to have been the servant of God to perform his will in the earth (1 Cor. 11:19; 2 Thess. 2:1-14; Ps. 76:10).

What are we to learn from this vision?

There are many, many things taught in this picture. But I want to leave with you just four things to remember for the comfort and strength of your soul.

1. The Lord our God is sovereign over all things. He is in control. He is performing his will.
2. Popularity is no indication of the will of God or the truth of God. If you would follow Christ, you must be prepared to swim against the tide, always be in the minority and always face bitter opposition from the world.

3. God's elect are secure at all times, being kept by the power of his grace (Rom. 8:28-39).

4. The religion of this world will prove in the end to be empty, frustrating and loathsome. Those who revel in it today will despise it at the last. But it will be too late!

There will be nothing but hatred in that day, when the lost mother meets her lost son, the lost wife meets her lost husband and the lost preacher meets his lost hearers in hell! In eternity, all who have served Babylon will despise her and will themselves be despised.

38.
Eternal security in Christ

Revelation 17:8

'The beast that thou sawest was, and is not; and shall ascend out of the bottomless pit, and go into perdition: and they that dwell on the earth shall wonder, whose names were not written in the book of life from the foundation of the world, when they behold the beast that was, and is not, and yet is' (Rev. 17:8).

The book of Revelation opens with a picture of the Lord Jesus Christ in the midst of his churches. It closes with a vision of all God's elect, the whole church of the redeemed, gathered before the throne of God and of the Lamb in glory. Everything in this book, from the first chapter to the last, is written to assure us of the eternal security and final perseverance of all who believe. God's church in this world is an elect, redeemed, sealed multitude whose names are written from eternity in 'the book of life of the Lamb slain from the foundation of the world' (Rev. 13:8).

In Revelation 17:8, the angel tells John that all who dwell upon the earth wonder at the beast and are deceived by the great harlot, Babylon, false religion, except those whose names were 'written in the book of life from the foundation of the world'. While others perish, they are secure. Though all others are deceived, they are secure. Though all others go down to hell under the wrath of God, those whose names are 'written in the book of life from the foundation of the world' are secure. I want to demonstrate from Scripture

that all true believers are eternally secure in Christ, being
kept by the power of God's grace.

Can a saved person ever be lost?

Is it possible for people saved by the grace of God, chosen
in everlasting love, redeemed by the blood of Christ and
born again by the power of the Holy Spirit, to be lost at
last? Can those who are 'called, chosen, and faithful' perish? Can those people, any of them, ever be lost? Can one
of God's elect go to hell? Is it possible for one of Christ's
redeemed ones to suffer the wrath of God? Is it possible for
one who is called by the Holy Spirit, regenerated and born
again by almighty grace, to fall away, draw back, depart
from Christ and perish at last? Let these questions be
answered not by the words, opinions, theories and doctrines of men, but by the Word of God alone, and the answer
is emphatically, unconditionally, unequivocally, 'No!' It is
not possible for a saved person to be lost. If we hear nothing
but the testimony of Holy Scripture, we cannot question
the eternal security of all God's saints.

'The righteous ... shall hold on his way, and he that
hath clean hands shall be stronger and stronger' (Job 17:9).
'The LORD will not cast off his people, neither will he forsake his inheritance' (Ps. 94:14). 'They that trust in the LORD
shall be as mount Zion, which cannot be removed, but
abideth for ever. As the mountains are round about Jerusalem, so the Lord is round about his people from henceforth
even for ever' (Ps. 125:1-2; see also Ps. 89:19-37). 'I will
make an everlasting covenant with them, that I will not
turn away from them, to do them good; but I will put my
fear in their hearts, that they shall not depart from me' (Jer.
32:40). Our Saviour promises, 'My sheep hear my voice,
and I know them, and they follow me; and I give unto them
eternal life; and they shall never perish, neither shall any

man pluck them out of my hand. My Father, which gave them me, is greater than all; and no man is able to pluck them out of my Father's hand. I and my Father are one' (John 10:27-30). In Romans 8:28-39, the apostle Paul tells us that God is for us in his sovereign providence (v. 28), in his saving purpose (vv. 29-30) and in his substitutionary provision (vv. 32-39). And, 'If God be for us, who can be against us?' '[God] shall ... confirm you unto the end, that ye may be blameless in the day of our Lord Jesus Christ. God is faithful, by whom ye were called unto the fellowship of his Son Jesus Christ our Lord' (1 Cor. 1:8-9). 'Faithful is he that calleth you, who also will do it' (1 Thess. 5:24; see also 1 Peter 1:2-5). All these texts of Scripture tell us one thing: God's elect are eternally secure in Christ. They shall never perish. 'The foundation of God standeth sure.' Salvation is the work of God alone. And that which God does is done for ever (Eccles. 3:14).

What is the basis of our assurance and security in Christ?

We have seen from the Scriptures that it is impossible for a saved person to be lost. We have the Word of God for it. Now, for the comfort and edification of your soul, let me go on to show why this is impossible.

1. The *perfection* of God's character guarantees the eternal security of his elect (Lam. 3:21-25).

2. God's *immutability* forbids any change in the objects of his love or in his attitude towards us (Mal. 3:6; Job 23:13; James 1:17).

3. God's *omnipotence* means that none can pluck us from our Saviour's hands (John 10:28-29; 1 Peter 1:5; Jude 24-25).

4. God's *mercy* will never turn to wrath.

5. God's *love* will never become hatred.

6. God's *faithfulness* will never cease.

7. God's *goodness* cannot fail.

8. God's *justice,* having once been satisfied for the sins of his elect, can never demand satisfaction from those for whom Christ died (Rom. 3:24-26).

> Payment God cannot twice demand,
> First at my bleeding Surety's hand,
> And then again at mine!

9. God's *eternal purpose*, which cannot be altered, frustrated, or defeated, guarantees the eternal security of his elect. The purpose of God according to election must stand. He will do all his pleasure. And his pleasure is the eternal salvation of his elect (Isa. 46:9-13; Eph. 1:3-14; 2 Thess. 2:13; John 6:37-40).

10. His *promises*, which are yea and amen in Christ, guarantee the eternal security of all believers (Heb. 13:5). He promises eternal life to all who believe (John 3:14-16). He promises to forgive all our sins (1 John 1:9).

11. The *finished work of Christ* guarantees the eternal security of God's elect. Christ has redeemed us (Gal. 3:13; Heb. 9:12). We cannot be unredeemed! Christ has sanctified us (Heb. 10:10-14). We cannot be unsanctified! Christ has justified us (Rom. 3:24). We cannot be unjustified! Christ has made us complete (Col. 2:10). We cannot be made incomplete! Christ has made us to be seated in heaven (Eph. 2:6). We cannot be unseated! Christ has blessed us (Eph. 1:3). We cannot be unblessed! Christ has 'made us meet [i.e. fit] to be partakers of the inheritance of the saints in light' (Col. 1:12). We cannot be made unfit!

12. The *present intercession* of Christ as our advocate in heaven guarantees the eternal security of God's

elect. His prayers on our behalf cannot be denied (John 17:24). His advocacy cannot fail (1 John 2:1-2).

13. The *seal of the Holy Spirit*, which cannot be broken, guarantees our eternal security in Christ (Eph. 1:13-14; 4:30). The seal preserves. The seal proves ownership. The seal is the earnest of our inheritance.

The basis of our assurance and security in Christ is not, in any way, dependent upon, or determined by, us. The whole basis of our security is our God, who he is, what he has done and what he is doing for us. Our good works do not make us more secure. And our evil works do not make us less secure. Our security is Christ! The security and welfare of the sheep are the responsibility of the Shepherd. Our relationship with the eternal God does in great measure determine what we do. But what we do in no way determines our relationship with the eternal God.

What about those who do depart from Christ and fall away?

I do not deny that many do depart from Christ, forsake the gospel, fall away from the faith and leave the church of God. Every pastor, every church, every believer is painfully aware of many who once walked in our company who now have left us. Our Lord experienced it (John 6:66); the apostles experienced it (2 Tim. 4:10), and we experience it today. Men and women depart from Christ and fall away for many reasons. The love of the world destroys some (Matt. 13:22). Trials overwhelm many (Matt. 13:21). Self-will has destroyed multitudes, like Judas. False doctrine ensnares some (Gal. 5:1-4). And gradual apostasy has claimed many souls by Satan's craftiness (Heb. 10:25-26). Yet it must be understood that those who depart from us, for whatever reason, never were truly of us (1 John 2:19). It is one thing to learn doctrine, but another thing to learn Christ. It is one thing to have an emotional experience, but another thing to be born again. It is one thing to change your life, but another thing to bow to the rule of Christ.

What are we to learn from these things?

A careful reading of Hebrews 10:35-39 teaches four things:

    1.There is a false faith by which many are deceived.
    2. False faith will, sooner or later, depart from Christ. Many, I fear, depart from Christ and will never know it until the Day of Judgement (Matt. 7:22-23).
    3. True faith will persevere to the end.
    4. 'Salvation is of the Lord!' (Jonah 2:9). Since salvation is of the Lord, we know that the salvation of God's elect is a matter of absolute certainty and that all who trust Christ are infallibly secure in him (Phil. 1:6).

39.

The Lamb and those
that are with him

Revelation 17:14

*'These shall make war with the Lamb, and the Lamb shall over-
come them: for he is Lord of lords, and King of kings: and they that
are with him are called, and chosen, and faithful'* (Rev. 17:14).

In Revelation 17, we are assured of the destruction of all
false religion, symbolized by Babylon, the great mother of
harlots. Though supported through the centuries by kings,
nations and empires, Babylon will fall at last. Though it is
maintained, enriched and adorned by Satan with the gaudy
ornaments of the earth, all false religion will be destroyed.
Though the kings and people of the earth drink from the
golden cup which she holds in her hand and are made drunk
with the wine of her fornication, the filthiness of the world's
religion (the abominations of free-will, works religion) will
be exposed at last. And those who have been deceived by it
will loathe it for ever. In the end, the truth of God must
prevail. The church of Christ will be victorious. The gates
of hell shall not prevail against her. The gospel of God's
free and sovereign grace, substitutionary atonement and
effectual mercy will certainly win the day. Christ will see
to it! In all things, 'We are more than conquerors through
him that loved us.' The message of this book, from beginning to end, is a message of victory through grace. Though
tried, persecuted, scorned, derided and afflicted, the church
of God will triumph over all her enemies. It is an assured

fact that 'The God of peace shall bruise Satan under your feet shortly' (Rom. 16:20).

Four truths revealed to John

In verse 14, the Holy Spirit inspired John to show us four things specifically revealed to him by the angel for the comfort and edification of God's saints in all ages.

1. The world always opposes and persecutes Christ and his church

When John saw the kings of the earth, whose rule and power are inspired by the hellish beast, the angel said, 'These shall make war with the Lamb.' These kings of the earth represent the secular, political, economic, philosophical, academic powers of the earth, acting in unison with, and by inspiration of, the great harlot. In other words, the world which is drunk with the false religion of Babylon always has been, and always will be, opposed to Christ, the church of God and the gospel of his free grace. The truth of God is never accepted, supported or maintained by popular opinion. If you follow Christ, you will have to fight against the world, specifically against the religion of the world. We must never seek to conciliate, or unite with, the enemies of Christ (James 4:4; 2 Cor. 6:14 – 7:1).

2. The Lord Jesus Christ will overcome all his enemies

'The Lamb shall overcome them' (cf. Isa. 45:22-25; Heb. 10:10-14; Phil. 2:9-11). Throughout the Word of God, and especially in this book, the Lord Jesus Christ is constantly referred to in his sacrificial character as the Lamb of God. And it is by virtue of his sin-atoning sacrifice that he must prevail over all his enemies. He will overcome some by the power of his saving grace and others by the rod of his wrath, but he will be victorious over all his enemies (Ps. 89:23).

3. Why Christ's victory is certain

Christ's conquest is a matter of absolute certainty because he is totally sovereign over all things. 'He is Lord of lords and King of kings' (John 17:2; Acts 2:36; Rom. 14:9). Divine sovereignty is essential to faith, hope and confidence in the promises of God. If God were not sovereign, we could not, with sanity, trust him implicitly. But we rejoice to know that the one whom we trust, into whose hands we have committed our souls, is absolutely, totally, universally sovereign over all things, always doing all things according to the good pleasure of his own will (Ps. 115:3; 135:6).

4. Our union with Christ

The one thing that distinguishes God's elect from all other people in the world is their relationship with the Lord Jesus Christ. Others make war with the Lamb. These are 'they that are with him'. They are one with him, united to him by grace from all eternity. It is their union with the Lamb that separates and distinguishes them from all others, makes them acceptable with God and secures their eternal salvation. God's elect are with Christ now, always have been with Christ and will be with Christ for ever (Eph. 1:6). We were with him as our surety in the covenant of grace. We were with him as our representative while he lived upon the earth. We were with him when he died as our substitute on the cross. We were with him when he arose from the dead and ascended into heaven as our mediator King. And we are with him in our hearts by faith and love. His cause is our cause. We are with our Lord in all that he does. In heart, will, purpose and desire, God's saints are with Christ.

Three works of grace in the believer

Now look at the last part of verse 14 and notice how the angel describes God's saints, identifying them by three distinct works of grace. Those who are with Christ 'are called, and chosen, and faithful'. With these three words all who are truly born of God are described. These three words write the biography of every redeemed sinner who enters glory by the merits of Christ. God's saints are called by the Spirit because they have been chosen by God, and they are faithful to Christ because they are called.

1. Called

All who are with Christ are with him by the almighty, effectual, irresistible call of the Holy Spirit in regenerating grace. Without question, there is a general call that goes out to all men, without qualification, every time the gospel is preached. By the power and authority of God himself, the gospel preacher commands all who hear his voice to repent and come to Christ in faith (Luke 24:47; Acts 17:30; Rom. 10:9-13,21). The preaching of the gospel is not an invitation to heaven. It is a divinely authorized command to faith! This call goes out to all who hear the gospel. But even this outward call is not universal (Matt. 11:20-26).

This call is necessary. Apart from this outward call, apart from the preaching of the gospel, there is no possibility of salvation (Rom. 10:17; James 1:18; 1 Peter 1:23-25). And all who hear this outward call, all who hear the gospel of Christ preached, are responsible to obey it and trust Christ (Rom. 10:21; John 3:36; 1 John 5:10). But this outward call alone will never produce faith in a sinner. 'Many are called, but few are chosen.' No matter how eloquent, sincere, earnest and convincing the preacher is, this outward call can never produce faith or save a sinner.

This text is talking about another call. Those who are 'the called' have been called, not by the voice of man, but by the voice of God the Holy Spirit. He uses the voice of a preacher, but the call is divine, inward, effectual and saving (John 6:63; 10:3; Ps. 65:4; 110:3). It is a personal call, a distinguishing call, a convincing call (John 16:8-13) and an effectual, irresistible call of love. It is this call of God that distinguishes the believer from the unbeliever (1 Cor. 1:26-31; 4:7; 15:10; Eph. 2:1-4).

2. Chosen

The call of the Spirit is the proof and evidence of our eternal election in Christ. Notice that in this verse calling is put before election, because we cannot know our election until we are called. But election took place long before we were called. The fact that we are called in time is the proof that we were chosen in eternity (1 Thess. 1:4-5). Divine election is a blessed, comforting, soul-cheering truth of Holy Scripture in which all true believers delight. As it caused David to dance before the ark, it causes our hearts to leap with joy before the Lord our God (Jer. 31:3; John 15:16; Rom. 8:28-30; 8:11-23; Eph. 1:3-7; 2 Thess. 2:13-14; 2 Tim. 1:9).

Notice particularly 1 Peter 1:2. Those who oppose the doctrine of sovereign election will usually run to this text and twist it to their own destruction, suggesting that election is based upon foreknown or foreseen faith. But that is totally to misrepresent what the apostle is saying. We are elect 'according to the foreknowledge of God the Father' — that is, according to God's purpose of grace in foreordination. Our election to eternal life is 'through sanctification of the Spirit'. God has chosen to bring us to heaven by the regenerating, sanctifying grace of the Holy Spirit, who gives us a new nature, imparting to us the righteousness of Christ in the new birth (Ezek. 36:25-27). And we were chosen 'unto obedience and sprinkling of the blood of Jesus Christ'. The text might legitimately be interpreted to say, 'We were chosen and foreordained to eternal life by God the Father, set apart, preserved and kept by God the Holy Spirit, until

the Lord Jesus Christ accomplished his obedience and death
as our substitute.' Those things certainly are true, and they
are taught elsewhere in the Scriptures. But Peter is telling
us that the object of God in our election was, and is, our
obedience to the gospel and the effectual application of the
blood atonement of Christ to our hearts by the Holy Spirit
through faith (see Heb. 9:14). God the Father chose us! God
the Son redeemed us! God the Spirit regenerated us, giving
us faith to obey Christ, trusting his blood for our complete
atonement! As the result of God's eternal, electing love,
grace and peace are multiplied to all God's elect (1 Peter
1:3-5). We rejoice in, and give thanks to, God for his eternal, electing love, mercy and grace in Christ Jesus. We know
our election because of our calling. And our calling makes
election precious.

3. Faithful

The sure and certain result of God's electing grace and the
Spirit's effectual call is faithfulness. Those who are with
Christ 'are called, and chosen, and faithful'. This simply
means three things. First, all who are called and chosen of
God *have faith in Christ*. It is the gift of God's grace in regeneration (Eph. 2:8-9). Secondly, all who are born of God
are *made faithful* by his grace. The saints of God are faithful, true, honest men and women (Eph. 1:1). They can be
trusted and depended upon. They are faithful stewards,
using whatever God puts in their hands for his glory and
his interest in this world (Matt. 25:14-30). All true believers are faithful to Christ, to his will, to his glory, to his
gospel, to his interests and to his people. And, thirdly, all
who are called by the Spirit *remain faithful*, persevering to
the end of their days by grace. They will endure their trials. They will overcome their temptations. They will triumph over their enemies. They will die in faith (Heb. 11:13).

40.

Christ destroys Babylon

Revelation 18:1-24

'And he cried mightily with a strong voice, saying, Babylon the great is fallen, is fallen, and is become the habitation of devils, and the hold of every foul spirit, and a cage of every unclean and hateful bird' (Rev. 18:2).

Satan has always opposed the Lord Jesus Christ. In the beginning, his heart was lifted up with pride against the Son of God. He inspired, organized and led a rebellion among the angels of heaven, attempting to overthrow God's throne, frustrate his purposes, destroy his works and prevent the triune God from executing and fulfilling his eternal covenant of grace. Though his revolt was totally unsuccessful (he did not even shake God's throne, much less overturn it! — See Isa. 14:24,26-27), yet the old serpent has never ceased to oppose the purpose of God. He knows he has only a short time before Christ casts him into the pit for ever (Rev. 12:12), yet he continues his rebellion. He continues to inspire, organize and lead men and women in rebellion against the God of heaven. And his primary means of opposition to Christ is organized false religion.

That religious system, inspired, organized and led by Satan, the religion of Antichrist, is portrayed as a great harlot patronized by the whole world and as a great city of worldwide influence and wealth. The name of that harlot and that city is Babylon. Babylon represents the world, especially the religious world, in opposition to Christ. The religions of the world have many names, but their essential tenets are always the same. The religion of the world, the religion of Antichrist, the religion of Babylon, is the religion of free will and salvation by works. The religion of Babylon, the hell-inspired religion of Antichrist by which the souls of deceived multitudes are destroyed, always proclaims that salvation is ultimately decided and determined by man. Free-will, works religion is a satanic invention and is damning to the souls of men. Both the preachers and the adherents of such religion, like Nimrod, are rebels against God, utterly lost, without the knowledge of the living God. And, like Nimrod, they shall all perish under the wrath of God.

This religion is popular. Men love it, support it, promote it and defend it. It has always been the religion of the world. It is wealthy. The world's most famous, most well-respected religious leaders are the servants of this great whore. And the religion of Babylon so thoroughly controls the minds of men that it controls the political, economic, academic and philosophical powers of the world. The whole world, by the deception of Satan, cherishes free-will, man-centred, Babylonian religion. But, thank God, the religion of Babylon, all opposition to the church of Christ, the truth of Christ and the glory of Christ, will one day be destroyed. That is the subject of Revelation 18.

An announcement, an admonition and a warning (vv. 1-8)

A great, mighty angel came down from heaven, whose glory lightened the earth. These mighty spirits, who were created by God to be ministering spirits to those chosen and ordained of God to be the heirs of salvation (Heb. 1:14), are also the instruments by which God executes his judgement upon his enemies. Those holy beings who, by divine direction, have protected God's church from their enemies in every age will destroy our enemies in the end.

The fall of Babylon is announced as if it had already occurred (vv. 2-3)

So sure and certain is God's judgement upon Babylon that it is recorded as a past event. Notice how the angel describes Babylon. It is not a literal city, but a religious system that encompasses and includes everything opposed to God. It is the habitation of devils, the home of every foul spirit and the cage of every unclean and hated bird! Babylon is the idolatrous religion of the world (Isa. 21:9; Jer. 50:2). The gods of Babylon are the dung-gods of free will and salvation by works. The dung of Babylon's religious solemnities has smeared and defiled the whole earth. Had it not been for the Lord's free, preserving grace, we would all have been swallowed up in Babylon. But God would not allow us to have our way (Jer. 51:7-10; 2 Thess. 2:10-13).

Yet even Babylon serves the purposes of God. Though the heresies of false religion are hatched in hell and set in opposition to the throne of God, they are under the rule of God and serve only to accomplish his purpose of grace towards his elect (1 Cor. 11:19; 2 Thess. 2:3). By the spreading fame and popularity of free-will religion, God's elect are proved. Though all the world goes after Babylon, God's own will not fall for her lies. When Babylon has served her purpose, she will be brought to utter destruction. By what means God will publicly destroy false religion, we are not told. But these things are plainly revealed: Babylon will fall suddenly. Her destruction will come from within (Rev. 17:16-17). And God's judgement upon Babylon is just and well deserved (v. 3). When the world's religious system is destroyed, the whole earth will be thrown into chaos and confusion, because it is the religion of the world that governs the economics, philosophy and politics of the world. When Babylon falls, everything falls.

An admonition from the mouth of Christ himself (v. 4)

This is a call which the Lord our God repeatedly issues to his church in all ages. It is an urgent call to separation: 'Come out of her, my people!' (See Isa. 48:20; 52:11; Jer. 50:8; 51:54; Zech. 2:7). The Lord does not say, 'Stay in Babylon and heal her.' He does not say, 'Find a way to get along with Babylon.' He does not say, 'Love Babylon, pray for Babylon and try to help Babylon.' God says, 'Come out of her, my people!' (Jer. 51:7-10). And all of God's people will deliberately come out of Babylon (2 Cor. 6:16-18). To remain a part of any church or denomination that denies the gospel of God's free and sovereign grace in Christ is to line up with the Lord's enemies and court eternal damnation. To come out of her is to have no fellowship with her, give no support to her, offer no hope to her and publicly repudiate her doctrines and practices by identifying with Christ, his gospel and his church.

A solemn warning (vv. 5-8)

A solemn warning is given to those who set themselves against Christ, his church and the gospel of his grace. The God of heaven is a God who can, must and will punish sin. Here the Lord himself tells us five things about divine judgement (v. 5):

> 1. God remembers all the iniquities of his enemies. He has forgotten the sins of his people, because they are thoroughly removed by the blood of Christ. But he will never forget any iniquity of his enemies.
> 2. God will punish sinners exactly in proportion to the evil they have done, according to strict justice

(vv. 6-7). There are no degrees of reward in heaven, but there are degrees of punishment. And the hottest fires of hell's lowest pit are reserved for those who despise the free grace of God and trample under foot the precious blood of Christ revealed in the gospel (Matt. 11:20-24).

3. Divine judgement comes suddenly, swiftly, without warning (v. 8).

4. It is thorough, complete, without mercy (v. 8).

5. God is both willing and able to punish sin (v. 8).

A threefold lamentation (vv. 9-19)

The kings of the earth, the merchantmen of the earth and the seamen of the earth, when they see Babylon fall by the hand of God, will all wail because of her fall.

The kings wail for Babylon (vv. 9-10)

The kings, the mighty men of power and influence in the earth, have lain in the bed of this great harlot for so long that they have come to love her and depend upon her. By yielding to her influence, honouring her name and defending her, they have made themselves rich and powerful. Slick politicians (of all parties) have always used religion to promote themselves. But when these mighty men see their whole religious foundation in ruins, they wail for her.

The merchants wail for her (vv. 11-16)

These merchants represent something more than businessmen. They represent all men and women who set their hearts on the wares and luxuries of this world. When everything they cherish crumbles before them, or becomes worthless in their eyes, they wail in agony (Luke 12:16-21).

Without question there is a direct reference here to false
prophets, preachers who for covetousness make merchan-
dise of men's bodies and souls, bringing them into the slav-
ery of the world's religion to enrich themselves (cf. v. 13;
2 Peter 2:1-3).

The seamen lament for her (vv. 17-19)

Like the kings and merchants, the seamen have spent their
lives seeking the wealth, power, luxury and pleasure of the
world. But when God brings everything to ruins, when men
see all their hopes and desires utterly destroyed, they weep
like babies in torment, with broken hearts. The destruction
of Babylon is the destruction of the world — its religious,
economic, political and philosophical foundations. When
the unbeliever sees everything he has lived for, worked for
and trusted in completely destroyed, he is utterly devas-
tated. Let all be warned: do not lay up treasures on earth
(Matt. 6:19-21). The fashion, the outward appearance and
the glamour of this world are all perishing (1 Cor. 7:31).
Make provision for your immortal soul (Mark 8:36-37).

A cause for great joy (vv. 20-24)

Babylon's fall and the world's destruction are God's just
retribution poured out upon those who have despised and
persecuted his elect throughout history. Therefore, all of
God's elect are called upon to rejoice over her.

This passage teaches us three things about the final destruction of Babylon:

1. It will be total, climatic and irreversible (vv. 21-22)

A mighty angel appears to execute God's judgement upon
Babylon. He picks up a huge millstone. With one mighty,

angry thrust, he hurls it into the sea and says, 'This is what will become of Babylon: it will be hurled into the sea of God's wrath for ever, never to be retrieved.' This wicked world, particularly, this religious world-system, with its leaders and its followers, as the centre of seduction, will perish for ever. Notice the symbolism that is used to express thorough destruction. All false religious comfort and hope, Babylon, will have gone! All joy, symbolized by music, will have gone! All skill, art, talent, craftsmanship and self-satisfaction will have gone! All food, symbolized by the mill, will have gone! All light will have gone! All relationships of love and unity will have gone!

2. It is a matter of strict justice (vv. 23-24)

Babylon's merchants are the men received and made great by the earth, both worldly and religious leaders! By her sorceries, the world has been deceived (Gal. 3:1). Babylon, primarily false religion, has upon her hands the blood of all God's saints and prophets (Luke 11:47-51).

3. It will be a cause for great joy (v. 20)

But why are God's saints called upon to rejoice when the wicked are damned? This joy is not at all a vindictive joy over the torments of personal enemies. It is a righteous agreement with God. It is God's saints taking sides with God, vindicating him in his justice and saying, 'Amen', to all that he does, because of their hearts' agreement with him (Ps. 139:21-22). God's saints will rejoice when God's enemies are destroyed, because God's name and honour will then be vindicated.

41.

Christ praised when the wicked are damned

Revelation 19:1-6

'And after these things I heard a great voice of much people in heaven, saying, Alleluia; Salvation, and glory, and honour, and power, unto the Lord our God: for true and righteous are his judgements: for he hath judged the great whore, which did corrupt the earth with her fornication, and hath avenged the blood of his servants at her hand. And again they said, Alleluia. And her smoke rose up for ever and ever' (Rev. 19:1-3).

Try to picture the scene John has described. Judgement has come. The wicked have been cast into hell. And the saints of God are singing and shouting the praises of God with joy because of his true and righteous judgements upon the wicked. What an awesome scene! As eternity commences, the saints of God in heaven are rejoicing and praising him for his condemnation of the wicked. This passage of Holy Scripture declares this fact most plainly: God's judgement of rebellious sinners, sentencing them to eternal torment, will be a subject of eternal praise among the redeemed.

Who will sing this song?

This song is sung by a great multitude in heaven. It is the same multitude we have seen throughout this book before the throne of God. It is the whole church of God's elect in

heaven (18:20; 19:1-4). This is that elect multitude who sing
the praises of God for his great salvation — the 144,000
sealed ones (7:3-4,9-10). These are the men and women
who have been redeemed by the blood of the Lamb out of
every kindred, tongue, people and nation on the earth, who
praise God for his distinguishing grace in Christ (5:9-10).
These are the blessed dead who have died in the Lord, having kept the commandments of God and the faith of Jesus
(14:3-8,12-13). This is that great multitude in every generation which has lived and died for the Word of God and the
testimony of his grace (6:9-11).

The day of retribution has come and these chosen, redeemed, saved, glorified souls are singing in the knowledge that the very souls for whom they once prayed and
laboured anxiously, with loving hearts, are suffering eternal torment. There is Christ, the Judge, passing sentence
on Jerusalem, for whom he once wept. There is Paul, joining in the song of praise as his kinsmen, for whom he was
willing to die, are enduring eternal punishment. There is
David, singing praise while Absalom, for whom he once
shed bitter tears, is among those cast into hell. All the prophets are singing! All the apostles are singing! All the saints
are singing! All the angels are singing! All are praising God
because of his judgements upon the wicked!

Why will God's elect sing his praises when the wicked are damned?

Obviously, it is not because they love to see human pain,
or because they are mean and vindictive. Rather, it is because in that day, they will have the mind of God. 'The
righteous Lord loveth righteousness.' It is only right for the
righteous God to punish sin and God's people will concur
wholeheartedly in his condemnation of it. God has made
all things for himself, for the glory of his name. All must

serve the cause of his glory. All must bring glory to the God of heaven, either in salvation, or in damnation. All who refuse to trust Christ and be saved by God's free grace must endure the condemnation their sin has brought upon them and in this way bring glory to God. Yes, even the damnation of the wicked will be a source of eternal praise to God because by their eternal ruin wicked men will magnify the justice, majesty and power of God. And the eternal ruin of the wicked in hell will be an eternal reminder to the saints of the debt we owe to God for his matchless grace!

What is the theme of this song? (v. 3)

The word 'Alleluia' means, 'Praise Jehovah!' So the theme of this song is the praise of the Lord our God for all that he is and all that he does. 'Alleluia' is an expression of great joy. It appears that the saints in heaven never grow weary of their heavenly employment. Again and again they sing, 'Alleluia!' 'Amen!' 'Alleluia!' 'Praise the Lord!' It is the great joy of God's saints in heaven to praise God for his wonderful works.

This word, 'Alleluia', is also an expression of admiration and wonder. Every glorious view of Christ, every act of his hand, every word of his mouth, every revelation of his character, every display of his majesty, greatness, power and glory causes the souls of the redeemed to burst out with another song of praise, saying, 'Alleluia,' for his salvation (v. 1), his attributes (v. 1), his judgements (vv. 2-4) and his sovereignty (v. 6).

What is the occasion of the song?

What is the event that causes God's saints to burst out in this joyful praise? Here God's saints are shouting, singing and rejoicing over the fall of Antichrist, Babylon — all false religion. Babylon is the mixing of everything together, stirring it well and calling it Christianity. It is the religion of the world. If other sins are damning their thousands, religion today is damning its tens of thousands. But one of these days God is going to judge once and for all this thing called 'religion', which has corrupted the earth with her fornication and persecuted his saints in every age. In our text, God has finally caught up with religion. And after Antichrist, Babylon and all the promoters and followers of false, man-centred religion are cast into hell, God is still on his throne. The saints are happy about that, and shout, 'Amen! Alleluia!' The world will mourn for ever over Babylon's fall. But the saints of God will rejoice for ever over her fall, for then God will have 'avenged the blood of his servants at her hand'. The people who are singing are the saints of God. The theme of their song is the praise of God. The occasion for their song is the judgement of God.

What does this song teach us?

This song of praise to Christ is a song about God's just condemnation of rebel sinners to the torments of hell. Here God's saints are singing, and singing with joy, at the same time as men and women who refused to bow to and trust the Lord Jesus Christ are suffering eternal damnation. Surely, the fact that this song is recorded upon the pages of inspiration is meant to be a special means of instruction. Here is an awesome fact: when the wicked are damned, the saints will sing. What are we to learn from this fact?

1. There is an appointed Day of Judgement when God will judge all men by the man Christ Jesus (Ps. 7:11-13; 11:5-7; Acts 17:31; 2 Cor. 5:10-11; Heb. 9:27).

The first message of the cross is this: a holy, right-eous and just God must punish sin. God's law must be honoured. His righteousness must be vindicated. And the Judge who will execute wrath upon guilty sinners is that one who was made to be sin and died in the place of sinners, Jesus Christ our Lord (John 5:22).

2. There is a place of eternal torment, where every rebel, every unbeliever, will suffer the wrath of God (Luke 16:23). I don't know what hell is or where hell is. But hell is real, more real than anyone has ever imagined. Hell is a place of endless pain, agony and torment, where men and women suffer for ever the just and righteous retribution of God's holy wrath.

3. The judgement of the wicked and the eternal torments of the damned will take place in the sight of the redeemed (Matt. 25:31-46; Luke 13:28; 16:22-23; Isa. 66:23-24; Rev. 14:10). Hell will be within the very sight of heaven! The wicked will be cast into hell before the eyes of the redeemed! In that awesome day, pastors and congregations will stand face to face be-fore the bar of God and witness one another's con-demnation or acquittal. Parents will be witnesses to the condemnation or acquittal of their children. Chil-dren will stand to witness the condemnation or ac-quittal of their parents. Husbands and wives will wit-ness each other's condemnation or acquittal. And it will be no matter of grief to the righteous to see the wicked condemned, for we shall see their sin for what it is and acknowledge that their condemnation is just. We shall see them condemned (Ps. 91:7-8). We shall see the terror on their faces. We shall hear their screams and cries of agony. Yet we shall not shed a tear. Our tears will be over. Our sorrows will be past (Rev. 21:4). Indeed, when the wicked are cast into hell,

we shall concur with the sentence and say, 'Amen! Alleluia!'

4. The judgement of God upon the wicked, so far from causing grief among the saints, will be a matter of everlasting joy to the redeemed (18:20). God's right-eous judgements will be a matter of endless praise in heaven. We shall sing and shout, 'Hallelujah!' (Exod. 14:30 – 15:1). And the smoke of their torments, rising up for ever, will be cause for endless praise to our God, marking as it does God's final glorious triumph over his enemies, and ours.

42.

Christ our omnipotent, reigning God

Revelation 19:6

'And I heard as it were the voice of a great multitude, and as the voice of many waters, and as the voice of mighty thunderings, saying, Alleluia: for the Lord God omnipotent reigneth' (Rev. 19:6).

This passage refers to that blessed day that is yet to come when all opposition to Christ has been eliminated from the earth, when Babylon has been cast into the sea of God's wrath. It refers to that day when 'The kingdoms of this world become the kingdoms of our Lord and his Christ', when the knowledge of the Lord will cover the earth as the waters cover the sea, and 'Nations shall learn war no more.' But the doctrine taught in our text is a blessed truth in all ages: 'The Lord God omnipotent reigneth!' For ever, before the worlds were made and for ever after the worlds are dissolved, at all times and in all places, from the beginning to the end, 'The Lord God omnipotent reigneth!' All God's saints, in all ages, rejoice to sing with unison this great Hallelujah chorus: 'Alleluia, for the Lord God omnipotent reigneth!'

'The Lord God omnipotent' refers to the Lord Jesus Christ, our Saviour. Many of the heathen religions of the world teach that God reigns. The Jews firmly hold to the truth that God reigns. But the doctrine of the Bible, the doctrine of the gospel, the doctrine of this text is that the Lord God omnipotent, the triune Godhead, exercises his sovereign dominion and government over all the universe in the person of his Son, Jesus Christ, our Saviour. 'The Father loveth the Son, and hath given all things into his hand' (John 3:35). Our Lord Jesus assured his disciples, 'All power is given unto me in heaven and in earth' (Matt. 28:18). Jesus Christ has taken unto himself, by divine right and by merit of his obedience as the sinner's substitute, all power, authority and dominion. He has the right to reign as sovereign, absolute Lord over all things because he is God. And as a man he earned the right to reign over all things by his obedience unto death. Christ's universal dominion is the effect and reward of his accomplished redemption. The sovereign dominion of the Lord Jesus Christ is a matter of joyful, heartfelt praise among the redeemed.

Who is this great King?

I have already said that this King is Jesus Christ, the Son of God, the incarnate God-man, the mediator between God and men. He is the very same man who died as the sinner's substitute, the one whom the Jews crucified. He is the 'faithful and true witness'. He is the Lamb of God. 'His name is called the Word of God.' He is 'King of kings and Lord of lords'. This great King is our Saviour. But let it never be forgotten that this man is 'the Lord God omnipotent'! His name is El-Shaddai, God Almighty. He is the Lord Jehovah with whom is everlasting strength (Isa. 26:4). He is the God with whom all things are possible and nothing is impossible (Matt. 19:26; Luke 1:37; Ps. 139:14-17).

Jesus Christ is, himself, the eternal God

He is not a god, or one like unto God, or a creature of God. He *is* God manifest in the flesh (1 Tim. 3:16; Col. 2:9; Rom. 9:5; 1 Tim. 6:14-16). We worship one God in the trinity of his sacred persons (1 John 5:7). We worship, trust and love the Father, the Son and the Holy Spirit. But we recognize that we have no knowledge of God the Father, Son and Holy Spirit except as they are revealed in the person and work of Christ, our divine mediator (John 1:18; Heb. 1:1-3). All that the Father says or reveals he says and reveals by the Son. All that the Father possesses or gives is in Christ the Son. All that the Father does, he does through the Son. All that the Father receives from his creatures, he receives through the Son. As for the Holy Spirit, he is the Spirit of Christ, leads men to Christ, speaks only of Christ and magnifies none but Christ. The holy, triune God has put all things in the hands of Jesus Christ, the mediator, that he might have all honour, pre-eminence and glory (Matt. 11:27; John 5:19-24; 14:6-9; Col. 1:17-18).

This great God is the one who lived, died, arose, intercedes and reigns in heaven as our Saviour. Our Saviour is, and must be, both God and man in one glorious, indivisible person. Were he not man, his work could not be imputed to man. Were he not God, his work could not be worthy of, or satisfy, God. God came into this world as a man to save men (Matt. 1:21-23). God lived as a man in perfect righteousness to establish righteousness for men (Isa. 42:4). God died upon the cross as a man, under the wrath of God, to satisfy the justice of God and put away the sins of men (Acts 20:28; Heb. 9:24). God arose from the tomb in the body of a man, ascended back to heaven and reigns upon the throne of glory for the salvation of men (Heb. 10:5-14). Our great King is God. And our great God is a man! His name is Immanuel. He is one of us, bone of our bone and flesh of our flesh (1 John 1:1-3).

Our God, Jesus Christ, is omnipotent

He has all power. Therefore, he is able to do whatever he is pleased to do in all things. And he always does exactly that which pleases him (Ps. 115:3; 135:6; Isa. 46:9-11).

Omnipotence is essential to divinity. A weak, helpless, frustrated, defeated God is an absurdity. If there is anything God cannot do, which is consistent with his nature, if there is any power greater than his power, any will greater than his will, any desire of his being that he does not satisfy, any purpose that he does not accomplish — then God is dead, there is no God, the universe is in chaos and man is without hope! A god who is not omnipotent is no God at all. Only a fool would worship, trust and serve a weak god. We worship the sovereign, eternal, unchangeable, omnipotent God of glory, Jesus Christ!

You can trust an omnipotent God, for 'None can stay his hand, or say unto him, What doest thou?' (Dan. 4:35). He created the world out of nothing, by his omnipotent word (Gen. 1:1; Isa. 45:12; John 1:1-3; Heb. 11:3). He upholds, sustains and rules the world, by his omnipotent power (Col. 1:16-17; Heb. 1:3). He saves sinners by his omnipotent grace (Ps. 65:4; 110:3; 1 Peter 1:5). This is our great King, Jesus Christ, 'the Lord God omnipotent'. We rejoice in him. He is God. He is man. He is the omnipotent God-man, in whom we safely trust.

How did he come to be such a King?

Without question, the Lord Jesus Christ has always been the King of the universe. His kingdom is an everlasting kingdom. He is King by divine right, because he is God. He is King by divine decree, because he was ordained by God before time began to be a mediator King in the covenant of grace. And he is King over all things, by right as the Creator and Owner of all things. But this text speaks specifically of Christ in his mediatorial character as the King, Ruler and sovereign Monarch of all the universe. As our mediator, the Lord Jesus Christ earned the right of sovereign dominion over all things by his obedience to God as a man (Ps. 2:6-8; Isa. 53:9-12; Dan. 7:13-14; John 17:2; Acts 2:29-36;

5:31; Rom. 14:9; Phil. 2:9-11). Our Lord's government of the universe in the nature of man is the reward of his obedience unto death as our substitute.

He lived to establish righteousness for us. He died to satisfy justice for us. He rose from the dead to demonstrate the accomplishment of redemption by his one great sacrifice for sin. He reigns in heaven over all flesh to apply the benefits of his obedience to God's elect, by the effectual grace of his Spirit. He will come again to gather his redeemed ones to himself in resurrection glory. And in the end, Christ the Mediator will present all his people before the throne of God in perfect salvation (1 Cor. 15:24; Jude 24-25). Then the purpose of God in the covenant of grace will be complete.

What is the extent of our Lord's dominion?

'The Lord God omnipotent reigneth!' The Lord Jesus Christ reigns as sovereign King today! The text does not say, 'The Lord God omnipotent will begin to reign.' It says, 'He reigneth!' The fall of Babylon is not the beginning of his reign, but the consummation of his reign. We are not waiting for some future age when Christ will become a King. Christ is King today. He reigns as King today over all things.

Heaven

The Lord Jesus reigns in heaven with undisputed sway. He is seated now at the right hand of the Majesty on high. There, in heaven's glory, Immanuel reigns as King (Heb. 1:3; 10:12-13). All the holy angels, seraphim and cherubim, bow before his august throne with delight, sing his praise and rush to do his will (Isa. 6:1-7). All the redeemed of the Lord, those spirits of just men made perfect, delight to honour, adore, worship and serve Christ as their rightful King. In the splendours of the celestial worlds, one spot transcends all others in beauty, glory and praise. And that spot is the throne of grace upon which Christ sits as King. But do not imagine, as so many do, that our Lord's dominion is limited to the world above.

Earth

The Lord Jesus Christ reigns today as sovereign Monarch over all the earth (Isa. 40:12-31; 45:5-12; Dan. 4:35-37). There is absolutely nothing and no one in the world which is not under the absolute rule of the Lord Jesus Christ. He is King everywhere and over all things. Our Saviour is the King! Our God is in charge! (Rom. 11:36). He rules over all the physical world (Nahum 1:3; Exod. 9:29; Matt. 5:45; Gen. 41:32; Amos 4:7; Acts 14:17); all the animal world (Gen. 31:9; Ps. 104:21; Dan. 6:22; Matt. 6:26; 10:29); every nation in the world (1 Chr. 16:31; Ps. 33:10; 47:7; Dan. 2:21; 4:17; Amos 3:6); and all men in this world (Exod. 11:7; Ps. 37:23; Prov. 16:9; 21:1). Even the evil deeds of evil men are under our Lord's dominion (Ps. 76:10; Exod. 14:17; 2 Sam. 16:10-11; John 19:11; Acts 2:23; 4:27-28).

Hell and the powers of darkness

Even the kingdom of darkness and hell itself is under the total dominion of our Lord Jesus Christ. He holds the keys of death and of hell. He reigns in the regions of the damned, over the demons of hell and over the prince of darkness. Satan is under his control and acts as his instrument (Job 1:6-12; 2:1-10; 2 Cor. 12:7). The demons must obey when he commands (Matt. 8:28-32; Mark 1:23-27). From the bottomless pit to the highest heaven, Jesus Christ reigns as King. 'The Lord God omnipotent reigneth!'

The hearts of his people

Particularly, Christ is King in Zion. He is the Sovereign over everything, but he is acknowledged as King in Zion. Not only does he reign in his church and in the hearts of his own people by right, but he also reigns with the full consent of his subjects (Matt. 23:8-10). Every believer is a voluntary bond-slave to Christ as his King. As John Newton says, 'He reigns in the hearts of his people. There he writes his precepts, impresses his image, and erects his throne; ruling them, not merely by an outward law, but by an inward secret influence, breathing his own life and Spirit into them; so that their obedience becomes, as it were, natural, pleasurable, and its own reward. By the discoveries he affords them of his love, he wins their affections, captivates their wills, and enlightens their understandings. They derive from him the "spirit of power, of love, and of a sound mind", and run with alacrity in the way of his commandments.'

What is the purpose of his reign?

The object of Christ in his sovereign, universal rule of all things is the eternal good of his elect (Rom. 8:28). 'The Lord God omnipotent reigneth,' so that he may accomplish his eternal purpose of grace towards his chosen, redeemed people (John 17:2). Let him do what he deems good, for what he does is good, always good, only good and eternally good for his elect. How we ought to trust him! (Prov. 3:4-6). He loves us. He lived for us. He died for us. He reigns for us. We can trust a King whose throne is erected and dedicated for our good!

43.

The Lamb and his wife

Revelation 19:7-10

'Let us be glad and rejoice, and give honour to him: for the marriage of the Lamb is come, and his wife hath made herself ready' (Rev. 19:7).

Revelation 19:7-10 describes that blessed, glorious day when the marriage of Christ and his chosen bride, the church of the living God, which he purchased with his own blood, will be fully consummated. When Babylon has fallen, when the wicked and unbelieving have been destroyed by the power of his wrath, in the end of the world, God's elect will be gathered to the great marriage supper of the Lamb and will be publicly united to Christ our Husband in perfection (Eph. 5:25-27). This is what is described in Revelation 19:7-10.

Throughout the Scriptures the relationship of a bridegroom and his bride is used to portray that between Christ and his church (Isa. 50:1; 54:1; 62:5; Jer. 2:32; Hosea 2:19-20; Matt. 9:15; John 3:29; 2 Cor. 11:2; Eph. 5:32; Rev. 21:9). In fact, the marriage of a man and woman was intended from the beginning to be a picture and type of the union of Christ and his bride, the church.

Marriage customs in Bible times

William Hendriksen helps us in our understanding of this majestic passage of Scripture by describing the marriage customs prevalent among the Jews during the time in which the apostle John lived. Hendriksen tells us that in a typical Jewish marriage there were four distinct elements.

1. The betrothal

This might be compared to engagement as we know it today, but it was much more binding. In the betrothal the terms of the marriage were publicly accepted and God's blessings were pronounced upon the union. From the day of the betrothal the man and woman were looked upon as husband and wife. They were legally married (Matt. 1:18-19).

2. The interval

There was an interval between the betrothal date and the wedding feast. Sometimes this interval was very long and sometimes very short. During this interval, the groom paid a dowry to the bride's father for the honour of receiving her hand in marriage (Gen. 34:12). The dowry might be paid in money, cattle, property, or even service (Gen. 29:20).

3. The wedding procession

At the close of the interval, the bride would prepare and adorn herself for her wedding. The groom, arrayed in his finest garments and accompanied by his friends, would go in a grand procession to the home of his bride, singing as they went. Once he received his bride, they would return in another grand procession, either to his or to his father's home (Matt. 25:1; John 3:29; S. of S. 3:6-11).

4. The wedding feast

The wedding feast was a lavish, extravagant banquet, provided entirely by the groom and his father (Matt. 22:2-4).
Usually these marriage suppers would be celebrations lasting at least seven days. At the wedding feast the bride and
groom were publicly and permanently united. It is the wedding feast itself which is described in Revelation 19:7-10.
This is no ordinary wedding feast, but 'the marriage supper of the Lamb'. Here we are informed that there is a day
appointed when the Lord Jesus Christ will gather his bride
out of the world and bring her into his Father's house for a
glorious everlasting wedding feast.

The marriage of the Lamb

The marriage of the Lamb is presented to us as a matter of
great joy in heaven (v. 7). Everything in heaven has been
anticipating this great event since the beginning of time.
When it finally comes, the angels will call for all the heavenly hosts (elect angels and saved sinners) to rejoice and
give honour to Christ, the Lamb of God. God the Father
planned everything from eternity for this great day. God
the Spirit is the earnest of this day in the hearts of his saints.
God the Son sees this great day as the day of his joy and
satisfaction. The angels of heaven and the glorified spirits
of the redeemed anxiously await this great day. And God's
saints living upon the earth all live in the blessed hope of
this glorious day.

Today, the church is betrothed to Christ (2 Cor. 11:2)

Though the marriage has not yet been brought to this glorious consummation, our union with the Son of God is a
matter of legal record in heaven. Christ is our lawful

Husband and we are his lawful, betrothed wife. He pledged his troth to us in eternity past in the everlasting covenant of grace (Hosea 2:16 – 3:3). Having betrothed himself to us before the foundation of the world, our dear Husband paid a dowry for his bride, the church. The dowry was his own lifeblood, paid to satisfy the debt we owed to God's offended justice.

> From heav'n he came and sought us
> To be his holy bride,
> With his own blood he bought us,
> And for our life he died!

As Christ pledged his troth to us in eternity, so we who believe pledge our troth to him in faith. Faith in Christ is nothing less than the wilful, deliberate consecration of our hearts to him (Rom. 7:4). By faith we are wedded to the Son of God.

This age in which we now live is the interval of separation

Our Saviour has gone to prepare a place for us in the Father's house. It was expedient for us that he go away. But as soon as the appointed time of separation is over, Christ Jesus will come again to receive us unto himself (John 14:1-3; 16:7). During this interval, Christ's chosen bride must make herself ready. But how do fallen, sinful men and women make themselves ready for marriage to the Son of God? They bathe themselves in the fountain of his blood and put on his robe of righteousness by faith.

At the end of time Christ will come in a great, glorious procession from heaven, accompanied by his heavenly angels, to receive his bride, the church (Matt. 25:31-34). He will gather the bodies of his sleeping saints and those who are yet living upon the earth unto himself. Then the wedding feast will begin. It is a feast that will last not for a

week or two, but for eternity! This feast will be the climax
of God's everlasting purpose of grace. It will be a holy,
blessed, everlasting, perfect union of Christ and his church,
an endless, joyous honeymoon for the Son of God and his
bride. All the promises of God in the gospel will be fully
realized in this great wedding feast.

The beauty of the bride

The bride's beauty is displayed in verse 8. Before the marriage supper takes place, the bride must be prepared. This
is no ordinary bride. Her attire is no ordinary attire. Her
beauty is no ordinary beauty. She has no natural beauty,
but God's sovereign grace has made her beautiful. Here is a
great contrast: the great harlot (Babylon — the false church,
representing all false religion) was arrayed in the gaudy
tapestry of the world (Rev. 17:4); but the bride of Christ is
arrayed in garments of purity, righteousness and light —
the garments of salvation.

The wedding garment

Her wedding garment of 'fine linen, clean and white' is
called 'the righteousness of saints'. This garment does not
represent the personal righteousness and good works of
believers (see Isa. 64:6). Without question, God's saints do
walk in righteousness and perform good works as the general tenor of their life in Christ, but these things have
nothing to do with our acceptance with God. Our righteousness cannot be compared to 'fine linen, clean and
white'.

This 'fine linen, clean and white,' represents the righteousness of Christ, given to all believers by God's sovereign grace (Isa. 61:10; Ezek. 16:6-14; Zech. 3:1-5). Christ's
righteousness is imputed to his people in justification (Rom.

4:3-5,22-24), and his righteous nature is imparted to them
in regeneration (Col. 1:27; 2 Peter 1:4; 1 John 3:5-9).

The blessedness of the called

This blessedness is declared in verse 9. Many are bidden
to the marriage by the preaching of the gospel. But there is
no blessedness in that outward call. In fact, to be bidden
and yet refuse to come will only add to one's eternal condemnation (Luke 14:15-24). However, those who are 'the
called', being compelled by God's irresistible grace, effectually called by the sovereign power of the Holy Spirit to
come to 'the marriage supper of the Lamb', are here pronounced 'blessed'. And blessed they are! Grace made them
willing to come who otherwise would never have come
(Ps. 65:4; 110:3). Their sins are all washed away (Jer. 50:20).
They have on the wedding garment of Christ's imputed
righteousness.

And with his spotless garments on
They are as holy as God's own Son!

In Christ, because of Christ, they are worthy of heaven's
glory (Col. 1:12). 'These are the true sayings of God.'

The testimony of Holy Scripture

The testimony of Holy Scripture must always be kept and
followed (v. 10). Filled with wonder and ecstasy, John fell
down to worship the one who showed him these things.
Perhaps he mistook the glorified messenger for his glorified Lord. We are not told. But he was sharply rebuked for
his error. In the rebuke John received, four things are clearly
taught:

1. God alone is to be worshipped, never angels or men.

2. All true believers are one in Christ and equal in him.

3. All God's servants in every age proclaim one message: 'the testimony of Jesus'. We preach Christ!

4. The spirit, the inner content, of all Scripture is the testimony of the Lord Jesus Christ (John 5:39; Luke 24:27,44-47).

Christ crucified is 'all the counsel of God' (1 Cor. 2:2; Acts 20:27). The purpose of Holy Scripture is to show chosen sinners who Christ is and what he has done and bring them to this great wedding feast robed in his righteousness.

44.

The marriage supper of the Lamb

Revelation 19:7-9

'Let us be glad and rejoice, and give honour to him: for the marriage of the Lamb is come, and his wife hath made herself ready. And to her was granted that she should be arrayed in fine linen, clean and white: for the fine linen is the righteousness of saints. And he saith unto me, Write, Blessed are they which are called unto the marriage supper of the Lamb. And he saith unto me, These are the true sayings of God' (Rev. 19:7-9).

These verses do not explain this glorious event; they only describe the glory of it. The fact that there will be a marriage supper is revealed. That it will be a glorious, everlasting celebration of salvation completed is evident. But the details are hidden from our eyes for now. We shall not pry into that which God has not revealed, but it will be profitable for our hearts reverently to rehearse and meditate upon that which he has revealed.

In the last day there will be a public wedding of Christ and his church, a blessed and eternal union in which Christ and his people will be made perfectly one. This is called 'the marriage supper of the Lamb'.

This marriage of the church to Christ will be the final consummation of the whole work of redemption. The whole church of Christ will be perfectly united to her divine Husband, and they will be perfectly one for ever, even as the Son is one with the Father. That defies understanding, explanation, or even imagination. But it is plainly revealed in the Word of God that we shall for ever be perfectly one with our Redeemer, as really and truly one with him as he is one with the Father! (See John 17:20-23).

The procession

When the Lord Jesus comes the second time with power and great glory to marry his beloved Bride, there will be a grand and glorious series of events which will immediately precede 'the marriage supper of the Lamb'. These events are recorded in verses 1-6. What will happen just before the great wedding? What are the events leading up to it?

1. The destruction of Babylon, the harlot church (vv. 1-2)

Actually, the destruction of Babylon is recorded in Revelation 18. Here it is celebrated — yes, celebrated — by all the saints of God and all the heavenly angels. As we have already seen, Babylon represents all false religion. Any church which mixes anything with the blood and righteousness of Christ for the sinner's acceptance with God is a harlot, apostate church. Any church that mixes anything with the grace of God for the salvation of sinners is a harlot church. Salvation by grace alone, through the merits of Christ's righteousness and shed blood, is the one essential criteria for all true Christianity. By this doctrine every church stands or falls. The lifeblood of God's church is the precious blood of Christ's effectual atonement for sin.

The sooner Babylon falls, the better. Babylon constantly makes war with the Lamb (17:14). Her most vile, obnoxious weapons of warfare are now, and always have been, the doctrines of free will, salvation by works, ceremonialism and legalism. The great harlot is always opposed to pure, free, sovereign grace. She always mixes something with faith, and even makes faith itself a meritorious work of the flesh by which men save themselves. Be warned: those who point men anywhere away from Christ for anything, point men to Antichrist, Babylon and destruction. Everything that is set up in opposition to Christ's one, great, all-sufficient, effectual sacrifice for sin must be cast down to hell. In the church of God, Christ is all. Any church that makes Christ less than everything is a harlot church, full of corruption, fornication and wickedness. From hell she arose, and to hell she must go! The glory and the honour of the true church of Christ will be known only when Babylon, the harlot church, is cast into hell.

2. A call to worship (v. 5)

We are not told whose voice this is, so it is best not to guess. But the one speaking calls on everybody to 'praise our God'. And we shall indeed praise him (v. 6). We shall praise him for the vindication of his justice, his truth, his saints, his Son and his throne.

These are the things which will immediately precede 'the marriage supper of the Lamb'. It will be a glorious procession pointing everybody to the Bridegroom, our Lord Jesus Christ. In this wedding procession it is not the bride, but the Bridegroom, who gets all the attention. It is not the bride, but the Bridegroom, who is honoured, adored and praised.

Once the grand and glorious procession is over, the Lamb and his wife will come together for their wedding.

The wedding

'Let us be glad and rejoice, and give honour to him: for the marriage of the Lamb is come.' We frequently hear about this marriage supper. It is mentioned many times in the Scriptures. But many people have very vague, not to say perverted, ideas about it. While we cannot be sure about everything that is going to happen on that great day, we can be certain of the meaning of this long-awaited event.

1. It is the glorious consummation of the everlasting covenant

It is the result of the Father's gift to his Son in the eternal covenant of grace (Ps. 2:8; 89:23-29; John 17:6,24). God the Father chose to save some of Adam's race, and those chosen ones were given to Christ, as a mediator and surety, to save (John 6:37-40). For those elect ones, Christ entered into a covenant of redemption, in which he pledged himself in due time to assume their nature, establish righteousness on their behalf, pay their debt, give them life and bring them to heaven in glorious union with himself! That which was arranged and settled by the triune God in eternity, in the covenant of his grace, is brought to its ultimate end when the Lamb takes all that the Father gave him into glorious, perfect union with himself.

2. It is the blessed consummation of our hearts' betrothal to Christ

Though Christ betrothed himself to us in eternity past, we betrothed ourselves to him in time, when we believed him. Faith is the betrothal, the commitment of our hearts to Christ as our beloved Husband. When the Spirit of God showed us the beauty of Christ and the glory of his grace, he conquered our hearts (Ps. 65:4). He made us willing to commit ourselves to Christ as our Husband. Though we are betrothed to Christ, he has not yet brought us to the Father's house. But our beloved Husband will surely come and bring us to his Father's house, when all things are ready (John 14:1-4).

3. It will be the perfecting of his body, the church (Eph. 4:12-13)

Today, our Lord is still forming his church, his body, his bride. It is not yet complete. Even the church in heaven is not yet perfect. It is written, 'They without us should not be made perfect' (Heb. 11:40). But there is a day of perfection coming! That will be the day of our home-going. That will be the day of our resurrection (1 Cor. 15:51-58), glorification (Rom. 8:30; 1 John 3:2) and presentation (Eph. 5:25-27). That will be the day of our coronation (Rev. 2:10; Ps. 45:11-17). The church is the bride of the great King. He will set a crown upon her head and make all creation bow at her feet, for the honour he has put upon her. And that will be a day of glory and bliss which will never end (Rev. 21:1-7).

The Bridegroom

Try to fix your mind upon the Bridegroom, our Lord Jesus Christ. On that most glorious of days, he will appear in his most glorious, most honourable, most dazzling character. What will it be? How will he appear? This is the marriage supper of the Creator, the King, the Ruler, the Sustainer, the Governor, the God of the universe. But when he comes to show forth all the splendour and glory of his being, he appears as 'the Lamb'! It is 'the marriage supper of the Lamb'!

Throughout the book of Revelation, our Lord is worshipped as 'the Lamb'. He is repeatedly referred to by this name. The Lamb is the sacrifice by which justice is satisfied and sin is put away (John 1:29). Whenever we read of Christ, or see Christ, as 'the Lamb', it is to remind us of his sufferings and death in our place as our great substitute to put away our sin.

The first time we looked to him, we looked to him as 'the Lamb'. We are looking to him now as 'the Lamb'. And when we see him as he is, in all the glory of his being, we shall see him as 'the Lamb'. Our Saviour was the Lamb slain in the eternal covenant. It was as the Lamb that our Lord proved his love for us. It was as the Lamb that our Saviour won our hearts and first caused us to love him. As the Lamb our Lord Jesus came into the closest possible union with us. When he was numbered with the transgressors, the Son of God came nearer to us than at any other time! (2 Cor. 5:21; Ps. 40:12). We never feel nearer to, or more perfectly one with, the Son of God than when we see him as the Lamb. And when we see our dear Saviour on his glorious wedding day and ours, we shall be wedded to him, worship him, adore him and embrace him as the Lamb! This will be heaven! This will be an endless feast of love! This will be the glory of God.

The bride

As the beauty of the bride is described we must not fail to observe that the description is really of the beauty and the glory of the Lamb. Her beauty is his beauty, which he has put upon her. 'His wife hath made herself ready. And to her was granted that she should be arrayed in fine linen, clean and white: for the fine linen is the righteousness (literally, righteousnesses) of the saints.'

1. The bride prepared herself for this glorious event

We are told, 'His wife hath made herself ready.' What does that mean? How do we make ourselves ready for heaven's glory? She has willingly, of her own accord, given herself to Christ, to be his for ever. She has come out of Babylon

and put away from herself the corruptions of the great harlot. She has washed herself from all uncleanness in the
fountain of his blood. And she has put on the Lord Jesus
Christ by faith.

2. Her garments were given to her

But notice that her gorgeous apparel was given to her as a
free gift of sovereign grace, as a royal grant from the King of
heaven. All that she carries with her to heaven was given
to her. All that she wears was given to her. She brings
nothing of her own, and wears nothing of her own. In fact,
she is there altogether by the grant of heaven. The garment
she wears is 'the righteousnesses' of the saints. I grant that
the word 'righteousness' should be written in the plural,
but I do not grant that it should read, 'the righteous deeds
of the saints'. 'The righteousnesses of the saints' are all
aspects of the righteousness of Christ given to us by God's
almighty grace:

> There is the righteousness of our forgiveness by
> the blood of Christ (Rom. 3:24-26; 1 John 1:9) — *a
> righteous pardon*!
> There is the righteousness of our justification and
> acceptance with God by the imputation of Christ's
> righteous obedience to us (Rom. 5:19) — *a righteous
> robe*!
> And there is the righteousness of our new nature,
> the righteous nature of Christ imparted to us in re-
> generation (2 Peter 1:4; 1 John 3:8-9) — *a righteous
> nature*!

Here we wear a filthy robe of sinful flesh. But there we
shall wear the robe of perfect righteousness, even the
righteousnesses of the saints, without spot or wrinkle. This
is the free gift of God's almighty grace.

This is 'the marriage supper of the Lamb.' Will you be there? I bid you come to the marriage. There is plenty of room. But you dare not come without the wedding garment. May God grant to you 'the righteousness of the saints', which is the pardon of sin by the blood of Christ, perfect righteousness by divine imputation and eternal life by the power of his grace.

45.
Christ the man of war

Revelation 19:11-16

'And I saw heaven opened, and behold a white horse; and he that sat upon him was called Faithful and True, and in righteousness he doth judge and make war' (Rev. 19:11).

When Moses saw Pharaoh and his armies drowned in the Red Sea and the people of God standing safely upon the shores of deliverance, he sang, 'The LORD is a man of war' (Exod. 15:3). How often our Saviour proves himself to be just that!

In the Garden of Eden our Lord foiled the schemes of the old serpent, and out of the Fall accomplished his own purpose, promising redemption to the fallen pair (Gen. 3:15; Isa. 14:24,26-27). Throughout the history of the Old Testament we see our great God illustrating his redemptive purpose in the deliverances of the chosen nation from the hands of their enemies. Then, at last, Christ came to deliver and save his people from sin, Satan and the curse of the law (Matt. 1:21). In the wilderness of temptation Christ Jesus overcame the temptations of the devil (Matt. 4:1-11). He met the accuser in Gethsemane again and overcame his power (Matt. 26:38-46). Then, at the appointed hour, the Son of God thoroughly routed his enemy and ours, stripped him of his possessions and accomplished redemption for God's elect by his death upon the cross as their substitute

(John 12:31-33; Rev. 20:1-6). Having accomplished eternal redemption for us, the Lord Jesus Christ took away our sins and carried the prince of darkness into everlasting captivity. He rose on high, was enthroned as the King of glory, and reigns for ever to save his redeemed ones (Ps. 68:18-20).

Yet, even now, 'The LORD is a man of war.' He rides forth in majesty, power and great glory, 'conquering and [still] to conquer' (Rev. 6:2). The Son of God has a controversy with his fallen creatures. The controversy is over his lordship. But the end of that controversy is not in doubt. It is written: 'His foes shall become his footstool.' Either by the irresistible power of his grace, or by the irresistible power of his wrath, King Jesus will defeat all his enemies and cause them to bow before his throne, acknowledging that it is right for him to be Lord (Ps. 89:21-25; Isa. 45:20-25; Phil. 2:9-11). In Revelation 19:11-16 John sees 'heaven opened'. Not a window, or a door, but heaven itself is opened, and the Lord Jesus Christ comes forth riding upon a white charger, like a mighty man of war. Four things are clearly revealed in this symbolic picture.

Christ is a mighty conqueror (vv. 11-13)

John had seen the Lord Jesus in his humiliation and even leaned upon his breast. Now he sees Christ in his glory as the Captain of our salvation, the King of kings and Lord of lords. But he sees a warfare on the earth. The seed of the woman and that of the serpent are in conflict. Truth and error are engaged against one another. The kingdom of light and the kingdom of darkness are involved in a war. Sometimes, when we see this warfare, we tremble. But John saw and described it from heaven's vantage-point. He wrote down what he saw that we might take courage. If we are soldiers enlisted under the banner of Christ, pledged to the

advancement of truth, sworn to the precious blood of atonement, the glorious doctrines of the gospel and the honour
of Christ, it will do us good to rise with John above the
mists of the earth and see this warfare from heaven's viewpoint. Though the battle must rage until Armageddon is
over, there is no cause for fear. The ark of God is safe. The
cause of Christ is secure. The church of the living God will
overcome her enemies. The truth of God will prevail.

Our mighty Saviour comes forth riding upon a white horse

Of course, the picture is purely symbolical. The Son of God
does not ride through the air upon a white horse! This picture of Christ charging his foes upon a white horse suggests four things:

　　1. Christ Jesus rides forth upon a white horse as
　　the leader of a great army because he is highly hon-
　　oured in heaven. God the Father has given him the
　　place of highest honour (Phil. 2:9-10; Col. 1:18). The
　　holy angels extol him above all others (Rev. 5:11-12).
　　All the saints in heaven and on earth honour Christ
　　as precious above all (1 Peter 2:7).
　　2. This white horse represents our Saviour's power
　　and dominion as our great Captain (John 17:2). The
　　horse is a symbol of power (Job 39:19-25).
　　3. The horse also symbolizes speed (Zech. 10:3).
　　The Word of God runs swiftly through the earth ac-
　　cording to his sovereign will. He only wills it, and
　　his gospel is spread to the uttermost parts of the earth.
　　The church of God is made a swift running horse for
　　the spread of the gospel.
　　4. This white horse represents the certain victory
　　of our Saviour (Rev. 6:2). The Lion of the tribe of Judah
　　will indeed prevail!

He is as good as he is great

Here is a conquering man of war who is altogether good. He who is vested with total power is perfectly good.

He is called 'Faithful and True'. He is faithful and true to his Father, to fulfil all his covenant engagements; to his people, to fulfil every word of promise; and to his enemies, to fulfil every threat of wrath against them.

His warfare is carried on in righteousness: 'In righteousness he doth judge and make war.' As C. H. Spurgeon says, 'Christ's kingdom needs no deception: the plainest speech and clearest truth — these are the weapons of our warfare.' The Son of God defeated Satan by bringing in everlasting righteousness. He conquers the hearts of chosen sinners by the proclamation of righteousness in the gospel. And on the last day, he will judge everyone in perfect righteousness.

'His eyes were as a flame of fire', to discover the hearts of men, to understand the plots of Satan and all his enemies, to consume those who oppose him and to melt the hearts of his people (Luke 22:61). Those flaming eyes represent the purity of our Lord in all his being and in all his works.

'And on his head were many crowns.' Our mighty defender is the crowned King of the universe. He wears the crown of creation (Col. 1:16-19), the crown of providence (Rom. 14:9) and the crown of grace (John 5:21). Christ rules everywhere. He rules everyone. He rules everything. And he rules always!

His clothing is glorious

'He was clothed with a vesture dipped in blood.' Whenever we think about our great God and Saviour, believers rejoice to see his whole being dipped in blood. We must never think about him, or anything he does, without seeing him dipped in blood. Our Shepherd is a blood-red Shepherd. Our great Prophet is one whose words are written in his own blood. Our King wears a crown won by his own blood. Our heavenly Advocate pleads his blood for us at the throne of God. The Lord Jesus Christ is seen best, and seen in his truest glory, when he is seen as the sin-atoning sacrifice for God's elect. It is impossible to understand anything about him or about his works until he is seen as one whose 'vesture [is] dipped in blood'. The greatest thing he ever did, his greatest glory and the key to understanding both who he is and what he does, is revealed in these words: 'He laid down his life for us' (1 John 3:16). We cannot think, talk, sing, or preach too much about his blood. His blood is our life. His blood is our gospel. His blood is that which attracts sinners to him (John 12:32). His blood is our motive and example (1 Peter 2:21-24).

His name sets him apart from all others

'He had a name written that no man knew, but he himself' (v. 12). 'And his name is called The Word of God' (v. 13). Those two statements do not contradict one another. Our Saviour himself declared, 'No man knoweth the Son, but the Father' (Matt. 11:26). Christ is called 'the Word of God' because he is the embodiment and revelation of the glorious, triune God (John 1:1-3,14-18; Col. 2:9-10). He sets before us, in human form, the mind, will, heart, nature and glory of God. We know these things. Yet we recognize such mysterious and majestic mystery in him that we readily acknowledge our ignorance concerning him. Our great Saviour is unspeakably, unknowably glorious. Who can understand and know the mystery of his person, the depth of his love, the wonder of his redemption, the treasure of his grace, or the blessedness of his peace?

The army he leads

The armies that follow him are the saints of God, sinners saved by the great man of war (v. 14). 'These are they which follow the Lamb whithersoever he goeth' (Rev. 14:4). The church of God is a mighty army, steadily advancing through this world under the direction of Christ himself.

God's church marches as many armies under one great Captain

Though we are one in Christ, the church of God scattered throughout the earth, through all the ages of time, is made up of many armies. At any one time, in any given place, it seems to be a small army of rag-tag nobodies. But God's church is many. And this army is strong beyond imagination. All the battalions of Christ's kingdom are engaged under one banner (the cross), fight under the direction of one King (Christ) and fight for one cause (the glory of God).

All who follow Christ are mounted, like him, upon white horses

As he fares, so they fare, for they are all one with him. These white horses mean the same thing here as when we see Christ himself upon a white horse. They represent high honour, great power, wonderful speed and certain victory.

All who follow Christ in this mighty army are well armed

They have neither sword, nor spear, nor bow, nor gun. They do not even have a little weapon hidden away in case of an emergency. There are no emergencies for Christ and his people! Their only armour is the bright white righteousness of Christ. They are 'clothed with fine linen, white and clean'. Christ is our strength, our defence, our refuge and our shield. We march with him through this world, in hostile

enemy territory. But we are never the ones who do battle.
We are engaged in the warfare, yes, but 'The battle is the
Lord's' (2 Chr. 20:15-17). Therefore, we are assured and
confident of victory (Rom. 8:36-39). Until our Captain is
taken, not one of his recruits can fall (Matt. 16:18).

> Rejoice, believer, in the Lord,
> Who makes your cause his own;
> The hope that's built upon his Word
> Cannot be overthrown!
> As surely as he overcame
> And triumphed once for you,
> So surely you that love his name
> Shall triumph in him too!

The warfare he wages

The warfare he wages is altogether spiritual (v. 15). As we
look through the ranks of these great armies, there is not
one weapon among them. But there is a sword, not in the
hand, but in the mouth of our great man of war, the Lord
Jesus Christ. The sword by which our Saviour conquers
the hearts of men is the gospel of his grace (Heb. 4:12). Our
warfare is not physical, but spiritual. Our only weapons
are the Word of God and prayer (2 Cor. 10:4). We are not
sent into the world to reform men's lives, or even to reform
society. We are sent to preach the gospel for the conversion
of sinners, for the saving of God's elect. Our only mission
is the preaching of the gospel. Those who are not subdued
by the gospel, our Lord will subdue by the iron rod of his
inflexible justice. And in the end he will tread his enemies
beneath his feet in the winepress of the fierceness of the
wrath of God.

The cause of this warfare

The cause of this warfare is rebellion against Christ the King
(v. 16). The Lord God is determined to make all creatures in
heaven, earth and hell bow to his Son. All Christ's enemies
will be made his footstool (Ps. 110:1; Heb. 10:13). Every
creature will be compelled, either by the gospel of the grace
of God or by the iron rod of his justice, to bow before the Lord
Jesus Christ and confess that he is, and rightfully deserves to
be, 'King of kings and Lord of lords'. Christ the mighty man of
war will indeed win the day (Isa. 45:22-25).

46.
Christ — the Word of God

Revelation 19:13

'And he was clothed with a vesture dipped in blood: and his name is called The Word of God' (Rev. 19:13).

'His name is called The Word of God'

The doctrine declared by this name given to our Saviour is of immense importance. All our knowledge of God, all our hopes of grace and life, all our salvation is wrapped up in the fact that the Lord Jesus Christ is the Word of God. In the New Testament, our Saviour is frequently referred to as the Word of God (John 1:1-3; Heb. 4:12-13; 2 Peter 3:5; 1 John 1:1-3; 5:7).

Some, seeking to undermine the inspiration and authority of the Scriptures, have suggested that the apostles got their idea of the eternal Logos, the eternal Word, from the writings of Plato. But that is not accurate. Plato got his idea of the eternal Word from the writings of the Old Testament Scriptures and from the writings of the ancient Jewish theologians who expounded them (Ps. 138:2). Those ancient Jewish writers frequently referred to the Messiah (the Christ) as the Word of God. So the apostles, especially when writing to Jewish believers, used that name to refer to Christ, being inspired to do so by God the Holy Spirit. What is the significance of this name? Why is the Lord Jesus Christ called 'the Word of God'?

He is the Son of God (John 1:1)

As the word, whether silent or expressed, is the product of the mind, the image of it and equal to it, so the Lord Jesus Christ is the only begotten Son of the Father. He is the express image of the invisible God. Indeed, Jesus Christ is God, in all things co-eternal, co-equal and one with God the Father and God the Holy Spirit. 'In the beginning was the Word, and the Word was with God, and the Word was God. The same was in the beginning with God' (John 1:1-2). Notice John's language: 'The Word was God.' He could not be more emphatic and clear in teaching both the deity of Christ and the doctrine of the Trinity. Quite literally translated, the text reads, 'God was the Word. The same was in the beginning face to face [as an equal] with God.' Yet, as the word and the mind are distinct from one another, so the Father and the Son are equal, but separate and distinct persons within the triune Godhead. 'There are three that bear record in heaven, the Father, the Word, and the Holy Ghost: and these three are one' (1 John 5:7). So when the Scriptures declare that Christ is the Word of God, they are telling us that:

    1. He is God (Heb. 1:8).
    2. He is the only begotten of the Father (John 3:16).
    3. He is a distinct person, separate from the Father and the Spirit (John 14:16-17; 2 Cor. 13:14).
    4. He is one with the Father and the Spirit in the sacred Trinity (Deut. 6:4).

The doctrine of the Trinity is a vital doctrine of the gospel. It is a doctrine taught through the current of Holy

Scripture and by universal consent of all the inspired writers. It is written as with a sunbeam through the Word of God. The Trinity of persons in the eternal Godhead is displayed in all the works of God revealed in Scripture: creation, providence and grace. The ordinances of divine worship, the mediatorial work of Christ, the songs and prayers of God's elect and the benedictions of grace all show forth the tri-unity of the Father, Son and Holy Spirit in the one God. But the doctrine is plainly stated in the text referred to before: 'There are three that bear record in heaven, the Father, the Word, and the Holy Ghost; and these three are one' (1 John 5:7). 'This text is so glaring a proof of the doctrine of the Trinity,' writes John Gill, 'that the enemies of it have done all they can to weaken its authority, and have pushed hard to extirpate it from a place in the sacred writings.' Almost all modern translations of the Bible either omit this verse altogether, or put in a footnote saying that it should be omitted. But the objections raised against its inspiration are groundless. There was never any dispute about it until Erasmus mistakenly omitted it from the first edition of his translation of the New Testament. We worship one God in the Trinity (tri-unity) of his sacred persons. And the Second Person in the triune Godhead is called 'the Word of God'. He is Jesus Christ, the eternally begotten Son of God. The man Christ Jesus is God manifest in the flesh (1 Tim. 3:16). He so thoroughly reveals God that he says, 'He that hath seen me hath seen the Father' (John 14:4-11). Indeed, all the fulness of the incomprehensible God 'dwelleth in him bodily' (Col. 2:9).

He is the living Word of whom the written Word speaks

I cannot stress this fact too much. The Bible is not a book of history, a book of morality, or even a book of theology. It is a book about the Son of God. This is exactly what our Lord taught his disciples on the Emmaus road (Luke 24:27,44,45). Jesus Christ is 'all the counsel of God' (Acts 20:27; 1 Cor. 2:2). All the Old Testament Scriptures promise and portray him. The four Gospels present him. Acts, the epistles and the book of Revelation proclaim and praise him.

No man preaches the Bible except as he preaches Christ. No man teaches the Bible except as he teaches Christ. And no one understands the Bible except as he understands how it directs him to, and shows him the glory and beauty of, the Lord Jesus Christ. The Word of God is like that box containing precious spikenard which the woman broke to anoint the Saviour. When it was broken open, 'The house was filled with the odour of the ointment' (John 12:3). God's servants, in preaching and teaching the Scriptures, break open the precious Word containing Christ crucified, and, as they do, the house is filled with the sweet aroma of Christ. Cherish the Bible. Read it diligently and carefully. It is the inspired Word of God, infallible and without error. But it is to be cherished because of the person revealed in it. Take Christ out of the Book of God and you have nothing left but processed wood in leather bindings with gilt edges. Christ crucified is the key that unlocks the treasure chest of Holy Scripture, and Christ crucified is the treasure contained in that chest.

The works ascribed to him

He is the Word of God who spoke for God's elect in the council of peace and covenant of grace before the world began (Ps. 40:6-8; Heb. 10:5-10). In the council chambers of the triune God, the Lord Jesus Christ spoke for us as our surety, agreeing to do all his Father's will for the accomplishment of our salvation. His blood is the blood of the everlasting covenant (Heb. 13:20). His blessings are all covenant blessings, bestowed upon those whom God had chosen from eternity because of Christ's word of promise as our surety (Eph. 1:3; 2 Tim. 1:9; Heb. 7:22). His delights were with his people from everlasting (Prov. 8:31). Because of his wise representation of us as our wisdom, upon the ground of his Word, God's elect were 'accepted in the Beloved' (Eph. 1:6), before the world began.

Christ is the Word of God by whom all things were created (John 1:3; 2 Peter 3:5). Evolution is a myth, invented and perpetuated by atheism. Christ our God is the Creator of all things. He spoke all things into being out of nothing. As he spoke all things into being, so he constantly upholds all things by the word of his power (Heb. 1:3). The 'laws of nature' and 'balance of nature' by which men imagine the world is sustained are nothing less than the execution of Christ's mighty word. The sun will burn as long as he fuels the candle. The earth will stand as long as he holds it up in the midst of nothing upon the foundation of his word.

As the Word of God, Christ is both the revelation of God's being and the interpreter of his will (John 1:18). It is not possible for man to know God apart from Christ, the Word. No man can know the mind of another, unless he expresses his mind in his word. And no man can know the mind of God, except by God's revelation of himself in Christ, his Word. Christ has, by his doctrine, his life and his sin-atoning sacrifice, shown us that God is holy, that he delights in mercy and that he saves his people graciously, upon the grounds of justice satisfied (Rom. 3:24-26).

It is as the Word of God that the Lord Jesus acts as our Advocate in heaven (1 John 2:1-2). He speaks to God the Father on behalf of all his chosen, redeemed people (John 17:9,20). Our Advocate is one whom God will hear — 'Jesus Christ the righteous'. He pleads with God for us for the non-imputation of sin to his redeemed. The basis of his plea is his shed blood. 'He is the propitiation for our sins.'

Christ, the Word of God, is the one by whom we are given, and preserved in, eternal life (Heb. 4:12-13). As in

the old creation, so in the new creation of grace, all things
have their being by Christ, the Word of God. Notice what
the Holy Spirit tells us about Christ as the Word of God in
Hebrews 4. He is living, powerful, dividing and discerning
(vv. 12-13). He is in the heavens (v. 14). He sympathizes
with us (v. 15). He is ready, willing and able to help us in
time of need (v. 16).

Jesus Christ is 'the Word of God'

Christ's person is a revelation of God. Christ's work is a
revelation of God. He is in the Father, and the Father in
him. His words and works are the words and works of the
Father. In the manger, he showed us God. In the synagogue
of Nazareth, he showed us God. At Jacob's well, he showed
us God. At the tomb of Lazarus, he showed us God. On
Olivet, as he wept over Jerusalem, he showed us God. On
the cross, he showed us God. In the tomb, he showed us
God. In the resurrection, he showed us God. If we say with
Philip, 'Show us the Father, and it sufficeth us,' he answers,
'Have I been so long time with you, and yet hast thou not
known me ...? He that hath seen me hath seen the Father'
(John 14:8,9). As Horatius Bonar says, 'This God whom
Christ reveals, as the God of righteous grace and gracious
righteousness, is the God with whom we have to do.'

He is God's exalted Word, exalted above all his name
(Ps. 138:2). He is the one exalted in the written Word. Let
us ever exalt him as the Word of God because he is the Son
of God, because he is the one of whom all the Scriptures
speak, and because he is the one by whom God is made
known to us and in whom we are made known to God!

47.

Christ and Armageddon

Revelation 19:11-21

'And I saw an angel standing in the sun; and he cried with a loud voice, saying to all the fowls that fly in the midst of heaven, Come and gather yourselves together unto the supper of the great God' (Rev. 19:17).

Armageddon is not a military conflict between earthly nations. It is not a nuclear war. It is a spiritual conflict. It is represented in every battle throughout history between Christ and Satan, the seed of the woman and the seed of the serpent (Gen. 3:15), the kingdom of light and the kingdom of darkness, the church and the world, truth and error, righteousness and evil, the worshippers of God and false religion. Whenever the people of God are oppressed and persecuted, the Lord reveals his power and defeats our enemies. That is Armageddon (Judg. 5:19-20). It is a battle which began in the Garden of Eden, has continued throughout the ages and will be consummated at the glorious second advent of our Lord Jesus Christ. That is what is described in Revelation 19:11-21.

This is a picture of our Lord's second coming for judgement. He comes to judge and make war. We have seen Babylon destroyed. We have heard the shouts of 'Hallelujah!' in heaven because of God's righteous judgement. But, before that final judgement comes, the beast, the false prophet and Satan himself must be destroyed. This will be the consummation of the battle that began in the garden. This is Armageddon. When our Lord Jesus Christ comes the second time in power and great glory, Satan's opposition to Christ and his church will cease for ever. Satan's power to deceive will be completely destroyed. His power to hurt God's creation will be ended for ever. Every influence of the Evil One will be cast with him into hell!

Let's look at this final battle of Armageddon. In that last day, the events will take place in a moment, in the twinkling of an eye. Christ will come to forcibly take possession of the earth, to rid it of all evil, and to make all things new. When he comes, our Lord will find the kingdoms of this earth mustered in confederate rebellion against him. By the might of his sovereign word and ineffable glory he will destroy them completely in this battle of Armageddon (Rev. 16:15-16).

The glorious advent of our Lord Jesus Christ (vv. 11-16)

What John sees here is that of which Enoch prophesied before the flood (Jude 14-15). In these verses the Holy Spirit gives us eleven things to describe the Second Coming of Christ.

1. Our Lord Jesus will come forth out of heaven (v. 11)

His name is not mentioned, but we know who he is by the marks and inscriptions he bears. All that is said of this great, coming Conqueror clearly identifies him as that same Jesus whom John had seen ascending into heaven (Luke 24:50-52; Acts 1:9-11). The Second Coming of Christ is announced by the opening of heaven: 'I saw heaven opened.' This is not a secret thing, known only to a few chosen people. This is the rending of the heavens that will take place at the glorious appearing of the great God, our Saviour. In that last Great Day, the very heavens will be opened, and Christ will appear to judge the world and to be glorified in all his saints (2 Thess. 1:7-10). The Lamb, being married to his chosen, redeemed bride, will leave his Father's house and come with his saints to take possession of the earth.

2. He will come riding upon a white horse (v. 11)

As we saw earlier, this white horse is purely symbolical. It represents royalty, judgement and war, righteousness, justice and truth, honour, majesty and victory. White is the colour that symbolizes the purity of Christ and the purity of his judgement. When he comes forth to conquer, he is upon a white horse (Rev. 6:2). When he comes to reap his harvest from the earth, he sits upon a white cloud (Rev. 14:14). And when he comes to sit in judgement, he sits upon a great white throne (Rev. 20:11). The horse symbolizes power and majesty. And its white colour symbolizes purity and truth.

3. He is called 'Faithful and True' (v. 11)

He is seen in sharp contrast with those whom he comes to judge and destroy. The dragon is the deceiver. The beast, the false prophet and Babylon represent all false religion. Those who follow them are false worshippers. But here is one who is absolutely true and faithful.

4. He will judge and make war in righteousness (v. 11)

In his letter to the Laodicean church, he was called 'the faithful and true witness' (Rev. 3:14). As such, he reproved his church and instructed his friends. Here he is the faithful and true Warrior and Judge for the everlasting destruction of his enemies. Righteousness cannot tolerate iniquity.

Justice cannot be at peace with sin. Sin must be destroyed.
God's mercy, slighted and abused by men, brings forth the
executioner of justice. The world banded together in arms
against God's sovereign throne, and now God sends forth
his King, Jesus Christ, to squash the rebellion and to execute absolute justice upon his enemies. Divine judgement
will be exactly according to God's law and justice (2 Cor.
5:10; Rev. 22:11). This horrible vengeance and wrath of God
upon men will be the result of man's wilful, deliberate rebellion against the claims of Christ in the gospel (Ps. 2:1-12;
Prov. 1:23-33; see Matt. 22:1-7). When Christ makes war
with men, it is because they will not surrender to him and
have his terms of peace. His warfare and judgement are
acts of righteousness.

5. His eyes are a flame of fire (v. 12)

In order to judge righteously, he must see all things perfectly. And he does. He searches the depth of the heart,
looks behind the mask of hypocrisy, penetrates the darkness of secrecy and sees the very thoughts and intents of
the heart. His eyes possess omniscient perception and break
out against his enemies with indignation and wrath. And
his wrath upon his enemies is as irresistible as his grace
towards his elect, because this mighty warrior is the Sovereign of the universe.

6. He wears the crowns of total, universal sovereignty (v. 12)

He is not only the Judge and the General, but also the sovereign King. Remember, he won these crowns by his obedience to his Father's will as our substitute (John 17:2). When
David conquered the Ammonites he took the crown of the
defeated king and placed it upon his own head, in addition
to the crown he already had as King of Israel (2 Sam. 12:30).
In the same sense, Christ has, by virtue of his conquests,

taken all the crowns of the universe and placed them upon his own head, in addition to the crown he possesses as God and Creator of all things. And he is coming to make war with, and execute judgement upon, those who dispute his right to total sovereignty (Isa. 45:9).

7. He is one whom no man can know (v. 12)

He has a name 'that no man knew, but he himself'. It is true, we know him by divine revelation. We know him by faith. But we could not know him had he not been revealed to us by God's almighty grace (Matt. 11:27). Yet this text implies much more. The Lord Jesus Christ, this God-man who comes to judge and make war, possesses such ineffable greatness and glory that no man has any idea how great and glorious, awesome and majestic he is who comes to judge and destroy the wicked (1 Tim. 6:14-16).

8. He is the one who shed his blood for sinners (v. 13)

He who comes to judge sinners in the wrath of God is the Christ who was judged for sinners in the wrath of God. I cannot agree with those who say the bloodstains on his garment have no reference at all to our Saviour's sacrifice for sin. These stains are not the blood of men whom he treads in the winepress of God's wrath. They are the blood of the one who has trodden the winepress of the wrath of God alone (Isa. 63:1-5). As he comes forth to judge and make war his garments are already stained! The primary issue of the judgement and warfare is these blood-stained garments! Christ comes to judge and make war with those who spilled his blood, despised his blood and counted his blood a use-less thing — in other words, with unbelievers. He who comes to judge the world is the Lamb of God, whom the world despises (Isa. 63:6).

9. He is the Word of God (v. 13)

Jesus Christ is the Word of God incarnate (John 1:1-14). He is the true and only expression of the eternal, triune God. He is the living Word of whom the written Word speaks and in whom the written Word is fulfilled. When he comes in judgement, he will reveal the righteousness, justice and truth of God.

10. He comes to destroy his enemies (v. 15)

In that dread day the Word of God will be an instrument of wrath and destruction. It will be the sharp sword of almighty justice, proceeding out of his mouth (Isa. 11:4). Do you see the ease with which Christ will destroy his enemies? He speaks, and it is done. He commands, and it is accomplished.

11. He is the King of kings and Lord of lords (v. 16)

This name tells of the majesty and dominion, glory and power of him who bears the sword of judgement and the rod of wrath (see Ps. 45:1-6). For ages the beast and the false prophet have attacked the throne of the King. The nations of the world have formed a league with hell against omnipotence. But now the Lion of the tribe of Judah comes forth to meet his enemies (Ps. 21:9). These eleven things describe the glorious second advent of Christ. But when he comes, he will not be alone. He comes with ten thousands of his saints.

The armies that follow him (v. 14)

When our Lord comes from heaven in flaming fire, taking vengeance upon those who do not know God and do not obey the gospel, his bride, the church, all the hosts of his elect, will be with him. No one can say precisely how this rapid succession of events will take place. But John appears to be speaking now of those events which will take place immediately preceding the final judgement and the great Hallelujah songs described in verses 1-10. The order of events appears to be as follows:

1. Christ will come (1 Thess. 4:16).
2. The dead in Christ will be resurrected (1 Thess. 4:16).
3. The living believers will be translated to heaven to meet the Lord in the air (1 Thess. 4:17).[1]
4. Christ will come to judge and make war with the armies of heaven, all his saints following him (2 Thess. 1:7-10). Christ is the head, the leader, the captain of these armies. He comes first. The saints follow in his train. The promise from the beginning was that the seed of the woman would crush the serpent's head. Here it is done! Christ is the Seed of the woman. And we who believe are his seed. Though the work is his and the battle is his, we shall follow him in the victory (Rom. 16:20; Rev. 17:14).

They ride on white horses

All those called, chosen and faithful ones will ride like their King upon white horses. Horses and chariots of fire took Elijah up to heaven. Horses and chariots of fire protected Elisha at Dothan. And white horses, symbolically, will bring the saints from heaven with our great King, for the final subjugation of the world to his authority. It is up to the

---

1. We shall meet our Lord in his descent, and return with him to destroy the wicked (Compare the usage of the word 'meet' in Acts 28:15-16).

bridles of these horses that the blood will flow in that day (Rev. 14:20).

They are 'clothed in fine linen, white and clean'

All the saints of God are clothed with the righteousness of Christ, perfectly pure and clean before God. Perhaps the psalmist had this very scene in mind when he wrote, 'The righteous shall rejoice when he seeth the vengeance: he shall wash his feet in the blood of the wicked. So that a man shall say, Verily there is a reward for the righteous: verily he is a God that judgeth in the earth' (Ps. 58:10-11). It is certain that Paul had this in mind when he declared that 'The saints shall judge the world' (1 Cor. 6:2). Notice that in that day the saints will wear no armour. They are now immortal. They cannot be hurt. We shall not be the executioners of vengeance. That belongs to Christ alone. But we follow the achievements of his sword and rejoice in the victory.

The enemies Christ comes to destroy (v. 19)

The beast represents all anti-Christian government, philosophy and power which has persecuted the church of God through the ages. The kings of the earth represent the nations of the world, arrayed in opposition to God, under the strong delusion of the beast and the false prophet, who represent all the religion of Antichrist (see Rev. 16:12-16). Demonic spirits, working demonic miracles, lead men and women in demonic religion in the name of Christ against Christ and the gospel of his grace. And those who are set in battle array against Christ think they are doing God service (see 2 Thess. 2:3-12). The preachers of free-will, works religion are demonic spirits, serving the cause of Antichrist to keep sinners from Christ (2 Cor. 11:1-3,13-15). All who embrace the religion of free will and salvation by works, under any name, are under the power of a lie and a strong delusion. They are in the religion of Antichrist, fighting against God. Those are the forces of Armageddon gathered against Christ whom he comes to destroy. With one accord, in one hell-inspired confederation, the governments of the world, the educators of the world, the philosophers of the world and the religions of the world are gathered against the Lamb of God to make war. But their confederation is useless! (See Ps. 2:1-12).

Our Saviour's conquest will be thorough (vv. 17-21)

The whole world of unbelief is gathered against Christ and his church to do battle. But the battle will end quickly and decisively by the glorious appearing of Christ. At his second coming, Satan's persecution of the church and his power to deceive will end for ever! Every influence of Satan will be cast with him into hell, never to appear again outside the pit of the damned. Hallelujah! Even now, Christ's victory over the beast and the false prophet is so certain that the angel is seen standing in the sun, calling the birds of prey to gather for a feast upon the carcasses of the Lord's enemies (see Matt. 24:24-28).

So easily will our Lord defeat those who oppose him that we are told, 'He that sitteth in the heavens shall laugh: the Lord shall have them in derision' (Ps. 2:4). For six thousand years, God has been longsuffering and patient, and men have despised his goodness. Now Jehovah laughs! For six thousand years God has sent light and truth to men who despised it. But now he laughs! For six thousand years God has offered terms of peace, which men have despised. But now he laughs! What a horrible day! God comes in judgement, laughing at his enemies!

First, *the beast and the false prophet* will be taken (v. 20). The governments and religions of Antichrist will be suddenly, thoroughly destroyed. Only at the moment of judgement will men see the futility of intellectualism, materialism, free-will teaching, ritualism and legalism. The philosophical, political and religious leaders of the world will be cast alive into hell, and with them all the delusions of Antichrist.

Then *those that have been deceived*, because they would not obey the gospel, will be destroyed for ever (v. 21). Thus this present world shall end! The only thing left to be seen is the fate of the devil. Babylon is gone! The beast is gone! The false prophet is gone! Only the dragon remains. And his ruin is described in chapter 20. Then we shall see the glorious pictures of heavenly, eternal bliss awaiting the saints of God.

48.

Christ's dominion over the prince of darkness

Revelation 20:1-3

'And he laid hold on the dragon, that old serpent, which is the Devil, and Satan, and bound him a thousand years' (Rev. 20:2).

The book of Revelation gives us seven visions of the person and work of Christ in this gospel age. In these seven visions the Lord revealed to John what he had done, is doing and will yet do for his church, in his church and with his church. The whole purpose of the book is to assure God's children in this world of their ultimate conquest over the world, the flesh and the devil. This blessed book is 'the Revelation of Jesus Christ'. By revealing to us who he is and what he does, our Lord calls us to look unto him with confident faith at all times, and assures us that we are 'more than conquerors through him that loved us'. The seven visions which John saw and recorded by divine inspiration are set before us in consecutive order in the twenty-two chapters of this book:

> 1. Christ in the midst of his churches, the seven golden candlesticks, in this world (chs. 1-3).
> 2. Christ opening and fulfilling the seven-sealed book of God's sovereign, eternal purpose (chs. 4-7).
> 3. Christ answering the prayers of his people, protecting them from their enemies and vindicating them

by executing the seven trumpets of judgement in his providential rule of the universe (chs. 8-11).

4. Christ and his church persecuted by Satan, world government and false religion (chs. 12-14).

5. Christ sending his angels to pour out the seven vials of his wrath upon the earth (chs. 15-16).

6. Christ's conquest over Babylon, the beast and the false prophet (chs. 17-19).

7. Christ's dominion over, and destruction of, Satan and the glory of the new Jerusalem (chs. 20-22).

These seven visions each cover the whole gospel age from the first to the second coming of Christ. They do not represent different ages, dispensations, or prophetic events. They all tell the same story. They all tell us what our Lord has done, is doing and will yet do for the salvation of his people. The use of the word 'seven' is striking. There are 'seven golden candlesticks', 'seven stars', 'seven seals', 'seven trumpets', 'seven angels', 'seven vials'. Seven is the number of perfection, completion and satisfaction. And in each of these seven visions, the Holy Spirit assures us of the perfect rule of Christ as the Monarch of the universe for the complete victory and eternal salvation of his church.

In Revelation 20 the final vision begins. Chapter 19 brought us to the very end of world history, to the final Day of Judgement. In chapter 20 we return to the beginning of the gospel age once again. In this vision we see once more the accomplishments of Christ's first advent, and we are carried through to the final conquests of his second advent. Revelation 20:1-3 reveals the binding of Satan which was accomplished by the work of Christ in his first advent. The sequence of events is clear:

1. Our Lord's first advent is followed by a long period of time, represented by a 'thousand years', in which Satan is bound.

2. At the close of this gospel age Satan is loosed for 'a little season'.

3. The loosing of Satan is followed by Christ's glorious second advent to judge the world and make all things new.

It should be clear to anyone who reads Revelation 20 that the language is figurative, as it is in all the pictures we have seen. 'The thousand years' are no more a literal period of time than 'the great chain' is a literal chain. As 'the chain' represents restraining power, 'the thousand years' represent a long period of time — that whole span of time between Christ's first and second coming. It is also obvious that 'the thousand years' precede (they do not follow) the Second Coming of Christ. In other words, we are now living in this 'thousand-year' period which began with the incarnation of Christ. The 'thousand years' are this present gospel age. They do not begin at Christ's second coming; they end at his second coming (see v. 11). Our Lord Jesus Christ has so thoroughly bound the prince of darkness that he has total dominion over him (see vv. 1-3).

The purpose of our Lord's incarnation (v. 1)

This great and mighty angel, whom John saw come down from heaven, is the Lord Jesus Christ himself, the Angel of the covenant, the Angel of God's presence (10:1-7; 18:1). He alone has the keys of death and hell (1:18). No creature could ever bind the devil, or even hinder his influence. He was the greatest, most powerful creature of the Almighty. None but Christ, the Creator, could bind him. We know that the primary purpose of our Lord's incarnation was the redemption and salvation of God's elect by the merits of his blood and the power of his grace (Matt. 1:21; 1 Tim.

1:15). But in order to accomplish our salvation Satan had to be bound. And here we see Christ coming with the key of the bottomless pit and a great chain in his hand. He is coming to shackle a treasonous rebel and lock him away! The Scriptures plainly tell us that one purpose of our Lord's incarnation and birth was to make war with, conquer and bind the prince of darkness (Gen. 3:15; 1 John 3:8; Rev. 12:5-11).

The character of our great enemy (v. 2)

Satan is too wise, too crafty, too strong and too cunning for any of us to resist him, overcome him, or avoid his blinding delusions. And this great rebel against God is full of enmity, anger, wrath and malice towards the souls of men. He knows that by the merits of Christ and in union with Christ, we shall have the place he desired. We shall sit with Christ upon the very throne of God and judge the world (Rev. 3:21; 1 Cor. 6:2). Satan's hatred for God's elect is fuelled by envy and jealousy. Let us ever beware of this great enemy.

In this passage his character is revealed in four names:

1. 'The dragon'

He is a beast of ferocious power in the earth. He is the instigator of all rebellion against, and opposition to, God, holding power over the minds of men, taking them captive at his will. The governors, kings and rulers of the earth are his willing subjects, by whom he breathes out the fires of persecution upon God's saints. Since the days of Nimrod, he has led the kings of the earth in a confederation against the Lord and his Christ. And he will continue to do so, as God permits, until the time of Armageddon.

2. 'The old serpent'

He is old, very old. He has been around since the beginning of history. And he is the serpent. He is best represented
by the slithering, crooked, deceiving serpent, with his subtle, hidden poison and deadly malignity. It was the serpent
who deceived our first parents and seduced them into sin
and death. It is the serpent who today deceives the souls of
men and women with presumptuous pride, false doctrine,
perverted wisdom and unbelief. And it is the serpent who
corrupts, divides and seeks to destroy the church of God.

3. 'The devil'

The word 'devil' means 'slanderer, liar'. This has been his
character throughout history. 'He was a murderer from the
beginning, and abode not in the truth, because there is no
truth in him. When he speaketh a lie, he speaketh of his
own: for he is a liar, and the father of it' (John 8:44). He
slanders God to man: 'Yea, hath God said ...?' (Gen. 3:1-5).
And he slanders man to God (Job 1:9-11). The devil twists
and perverts all — God's Word, his providence, his gospel
and his grace!

4. 'Satan'

The word 'Satan' means 'accuser'. He is one who waits to
entrap, to oppose, to disable, to bring disaster and to destroy. He is a ready, vicious, unrelenting adversary. He opposed God in the beginning. He opposed Christ upon the
earth. And he opposes God's elect from the cradle to the
grave.

Child of God, this is the character of your soul's great
enemy. He is a powerful dragon, a subtle serpent, a deceiving slanderer and a bitter, relentless adversary. But our Saviour is mightier than our adversary! Satan is too great for
us, but he is not too great for our Lord Jesus Christ.

The binding of Satan by Christ (vv. 2-3)

John saw the Lord Jesus come down from heaven with a key to lock the bottomless pit and a chain to bind the devil (9:1,11; 11:7). This bottomless pit has a lid upon it that can be locked and sealed. Remember, this is only a picture, a figurative symbol, nothing more. But it tells us of the work of Christ. He laid hold upon Satan, overpowered him, rendered him helpless and bound him securely with the mighty chain of his sovereign power. He cast him into the bottomless pit, locked the lid and sealed it for a thousand years, more literally, 'for the thousands of years'. What does this mean? How did this binding of Satan take place? You will remember that when our Lord Jesus began his public ministry, the Pharisees accused him of casting out demons by the power of Satan. His answer was: 'How can one enter into a strong man's house, and spoil his goods, except he first bind the strong man? And then he will spoil his house' (Matt. 12:29). That word, 'bind', is exactly the same in Matthew 12:29 and in Revelation 20. And it is talking about the same thing.

1. The temptation in the wilderness

The binding of Satan began when our Lord triumphed over him in the wilderness of temptation (Matt. 4:1-11; Luke 4:1-13). When Satan met Christ Jesus in the wilderness, he was foiled by the Word of God. As a result of this triumph, our Lord, having bound the strong man, began to spoil his goods, casting out demons. In the words of William Hendriksen, 'The power and influence of Satan over the deluded masses was beginning to be curtailed.'

2. Gethsemane

In the garden of Gethsemane our Lord Jesus again broke the power of Satan by faith and prayer (Matt. 26:36-46). In

that dark, cold night, Satan came to oppose our dear Saviour, taunting him with the hideous load of sin that must
be put upon him, tormenting him with the anticipation of
being made sin, being made to suffer the wrath of God and
being forsaken by the Father. He was trying to keep the Lord
from the cross. And our Saviour's tender, holy, human soul
was crushed with sorrow. But he rose in triumph after he
prayed (Heb. 5:7-9). In confident faith, he rose up to lay
down his life for his sheep (Heb. 12:1-2).

3. The cross

Then our great Saviour crushed the serpent's head, bound
him as a wild beast and cast him into the bottomless pit by
his glorious, triumphant death upon the cross (John
12:28-32). By his death upon the cursed tree, our Lord broke
the arms of Satan's usurped dominion over the nations of
the world and began to draw all men unto himself, Gentiles as well as Jews. The light was taken from the Jews who
despised it, and sent to the Gentiles who never had it, that
God's elect in every nation might see the light of the glory
of God in the face of Jesus Christ and be saved.

4. The ascension and exaltation of Christ

When our Saviour ascended up to heaven and was exalted
as King over all things, he brought Satan into captivity under
his sovereign rule (Ps. 68:18-19; Col. 2:13-15; Rev. 12:5-11).
The Son of God has always ruled Satan, as he has ruled all
things, by virtue of his total sovereignty as God. But now,
he has, as the God-man, our mediator, taken away Satan's
power to deceive the world so that he might gather his elect
out of every nation in the world.

Satan is bound today!

Every text of Scripture which speaks of the binding and captivity of Satan refers to and is associated with our Lord's first advent, his life, his death and his exaltation. This is a glorious, comforting gospel truth which few people seem to apprehend. We are not awaiting the day when Satan will be bound and Christ will be King. Jesus Christ is the sovereign King over all things today! And Satan is bound already!

He is under Christ's control

Our great adversary is under the total rule and control of our dear Saviour. He cannot harm us! His temptations are under the rule of Christ! His assaults are under the rule of Christ! Even his roars are under the rule of Christ! This binding of Satan is not the same as his destruction. That comes later, at the Day of Judgement.

His power to deceive is restrained

This binding of Satan is specifically the destruction of his power, or the restraint of his power, to deceive the nations. Satan's influence in the world is not destroyed, but curtailed, so that he is unable to prevent the spread of the gospel, the salvation of God's elect and the progress of Christ's kingdom in the nations of the world. Satan cannot prevent, or withstand, the increase and completion of Christ's church in this world (Matt. 16:18).

He is bound through the preaching of the gospel

Satan is also bound today by the power of Christ, through the preaching of the gospel (Luke 10:16-20). As we preach the gospel of the grace of God, when it is effectually applied to the hearts of men and women by the Holy Spirit, Satan is bound and his house is spoiled!

I do not say, by any means, that Satan is bound with reference to all men, but, in so far as God's elect are concerned, Satan is bound everywhere. He cannot stop the progress of the gospel until the thousand years are finished, until the church of Christ is complete and all God's elect are saved. But then he must be loosed for 'a little season'.

The loosing of Satan

There will be a little season of great deception at the close of this present gospel age (v. 3). John tells us that Satan 'must be loosed a little season'. The Lord Jesus will once again allow Satan freedom to deceive the nations of the world, because they would not believe the gospel, nor receive the love of the truth (2 Thess. 2:1-12). In that little season, there will be a famine of the Word of God (Amos 8:11-13). In that little season, the world will be zealously religious, but utterly ignorant of the true and living God, deceived with false religion (2 Thess. 2:1-12; Rev. 16:12-14). But God's elect will not be deceived (2 Thess. 2:13-14). His people are safe. They shall not be moved away from the hope of the gospel (1 John 2:20-29). Child of God, rejoice! Satan is bound as far as you are concerned! He cannot harm you. He cannot accuse you before God. He cannot bring you into condemnation. He cannot prevent the success of Christ and his kingdom! Soon God will bruise Satan under your feet (Rom. 16:20; Rev. 12:11-12).

49.
Living and reigning with Christ

Revelation 20:4-6

'Blessed and holy is he that hath part in the first resurrection: on such the second death hath no power, but they shall be priests of God and of Christ, and shall reign with him a thousand years' (Rev. 20:6).

What happens to a believer when he dies? Where does he go? What is his condition? What does he do? How many times we have asked ourselves these questions! One of our loved ones is taken from us, a man or a woman who loves Christ, or a child, who is loved, chosen and redeemed by Christ, is taken out of this world. We go to the funeral parlour, pay our last respects, hold them in precious, honourable memory and weep for the aching void in our hearts. Finally, we take them to the cemetery, bury their bodies in the earth and say goodbye. We have laid the precious body of a dear friend, a loving companion, an aged parent, or a beloved child in the ground. Then we go home. All the friends are gone. The rest of the family has gone home. And we sit alone. In the middle of the night, in the still hours of the early morning, as we wipe away the tears, these questions arise in our hearts: 'Where has my beloved one gone? What is his condition now? What is she doing? Do they yet see us? Do they still hear us?' Like Martha, we know that they will rise in the resurrection at the last day (John 11:24), and we comfort ourselves with the hope of the resurrection. But what about the time between death and the resurrection of the body?

Our Lord has not left us in the dark. He has supplied us with answers to these questions in Revelation 20:4-6. We have seen that 'the thousand years' in Revelation 20 refer to the whole gospel age in which we live. They represent not a literal number of years, but the whole span of time between Christ's first advent and his second advent. These thousand years have a glorious meaning for God's people on the earth. During this time Satan is bound, the gospel is preached and God's elect are gathered from the four corners of the earth. The body of Christ, the church, is being completed. The kingdom of God is going on from victory to victory. But the glories of heaven far transcend those of God's saints upon the earth during this period. Revelation 20:1-3 describes the advance of the church in the world during the gospel age. But verses 4-6 describe the condition of the victorious saints in heaven today.

In order to grasp the meaning of these verses, we must go back in our minds to the first century, and try to see these things as John and those early believers saw them. Roman persecutions are raging against the young church. Martyrs, one after the other, are being beheaded. Paul and James have already been slain. Why? Simply because they refused to say, 'Caesar is Lord,' and refused to drop incense upon the altar of a pagan priest. They were not slain for worshipping Christ, but for refusing to participate in, or give credibility to, any worship except the worship of Christ. Because of their allegiance to Christ alone, and the gospel of God's free and sovereign grace in him, multitudes of believers were burned at the stake and thrown to wild beasts in the Roman amphitheatres. But our Lord was not unmindful of his persecuted saints. He sustained them for their trials and gave them grace and strength to remain faithful to the end.

It was for the comfort and strength of these afflicted saints that our Lord gave us this vision of 'the souls of them that were beheaded for the witness of Jesus, and for the word of God, and which had not worshipped the beast, neither his image, neither had received his mark upon their foreheads, or in their hands'. In this vision our Lord describes the slain martyrs, together with all the departed saints who had faithfully confessed Christ upon the earth, as kings reigning with Christ in heaven (1:6; 5:10). It is as though the Lord is saying, 'In the world you will have tribulation; but, in that better land above, all the saints live and reign with Christ.' What comfort! Our departed friends, loved ones and companions in the grace of God are living and reigning with Christ right now. 'Truly,' writes William Hendriksen, 'the sufferings of this present time are not worthy to be compared with the glory which is revealed to the souls of believers reigning with their exalted Lord in heaven!'

Whom did John see?

Those who die without Christ perish without Christ and enter the eternal torments of the damned in hell. If you do not know, trust, love and worship the Lord Jesus Christ in this world, when you die you will be in hell. If you die without Christ, you will suffer for ever the just wrath of God. If you refuse to trust Christ, God will refuse to be merciful to you. Not all people go to heaven when they die. But there are some in this world who do enter into eternal life when their bodies die. Who are they?

1. Men and women who have given their lives for Christ

Our text speaks specifically of these martyrs who were beheaded for Christ. But they represent all who die in faith.

In fact the very word for 'witness' (Acts 1:8), which all believers are, is 'martyr' . A martyr is one who sacrifices his
life for a noble cause. He lays down his life for the cause
that is more precious to him than life itself. That is exactly
what every believer is — one who lays down his life for
Christ and gives his life to Christ. Faith in Christ is nothing
less than the surrender of one's life to the Lord Jesus Christ
(Matt. 10:39; 16:25; Mark 8:34; Luke 9:23-26; 17:32-33; John
12:25-26). These people had given their lives *to* Christ, and
they had given their lives *for* Christ.

2. Men and women who had been beheaded

What was there about these people that so enraged their
enemies and brought such severe persecution upon them?
Were they rebels, traitors, murderers? What had they done?
How were their lives characterized? They boldly confessed
Christ and the gospel of his grace in the face of his enemies
— 'for the witness of Jesus'. They so confessed Christ as to
make all men see that any religion opposed to Christ and
the gospel doctrine of salvation by grace alone, through
faith alone, in Christ alone, is false religion, damning to
the souls of all who believe it (see Acts 4:8-12). These saints
were martyred because they rejected and refused to participate in, support, or approve of any doctrine or worship
which is contrary to the Word of God. They believed the
doctrine of the Word, worshipped the Christ of the Word,
practised the ordinances of the Word and lived by the rule
of the Word. They might have saved their lives, but for one
thing — these servants of Christ refused to give any credibility to any false religion in any form. They would not
worship the beast! Cost what it may, they could not, in good
conscience, worship any false god, under any image, by
any name, or embrace as their brethren those who did.
These are the people John saw. They were martyrs, men
and women who had given their lives *to* Christ. And many
of them were required to give their lives *for* Christ.

Where were these saints seen?

They were no longer on the earth. Their bodies had been buried, or burned, or eaten by wild beasts. Yet John saw them alive! Where? They were all sitting upon thrones. What does that mean?

For one thing, it means that they were in heaven! Throughout the book of Revelation, the throne of Christ and his people is in heaven (Rev. 1:4; 3:21; 4:2-6,9-10; 5:6,7,11,13; 6:16; 7:9-11,15,17; 8:3; 12:5; 14:3, 5; 16:17; 19:4,5; 20:4,11; 21:5; 22:1,3). 'Comfort one another with these words.' Those who sleep in Jesus are in heaven to-day, sitting with him upon his throne! For another thing, it means that they are actively engaged with Christ in the rule of the world. 'They lived and reigned with Christ a thousand years.' I do not know the full meaning of that statement. But I do know this: the saints of God in heaven are already victorious, out of the reach of harm. And I know that they are still very interested in God's saints upon the earth. Without us, they are not complete (Heb. 11:40; 12:1). And it means that they are perfectly happy, content and satisfied. The saints in heaven have attained that which they had long desired and sought. They are with the Lord Jesus Christ (Phil. 3:8-14). For the believer, death is a great honour, a great privilege and a great reward, not a thing to be dreaded and feared, but anxiously anticipated. It will be a welcome relief to lay aside this cumbersome body of flesh!

What are the saints of God doing in heaven?

Many have the idea that God's saints are floating around on clouds, strumming harps and singing, with nothing to do. According to this vision they are very busily engaged in the most important affairs of the universe. They are judging the world with Christ. The ransomed souls in heaven not only praise Christ for his righteous judgements, they actually participate in them. These saints in glory are constantly pictured as taking part in all that Christ does. They sit with him in his throne (3:21). They stand with him on Mount Zion (14:1). They worship at his throne (5:8-10). They sing before his throne (14:3; 15:3). They see his face (22:4).

They are living with Christ

'They lived and reigned with Christ a thousand years' (see Rev. 7:9-17). The saints in heaven respond in a perfect manner to their perfect environment. That is living!

They are sharing the royal glory of Christ

Not only do they behold his glory, they share his glory as the divine Mediator, our covenant Head! (John 17:22-24). All their prayers are answered. All their desires are constantly fulfilled. All their troubles are over (sin, unbelief, temptation).

How are the saints in heaven described?

Sometimes the best way to see something is by contrast. So in this vision the bliss and glory of the saints in heaven is contrasted with the condition of the lost: 'But the rest of the dead lived not again until the thousand years were finished.' Does that mean that those who die in unbelief simply cease to exist when they die, or that their souls sleep with their bodies in the earth? Certainly not! (Remember the rich man in Luke 16.) John simply means us to understand that those who die without Christ cease to live. They exist in hell. But they do not live. Their existence is eternal death. In hell they await their final judgement, when both body and soul will suffer the infinite wrath of God for ever!

But the saints in heaven live! After the resurrection of the body their bliss will be increased, but even now, they live. They have eternal life! 'This is the first resurrection!' The first resurrection is a spiritual resurrection. It is the resurrection of sinners from spiritual death to spiritual life in Christ (John 5:25). This first resurrection begins in the new birth. It is completed in the translation of the soul from this body of sin and this sin-cursed earth to God's holy heaven. It will be followed by the resurrection of the body to immortal glory at Christ's second coming. The Word of God teaches us three things about the resurrection of God's elect:

1. We have been raised representatively in Christ (Eph. 2:5).
2. We have been raised spiritually by the power of God the Holy Spirit (John 5:25; Eph. 2:1-3).
3. We shall be raised bodily when our Lord comes again (1 Thess. 4:17).

The blessedness of all who are born of God (v. 6)

Here John gives us a word of comfort and assurance regarding ourselves, even while we live in this world. If we are born of God, if we have part in the first resurrection, then we are blessed (Eph. 1:3). We are holy (saints), made holy by the righteousness of Christ imputed to us in justification and imparted to us in regeneration. Over us the second death, the everlasting wrath of God, has no power (Rom. 8:1,33-34). Soon, we shall be priests with God, serving him in the Most Holy Place. We too shall reign with Christ for a thousand years. That is to say, we too shall enter into heaven's glory and bliss when we leave this world. What a blessed hope this is! (See 2 Cor. 4:17 – 5:9).

50.

Christ our resurrection

Revelation 20:6

'Blessed and holy is he that hath part in the first resurrection: on such the second death hath no power' (Rev. 20:6).

Believers live in hope of the resurrection. With Paul, every believer might declare, 'If in this life only we have hope in Christ, we are of all men most miserable' (1 Cor. 15:19). In making that statement the apostle does not mean that the believer's life in this world is a sad, morbid existence, or that it is really more delightful and pleasurable to live in this world without faith in Christ. Nor does he imply that, were it not for the hope of eternal glory, the saints of God would prefer not to live as they do in obedience and submission to their heavenly Father. We do not serve our God for gain! Paul simply means that if there were no such thing as eternal life in Christ, no eternal bliss of life with Christ in glory and no resurrection of life at the last day, then believers would be the most miserably frustrated people in the world. We would never have that which we most earnestly desire. We would never enjoy that for which we are most ambitious. We would never see the end of our hope. We would never embrace Christ, or be embraced by Christ. We would never see our Redeemer. A more distressing thought cannot be imagined. Nothing could be more cruel and miserable than to live in hope of seeing Christ, being like Christ and spending eternity with Christ, only to die like a dog! 'If in this life only we have hope in Christ, we are of all men most miserable.' What a horrible thought! What a tormenting supposition! But it is not so! We live in hope of the resurrection (Job 19:25-27). The believer is calm in sickness, peaceful in sorrow, at ease in trial and afflic- tion, confident in bereavement and serene in death because he lives in hope of the resurrection. This is not some fool- ish philosophy. It is not a mere religious tranquillizer by which he is enabled to cope with the trials of life. This is the clear, calm, confident assurance of the believer's heart. It is the necessary, inevitable result of faith in Christ, who declares, 'I am the resurrection, and the life, he that believeth on me, though he were dead, yet shall he live: and whosoever liveth and believeth in me shall never die' (John 11:25-26).

The hope of the resurrection is much more than belief in a point of orthodox doctrine. It is a matter of faith and hope in a person, the Lord Jesus Christ. Christ is himself our resurrection. He is the resurrection and the life of all who trust him. Though believers do die physically, we shall never really die. The death of the body is, for the believer, merely an elevation in life. And even these bodies will be resurrected with Christ at the last day (John 5:28; Phil. 3:20-21). 'Blessed and holy is he that hath part in the first resurrection: on such the second death hath no power.' As we saw in our previous study, this hope of the resurrection is based upon three things: the representative resurrection of God's elect with Christ, the spiritual resurrection of every believer in Christ and the revelation of God concerning the resurrection.

The representative resurrection of God's elect with Christ

We live in hope of the resurrection, because we know that God's elect have been resurrected representatively with

Christ: 'God, who is rich in mercy, for his great love wherewith he loved us, even when we were dead in sins, hath quickened us together with Christ, (by grace ye are saved) and hath raised us up together, and made us sit together in heavenly places in Christ Jesus' (Eph. 2:4-6). The new birth, our spiritual resurrection, is the result of our having been resurrected with Christ representatively, even as our ultimate glorification will be the result of our having already been glorified in Christ our representative (Rom. 8:30).

When the Lord Jesus Christ rose from the grave he did so, not as a private individual, but as a public representative, as the representative of God's elect. All that Christ, the God-man, has done and experienced, all of God's elect have done and experienced in him, by virtue of our representative union with him. His obedience to the law of God was our obedience (Rom. 5:10,18-21). His death as a penal sacrifice for sin was our death (Rom. 6:6-7,9-11; 7:4). His resurrection was our resurrection. In all things Christ is our representative.

An indisputable fact

The resurrection of Jesus Christ from the dead is an indisputable fact of revelation and history upon which we rest our souls. If anyone could disprove the resurrection of Christ, he would disprove the gospel: 'If Christ be not raised, your faith is vain; ye are yet in your sins' (1 Cor. 15:17). But no one can ever disprove the resurrection of Christ. It is one of the best-attested facts in history (1 Cor. 15:1-8).

Because he rose, we too will rise

The bodily, physical resurrection of the Lord Jesus Christ necessitates the resurrection of all who are in Christ. That which has been done for us representatively must be experienced by us personally. Otherwise, the representative work of Christ would be meaningless. All believers are members of Christ's mystical body, the church (1 Cor. 12:12,17). If one member of the body were lost, the whole body would be maimed. If one member were lost, the head would not be complete (Eph. 1:22-23). Our bodies of flesh must be fashioned like unto his glorious body (Phil. 3:21). Christ was raised as the first-fruits of those that sleep (1 Cor. 15:20). If he is the first-fruits, the full harvest must follow. All those saints whose bodies sleep in the earth will be raised from death to life, even as Christ was raised from death to life.

Christ is the Second Adam. As we have borne the image of our first covenant head, Adam, we must also bear the image of the second (1 Cor. 15:21-23,47-49). Otherwise, his headship would be meaningless.

Our Lord Jesus Christ has obtained the victory over all that could hinder the glorious resurrection of his people. He put away our sins by the sacrifice of himself. He took Satan into captivity by his death upon the cross. He delivered us from the curse of the law by being made a curse for us. He spoiled death, hell and the grave by his triumph over them. By all of this he has delivered his people from the fear of death (Col. 2:13-15; Heb. 2:14-15).

We are also assured of the resurrection because the covenant engagements of Christ as the surety of God's elect require their resurrection (John 6:37-40). In that great and glorious resurrection day, our great Saviour will present all the host of his redeemed ones holy, unblameable and unreprovable to God his Father (Eph. 5:27), saying, 'Behold, I and the children which God hath given me' (Heb. 2:13). Then 'There shall be one fold and one shepherd' (John 10:16).

The spiritual resurrection of every believer in Christ

We live in hope of the resurrection, because we have experienced the resurrection of Christ in regeneration. The new birth is nothing less than a resurrection from the dead. It is a spiritual resurrection. This is the resurrection of which John speaks in Revelation 20:6: 'Blessed and holy is he that hath part in the first resurrection: on such the second death hath no power.' Like all other people, God's elect are born in spiritual death and deserving of eternal death. In regeneration, God the Holy Spirit, by invincible, irresistible grace, gives them life in Christ. He raises them from death to life. Never in the Scriptures is the new birth attributed to the free will of man, or even to his faith. It is the work of God the Holy Spirit. Only the omnipotent God can give life to dead sinners (John 3:3-8). The new birth is always spoken of in the Scriptures as a resurrection (John 5:25; 11:25-26; Eph. 2:1-4). It is not a decision, but a resurrection. It is not a reformation, but a regeneration. It is not a new start in life, but an entirely new life!

The Word of God gives numerous illustrations of the new birth, this spiritual resurrection, by the power of God. Ezekiel's description of the deserted infant, cast off, polluted in its blood, naked in its loathsomeness and dead, but raised to life by the word of God's power in the time of love, is a vivid picture of the new birth (Ezek. 16:1-8). The prophet's vision of dry bones, caused to live by the preaching of God's Word and the power of God's Spirit (Ezek. 37:1-14), is certainly intended by God to be an illustration of our regeneration by the power of the Holy Spirit through the preaching of the gospel. But there is not a clearer, more instructive picture of the believer's spiritual resurrection in Christ than the story of the resurrection of Lazarus in John 11. Five things are revealed about Lazarus and his resurrection which are reflected in the spiritual resurrection of every believer.

1. His condition

Lazarus was dead (John 11:14), and so were we when the Lord God came to us with his saving grace. God could have prevented Lazarus' death and could have prevented our death in Adam, but he allowed it, as he allowed the death of Lazarus, that he might glorify himself in delivering us from death to life by the power of his grace (John 11:4; Eph. 2:7).

2. His calling

The Lord Jesus 'cried with a loud voice, Lazarus, come forth. And he that was dead came forth' (John 11:43-44). Someone said, 'There was such power in the Saviour's voice that when he cried, "Come forth," had he not specified, "Lazarus, come forth," the whole cemetery would have been emptied!' Our Lord's call to Lazarus was a personal, particular and powerful call. He called Lazarus. He called Lazarus alone. And Lazarus came forth. He was raised from the dead by the effectual power of the Saviour's voice. There is a general call in the gospel that goes out to all men indiscriminately whenever the gospel is preached, and all who hear are responsible to obey. But dead sinners cannot and will not 'come forth' — they will never live before God until God the Holy Spirit calls them by the effectual, irresistible, life-giving call of his sovereign power. At God's appointed time, in 'the time of love', he will call every chosen, redeemed sinner. When that time comes, when he calls, the dead will live. 'It is the Spirit that quickeneth; the flesh profiteth nothing' (John 6:63).

3. His conversion

'He that was dead came forth, bound hand and foot with grave-clothes: and his face was bound about with a napkin. Jesus saith unto them, Loose him, and let him go' (John

11:44). As the grave-clothes that bound Lazarus had to be taken away, so conversion always follows calling. When sinners come to Christ and are taught by him, the grave-clothes of ignorance, superstition, tradition, religion and fear fall away.

4. His communion

When the Lord Jesus was in Bethany, 'Lazarus was one of them that sat at the table with him' (John 12:2). Saved sinners, being raised from death to life in Christ by the power and grace of God, live in communion with Christ. Their communion is sometimes interrupted by their sin, or by the Saviour's hiding his face from them for a season in loving chastisement (S. of S. 5:2-8; Isa. 54:7-10), but he will not forsake his own, neither will he let them forsake him (Jer. 32:38-40). The general tenor of their lives as believers is to walk with Christ. They live in the Spirit (Rom. 8:9,14), in blessed communion with the Son of God.

5. His conflict

Because of Lazarus many others believed on the Lord Jesus Christ. Therefore, the Jews sought to kill him (John 12:10-11). And anyone in this world who lives with Christ and serves him will be the object of the world's scorn and persecution. 'In the world ye shall have tribulation' (John 16:33). 'Yea ... all that will live godly in Christ Jesus shall suffer persecution' (2 Tim. 3:12).

The revelation of God concerning the resurrection of our bodies

There will be a resurrection of life at the Second Coming of Christ (1 Cor. 15:35-44,51-58; 1 Thess. 4:13-18). The Word of God does not teach a secret rapture of the church, but a glorious resurrection of the just. The fact is, God's elect never really die. Our Lord said, 'Whosoever liveth and believeth in me shall never die' (John 11:26). For the believer, the death of the body is only a temporary thing. When Christ comes again our bodies will be raised in immortality, made like unto his glorious body (Phil. 3:21).

Immediately following the resurrection of the just, there will be a resurrection of the damned (John 5:28-29). When Christ comes, the dead in Christ will be raised; then the saints who are living on earth at the time will be translated — that is, glorified; and then the wicked will be raised to judgement. Believers will be raised by virtue of their union with Christ in order to be judged (declared justly righteous) and rewarded with all the fulness of everlasting glory. The wicked, the unbelieving, will be raised by the power of Christ in order to be judged (declared justly condemned) and have the sentence of God's wrath executed upon them. The righteous will be raised in love to a great wedding feast. The wicked will be raised in wrath, to everlasting condemnation. Soon you and I will stand before the living God in judgement. 'Prepare to meet thy God!'

51.

Christ turns Satan loose
for 'a little season'

Revelation 20:7-10

'And when the thousand years are expired, Satan shall be loosed out of his prison' (Rev. 20:7).

Our Lord Jesus Christ, by his death upon the cross, defeated Satan and bound him with a great chain. The purpose of this binding was 'that he should deceive the nations no more'. As the result of Satan's binding, the glorious gospel of Christ has been carried into the four corners of the earth. Our Lord has been gathering his elect out of the four corners of the earth for two thousand years. Yet he told us that when the time appointed (symbolized by the thousand years) was fulfilled, Satan must be loosed for 'a little season' (Rev. 20:3).

The Holy Spirit teaches us four things about this 'little season'

First, at the end of this present gospel age, just before the coming of Christ, Satan will once again be turned loose upon the nations of the world (v. 7).

Second, he will be allowed to deceive the nations of the world with false religion once more (v. 8). Gog and Magog represent all the nations of the world set in opposition to Christ, his church and the gospel of his grace. The terms 'Gog and Magog' are borrowed from Ezekiel 38, but John never expected anyone to take them to mean Russia, China, or any other literal nation! He tells us plainly that Gog and Magog represent the nations of the world under the influence of satanic deception (see v. 8!).

Third, under the satanic delusion of false religion, all the nations of the world will rise up in opposition to Christ, his gospel and his church (v. 9). Here again we are warned about the great battle of Armageddon. This is the same battle described in Revelation 16:12-16 and 19:19-21. It is the final assault of Satan against the Lord Jesus Christ. The meaning of the vision is clear: towards the close of this gospel age, before Christ comes in glory, Satan will deceive the world with a false gospel, a false Christ, a false god, a false spirit and a false faith; and the world, in the name of Christ, will turn in violent persecution against Christ's kingdom.

Fourth, Satan's last assault, like all that have preceded it, will be foiled in the end (v. 10). The purpose of God will not be frustrated. The truth of God will not be overturned. The saints of God will not be deceived. The church of God will not be harmed. The Christ of God will thoroughly defeat his enemies. The punishment of the beast and the false prophet has already been described (Rev. 19:20). Here John assures us that Satan, the beast and the false prophet will all be cast into the lake of fire. In that horrible place of damnation they will be unceasingly tormented for ever. This battle will end in swift and decisive victory for us when Christ comes in power and great glory (2 Thess. 2:8).

Here are seven things that need to be understood by all who seek to serve God in this generation.

1. We are living in an apostate religious world

The New Testament teaches us plainly that before Christ comes, as this dispensation is drawn to a rapid conclusion, there will be a general, universal, wholesale departure from the faith of the gospel. It is true, this departure from the gospel began during the days of the apostles. Satan has been around from the beginning. Antichrists were abundant even in the apostolic age (1 John 4:1-3). Yet never before in history have almost all professedly 'Christian churches' of the world so openly denied the gospel of Christ and so unanimously accepted, promoted and preached the lies of Satan. Never before have the philosophy of the world and the religion of the world been so completely united. I am not referring to the apostasy of Rome. Romanism has always been apostate. Papacy was antichrist from the beginning. But in our day, the children of Rome are rapidly returning to their harlot mother, not in name, but in doctrine. The major tenets of virtually all organized 'Christian' religions are purely Roman doctrines. These are things held in common, throughout the world by Presbyterians, Baptists, Methodists, Anglicans, Campbellites, Pentecostals, Mormons, Russellites, liberals, conservatives and fundamentalists, Catholics and non-Catholics, Protestants and non-Protestants. They are even held in common by Jews, Muslims, Hindus and Buddhists. The universally embraced heresies of this apostate age are salvation by free will, justification by works, asceticism (the teaching that evil is in things, not in us!) and rewards, or loss of rewards, in heaven based on works.

No one can know for certain, but it may be that we are now living in the day of Satan's 'little season'. Professing Christianity is in a state of almost total apostasy. There is a remnant according to the election of grace. There are a few individuals and churches scattered throughout the world who believe and preach the truth of God. However, by comparison, they are a very small remnant. The nations of the world have been deceived with the satanic lie of free-will, works religion. This is precisely what God told us would happen in these last days. These are perilous times for the souls of men (1 Tim. 4:1-5; 2 Tim. 3:1-13; 4:1-4; 2 Thess.

2:1-8). Our Lord said, 'I am come in my Father's name, and ye receive me not: if another shall come in his own name, him ye will receive' (John 5:43). It has come to pass. False prophets come in their own name, and men and women flock to hear them, while angrily rejecting the gospel of God's free and sovereign grace in Christ.

2. The apostate religion of this world is the result of God's judicial reprobation

Rolfe Barnard once said, 'This is a reprobate age, an age that cannot be explained apart from the judgement of God.' Here is one of the most solemn things set forth in all the Word of God. When God gives men the light of the gospel and they refuse to walk in it, they are in danger of being reprobate, cast off and deceived by Satan. And this is the work of God! (See Hosea 4:17; Matt. 23:37-38).

3. Reprobation is the work of God

It is the work of God, fixing it so that those who will not receive the truth cannot receive it (Prov. 1:23-33). It is the Lord Jesus Christ himself who turns Satan loose upon the nations for a little season (Rev. 20:3,7). It is God the Holy Spirit who ceases to restrain the powers of darkness (2 Thess. 2:7-8). It is God the Father who sends men a strong delusion, that they might be damned (2 Thess. 2:9-12).

I cannot imagine anything more solemn. The Scriptures tell us that God Almighty sovereignly employs Satan and his hellish religion to secure the damnation of those who hear, but will not receive, the love of the truth! God will not trifle with those who trifle with his Son and the gospel of his grace.

4. How we may identify the messengers of Satan

There are three marks by which the messengers of Satan, by whom the nations of the world are deceived, may be identified:

>   1. Their enchanting miracles (2 Thess. 2:9; Rev. 16:13-14);
>   2. Their evident motives (2 Peter 2:3);
>   3. Their enticing message.

Some of these false prophets have all three marks, some have two, some only one. But every false prophet can be identified by these three marks. He may, or may not, pretend to have apostolic gifts. He may, or may not, be an evidently covetous man. But every false prophet in the world has the same message. He will always mix something, somewhere, with the work of Christ (2 Cor. 11:1-3,13-15). Every false prophet and every false religion, every satanic delusion, makes salvation, acceptance with God and eternal life, to one degree or another, dependent upon man. Somewhere or another, by one means or another, at one point or another, all false religion makes salvation conditional upon something done by the sinner. Any man who preaches conditional grace is a deceiver of men, an instrument of Satan for the damning of men's souls. Salvation is conditioned upon the work of Christ alone! Christ alone is our Saviour (1 Cor. 1:30). And salvation in Christ is by the free grace of God alone (Eph. 2:8-9).

5. God's saints in these dark days have great cause for thanksgiving

If you are one of God's elect, a trophy of his almighty grace, snatched out of this apostate religious world, you have something for which to be thankful (2 Thess. 2:13-14). What an outpouring of praise and thanksgiving must have erupted in the hearts of the Thessalonian believers when they read these verses! Rejoice and give thanks to God for his unspeakable grace and abundant mercy. He has chosen us as the objects of his love. He has redeemed us by the blood of his dear Son (2 Cor. 5:21). He has caused us to hear the gospel (Rom. 10:17; Amos 8:11-12). He has called us by the power of his Spirit (Ps. 65:4). He has given us faith in Christ and saved us from eternal ruin by his omnipotent grace (Eph. 2:1-5, 8-9). And he has kept, and will keep, us from the apostasy of this age (1 John 2:19-28).

6. These days of darkness place us in a position of great responsibility

We must hold fast the form of sound words that we have received (2 Tim. 1:13) and earnestly contend for the faith (Jude 3). We must in these dark days, as never before, make known to men and women who are bound for eternity the gospel of God's free and sovereign grace in Christ (2 Tim. 4:1-5). There is no hope for any apart from the knowledge of Christ in the gospel.

7. There is no cause for despair (Rev. 20:10)

Satan will certainly fall. The truth of God will prevail. The church of God is safe. God's elect cannot be deceived by Satan's lie (Matt. 24:22-24; Mark 13:20-22). The day of victory is at hand. When God our Saviour has finished with our adversary, the devil, he will cast him into the lake of fire, where he can do no more harm.

52.

Christ and the judgement of the great white throne

Revelation 20:11-15

'And I saw a great white throne, and him that sat on it, from whose face the earth and the heaven fled away; and there was found no place for them' (Rev. 20:11).

When will the Day of Judgement be? Who will be judged? Who will be the judge? Will there be one judgement or two? Will there be one judgement for believers and another for unbelievers? Will we be judged first by Christ for our sins and second for our works as believers? These are questions about which there is much needless confusion. A careful study of the teachings of the Word of God about the Day of Judgement will help to clarify our thinking about that great day.

No text in the Bible more clearly teaches us what will happen on that day than Revelation 20:11-15. Read that passage carefully. This is the throne of judgement before which we all must appear in the Last Day. It is called 'a great white throne', to set forth the power, holiness and sovereignty of the one who sits upon it. It is called 'great' because it is the throne of the omnipotent God. It is called 'white' because it is pure, spotless, righteous and just. Nothing proceeds from this throne but justice and truth. It is called a 'throne' because the Judge who sits upon it, before whom we all must stand, is the holy, sovereign Lord God. In the last day, when time shall be no more, we must all appear before the august, great, white throne to be judged by God, to be judged according to the strict and exact righteousness and justice of the thrice-holy God!

However, while the Word of God constantly warns the wicked of the terror of divine judgement and the everlasting wrath of God, the Day of Judgement is never described as a terror to believers, or even a thing to be dreaded by us. Rather, for the believer the Day of Judgement is always set forth as a matter of anticipated joy and glory. On this earth God's saints are constantly misjudged. His servants are maligned and slandered by reprobate men. But in that last great day, God Almighty will vindicate his people and exonerate his servants (1 Cor. 4:3-5). In the Word of God we do not find God's saints dreading that day, but looking forward to it, even anticipating it, with peace. If, as believers, as sinners saved by God's free and sovereign grace, through the sin-atoning blood and imputed righteousness of the Lord Jesus Christ, we understand what the Bible says about that great day, we shall look forward to it, too. With this in mind, let's see what the Bible teaches about the judgement of the great white throne. I do not claim to be an expert on prophetic matters, but I do know that there are five truths clearly revealed in the Word of God about things to come.

1. The Lord Jesus Christ is coming again

Do not concern yourself about the signs of the times and those things which men imagine are indications of the last days. There is very little, if anything, of spiritual value to be gained by studying all the books ever written on prophetic issues. They all have to be rewritten as soon as the predicted events have failed to come to pass! We are never commanded to look for signs of our Lord's coming.

We are commanded to be looking for *him* to come! Get this one blessed fact fixed in your mind — Jesus Christ, our

Lord, our Saviour, the Son of God, is coming again! The Son of God is personally coming again to this earth (Acts 1:9-11). That very same God-man who was born at Bethlehem, who lived as our representative, and died as our sin-atoning substitute on the cross is coming to this earth again. He said, 'I will come again' (John 14:3). The apostle Paul wrote, 'The Lord himself shall descend from heaven' (1 Thess. 4:16). He said, 'The Lord Jesus shall be revealed from heaven' (2 Thess. 1:7; Job 19:25-27). He came once in weakness; he is coming again in power. He came once in humiliation; he is coming again in glory. He came once to be despised; he is coming again to be admired. He came once to suffer; he is coming again to conquer.

The Second Coming of Christ will be sudden, unannounced, unexpected and climatic. Christ will come as a thief in the night, without warning (1 Thess. 5:2). He said, 'I will come on thee as a thief, and thou shalt not know what hour I will come upon thee' (Rev. 3:3). The Lord does not tell us to look for the tribulation, or the regathering of Israel, or the rebuilding of a Jewish temple. He tells us to look for him! If you look for signs and times and seasons, you will be shocked when Christ comes. The only things mentioned in the Word of God that will announce the Lord's coming will be 'a shout, the voice of the archangel and the trump of God' (1 Thess. 4:16). No man knows the day or hour of our Lord's coming, and that is best (Matt. 24:36; Mark 13:32; Acts 1:7).

If we knew the day or hour, we would become irresponsible and negligent with regard to our daily duties. Do not seek to know when Christ is coming. Be content with his promise, and wait for his appearing. Yet we must always look for our Lord Jesus to appear at any moment. 'Behold, he cometh'! (Rev. 1:7). Be on tiptoe with faith and expectation as you look for him. All will be taken by surprise except those who are expecting him to appear. Like those Thessalonians who believed God, we must constantly 'wait for his Son from heaven' (1 Thess. 1:10). Faith is ever 'looking for that blessed hope and the glorious appearing of the great God and our Saviour Jesus Christ' (Titus 2:13). Christ is coming now. Soon he will appear. And when the Son of God appears he will bring with him a crown of righteousness, immortality and life for all who love him and look for his appearing (2 Tim. 4:8; James 1:12).

2. The dead will be raised at his coming

When Christ comes, there will be a great, general resurrection of all who have ever lived upon the earth (Rev. 20:13; John 5:28-29).

First, all who have died in faith will be raised from the grave. All will be raised, but the saints of God will have distinct priority in the resurrection. 'The dead in Christ shall rise first.' The bodies of God's saints will be raised from their graves and reunited with their souls (1 Thess. 4:13-18). All the Old Testament saints and all the saints and martyrs of this age, all who sleep in Jesus, will be raised from their graves!

Then, immediately after the sleeping saints rise, all believers living upon the earth will be changed and caught up to meet the Lord in the air (1 Cor. 15:51-58). As our Lord descends in the brilliant glory of his second coming, we shall go out to meet him and return with him, as he comes with all his saints to burn up the earth, destroy the wicked and make all things new. What a day that will be!

After that, after the Son of God has gathered all the ransomed bodies of his elect from the earth, after he has destroyed all the wicked with the brightness of his coming, all the wicked will be raised. There is a resurrection for the wicked, too. But for those who do not believe, there is no music in the resurrection. The Lord himself will issue a summons they cannot resist. They will stand in terror before him whose grace they have despised and against whom they have sinned! The body and soul now united in sin will be united in horror to be judged by God and suffer his wrath in hell for ever!

3. All men will be judged

Immediately after the resurrection, we must all be judged by God according to the record of our works (Rev. 20:12-13). 'It is appointed unto men once to die, but after this the judgement' (Heb. 9:27). The Judge before whom we must stand is the God-man, whom we have crucified (John 5:22; Acts 17:31; 2 Cor. 5:10). We shall be judged out of the books, according to the record of God's strict justice. When the books are opened, what shocks of terror will seize the hearts and souls of those who have no righteousness and no atonement before the holy Lord God! With the opening of the books, every crime, every offence, every sin they have ever committed, in mind, in heart and in deed, will be exposed! 'Judgement was set; and the books were opened' (Dan. 7:10). I realize that this is figurative language. God does not need books to remember man's sins. However, as John Gill wrote, 'This judgement out of the books, and according to works, is designed to show with what accuracy and exactness, with what justice and equity, it will be executed, in allusion to statute-books in courts of judicature.'

In the Scriptures God is often represented as writing and keeping books. And according to these books we shall all be judged. What are the books?

The book of divine omniscience (Mal. 3:5);
the book of divine remembrance (Mal. 3:16);
the book of creation (Rom. 1:18-20);
the book of God's providence (Rom. 2:4-5);
the book of conscience (Rom. 2:15);

the book of God's holy law (Rom. 2:12 — This book of
the law has two tables: the first table contains all
the sins of men against God (Exod. 20:3-11); the
second table contains all the sins of men against
one another (Exod. 20:12-17);
the book of the gospel (Rom. 2:16).

But there are some against whom no crimes, no sins, no
offences can be found, not even by the omniscient eye of
God himself! 'In those days, and in that time, saith the LORD,
the iniquity of Israel shall be sought for, and there shall be
none; and the sins of Judah, and they shall not be found:
for I will pardon them whom I reserve' (Jer. 50:20). Their
names are found in another book, a book which God himself wrote and sealed before the worlds were made. It is
called 'the book of life'. In this book there is a record of
divine election, the name of Christ, our divine surety, a
record of perfect righteousness (Jer. 23:6; cf. 33:16), a record
of complete satisfaction and the promise of eternal life.

The question is often raised: 'Will God judge his elect
for their sins and failures, committed after they were saved,
and expose them in the Day of Judgement?' The only reason that question is ever raised is because many retain a
remnant of the Roman doctrine of purgatory, by which they
hope to hold over God's saints the whip and terror of the
law. There is absolutely no sense in which those who trust
Christ will ever be made to pay for their sins! Our sins
were imputed to Christ and shall never be imputed to us
again (Rom. 4:8). Christ paid our debt to God's law and
justice, and God will never require us to pay. The God who
has blotted out our transgressions will never write them
again. He who covered our sins will never uncover them!
The perfect righteousness of Christ has been imputed to
us. On the Day of Judgement, God's elect are never represented as having done any evil, but only good (Matt.
25:31-40). The Day of Judgement will be a day of glory and

bliss for Christ and his people, not a day of mourning and sorrow. It will be a marriage supper. Christ will glory in his church. God will display the glory of his grace in us. And we shall glory in our God.

4. The righteous will enter into eternal life

Those who are found perfectly righteous, righteous according to the records of God himself, will enter into eternal life and inherit everlasting glory with Christ. Those that have done good, nothing but good, perfect good, without any spot of sin, wrinkle of iniquity, or trace of transgression, will enter into everlasting life (Rev 22:11). Who are these perfectly righteous ones? They are all who are saved by God's free and sovereign grace in Christ (1 Cor. 6:9-11; Rom. 8:1,32-34). Though there will be degrees of punishment for the wicked in hell, because there are degrees of wickedness, there will be no degrees of reward and glory among the saints in heaven, because there are no degrees of redemption and righteousness. Heaven was earned and purchased for all God's elect by Christ. We were predestined to obtain our inheritance from eternity (Eph. 1:11). Christ has taken possession of heaven's glory as our forerunner (Heb. 6:20). We are heirs of God and joint-heirs with Jesus Christ (Rom. 8:17). Our Saviour gave all the glory he earned as our mediator to all his elect (John 17:5,20-22). And in Christ every believer is worthy of heaven's glory (Col. 1:12). Glorification is but the consummation of salvation, and salvation is by grace alone! That means that no part of heaven's bliss and glory is the reward of our works, but all the reward of God's free grace in Christ! All spiritual blessings are ours from eternity in Christ (Eph. 1:3).

5. The wicked will be cast into hell

All who are found guilty of sin in that great and terrible Day of Judgement will be cast into the lake of fire and there be made to suffer the unmitigated wrath of Almighty God for ever. One by one, God will call the wicked before his throne and judge them. As he says, 'Depart ye cursed,' he will say to his holy angels, 'Take him! Bind him! Cast him into outer darkness!' In that day there will be no mercy, no pity, no sorrow, no hope and no end for the wicked! To hell they deserve to go! To hell they must go! To hell they will go!

Let all who read these lines beware. Unless you flee to Christ and take refuge in him, in that great day the wrath of God will seize you and destroy you for ever! I beseech you now, by the mercies of God, be reconciled to God by trusting his beloved Son! In that great and terrible day let us be found in Christ, not having our own righteousness, but the righteousness of God in Christ.

53.

Christ will make all things new

Revelation 21:1-8

'And I saw a new heaven and a new earth: for the first heaven and the first earth were passed away; and there was no more sea' (Rev. 21:1).

It is impossible for us to grasp the fulness, splendour and glory of the vision John had before him when he wrote Revelation 21. The things described in this chapter are truly glorious. By the time we reach this point, the Lord Jesus Christ has already come in power and great glory. At his coming, our Saviour purged the old creation with fire. The final judgement of the great white throne is over. Then, John writes, 'I saw a new heaven and a new earth.'

Our Lord Jesus Christ will make all things new. When he comes the second time, in the glory of his second advent, the universe in which we now live will be dissolved with fire, and thus purged of all the consequences of sin. The slime of the serpent will be erased from God's creation. The heavens will depart as a scroll when it is rolled together. And every mountain and island will be removed out of their places (Rev. 6:14). Peter wrote, 'The day of the Lord will come as a thief in the night; in which the heavens shall pass away with a great noise, and the elements shall melt with fervent heat, the earth also and the works that are therein shall be burned up' (2 Peter 3:10). Every trace of sin upon the handiwork of God will be removed.

Then the Lord Jesus Christ will create a new heaven and a new earth (Isa. 65:17; 66:22; 2 Peter 3:11-13). He will redeem the earth itself from the bondage of corruption by his transforming power and make this earth a suitable habitation for his glorified saints (Rom. 8:20-23). In these eight verses John describes five things revealed to him by the Spirit of God.

1. The new creation (v. 1)

The old world, with all its sorrows and troubles, this world of care, will pass away to make room for an entirely new world: 'I saw a new heaven and a new earth!' The word that is used here implies that John saw a new creation, but not another creation. What the apostle saw was heaven and earth completely purged of sin and regenerated, renewed and rejuvenated by the power of God. In this new creation, all the potentialities of nature, so long held in bondage by sin, will be fully realized. All the curse of sin will be removed from the earth. Weeds, thorns and thistles will be no more. The old order of the world will vanish away. All rebellion against the throne of God will be ended!

'And there was no more sea.' The sea is a constant emblem of trouble. The raging, roaring, tempest-tossed waves of the sea represent the agitation and unrest of the world in opposition to Christ. The beast, symbolically, arose out of the sea. The great harlot (the religion of Antichrist) and all the nations of the world are found in the sea (Rev. 13:1; 17:15).

In Christ's new creation, everything will be peace. When this earth is restored to its pristine beauty, it will be a glorious habitation for the glorified sons of God. As Eden was the garden of the Lord, perfect and glorious, a home well suited for our sinless parents, the whole world will then be a home well suited for God's sinless people when it is delivered from the bondage of corruption. This new creation

will be the eternal home of all who have been made new
creatures in Christ (2 Cor. 5:17). 'We, according to his promise, look for new heavens and a new earth, wherein dwelleth
righteousness' (2 Peter 3:13). This will be the ultimate consequence of Christ's redemptive work and God's transforming grace. Christ gave us a new standing in redemption, a
new nature in regeneration and will give us a new creation
in eternity.

2. The new Jerusalem (v. 2)

'The holy city, new Jerusalem,' is not a literal walled city.
It is the church of the living God in its complete, perfect
state. John describes the new Jerusalem (God's glorified
church) more fully later. For now he simply tells us three
things about it.

The church of God is 'the holy city, new Jerusalem'

It is called 'new' to distinguish it from the earthly Jerusalem, the symbolical Old Testament centre of worship. It is
'holy' because it has been purged and cleansed of all sin by
the blood of Christ and the power of his grace. It is evident
from the Scriptures that 'the holy city, new Jerusalem' is
the whole church of God's elect (Ps. 48:1-2; Isa. 26:1-2; 40:9;
Gal. 4:26; Heb. 12:22-24). It is called a 'city' because a city
is a place of permanent residence, made up of a great
number of people, and a place of security and safety. This
'holy city' will be our home, the place of our family and of
our most intimate fellowship (Heb. 11:16).

This 'holy city' comes down from God out of heaven

When Christ comes again to the earth all the saints of God
will come with him into his new creation (Dan. 7:13-14,18;
Jude 14).

The church of God is 'prepared as a bride adorned for her husband'

This describes the church in her eternal, glorified state, beautified with all the perfection of holiness, in perfect conformity to the Lord Jesus Christ. This was the object of God the Father in election (Eph. 1:4; Rom. 8:29-30), the goal of God the Son in redemption (Eph. 5:25-27) and the objective of God the Holy Spirit in regeneration (Eph. 1:13-14). This great, glorious event will be the final, climatic result of Christ's work as our Saviour and surety (Heb. 2:13).

3. The divine presence (v. 3)

This will be the glory of heaven, the joy of the saints and the delight of the new creation. The Lord our God, in the person of Jesus Christ his Son, will be immediately and eternally present with his people. God will eternally dwell among men. The spiritual presence of Christ with his church is her glory in this world (John 14:23). In the midst of all our troubles, the Lord is with us (Isa. 43:1-5; Heb. 13:5). He graciously visits his saints in our assemblies in the sweet manifestations of his presence through the ordinances of divine worship (Matt. 18:20). But, blessed as our fellowship is now, it cannot begin to compare with the presence of God which we shall enjoy in the new creation. God himself will be with us for ever. His presence with us and our communion with him will never be interrupted. This is the heaven of heaven. In that blessed state, we shall enjoy perfect communion with Christ, perfect commitment to Christ and perfect conformity to Christ for ever. In that state, our covenant interest in, and relationship to, the triune God will be perfectly revealed, realized and enjoyed. We shall find eternal delight and satisfaction with God. And God will find eternal delight and satisfaction with us!

4. The bliss of eternity (v. 4)

In that day, trouble will be no more. God will wipe away
all tears from our eyes. We have many tears to shed here.
Our sins, our afflictions, our heartaches, the struggles of
our souls, the troubles of God's church in this world and
the perishing souls of lost friends and relatives all cause
our cheeks to burn with tears. But God will dry our tears
with the knowledge of complete forgiveness, acquiescence
in his perfect will and the accomplishment of his glory in
all things. All possible causes of future sorrow will also be
removed. In the new creation there will be no possibility of
pain, sorrow, crying, or death, because there will be no more
sin. In that state, as we have seen, the very consequences
of sin will be gone. There will be absolutely no sorrow of
any kind, 'for the former things are passed away' (Isa. 25:8;
35:10; 51:11). That one statement destroys the teachings of
purgatory, degrees of reward in heaven, mourning in heaven
over the lost and even weeping in heaven over past sins.
There will be nothing for God's saints in eternity but an
everlasting fulness of glory and joy.

5. The divine assurance (v. 5)

These blessed promises of glory to come are here assured
to us by the oath of him who is 'faithful and true'. Our
Saviour says, 'Behold, I make all things new!' The language
is in the present tense. He is now making all things new by
his providence and grace (Rom. 8:28; 11:36; 2 Cor. 5:17).
Soon his work will be done. When that great day comes, he
will declare, 'It is done!' All that was purposed and planned
by God the Father before the world began, all that Christ
agreed to as our surety in the everlasting covenant, all that
he came into this world to accomplish, will be done when

time is no more. God's works will be finished exactly as he purposed. Everything that has been, is now, or will be in the future will serve his glorious purpose and ultimately glorify him. Everything, in the end, will prove to have been the work of God for the salvation of his people. It is written: 'All things are of God' (2 Cor. 5:18). And when our dear Saviour has made all things new, when the triune God has finished his work, we shall see that it has been so (Rom. 8:28-30).

54.

Christ makes all things new

Revelation 21:5-8

'And he that sat upon the throne said, Behold, I make all things new. And he said unto me, Write: for these words are true and faithful' (Rev. 21:5).

We rejoice to know that the Lord Jesus Christ will soon come again and that when he comes, he will make all things new. He will create 'a new heaven and a new earth'! As we saw in our previous chapter, this is what John saw and described in Revelation 21:1-4. The believer anticipates, with anxious heart, that great day when our God makes his creation new. We look forward to that new heaven and new earth 'wherein dwelleth righteousness'. However, it must never be forgotten that the Son of God exercises his renewing, creative power in this day. The basis of our confidence regarding the new creation of heavenly glory is our experience of the new creation of grace.

First, in verses 1-4, John saw the new heaven and new earth that Christ will make. Then he heard the Son of God declare, 'Behold, I make all things new!' It is as though our Lord were saying, 'John, the promise of a new heaven and a new earth should not take you by surprise. These things should not astonish you. Behold, I am making all things new right now by my saving, renewing, regenerating grace.' Every time he saves a sinner by his almighty grace, he makes all things new for that sinner, and when he comes at the Last Day he will make all things new in God's creation.

The announcement of grace

'He that sat upon the throne said, Behold, I make all things new.' With these words the Lord Jesus Christ, our Saviour, announces his great work of grace. Meditate upon each word carefully.

'He that sat upon the throne' is Christ himself, the great God-man, the exalted mediator, the Redeemer and King of his people. He sat upon the throne of universal dominion for ever as God (Heb. 1:8). He sits upon the throne now as the Lamb of God, upon the basis of his mediatorial accomplishments as the sinner's substitute (John 17:2). He sits upon the throne because his work of redemption is finished (Rom. 8:34). He sits upon the throne with the ease of an absolute monarch, possessing total sovereignty, without the slightest possibility of his throne being toppled or his decrees being nullified (Isa. 46:10).

'He that sat upon the throne said, Behold! [Give me your attention. Hear what I say. Give thoughtful consideration to my words. I am doing wondrous things for the sons of men.] I make all things new!' Christ, the Creator and Sustainer of all things in the physical creation, is the one who makes all things in the new creation. Nothing is attributed to the will of man. The Son of God says, 'I make all things new!' Whatever this new creation is, he assures us that it is his work alone, accomplished by his power, according to his purpose, arising from his grace and performed for his praise. The apostle Paul uses similar language in 2 Corinthians 5:17: 'If any man be in Christ, he is a new creature: old things are passed away; behold, all things are become new.' The new creation is accomplished by the merits of Christ's obedience and the power of his Spirit through

the preaching of the gospel of his grace and glory. Everything in the new creation comes from him, is centred on
him and directs our hearts to him. He says, 'I make all things
new!' In the new creation, we are the beneficiaries of a
new covenant (Jer. 31:31-34; 32:38-40), the recipients of a
new nature (2 Peter 1:4; 1 John 3:9-10), given a new relationship (1 John 3:1-2), brought into a new family (Eph.
3:15; Mark 3:31-35), made to worship in a new way (Heb.
10:19-24) and granted a new record in heaven (Isa. 43:25;
44:22; Jer. 50:20).

The new covenant is the everlasting covenant of grace
made between God the Father, God the Son and God the
Holy Spirit before the world began. In that covenant the
salvation of God's elect was secured by the covenant promises of the three persons of the Godhead to one another.
The new nature created in the believer is the nature of Christ
himself, a holy nature. Christ does not repair the old nature.
He gives his people a new nature. The old nature remains
with us, so that we cannot do the things we would. Sinless
perfection is impossible, even for a moment! But there is in
every believer a new nature that brings forth fruit unto God
(Gal. 5:22-23).

Our new relationship with God is one of sonship. God
no longer deals with us as with slaves under the yoke of
the law, and we no longer serve God as slaves by the con-
straint of the law. We are the sons of God! Can you imagine
anything more ennobling? Being the sons and daughters of
God, we are now members of a new family, the family of
God. Our family is a large one. It includes the whole church
of God's elect. And it is well supplied, for God himself is
the one who provides for us. All the members of this family, all whose names are written in heaven, worship God in
a new way. We come to God by faith in Christ, trusting the
merits of his blood. We are all priests unto God. We do
business in the holy place personally and are accepted there
in Christ.

In this new creation, 'Old things are passed away; behold, all things are become new.' That means that our old
record of sin is gone. Christ has purged away our sins by
the blood of his cross. It also means that we have a new
record in heaven. In the books of God we are declared to be
perfectly righteous, because we have been made the righteousness of God in Christ by divine imputation (2 Cor. 5:21).

The assurance of grace

Having made this marvellous declaration of grace, anticipating our hesitancy to believe such great things, our Saviour gives us this perpetual word of assurance: 'And he said
unto me, Write: for these words are true and faithful.'
Whether you are a young believer, one who has just come
to Christ, or one who has been in Christ for many, many
years, before God all things are new — perpetually new,
immutably new, eternally new! Your feelings will fluctu-
ate, your failings will be many and your experiences will
often appear to contradict God's work of grace and word of
promise, but the new creation does not depend upon you.
It depends only upon the truth and faithfulness of our great
God and Saviour (2 Tim. 2:12-13,19). The Lord God will
never disown his child, disinherit him, cease to be gracious to him, or change his record in heaven. He will not
impute sin to the one he has forgiven (Rom. 4:8). Because
the new creation is God's work, it is for ever. Nothing can
be taken from it. Nothing can be added to it (Eccles. 3:14).

The accomplishment of grace

Read these next words and rejoice: 'And he said unto me, It
is done'! The gospel of Christ is good news to sinners who
can do nothing for themselves, because it declares that the

whole work of grace is done. The whole business of making all things new is finished. It was done before the world
began. All the blessings of grace and salvation were fully
given to God's elect in Christ before the world began (Eph.
1:3; 2 Tim. 1:9). In him, according to God's everlasting purpose of grace, we were predestinated, called, justified and
glorified from eternity (Rom. 8:28-30). The work was done
when Christ died. When our Saviour cried, 'It is finished'
(John 19:30), he declared that the whole work of righteousness and redemption, the whole accomplishment of God's
will by which we are sanctified and made perfect (Heb.
10:5-14), was completed. The work is done when the
chosen, redeemed sinner believes on the Lord Jesus Christ.
Our faith adds nothing to what Christ has done. Faith receives Christ and all that he has done. Yet no one has any
right to claim Christ and grace until he believes. 'He that
believeth on the Son hath everlasting life: and he that
believeth not the Son shall not see life; but the wrath of
God abideth on him' (John 3:36). If you believe on Christ,
you are a new creature in Christ. Your faith in him is the
fruit of his creation, the gift of his grace and the evidence
of your election, redemption and calling.

The accomplisher of grace

Once more the Lord Jesus declares, 'I am Alpha and Omega,
the beginning and the end.' Staying with the context, we
see that he is telling us the whole work of making all things
new is his alone. He is the beginning of the new creation
and the end of it. To put it another way, 'Salvation is of the
Lord!' He planned it. He purchased it. He performs it. He
preserves it. And he perfects it. Therefore, he alone is to
have the praise of it, 'that, according as it is written, He
that glorieth, let him glory in the Lord' (1 Cor. 1:31).

The abundance of grace

In the new creation, grace is both abundant and free. The Son of God declares, 'I will give to him that is athirst of the fountain of the water of life freely.' John Gill accurately describes this spiritual thirst as the thirst of a needy soul for Christ himself, for pardon and righteousness, for communion with, and conformity to, Christ, a thirst for a greater knowledge of Christ and for the glories of his kingdom. This thirst the Lord Jesus promises to quench abundantly, with 'the fountain of the water of life', and 'freely', without money, without price, without qualification of any kind to be met by the sinner. In Christ, grace is free and abundant!

'He that overcometh shall inherit all things'

All believers will overcome sin, Satan and the world, because all believers are more than conquerors in Christ (Rom. 8:35-39). Overcoming by the blood of the Lamb, every child of God 'shall inherit all things'. We are 'heirs of God, and joint-heirs with Christ' (Rom. 8:17). That means that all that Christ possesses as our mediator we shall possess in him for ever. This one statement from the lips of our Lord should be sufficient to put to silence all questions about degrees of reward in heaven. The Son of God declares that every saved sinner 'shall inherit all things'!

'And I will be his God, and he shall be my son'

Christ himself, in whom we were adopted and by whom we have been purchased, is the mighty God and our everlasting Father (Isa. 9:6). We are his seed and his offspring. Here he promises us his perpetual presence, protection and provision for ever. In heavenly glory, he will see his seed with satisfaction, prolong his days and enjoy the fruit of his toil in us for ever. He will present us to himself in the perfection of holiness (Eph. 5:27) and present us to the Father (Heb. 2:13). Though now we are the sons of God, 'It doth not yet appear what we shall be' (1 John 3:2). But this we are assured of: Christ will be ours for ever and we shall be his for ever in the fulness and perfection of heavenly glory!

The admonition of grace

In verse 8, there is a strong word of warning and admonition. It is possible that someone may have read the pages of this book and yet not be a new creature in Christ. Be warned! Salvation is more than a profession of faith, a religious experience, doctrinal soundness, or a moral reformation. Salvation is a new creation (Gal. 6:15). You must be made a new creature, or you must die for ever. Are you a part of this new creation? Are you a new creature in Christ? If you are, do not ever forget where and what you were when God saved you (1 Cor. 6:9-11). Consecrate yourself to the Lord Jesus Christ, your gracious God and Creator. 'Ye are not your own. For ye are bought with a price: therefore glorify God in your body, and in your spirit, which are God's' (1 Cor. 6:19-20).

55.

Christ and the holy city, the new Jerusalem

Revelation 21:9 - 22:5

'And he carried me away in the spirit to a great and high mountain, and showed me that great city, the holy Jerusalem, descending out of heaven from God' (Rev. 21:9).

Throughout the book of Revelation we have seen vision after vision of the Lord Jesus Christ in his redemptive, saving, preserving grace. Every vision seen and recorded by John sets forth the whole history of redemption from the incarnation of Christ until the final consummation of all things at his glorious second advent. Each vision is historical, current and prophetic. And, as you read through the book, you get a sense of anticipation. Everything appears to be moving in one direction, with steady pace, towards a particular end. Really, history is not circular, but linear. All history moves in a direct line to one, glorious end, to accomplish one object. And that object is the complete revelation of God's glory in the salvation of his elect by Christ Jesus. This is the vision which John describes in Revelation 21:9 – 22:5.

In this passage of Scripture we have a beautiful, symbolic picture of the church of God, the Bride of Christ, as God views her. It is the holy city, the new Jerusalem. Remember, the picture is altogether symbolical. It is a picture of the church of God in her eternal, heavenly glory. But this vision of the church's triumphant glory is also a vision of the church's present glory in Christ. In Christ, by virtue of our union with him, the church of God, and every member of it, is perfectly and eternally complete (Col. 2:10). In this passage, John tells us twelve things about the church of the living God as she will be in that glorious state called 'the holy Jerusalem'.

1. The 'holy city'

The church of God is described as a city, the holy city, the new Jerusalem (21:10,16,18). The church is a community of men and women who have fellowship with God in the Lord Jesus Christ. This community will, in its ultimate fulness, be an enormous, flourishing city. It is called 'the holy city' because it has been purified and made holy by the blood of Christ. It is called 'the new Jerusalem' because it has been renewed by the grace and power of God the Holy Spirit. It is called a 'great city' because it is made up of a vast multitude which no man can number. The new Jerusalem is a radiant, highly valued city, a city of pure gold because God considers his church the most valuable thing in his creation. And it is described as a city four square (1,400 miles high, 1,400 miles long and 1,400 miles wide), complete and in perfect symmetry because it is altogether perfect (Ps. 48:12-14).

2. The Bride of Christ

This holy city, the church, is the Bride of Christ (21:2,9). The people of this city are the objects of his eternal love, the choice of his heart, the bride to whom he is betrothed, for whom the dowry of righteousness and redemption has been paid and whom he is coming to wed.

3. The light of the city

This city, the new Jerusalem, is a well-lit city (21:11,23; 22:5). The Lord God himself, as he is revealed and known in the sin-atoning Lamb, is the light of the city. Christ the light drives out the darkness of ignorance and the night of sorrow. It is only in Christ that the glory of God is seen in this world (2 Cor. 4:4-6). And it is only in Christ that the glory of God can be seen in heaven (Isa. 60:1,3,5,19-21). God is Spirit. We cannot see a spirit. But we shall see all the fulness of the triune God in the person of our Saviour, when we see him face to face (John 1:18).

4. The presence of God

The church is the temple of God, but here John tells us that God is the temple of his church (Rev. 21:22). It is true that God dwells in us, but we learn from this passage that we dwell in God! And, in eternity, we shall have the full manifestation and enjoyment of the atmosphere of God's being. The radiance of God's being will fill the entire city of God. It will be fully manifest everywhere, to everyone. There will be no back settlements in the heavenly Canaan, no dark corners in the new Jerusalem. All God's elect will dwell in the immediate, direct, presence of God for ever.

5. The security of the city

The new Jerusalem is a divinely secured fortress of grace (Rev. 21:12,17-18). Round about this city is a great high wall, a wall with four sides. It is an unseen wall, but it is a very secure wall. The wall of our salvation is our great God (Zech. 2:5). We are secured from all harm and all real danger by the purpose, purchase, power and promises of our God.

6. The foundations of the city

The foundations upon which this city is built are the twelve apostles of Christ (Rev. 21:14,19,20). Men and women come into this city, into this church of God, and enter into glory at last, by the preaching of the apostles, by the message they delivered — the gospel of Christ. The apostles were the messengers of the Lamb. Their foundations are really one — Jesus Christ himself (Eph. 2:20; 1 Cor. 3:9). In this great foundation, all the glorious attributes of God are revealed and set forth by many precious stones.

7. The gates of the city

This great city has twelve gates of pearl (Rev. 21:12-13, 21,25,27; 22:14-15). There are plenty of open gates on every side for all who will enter. But the gates are made and opened for a specific people. They are the ones whose names are inscribed upon them, 'the twelve tribes of the children of Israel', that is to say, God's elect. At every gate there is an angel, a messenger, calling for men to enter into the city. These messengers represent God's preachers. The gates are pearls, one pearl, even the Pearl of great price, Jesus Christ. He is the door, the only door, by whom we enter the city. The gates to the City Beautiful are never shut. Christ is an open door by whom sinners draw near to, and find acceptance with, the eternal God.

8. The street of the city

The street of the city is pure gold, transparent as glass (Rev. 21:21). There is only one street running through the city. It leads from every gate right up to the throne of God, the river of the waters of life and the tree of life. And that street is the pure, transparent, golden gospel of Christ. This street represents the gospel, the only way to God. It is pure and transparent. It has nothing to hide. And it is more valuable than all the gold of the earth.

9. The river of life

This great city is supplied with life by the river of the water of life, proceeding from the throne of God (Rev. 22:1; Ps. 46:4). The source of life is the throne of God. And the river of life is the Lord Jesus Christ, our Saviour.

10. The tree of life

In the midst of the city is the tree of life (Rev. 22:1-3). This represents the cross of Christ, the message of blood atonement by the crucified substitute (Gal. 3:13). It bears fruit regularly, at appointed times (Isa. 55:11). It bears abundant fruit. Its leaves (i.e., its doctrines) are for the healing of the nations. The message of redemption by Christ is the means by which God heals the souls of men (John 3:14-16).

11. The King on the throne

In the new Jerusalem God sits upon his throne (Rev. 22:3-4). There his sovereignty is acknowledged, his will is obeyed and his face is seen.

12. The inhabitants of the city

The inhabitants of the holy city, the new Jerusalem, are God's elect (Rev. 21:24,27). All whose names are written in the book of life (that is, all the elect), all who were redeemed by the blood of Christ, all who are justified and sanctified (saved and made holy) in Christ by the grace of God, all who believe on the Lord Jesus Christ, will be in the new Jerusalem and will reign for ever and ever with the Son of God! Will you be among the inhabitants of that city?

56.
Heaven — who shall enter in?

Revelation 21:27

'And there shall in no wise enter into it any thing that defileth, neither whatsoever worketh abomination, or maketh a lie: but they which are written in the Lamb's book of life (Rev. 21:27).

The church of God in this world is like the tabernacle in the wilderness. On the *inside*, it is lit up with the glory of God's presence. We are the temple of the living God. God dwells in our midst. God the Holy Spirit resides in the hearts of his people. And the one person who always attends the assembly of the saints is the Son of God, our Saviour, the Lord Jesus Christ. Wherever two or three gather in his name, he is present with them (Matt. 18:20). On the *outside*, God's church is guided and protected by the fiery and cloudy pillar of God's eternal providence. As God led Israel in the wilderness, fed them, protected them and defended them under the symbol of the fiery and cloudy pillar, so he leads, feeds, protects and defends his church today.

But, to all outward appearance, the church of God in this world seems a common, unattractive, despised thing. Insofar as the nations were concerned, the tabernacle was nothing but a crude tent. God was there, but they were unaware of it. The altar was there, but they had no use for it. The sacrifice of atonement was there, but they despised it. The mercy-seat was there, but they could not see it. All they could see was a poor, homeless people who had no

place to worship but a crude tent, and a people who claimed
to be the only true worshippers of God in the world. The
faithful Jews would not worship at any other altar. They
refused to acknowledge as brethren any who would not
worship their God. They acknowledged only one way of
salvation — blood atonement! For these things they were
always despised, persecuted and mocked by the world
around them.

The tabernacle in the wilderness was, in these ways, a
symbol and picture of God's church in this world. God
dwells in his church. Christ Jesus guides and protects his
church. But the world — and all the religions of the world
— mocks and despises the church of God. It will not always be so. There is a day coming when the tables will be
turned. In the last day the Lord God will reveal his glory in
his church and glorify his church before all the universe
(John 17:22-23; Eph. 2:7). In Revelation 21:10-27 John shows
us the glorified church of God in the Last Day (see Eph.
5:25-27). Christ loved his church, died to redeem it, sancti-
fies it and will perfect and glorify it.

In the Last Day, the Lord Jesus will present his church,
in all the resurrection glory he puts upon her, to the Father's
throne. And all the world will marvel at his glory and grace
revealed in his church. Look at John's description of her
glory. We shall be presented before the throne of God, before the adoring angels, before Satan and before the eyes of
the damned as a virgin bride (v. 9), the city of God (vv. 10-11),
a walled fortress (v. 12), a great, massive city (vv. 12-17), a
perfect, complete city (v. 16), an indescribably wealthy people
(vv. 18-21), a perfectly happy, satisfied people (vv. 22-23)
and a universally honoured, glorious church (vv. 24-26).

The church of God will be the crowning glory of the
new creation in eternity. 'As it is written, Eye hath not seen,
nor ear heard, neither have entered into the heart of man,
the things which God hath prepared for them that love him'
(1 Cor. 2:9). No tongue can tell, because no mind can

conceive, the glory that awaits the church of God in heaven's eternal bliss.

A solemn fact

But some will never enter into the glory and bliss of heaven: 'And there shall in no wise enter into it anything that defileth, neither whatsoever worketh abomination, or maketh a lie: but they which are written in the Lamb's book of life.' Heaven is an eternal state of perfect holiness into which nothing but perfect holiness can enter.

Here is a very solemn fact: 'There shall in no wise enter into it anything that defileth, neither whatsoever worketh abomination, or maketh a lie.' Heaven will never be polluted by sin. God almighty is holy, righteous, just and perfect. That which dwells with him for ever must be holy, righteous, just and perfect. In order for anything, or anyone, to enter heaven it must be perfect. Any lack of absolute, total perfection must exclude us for ever from the presence of God. Perfect holiness cannot tolerate anything less than perfect holiness. When sin defiled Eden, Eden was destroyed for ever because God will not tolerate sin. His law requires a perfect obedience from man and threatens any lack of perfection with death. And the law requires a perfect sacrifice for atonement. Even God's own dear Son, when he was defiled with sin, was forsaken by God and slain! God requires perfection. Heaven is a world of perfection. Defilement, abomination and deceit shall never enter into it. Sin shall never darken the kingdom of light or defile the City Beautiful.

It is not at all a matter of bigotry or harshness to declare that heaven shall never be defiled by sin. It is only a matter of righteousness and justice, to which every rational person must give assent. Everything in heaven, everyone in heaven and everyone going to heaven is in full agreement with this decree: 'There shall in no wise enter into it anything that defileth.' We have seen what sin has done to the world of the angels, the physical world and our fallen race. We do not want to see heaven ruined by it. The essence of heaven's bliss is the total absence of sin in that blessed state. God's saints are citizens of a land where there is no sin. We are going to an eternal world, where sin will never be found. One of heaven's greatest attractions and most cherished glories is total freedom from sin. There we shall enjoy perfect communion with, perfect conformity to, and consecration to, the Lord Jesus Christ. Should sin be permitted to enter, all would be ruined! Sin would disrupt the peace of heaven, destroy the joy of heaven and defile the beauty of heaven for ever.

This exclusion of sin from heaven is the exclusion of all who are sinners. 'There shall in no wise enter into it anything that defileth.' No person who defiles, no fallen spirit, no sinful man can enter the gates of the New Jerusalem. No tendency to sin, no thought of sin, no will to sin, no desire for sin can go to heaven. Were it possible for a sinner to go to heaven, he could never enter into the heavenly state. The essence of heaven is a condition, not a place. It is a condition of worship, holiness and delight in God. If a sinner could get to the place of heaven, he still could not be in the condition of heaven. He would be out of his element. Heaven would be misery for a sinful man if he should enter it in such a condition.

Our own hearts give full agreement with this exclusion: 'There shall in no wise enter into it anything that defileth.' If I might enter into heaven as I am at this moment, as I write these lines, with my sinful heart and nature, it would be a horrible crime for me to do so, for my presence there would defile the city of God. Just as a leper would not, and could not, enter the temple of God, lest he defile that holy place and all who were there, no sinner will be allowed to enter heaven. Just as we demand that those with a deadly disease be isolated from healthy society for the sake of the living, God demands that sinners be banished from himself and from his saints in heaven.

This exclusion of sin from heaven is the absolute exclusion of all who defile, make abomination, or make a lie. John is telling us that sinners of every kind must be excluded for ever from the paradise of God: 'There shall in no wise enter into it anything that defileth.' No evil thought, words, or deeds may enter heaven. Those who enter the city of God must be free of these things. If we are defiled by sin, in any way, we cannot enter heaven. No unclean thing shall enter the temple of God (Isa. 52:1).

'There shall in no wise enter into it anything that ... worketh abomination.' Abomination in Scripture usually refers to idolatry, the making of idols, the worship of idols and the service of idols (1 Kings 11:4-8). The most abominable thing in this world in the sight of God is false religion, idolatry. If a person's religion is false, if he worships strange gods, he cannot go to heaven. Should anyone ask, 'What is a strange god?' It must be answered, any god who wants to save, but lacks the power to save, any god who sends people he loves to hell, any god whose will is frustrated, whose purpose is defeated, whose power is limited, is a strange god.

'There shall in no wise enter into it anything that maketh a lie.' All false prophets and false teachers, inventors and perpetrators of religious lies will be excluded from the paradise of God (1 Tim. 4:1-2; 2 Thess. 2:11-12).

'There shall in no wise enter into it anything that defileth, neither whatsoever worketh abomination, or maketh a lie.'

A solemn conclusion

In the light of these things, it must be concluded that no human being can, in his natural condition, enter into heaven. All who are without Christ are without hope (Eph.

2:11-13). 'Flesh and blood cannot inherit the kingdom of God' (1 Cor. 15:50). Without Christ there is no hope of mercy, no blood atonement, no righteousness, no eternal life and no hope before God. Revelation 21:27 destroys for ever all hope of self-salvation (Jer. 13:9). Can a sinful man wash away his own sins? Can a dead man give himself life? Can a guilty man make righteousness for himself? If any of us are saved, we must be saved by grace (Eph. 2:8).

Even those who are saved by the grace of God must undergo a great change before we can enter into heaven. Many are of the opinion that God's saints in this world get riper and riper for heaven in progressive holiness and sanctification until at last they are ready for heaven. But it is not so. Though we are made perfectly righteous before God by righteousness imputed and imparted to us before we can enter into heaven, we must drop this robe of flesh in death. And our bodies must be transformed in the resurrection.

A word of hope

Yet the Holy Spirit gives us a blessed word of hope. I know that nothing evil shall enter heaven, nothing and no one who defiles, works abomination, or makes a lie shall enter heaven. No one has the right to enter by nature. And no one can ever earn the right to enter. But there is hope. God has written a book of election, and all whose names are written in that book will enter in. No one shall enter into heaven 'but they which are written in the Lamb's book of life'.

I want to know one thing: is my name written in that book? If it is, all is well. If it is not, I must be damned for ever. Is my name written there? I know this, if my name is written there it was written there in eternity (Rev. 13:8) because of a covenant (2 Sam. 23:5), and it was written there permanently. The Lamb's book of life is a book of election, a record of redemption and a promise of life.

I take the liberty of writing in the first person because I want all who read these lines to apply what is here written to themselves personally. I am confident that my name is written in that blessed book. Are you? I have this confidence for only one reason: I trust the Lord Jesus Christ. Trusting Christ I have life (John 3:36), and, by his grace, I have all that God requires for entrance into heaven (Col. 1:12; 2:9-10). In Christ I have complete atonement for all my sins (Rom. 5:10). In Christ I have perfect righteousness. He is the Lord my righteousness. His righteousness is as truly mine as my sin was once his (Jer. 23:6; 33:16; 1 Cor. 1:30; 2 Cor. 5:21). In Christ I am assured of a glorious change. When I die, as I soon shall, I shall depart this world of sin to be with Christ in heaven's world of holiness (2 Cor. 5:1-9). And when my Redeemer comes again I shall be in the resurrection of the just because in him I am totally justified before God (John 5:28-29; 1 Cor. 15:51-58).

If you believe on the Lord Jesus Christ, you too will enter into that glorious state called 'heaven' because, from eternity, your name was 'written in the Lamb's book of life' by the very finger of God. May God help you to believe!

57.

With Christ in heaven: paradise regained

Revelation 22:1-5

'And there shall be no more curse: but the throne of God and of the Lamb shall be in it; and his servants shall serve him' (Rev. 22:3).

When God created the first man, Adam, he placed him in the Garden of Eden. Eden was a place of innocence, abundance, life and joy. It was paradise on earth. But paradise was not complete for Adam until the Lord God had given him a woman to be his bride. So the Lord caused Adam to sleep in the earth and took a rib from his side. From Adam's wounded side Eve was made. She came from Adam. She was a part of Adam. Without Adam, Eve could never have lived. Yet without Eve, Adam could never have been complete.

Adam and Eve had for their home the paradise of God. There they lived in perfect harmony, holiness and happiness. But soon the serpent beguiled Eve and persuaded her to eat from the tree of the knowledge of good and evil. And Adam, when he saw what Eve had done, took the fruit of the tree in rebellion against God. Sin had entered the world. Paradise was lost. Fallen man was driven away from the presence of the Lord.

But, in the fulness of time, the Second Adam was born. Jesus Christ, the Son of God, came into the world to seek his beloved bride, his elect church. He came to recover for us what we lost in Adam. By his obedience unto death, he has regained for us all that we lost in Adam: righteousness, peace, life, fellowship with God, and paradise. And he has already entered the paradise of God as our representative, claiming it in the name of his people (Heb. 6:20). But, as Adam was incomplete without Eve, so Christ is incomplete without his beloved bride. The head must have the body. The bridegroom must have his bride. And Christ must have his church, 'which is his body, the fulness of him that filleth all in all' (Eph. 1:23). When Christ and his church are united in heaven, in the perfection of heavenly glory, paradise will have been fully recovered.

In this passage, John describes the holy city, new Jerusalem, using symbols drawn from the Garden of Eden (see vv. 1-5). The eternal, heavenly state of God's saints with Christ is paradise regained. Our Lord said to the thief on the cross, 'Today shalt thou be with me in paradise' (Luke 23:43). The apostle Paul was 'caught up into paradise' (2 Cor. 12:4). That blessed place and condition is described as 'the paradise of God' (Rev. 2:7). When God's saints leave this world, they enter into paradise, not purgatory; not limbo, but paradise! What is it like? In these five verses John shows us six things about paradise:

1. The river of paradise (v. 1)

The earthly paradise was watered by a mighty river, but it was only a river of water for the earth. The heavenly paradise is watered by the river of the water of life (v. 1).

The symbolism of the river

This river of the water of life is the everlasting love of God (Ps. 46:4). Like a river, the love of God is ever flowing towards his elect, abundant and free (Eph. 3:18-19). The streams of this river make glad the hearts of God's people.

442 Discovering Christ in Revelation

These streams, like the rivers in Eden, run in four directions across the earth. They are: eternal election, blood atonement, effectual calling, peace, pardon, justification and eternal life. Flowing to sinners from the river of God's everlasting love, through the mediation of Christ, these blessings of grace bring us eternal life. This river is called the 'river of the water of life' (Zech. 14:8-9; John 7:38-39) because the love of God is the source and cause of life, revives the saints with life and sustains them in life.

The purity of the river

God's love for us is a mighty, flowing river that is pure and clear as crystal. His love for us is pure, sincere, true, without hypocrisy. And the love of God is as clear as crystal. It is free, without motive or condition. It promotes purity. The gospel, which reveals it, is a gospel of purity and holiness. The grace which is the fruit of it is righteousness. And every discovery of this love compels and constrains us to consecrate ourselves to Christ in obedience, love and faith. The love of God is free from licentiousness and can never promote it.

The source of the river

The source of this great river of love is the throne of God and of the Lamb. God's love for us is not caused by, or conditioned upon, our obedience or love to him. His love for us precedes our love for him and is the cause of our love for him (1 John 4:19). God's love for us is not caused or conditioned even upon the obedience and death of Christ as our substitute. It was God's love for us that sent Christ to die for us and redeem us (John 3:16; Rom. 5:8; 1 John 3:16; 4:9-10). God's love for his elect is free. He said, from eternity, 'I will love them freely' (Hosea 14:4). God's love for us is like God himself — eternal, immutable and indestructible.

And the source and cause of his love is his own sovereign will and pleasure (Rom. 9:11-18). It cannot be attributed to anything else.

2. The tree of paradise (v. 2)

In the Garden of Eden there was a tree of life. Adam, by sin, lost his right to eat from that tree. In the paradise of God there is another tree of life. And that tree of life is the Lord Jesus Christ himself. He is that one in heaven who heals chosen sinners scattered through the nations of the earth by virtue of his finished work of redemption and by the power of his Holy Spirit. Christ, the tree of life, fills heaven. He is seen in the midst of the street and on both sides of the river. The city of God is full of Christ. That is the blessedness of heaven. Christ is there! Luther's doctrine concerning the ubiquity of Christ's physical body after his glorification may not be correct, but his heavenly body is such that he is immediately known and accessible everywhere and to everyone at all times. What mortal can imagine such a body? Our Saviour's immortal body, and the immortal bodies we shall have after the resurrection, will be free of all limitations and hindrances necessary to this earthly existence.

Christ, the tree of life, bears twelve manner of fruits. He bears fruit for the twelve tribes of the Israel of God. He has fruit sufficient for the whole Israel of God, the whole body of his elect. All fulness is in him. And we have our perfection and completion in him (John 1:16; Eph. 1:6; Col. 2:9). The fruit of this tree of life is abundant at all times. From it we obtain abundant, perfect righteousness (both for justification and for sanctification), plenteous redemption (from the curse of the law by Christ's atonement, from the dominion of sin by the power of his grace and from the very

being and consequences of sin by the resurrection of our
bodies) and eternal life, with all its blessedness in time
and eternity.

The leaves of this tree are for the healing of the nations.
The leaves of this tree are the blessed doctrines of the gospel — substitutionary redemption and imputed righteousness. Through the preaching of the gospel today, God sends
his grace into the nations of the world for the healing of
men's souls (Rom. 1:15-16; 10:17; 1 Cor. 1:21). And in heav-
en's glory the leaves of this tree, the blessed gospel of Christ,
will yet preserve all God's elect in life as the tree of life in
Eden would have preserved Adam in life (Gen. 3:22-24).
Even in that blessed, eternal state God's saints will be 'kept
by the power of his grace'. In a word, everything in Christ
will unceasingly contribute to, and secure, the everlasting
life and joy of God's saints in heaven.

3. The freedom of paradise (v. 3)

'And there shall be no more curse.' The curse of the law
cannot fall upon those who have been redeemed from it by
Christ's precious blood (Gal. 3:13). Where there is no sin,
there is no cause for the curse. And Christ has put away
our sins for ever. We shall not even suffer loss or be treated
any the less graciously because of our sin. Imagine that!
God will not impute sin to those for whom Christ has died
(Rom. 4:8), neither in this world, nor in the world to come.
In that blessed state awaiting us, there will be no possibility of a curse because there will be no possibility of sin.
Not only has the Son of God saved us from the Fall, he has
saved us from the possibility of another fall (John 10:28).
Consequently, in the holy city, new Jerusalem, there will
never even be the fear of the curse of God's holy law!

4. The throne of paradise (v. 3)

'But the throne of God and of the Lamb shall be in it.' It is the presence and stability of this throne that guarantee the security of God's saints and remove all possibility of curse from us. It is called 'the throne of God and of the Lamb' because God and the Lamb are one and God is seen, known and revealed only in the Lamb (John 1:14,18). This throne is the source of all things, the rule of all things and the end of all things (Rom. 11:36). This throne, a throne of free grace (Heb. 4:16) and sovereign dominion (Dan. 4:35-37), is the joy of all believers and the dread of all rebels.

5. The joy of paradise (vv. 4-5)

'His servants shall serve him.' In eternity we shall serve God our Saviour perfectly and perpetually. 'And they shall see his face.' Then, when we see him who loved us and gave himself for us face to face, we shall enjoy perfect communion with him, complete acceptance with God in him and with him, and full satisfaction in him. In heaven's glory he will make a full disclosure to us of himself, his works and his ways. And when we see his face, seeing all things as he sees them, we shall be filled with intense, indescribable delight! 'And his name shall be in their foreheads.' That simply means that we shall own and be owned by, shall accept and be accepted by, our God for ever. We shall confess him to be our God, and he will confess us to be his people for ever. 'And there shall be no night there.' There will be no darkness of any kind in heaven: no darkness of sin, sorrow, ignorance, or bigotry. In the new Jerusalem, there will be no need for secondary lights, no need for the symbolic ordinances that now contribute so much to our worship, neither believer's baptism (the confession of

Christ), nor the Lord's Supper (the remembrance of Christ). There will not even be a need of pastors and teachers to instruct, guide and correct us. The reason is this: 'For the Lord God giveth them light.'

6. The duration of paradise (v. 5)

'And they shall reign for ever and ever.' When the Lord Jesus Christ has presented his bride, his body, the church and kingdom of God in its entirety to the Father, holy, blameless, unreprovable and glorious, we shall reign with him for ever and ever (1 Cor. 15:24-28) in 'the glorious liberty of the children of God' (Rom. 8:21). Let these thoughts sustain, comfort and rejoice your heart, child of God, as you live in the hope of that city whose builder and maker is your God:

1. Our Adam, the Second Adam, the Lord Jesus Christ, is in paradise now.
2. From his wounded side God is forming a bride for him.
3. Paradise will not be complete for Christ until he has his beloved bride with him.
4. Christ will have his bride. Not one of God's elect, given to Christ in eternity, redeemed by Christ at Calvary and called by the Spirit of Christ in time, will be missing in the heavenly paradise.

58.

The throne of God and
of the Lamb

Revelation 22:3-4

*'The throne of God and of the Lamb shall be in it; and his servants
shall serve him'* (Rev. 22:3).

In this last chapter of Revelation the apostle John is describing the glory, bliss and beauty of heaven's eternal paradise. In verses 3 and 4 he shows us 'the throne of God and
of the Lamb'. Wherever heaven is, whatever heaven is, in it
'There shall be no more curse!' In the old paradise, the
Garden of Eden, there was a river and a tree of life. But the
paradise of God, which we shall inherit in the new creation, is infinitely better than Eden, for in the paradise of
God, 'There shall be no more curse!' There will be no curse
there because there will be no sin, the cause of the curse.
There will be no pain, sorrow and death, the results of the
curse. And there will be no possibility of curse — no devil,
no temptation, no weakness!

'The throne of God and of the Lamb shall be in it'

The name of the city of God is *Jehovah-shammah*, 'The
Lord is there!' God, in the Trinity of his blessed persons,
Father, Son and Holy Spirit, will be there upon the throne
of glory. And the Lamb, the sin-atoning sacrifice, the
mediator, the man Christ Jesus, will be there upon the throne

of glory. There is only one throne, for there is only one God. God and the Lamb are one (John 10:30; Col. 2:9).

'His servants shall serve him'

The highest, most constant desire of God's servants is that we may serve him. And this will be our delight in heaven's glory. In that blessed, eternal day we shall serve the Lord our God like the angels themselves, perfectly and perpetually. We shall worship him perfectly and perpetually. We shall do his will perfectly and perpetually. And we shall glorify him perfectly and perpetually!

'They shall see his face'

We shall see the face of the triune God, in all the fulness, majesty and splendour of his brilliant glory, as we behold the face of the Lamb, the Lord Jesus Christ. All his saints will see him as he is. When we see him, we shall be like him (1 John 3:2).

  1. To see his face is to enjoy intimate, personal, familiar communion.
  2. To see his face is to have the largest possible discovery of his love.
  3. To see his face is to have him clearly and fully revealed. It is to know him. It is to dwell in perfect light.
  4. To see his face is to attain perfect satisfaction (Ps. 17:15).

'His name shall be in their foreheads'

In that blessed, eternal day of heavenly glory, every child of God will be known to all the universe as one of God's elect. They will all be owned by God — publicly owned, gloriously owned, delightfully owned and eternally owned: owned by the Father as the objects of his love; owned by the Son as the purchase of his blood; owned by the Spirit as the fruit of his grace. In these two verses the Holy Spirit shows us the glory that awaits those who believe on the Lord Jesus Christ. Lift up the hands that hang down, strengthen those feeble knees, keep your eye upon the prize that awaits you, and run with patience the race that is set before you. Particularly as you run your race, as you endure hardness here, as you suffer adversity here, as you fight and war with sin, Satan and the world, I encourage you to fix your eye of faith upon 'the throne of God and of the Lamb'. Nothing is more comforting and encouraging to God's people in this world than the realization of our Saviour's mediatorial reign over all things.

Behold the Lamb of God!

We can never see and know God until we behold the Lamb of God. And we can never get a proper view of the throne of God until we behold the Lamb of God. So, in all things spiritual, the first order of business is to behold the Lamb of God (John 1:29). Before the world began God ordained that his dear Son would come into this world to die as an innocent victim, as a Lamb for the atonement of his people's sins (Rev. 13:8; 1 Peter 1:18-21). God has always had the Lamb before his eye. Everything he has ever done, is doing, or will yet do, is done for the sake of the Lamb.

In all the Old Testament Scriptures, the central figure in the revelation of God was the lamb of sacrifice. The first blood shed in the world was the blood of a lamb (Gen. 3:21). Abel offered God the blood of a lamb (Gen. 4:1-5). Abraham offered a lamb in the place of Isaac upon the mount (Gen. 22:8-14). When the judgement of God fell upon Egypt, Israel was saved by the blood of a lamb (Exod. 12:1-14). The prophet Isaiah vividly described the suffering and death of the Lord Jesus Christ as the substitutionary, sin-atoning Lamb of God (Isa. 53:1-12). When John the Baptist pointed to the Lord Jesus Christ and said, 'Behold, the Lamb of God, which taketh away the sin of the world,' his disciples knew exactly what he meant. He was saying, 'Behold, the Redeemer of whom God in the prophets spoke!'

The Lord Jesus Christ, as the Lamb of God, has taken away the sin of the world. The sins of God's elect throughout the whole world were at one time imputed to him. And he has effectually taken away their sins.

The 'world' here is the world of God's elect. Everybody in this world is redeemed, justified and saved, for the Lamb of God took their sins away. When the word 'world' is used in connection with the love and grace of God, or redemption, salvation, intercession and life in and by Christ, it is always to be understood in this sense (John 3:16; 1 John 2:1-2; 3:16; 4:9-10). We know that because God plainly asserts that he does not love, has not redeemed and will not save some people in the world (Ps. 7:11; Rom. 9:11-18). The Lord Jesus refused even to pray for the reprobate of the world (John 17:9,20). It is utterly foolish to imagine that he died to redeem those for whom he would not pray, and blasphemous to assert that he died to redeem and save those who yet perish under the wrath of God. The Son of God did not die in vain.

Christ has put away the sins of God's elect by the sacrifice of himself (Heb. 9:26; 1 Peter 2:24; 3:18; 4:1). He put our sins away by voluntarily suffering the wrath of God to the full satisfaction of justice, dying as the Lamb of God upon the altar of God, by the hand of God, for the people of God. 'Behold, the Lamb of God!' Jesus Christ is the Lamb appointed by God, anointed by God, approved by God, accepted by God and the Lamb who is God! To behold the Lamb of God is to trust the Lord Jesus Christ as the Lamb of sacrifice and atonement, by whose merit alone we have acceptance with God.

Behold the Lamb upon his throne!

Verse 3 speaks of 'the throne of God and of the Lamb'. There is only one throne, as we have already noted. Yet it is equally and fully the throne of God and of the Lamb, because God and the Lamb are one. The Lord Jesus Christ sits upon the throne in heaven by lawful right, both as God and as the Lamb. We have seen this many times in our study of Revelation, but it is one of those blessed facts of our faith that needs to be constantly brought to our attention.

As God, Jesus Christ always sat upon the throne of universal sovereignty, dominion and power. He is very God of very God, co-eternal, co-equal with the Father in all things. He possessed the glory of divinity from eternity, before ever the earth was made (John 1:1-3). But now, God sits upon his throne in the person of the sin-atoning, mediatorial Lamb, the God-man, Jesus Christ. By his obedience to God as our mediator and the merit of his blood as our sin-atoning Lamb, Jesus Christ has earned the right to rule the universe for ever as a man (John 17:2; Rom. 14:9). He is to God's elect what Joseph was to his people in Egypt (Gen. 41:43-44). Our Saviour rules over all creation (Eph. 1:22), all the details of providence, all his enemies and ours (2 Peter 2:1) and all the vast realms of grace (Ps. 68:18-20), for the salvation of his elect (John 17:2). His rule and dominion is unlimited, sovereign and everlasting (Dan. 4:35-37).

Behold the throne of God and of the Lamb!

Though it is the throne of God, it is none the less the throne of the Lamb. And though it is the throne of the Lamb, it is none the less the throne of God. What does that mean? It is a throne of august majesty, perfect holiness and strict justice. It is a throne of infinite mercy and sovereign grace (Heb. 4:16). It is an approachable, accessible throne. It is a throne of absolute safety and security. It is an appealing,

alluring, charming throne. Behold the throne of God and of
the Lamb with delightful, anxious hope and anticipation!
(Rev. 4:9-10). 'The throne of God and of the Lamb,' above
all other things, is what draws our hearts to heaven. Fix
your eyes constantly upon the Lamb upon the throne, and
be at peace.

59.

Face to face with Christ
our Saviour

Revelation 22:4

'And they shall see his face; and his name shall be in their fore-heads' (Rev. 22:4).

Heaven is set before us in the Scriptures by many pictures of bliss awaiting God's elect in eternity. Heaven is a place prepared for us. It is the everlasting kingdom. It is eternal glory. Heaven is our purchased inheritance. It is the city of God and of the Lamb. It is our home. Heaven is our final resting-place. These, and many other descriptive phrases, fill our hearts with joy and anticipation. But here is the greatest bliss of the eternal state, the consummation of glory, the very heaven of heaven: 'And they shall see his face.' When the Lord said to Moses, 'Thou canst not see my face and live,' he was speaking to a mere mortal upon the earth. Those words have no reference to those who have put on immortality and incorruption. In the coming glory-land every child of God will see the face of our God and live. Indeed, it is this sight of Christ which will be the essence and excellence of our life. We shall see face to face the one who is the brightness of the Father's glory and the express image of his person! This is the heaven that awaits us!

> Face to face with Christ my Saviour,
> Face to face, what will it be;
> When with rapture I behold him,
> Jesus Christ, who died for me?

What is this heavenly vision?

Some people have very earth-bound and unscriptural ideas about heaven. Some think of heaven only as a place where they can gratify their earthly desires. They seem to think only of the comforts and pleasures that heaven might bring to them in a natural, physical way. To them, the streets of gold, the gates of pearl and the walls of jasper are enough. I have even heard men talk about heaven as though it were a place that would gratify their religious pride and self-righteousness. Some religious denominations actually seem to imagine that their particular brand of religion will give them a place of superiority in glory and that the rest of God's saints will be beneath them and serve them!

All such worldly ideas of heaven must be rejected. However, there are many things in heaven that we shall see and enjoy. We shall see the holy angels who have ministered to us throughout our earthly pilgrimage (Heb. 1:14). Men and women of flesh and bones will commune with cherubim and seraphim. We shall see and know Gabriel and all the heavenly hosts. We shall see the patriarchs who served God in those early days of time. We shall even know those men and women who walked with God before the flood, such as Abel, Enoch and Noah. We shall see and know the apostles and prophets. Those martyrs with whose blood the pages of church history are written will be there. Those brethren with whom we have enjoyed sweet fellowship upon the earth will be there. And we shall see again our loved ones who fell asleep in Christ Jesus. Without question, in our glorified state, earthly ties will no longer divide us, but the saints in glory will know one another, just as Peter, James and John knew Moses and Elijah when they appeared with them on the Mount of Transfiguration.

Yet, for all of this, the greatest joy and fulness of heaven will be the fact that we shall see Christ himself face to face. That which we desire above all else in heaven is the sight of Christ. With the psalmist we most gladly declare, 'Whom have I in heaven but thee? And there is none upon earth that I desire beside thee' (Ps. 73:25). Christ is all in all to us here, and we long for a heaven in which he will be all in all to us for ever. Here upon the earth, it was a sight of Christ which first turned our sorrow into joy. The daily renewal of communion with Christ lifts us up above the cares of this world. Even here, we say, 'If we have Christ we have enough.' If Christ is all to us now, what will he be in glory? The paradise of God is a heaven of intense, eternal, spiritual fellowship with Christ. Heaven is a place where it is promised that 'They shall see his face.' Moses, we are told, saw his back parts. He saw the train of his majesty. But there we shall see his face. We shall literally see our Saviour's face. Though he is glorified, that very man who died at Calvary is upon the throne of glory. We shall see him, the God-man.

What a sight that will be for redeemed sinners! We shall see our well-beloved — his hands, his feet, his side, his head and his face. We shall literally see him who loved us and gave himself for us. Even sweeter is the fact that we shall enjoy a perfect, spiritual sight of our Redeemer. This text seems to imply a greater ability in the next world by which we shall be able to see Christ more fully. Here, upon the earth, the very best of us are only infants. Now we know in part. Now we see through a shaded glass. But in heaven, we shall see the Saviour face to face. And we shall know even as we are known. We shall see Christ in such a way that we shall know him. We shall know the heights, depths, length and breadth of the love of Christ that passes knowledge. We shall see the Saviour always. The saints in heaven will never cease to see him. We shall never cease to embrace our Saviour! It is not so now. Sometimes we are near the throne; at other times we are afar off. Sometimes we are as bright as the angels; at other times we are as dull as lead. At times we are hot with love, but at other times

we are cold with indifference. But the day will soon come,
when we shall for ever be in the closest possible associa-
tion with Christ. Then we shall see his face without ceasing. And we shall see our Saviour's face as it is now, in the
fulness of his glory (John 17:24). John gave us a little glimpse
of that in Revelation 1:13-16. Turn to that passage again
and rejoice in the prospect of this blessed hope.

How are we going to see Christ in glory?

The word 'see' in this text implies a clear, full, undimmed
sight of Christ. We shall see Christ clearly because everything that hinders our sight of him here will be removed.
Our sins and our old, sinful nature will be completely removed. All those earthly cares that now cloud our vision
will be taken out of the way. All our sorrows will be ended
(Rev. 21:4). And there nothing will stand between us and
our Saviour. In glory there will be no rival in our hearts.
We shall love Christ supremely. We shall see Christ personally. Now we see him by faith, but then faith will be
turned to sight, and we shall see Christ personally for ourselves. The language of Job is a proper description of the
future prospect that awaits every believer (Job 19:25-27).
    We shall see our Saviour in all the fulness of his person
and work. Fully beholding his glorious person, we shall
see him who is God over all and blessed for ever in the
perfection of his glorified manhood. In that day, we shall
see Christ in the fulness of his covenant engagements
and in the perfection of all his mediatorial offices as our
surety: Prophet, Priest, King, husband, shepherd and substitute. In the world to come, we shall see Christ in the
fulness of his saving grace. Then we shall know the meaning of electing love. Then we shall know the price of blood
atonement. Then we shall know the power of his priestly
intercession. Then we shall know the goodness of his

preserving grace. And when we see his face, our eyes will be full of adoration for him alone. In that world of glory to come there will be no voice heard that speaks of the power of man's free will, or the goodness of man's works. In that day we shall say, 'Not unto us, O Lord, not unto us, but unto thy name be honour, and power, and glory, and dominion for ever and ever' (Ps. 115:1; Rev. 1:5-6; 5:9-10).

Why will this vision of Christ be the greatest bliss and joy of heaven?

I have said that seeing Christ face to face is the heaven of heaven, the glory of glory. But why do we place such importance upon this one aspect of our eternal inheritance? The answer should be obvious. When we see him our salvation will be complete. Soon the resurrection day will come, and all men will see the great God and Saviour. When the wicked see his face, they will be consumed in his fierce wrath. But we shall see him and live. We shall be like the burning bush, glowing with the glory of God, but not consumed. We shall stand in the presence of God in perfect salvation. Every spot of sin will be eradicated from our souls. Our bodies will be made immortal, incorruptible, glorious. When we see his face we shall be conscious of his favour and enjoy perfect and uninterrupted fellowship with him. In glory, we shall walk with God perfectly. Not until we see his face will we fully know the meaning of being one with him.

When we see him there will be a complete transformation: 'We shall be like him, for we shall see him as he is.' We shall see things as he sees them, think as he thinks, will what he wills, love what he loves and hate what he hates — perfectly. When we see the face of the Son of God we shall be perfectly satisfied (Ps. 17:15).

To whom is this promise given?

The apostle tells us that those who will see the face of Christ are none 'but they which are written in the Lamb's book of life' (Rev. 21:27). Every one of those who are the objects of God's eternal grace will see his face. Every soul that was chosen by God in the council of love will see Christ in the courts of glory (Eph. 1:4). Everyone who was predestined to be a son of God will be his son (Rom. 8:29). Every soul for whom Jesus died at Calvary will see his face in heaven. They are accepted, pardoned, justified, sanctified and purchased. And they will see him (Isa. 53:10-12). Every man, woman and child who is called by the Spirit of God and regenerated by divine power will see his face (Eph. 1:13-14). Everyone that repents of his sin and believes on Christ will see him (John 1:12-13). Every heart that bows in submission to King Jesus will see the King in his beauty (Luke 14:25-33). Everyone who loves Christ will see Christ (2 Tim. 4:8). They may have been the vilest, most abominable wretches ever to walk upon the earth, but they are washed, they are justified, they are sanctified. And, 'They shall see his face!'

They will all with equal clearness see the face of Christ. I read of no secondary joys in heaven. There are no back streets in the new Jerusalem! I can find no more foundation in the Scriptures for the doctrine of rewards in heaven than I can for the doctrine of purgatory! All the saints of God will see the Saviour's face. What more can anyone want? The dying thief went with Christ to paradise, and so did Paul. Heaven is altogether the reward of grace, not of debt, and it will be possessed to the full by all the heirs of grace (Rom. 8:17). All the saved are loved by God with a perfect love. All were chosen in Christ. We all have the same blessings of grace in the covenant. We are all redeemed by the same blood. We are all accepted in the same righteousness.

We are all the sons of God upon the same grounds. And we all have the same hope of glory. Heaven was earned and bought for us by the Son of God, and it will be given to us in all its fulness. In this world of sorrow, comfort yourself with this hope: 'They' who believe on the Lord Jesus Christ 'shall see his face.'

60.

The Scriptures confirmed

Revelation 22:6-21

'And he said unto me, These sayings are faithful and true: and the Lord God of the holy prophets sent his angel to show unto his servants the things which must shortly be done' (Rev. 22:6).

In these verses, God the Holy Spirit confirms his holy Word to us, giving us distinct evidences of inspiration. This is God's own confirmation of the Holy Scriptures as his Word. God's last written word to man is a word of confirmation and ratification of the whole inspired volume. Many think these verses refer only to the contents of the book of Revelation. But John begins by telling us that what he is saying includes and completes God's revelation of himself by the holy prophets (v. 6). By divine arrangement, this is the last chapter of the Bible. What it says is true of the whole canon of Scripture from Genesis to Revelation.

Four facts about the Bible

Here are four facts about the Bible that need to be constantly and forcefully emphasized with clarity in the church of God today. Let all who believe God be fully persuaded of these things and seek to understand them clearly.

1. The Bible alone is the inspired Word of God (2 Peter 1:19-21)

'All Scripture is given by inspiration of God' (2 Tim. 3:16). Holy men of God, prophets and apostles, chosen, ordained and gifted by God, wrote the Scriptures as they were infallibly guided by the Spirit of God. Though these men were, for the most part, unknown to one another, though they lived in different lands, cultures and ages, though they were men of greatly varying natural abilities and lifestyles (kings, shepherds, fishermen, doctors, etc.), they all wrote of one person and declared the same message without the slightest contradiction (Luke 24:27,44-47). The person of whom the Scriptures speak is our Lord Jesus Christ (John 1:45; 5:39). The message the Scriptures declare is redemption by the blood of Christ (Luke 24:45-46), redemption purposed by grace, accomplished by grace, applied by grace and received by grace.

2. The Bible is to be honoured as the Word of God

This holy book, the Bible, is to be reverenced, honoured and esteemed by us as the Word of God (Ps. 138:2). David said, 'Thou hast magnified thy word above all thy name.' I know that men and women can be idolatrous and superstitious regarding the Word of God. But let us never depreciate, or in any way show any disrespect or disregard for, the Word of God. If God has magnified his Word above all his name, then surely those who know and reverence his name will reverence his Word. In an attempt to rebuke a superstitious attitude for the Scriptures, I have heard men say, 'Apart from the application of the Holy Spirit, this book is no more valuable than the morning newspaper.' Oh, no! Unlike any other printed word, there is a special blessing promised to those who read, hear, obey and keep the things written in this book. This blessed book is the Word of God (Heb. 4:12).

3. The authority of Scripture

We are required by God to submit to the total authority of
his Word (2 Tim. 3:16-17). Creeds and confessions are useful in their place, but the only rule of faith and practice in
the house of God must be the Word of God. We must not be
induced by anyone to pin our faith to the words of fallible
men. Faith simply submits to God's revelation. Faith does
not argue with God's Word, oppose God's Word, or ignore
God's Word. Faith believes the Word, submits to the Word
and obeys the Word. Faith holds God's book, the Bible, to
be singularly authoritative in all things. The Holy Scriptures alone are authoritative in the kingdom of God.

4. The life-giving Word

The Word of God is, by the blessing of God the Holy Spirit,
the instrumental source and cause of all spiritual life in
men (Heb. 4:12; James 1:18; 1 Peter 1:23-25; Rom. 10:17).
God saves his elect by the Word which he has given, through
the preaching of the gospel. He who preaches and teaches
the gospel of Christ fully preaches and teaches the Word of
God fully (cf. Acts 20:27; 1 Cor. 2:2; 1 Peter 1:25). That alone
is God's ordained means of grace (1 Cor. 1:21).

God's own confirmation of his Word

The Bible is, in its entirety, the Word of God, inerrant, infallible and immutable. Let us reverence and submit to it
as such. Here are fifteen facts that will help to strengthen
and confirm our faith in God's revelation of his Son, the
Holy Bible.

1. The one who gave it (v. 6)

The Bible is confirmed as the Word of God by the name of
the one who gave it. It has been given to us to us by our
mediator, Jesus Christ, who is the Lord God of the holy
prophets (Rev. 1:1). Christ is the living Word of whom the
written Word speaks (John 1:1-3). The whole revelation of
God to man is given in, by and through the mediatorial
man, Christ Jesus, the Son of God. And all that the Lord
God reveals is faithful and true. Not one word from God
has ever fallen to the ground — neither a word of prophecy, nor of promise, nor of threat.

2. The messengers God used (v. 6)

The Bible is also confirmed as the Word of God by the messengers God has employed to give it. The holy God gave his
holy Word to his holy angels, to give to his holy prophets,
to show his servants in every generation the mind and will
of God in all things spiritual. I do not know how the angels
are involved in giving us the Word of God, but they have
been (Gal. 3:19). Perhaps they are charged with secretly
protecting and preserving the Holy Scriptures for us.

3. The fulfilment of Scripture (vv. 6-7)

The Scriptures will soon be confirmed to all the world as
the Word of God by the accomplishment of all that has been
revealed in them. The Bible reveals certain 'things which
must shortly be done'. Though men scoff and mock, these
things will come to pass. Christ will come. There will be a
resurrection of the dead. This world will be destroyed, both
the religious and political systems of the world and the
material earth upon which we now live. We shall stand
before God in judgement. Our God will make all things new.
We shall spend eternity somewhere, either in heaven or in
hell.

4. Its honesty in exposing sin (vv. 8-9)

Another way in which the Bible is confirmed to us as the
Word of God is by its honesty and forthrightness in expos-
ing the sins of even its most eminent characters. The first
time John fell down to worship an angel, it might be over-
looked as a mistake. He may have thought the angel was
Christ himself (Rev. 19:10). But here, John's behaviour reveals the sinfulness and idolatry that is in the hearts of all
men. Even when he was in the Spirit, John was only a sinful man, prone to every imaginable evil.

Why does the Word of God so plainly and frequently
reveal the corruption and sin of God's elect?

> 1. To show us our depravity.
> 2. To show us that salvation is by grace alone
> (1 Cor. 4:7).
> 3. To show us that Christ alone is our righteous-
> ness (2 Cor. 5:21).
> 4. To keep us looking to Christ alone for all our
> salvation (1 Cor. 1:30).

5. It is open to public scrutiny (v. 10)

God's Word is not a secret revelation. It is open to all, for
all to read and hear. No part of God's truth is hidden from
anyone, and God's servants make no effort to hide it. All
the doctrines of the Bible are open for inspection. All the
prophecies of the Bible are open for scrutiny. All the Scriptures are open to be studied and believed (1 John 5:10).

6. The effect it has on those who hear it (v. 11)

To some it is a savour of life unto life, to others a savour of
death unto death (2 Cor. 2:15-17); but none hear or read the
Word of God without being affected by it.

7. The basis on which men will be judged (v. 12)

On the Day of Judgement the Book of God, and the gospel it reveals, will be the basis of judgement. On that great day the Lord Jesus Christ will dispense the rewards of justice according to the rule of Holy Scripture. Those who obey the gospel will be saved. Those who disobey the gospel will be damned.

8. Christ's coming for his people (vv. 13-14)

The Bible will be confirmed to all men as the Word of God by Christ himself when he comes to reward his saints. They will live who obey his commandments (1 John 3:23). But the only way any sinner can obey God's commandments is to believe on the Lord Jesus Christ (Rom. 3:28-31). All who do believe will eat of the tree of life by just right because in Christ they are worthy to do so (Col. 1:12). They will enter into the city of God.

9. The condemnation of those who reject it (v. 15)

The Bible will be confirmed as the Word of God, faithful and true, by condemning and banishing from heaven all who despise its message and reject its counsel.

'Dogs' are religious prostitutes, those who have prostituted the gospel for their own gain (Deut. 23:17-18; Isa. 56:10-11; Phil. 3:2). 'Sorcerers' are superstitious people, people who look to the stars, astrological signs, or palm readers for information, rather than to the Lord God. 'Whore-mongers and murderers' are profligate, lawless rebels. 'Idolaters' are worshippers of strange or false gods and materialists, who idolize things. 'Whosoever loveth and maketh a lie' refers to false prophets and their followers, all those who attempt to mingle works with grace and the will of man with the will of God in the affair of salvation (Gal. 1:6-8; 2 Thess. 2:10; 1 Cor. 15:22).

10. The preaching of the gospel (v. 16)

The Bible is confirmed as the Word of God to all who hear the gospel preached by the testimony of the Lord Jesus Christ through his messenger. It is Christ who speaks to us by his Word. The angel (that is, the preacher) is his messenger. His message is found and heard in his churches.

11. The open call to sinners issued by the Lord of glory (v. 17)

No matter how it is interpreted, this call is full of grace. The Spirit of God and the Bride of Christ say to the Lord Jesus, 'Come, fulfil your word.' The gospel preacher, the one who hears the Word of the Lord, stands upon the walls of Zion and says, 'Come...' — either, 'Sinner, come and welcome to Jesus,' or 'Lord Jesus, come to us poor sinners.' The Lord himself calls sinners ('Him that is athirst ...!' 'Whosoever will ...!') to come and take of the water of life freely.

12. The warnings given concerning Scripture (vv. 18-19)

God confirms the pages of Holy Scripture as his own Word by the solemn sanction he places upon every word, doctrine and precept revealed in its pages. Compare Deuteronomy 4:2 at the end of the law, and Malachi 4:4 at the end of the prophets, with Revelation 22:18-19 at the end of the apostolic writings. The warnings given here apply to the entire Bible.

13. The testimony of Christ himself (v. 20)

The Lord Jesus here declares that he will do what he has revealed and promised (John 14:1-3).

14. The hope and expectation of God's saints in this world (v. 20)

Having heard his Word, the whole church of God stands, as it were, on tiptoe and cries out expectantly, 'Even so, come, Lord Jesus!'

15. The benediction of grace with which it ends (v. 21)

The Bible ends with this final word from God to men. With it the Lord God gives clear testimony to the eternal Godhead of Christ. He is the Lord, the giver of all grace. God's final word is a word of grace and an assurance of grace. His final word is: 'Amen — so shall it be!'

61.

No changes in eternity

Revelation 22:11

'He that is unjust, let him be unjust still: and he which is filthy, let him be filthy still: and he that is righteous, let him be righteous still: and he that is holy, let him be holy still' (Rev. 22:11).

Read and pay attention to the words of the wise man when he says, 'In the place where the tree falleth, there it shall be' (Eccles. 11:3). Solomon's language is not hard to understand. His meaning is: 'Whatever your condition is when you die, that will be your condition throughout eternity.' Death changes nothing. There will be no changes in eternity. Whatever your spiritual condition is at the moment of death, that will be your spiritual condition throughout eternity. Whatever your state is before God when you die, that will be your state before God throughout eternity.

The judgement bar of God is not to be a trial to determine the guilt or innocence of those who stand before him. Judgement Day will *determine* nothing, but it will *show* the guilt or innocence of all who stand before him, and execute the penalty of justice upon the guilty and the reward of justice upon the righteous. Judgement will reveal everything, but will change nothing. I repeat myself deliberately: there will be no changes in eternity. Purgatory is a lie. Limbo is a delusion. 'In the place where the tree falls, there it shall lie!' In Revelation 22:11 the angel said to John, 'He that is unjust, let him be unjust still: and he which is filthy, let him be filthy still: and he that is righteous, let him be righteous still: and he that is holy, let him be holy still.' Here are four unalterable, inflexible, unbending statements of divine justice. They cannot change or be changed. We are told that 'Justice is blind.' Among men, that is questionable. But I assure you that the justice of God is blind to all those things that men consider mitigations of guilt. It does not take into consideration, or offer leniency upon the grounds of age, race, sex, environment, education, ability, or knowledge. It sees only two things: sin and righteousness, guilt and innocence, filthiness and holiness. Justice gives consideration to nothing else.

1. 'He that is unjust, let him be unjust still'

All who die in a state of guilt and condemnation, with the curse of the law and the wrath of God upon them, will spend eternity in a state of guilt and condemnation, under the curse and unmitigated wrath of God. It is written: 'He that is unjust, let him be unjust still.'

If you are without Christ, you are unjust, you are in a state and condition of non-justification. You have broken God's law. The guilt of sin is upon you. Oh, if you could understand what I am saying to you, you would tremble with fear! The wrath of God is upon you! You are cursed! You are condemned! The very same wrath of God that heats the fires of hell is upon you right now (Ps. 5:5; 7:11-13; 11:4-6; Ezek. 18:20; John 3:18,36).

Your unjustified condition, your state of condemnation, is a matter of righteousness, justice and truth. If God should seize you before you draw your next breath and cast you into hell, his judgement upon you would be exactly what you deserve. You have earned his wrath. 'The wages of sin is death' (Rom. 6:23; Ps. 51:1-5).

Here are three reasons why you ought to go to hell, three reasons why you ought to be damned for ever:

1. You were born in a state of guilt and condemnation (Rom. 5:12; Eph. 2:3).

2. You have personally broken every law of God, transgressed every commandment, and come short of every requirement of God from your earliest days (Rom. 3:23; Ps. 58:3).

3. You have repeatedly heard and rejected the gospel of the grace of God. You have repeatedly had Christ crucified set before you and have wilfully despised him (Prov. 1:23-33; 1 John 5:10).

My comments are particularly addressed to those of you who have been raised under the sound of the gospel, who still refuse to believe on and bow to the Lord Jesus Christ. You know the message of substitution, but you despise the substitute. You know the commandment and promise of God: 'Believe on the Lord Jesus Christ, and thou shalt be saved!' But you will not obey the commandment. And you despise the promise. You know that you can never be justified by your works, yet you will not acknowledge the evil of your 'good' works, confess your sin and trust Christ alone. If you die in your present condition, unjust, you will be unjust for ever. You are without hope, without life, without God, without Christ. Dare you die in such a state? If you do, there will be no mercy for you, but only wrath, no friend in heaven for you, but only enemies. You will remain unjustified for ever! The only change that will take place is this: when you wake up in hell, you will value justification by Christ more than anything and want it more than anything, but there will be no possibility of your obtaining it.

2. 'He which is filthy, let him be filthy still'

If you die in a state of filth, a depraved, defiled, degenerate sinner, you will be filthy for ever. It is written: 'He which is filthy, let him be filthy still.' 'Without holiness no man shall see the Lord.' As John Gill says, 'All mankind are originally, naturally, and universally filthy, or defiled with sin.' None of us likes to hear it, but it is true. And if I would be faithful to the souls of all my readers, I must tell you the truth.

If you are without Christ, you are filthy, so filthy that even your righteousnesses are filthy rags in God's sight (Isa. 64:6). No one likes to think of filth, come into contact with filth, see filth, smell filth, or touch filth. Have you ever smelled a filthy thing, or had to work in filth? If you have, the remembrance of it will be enough to make your stomach begin to churn. Yet the Word of God declares that you and I are by nature filthy. Our hearts are filthy (Mark 7:21-23). Our best deeds are filthy (Isa. 64:6). Our consciences are filthy and must be purged (Heb. 9:14). If you die in your filth, you will wallow for ever in your filth in hell. Death will not change you. The fires of hell will not purge away the filth of nature. 'He which is filthy, let him be filthy still!' There will be no regeneration of the heart, no repentance from sin, no renovation of the soul and no reformation of life in hell. The only thing that will change is this: in hell your lusts and filthy passions will be more acute than ever, but will remain unsatisfied. And the corruptions of your heart will torment you more, infinitely more, in hell than anyone has ever been tormented by conscience in this world.

The only one who can purge you from your filth is the Lord Jesus Christ. His blood has purged away the filth of every believer from the book of justice. Christ's blood, if you believe, will purge away the guilt of your filth from your conscience. In fact, your faith in him will be to you the evidence that his blood purged away your sins when he satisfied the justice of God for his elect at Calvary (Heb. 11:1). By the power, merit and virtue of his blood, the Son of God will purge away the filth of sin from our bodies in the resurrection. Believe on the Lord Jesus Christ, and be clean (Zech. 13:1).

3. 'He that is righteous, let him be righteous still'

All who die in a state of righteousness, justified and complete in Christ, will be righteous for ever and will enjoy the
just reward of perfect righteousness in eternal glory. It is
written: 'He that is righteous, let him be righteous still.'
That which God has given shall never be changed, lost, or
taken away (Eccles. 3:14; John 10:28-29; Rom. 11:29). Death
and judgement will not make you any more righteous than
you are at the moment you die. Nor will they make you one
bit less righteous than you are at the moment you die. Death
changes nothing. Judgement changes nothing. Eternity
changes nothing. Are you interested in being righteous
before God? If you are, let me show you six things from the
Word of God.

   1. You cannot make yourself righteous, no matter
what you do (Gal. 2:21).
   2. The only way any sinner can be made righteous
is by the righteous obedience of Christ being imputed
to him (Rom. 5:19). Just as Adam's sin was imputed
to us, the sins of God's elect were imputed to Christ,
and Christ's righteousness is imputed to every
believer.
   3. The only way you can obtain the imputed righteousness of God in Christ is by faith (Rom. 9:31-33).
Faith does not perform righteousness, or accomplish
righteousness, or merit righteousness. Faith receives
righteousness.
   4. If you believe on the Lord Jesus Christ, you are
perfectly righteous in him (1 Cor. 1:30; Jer. 23:6; 33:16;
Col. 2:10), immutably righteous, completely righteous
and eternally righteous.
   5. If you are now righteous in God's sight, if you
have received the righteousness of God by faith in
Christ, God in strict justice will reward you for the

perfect, righteous obedience of Christ when you stand before him in judgement (Col. 1:12). Looking on you in Christ and having imputed to you all that Christ did for sinners in his life and in his death, the Lord God will say to you in that day, 'Well done!'

6. If you have been made righteous by the imputation of Christ's righteousness to you, you will live soberly, righteously and in a godly manner in this world, for the glory of him who has made you righteous (Titus 2:11-14). Grace never makes saved sinners licentious, but righteous. God's saints are never perfectly righteous in this world. All true believers know and acknowledge that fact (1 John 1:8-10). But they are sincerely righteous, universally and in all aspects of life (Rom. 6:11-18).

4. 'He that is holy, let him be holy still'

If you die in a state of holiness, born again (regenerated and sanctified) by the Spirit of God, you will be holy for ever and will inherit the kingdom of holiness. Remember, that which God has done cannot be undone, made better, or made less (Eccles. 3:14). It is written: 'He that is holy, let him be holy still.'

Perhaps you wonder, 'What is the difference between righteousness and holiness?' The one is a matter of legal standing; the other is a matter of personal experience. All men without Christ are in a state of being unjust, a state of non-justification, condemnation and guilt before the law of God. That is man's standing before God. But his nature is 'filthy', the condition of his heart, the thought of his mind, the state of his soul, is 'filthy'. All who are in Christ, redeemed by his blood, are 'righteous'. Our legal standing before God is righteous, right in the eyes of the law, because Christ's righteousness has been imputed to us. We were made righteous by Christ's obedience. But 'holiness' is the believer's new nature in Christ. Holiness is not what we do. Holiness is what we *are* by the new birth. Holiness is the righteousness of Christ imparted to us in regeneration.

Holiness is that new nature given to every believer when he or she is born of God (1 John 3:9; 2 Peter 1:4; 1 Cor. 3:17). However, though God has given us a new, holy nature by the new birth, we still have the old nature of sin. This is the cause of that warfare that goes on in every believer's heart between the flesh and the Spirit (Rom. 7:14-25). The believer is not two persons, but one — one person with two natures. These two natures, so long as we are in this world, must be at war with one another (Gal. 5:17). The Spirit rules but never conquers the flesh in this world. Flesh will not submit to the Spirit, agree with the Spirit, or be at peace with the Spirit for a moment. When we die we shall not become any more holy than we now are; we shall simply cease to be bothered by this sinful, fleshly nature. In eternity we shall do what we now want to do (only and always that which is perfectly righteous), because we shall be what we now long, with all our hearts, to be — totally free from all sin! But death will make no changes. There will be no changes in eternity.

'He that is unjust, let him be unjust still: and he which is filthy, let him be filthy still: and he that is righteous, let him be righteous still: and he that is holy, let him be holy still.' 'In the place where the tree falleth, there it shall be.' Only one thing in this world is of any real consequence, because only one thing in this world is of any eternal consequence, and that is your relationship with the Lord Jesus Christ. Faith in Christ is the one urgent, eternal necessity of your soul. 'He that believeth and is baptized shall be saved; but he that believeth not shall be damned.'

62.

Our Lord's final beatitudes

'Blessed are they that do his commandments, that they may have right to the tree of life, and may enter in through the gates into the city' (Rev. 22:14).

A beatitude is the sure and certain promise of immortal bliss, eternal happiness and supreme delight. The Lord Jesus pronounced nine beatitudes in his Sermon on the Mount (Matt. 5:3-12). The apostle Paul, by divine inspiration, gave us what some have called 'the last beatitude' in Acts 20:35: 'Remember the words of the Lord Jesus, how he said, It is more blessed to give than to receive.' Everyone knows that in this world it is more blessed to be rich and have the means to give than it is to be poor and have nothing to give. But the words of our Lord mean that it is more blessed to give to others than it is to receive from them. It is more blessed to give what we have, be it little or much, for the good of others, than it is to increase what we have. Many give for the hope of gain, to get more. God's people give according to their ability, to do good, hoping for nothing in return. It is more blessed to give our labour to those who need it than it is to be paid for our labour by those who do not need it. It is blessed to give to, and labour for, those who are grateful and appreciative. But it is more blessed and honourable to give to, and labour for, those who are ungrateful and unappreciative, for then our gifts and our labours are to God alone.

Look again at Acts 20:35: 'I have showed you all things, how that so labouring ye ought to support the weak, and to remember the words of the Lord Jesus, how that he said, It is more blessed to give than to receive.' This tells us three things about the children of God in this world.

First, God's saints are honest, hardworking men and women. They work for their living. They work hard. They work for the glory of God (Eph. 6:5-8; 1 Thess. 4:11; 2 Thess. 3:10; 1 Tim. 5:8). God's people are not idle layabouts, but productive members of society.

Second, God's people work, not merely to enrich themselves, but to support the weak, the poor, the needy and the work of the gospel (Eph. 4:28). Believers are not greedy, grasping people, but generous, giving people. We work to support our families, the work of the gospel (churches, pastors, missionaries, etc.) and those who are not able to support themselves.

Third, God's saints in this world who give with willing and cheerful hearts are blessed by God. The fact that they give with willing hearts, freely and cheerfully, is proof that they are loved by God. Our giving does not cause God to love us and bless us with his grace, but it is a proof that he does love us and has blessed us (2 Cor. 9:7). Giving men and women will constantly be supplied by God with the ability to give (2 Cor. 9:8; Phil. 4:19; Luke 6:38). Generous, open-hearted and open-handed men and women, those who give willingly and cheerfully because they love Christ, are blessed with God's unspeakable gift, Jesus Christ, and everlasting glory in him (2 Cor. 8:9; 9:15). The text says giving men and women are 'blessed'!

These are the beatitudes of our Lord, his sure, unconditional promises of supreme happiness and eternal bliss to his people. These beatitudes and the blessedness they promise are not conditioned upon the character and conduct of those to whom the promises are made. Rather, their character and conduct are the result of the blessing bestowed (Eph. 1:3).

The promises in Revelation of supreme happiness and eternal bliss

Our Lord gives seven final beatitudes to his people in the book of Revelation. Here are the last seven beatitudes given to God's elect in the Word of God. Here, in the last book of the Bible, are seven sure and certain promises of immortal bliss, eternal happiness and supreme delight given to all who believe.

1. The promise is connected with the public ministry of the Word

'Blessed is he that readeth, and they that hear the words of this prophecy, and keep those things which are written therein (Rev. 1:3).

'Blessed is he that readeth.' John Gill suggested that the word 'readeth' here means to read with explanation. The faithful gospel preacher reads God's Word to the church and explains the meaning of the words. That is what it is to preach the Scriptures. And the man who does so is blessed by God, with grace, with gifts of knowledge and understanding (Jer. 3:15) and with the ability to preach the gospel, teaching the Word of God. That man is blessed by God in the preparation and in the preaching of God's message to his people (Eph. 3:8).

'Blessed are they that hear the words of this prophecy.' Those who hear the Word of God faithfully read and proclaimed are blessed in the providence of God, for this is the means of grace, the means by which God calls, comforts, corrects and cleanses his elect (Isa. 52:7; Rom. 10:14-17; Eph. 4:8-16; 5:26). Those who hear in faith with understanding hearts are blessed with divine grace and eternal life (John 3:5-7; 1 Cor. 2:9-14).

'Blessed are they that keep those things which are written therein.' Those who keep the Word in their hearts are the children of God. Their hearts have been prepared by grace. The Word has been sown in their hearts by grace. And they keep the Word by grace. They receive the Word as seed sown in good ground, and it brings forth fruit (Matt. 13:23). They receive the Word by the power and grace of God the Holy Spirit (1 Thess. 1:4-5).

2. The promise is to all who die in the Lord

'Blessed are the dead which die in the Lord from henceforth: Yea, saith the Spirit, that they may rest from their labours; and their works do follow them' (Rev. 14:13). There is a great, indescribable blessedness connected with death for the believer: 'Precious in the sight of the LORD is the death of his saints' (Ps. 116:15; see 2 Cor. 5:1-9).

'They rest from their labours' (see Heb. 4:9-11). As soon as a sinner comes to Christ in faith, he begins to keep a sabbath rest. Ceasing from his own works, he rests in Christ's purchase, trusting him alone for acceptance with God. That is what the Old Testament sabbath day typified. We also rest, at least in measure, in our Lord's providence (Rom. 8:28). But as soon as God's saints leave this world of woe, they enter into the perfect rest of his presence.

'And their works do follow them.' Our works do not go before us to prepare a place for us in heaven. Christ did that (John 14:1-3; Heb. 6:20). We do not carry our works with us as the ground of our acceptance with God or the basis for reward in heaven. Every believer knows that his righteousnesses are filthy rags before God (Isa. 64:6). But our works do follow us to heaven for the praise, honour and glory of Christ.

3. The promise is to those who persevere in the faith of Christ

'Behold, I come as a thief. Blessed is he that watcheth, and keepeth his garments, lest he walk naked, and they see his shame' (Rev. 16:15). God's saints live in anticipation of

Christ's coming to carry them home. We look for his second coming at any moment, and we look for him to come and carry us away by death at any moment. We are watching for him. We do not watch for him as we ought, but we do watch for him in faith. This is the constant life of faith. Faith never quits. Thus we keep our garments, the garments of salvation, persevering in faith (Matt. 10:22; 1 Cor. 15:1-3; Heb. 3:14; 10:23). Those who do not persevere unto the end, those who cast away the faith of Christ, never truly knew him. Being found naked, they will be ashamed and cast away for ever (Matt. 22:12-14).

4. The promise is to all who are called to the marriage supper of the Lamb

'Blessed are they which are called unto the marriage supper of the Lamb' (Rev. 19:9). The call spoken of here is the effectual call of grace, by which God the Holy Spirit brings chosen, redeemed sinners to Christ, creating faith in them by his irresistible power (Ps. 65:4; 1 Cor. 1:26-31). This is that distinctive, distinguishing call which separates the precious from the vile (Rom. 8:29; 1 Cor. 4:7).

5. The promise is to those who are born of God

'Blessed and holy is he that hath part in the first resurrection: on such the second death hath no power, but they shall be priests of God and of Christ, and shall reign with him a thousand years' (Rev. 20:6). This is not a promise to be fulfilled in some future millennial kingdom. The first resurrection is a spiritual resurrection. It is the new birth (John 5:25; Eph. 2:1-5). All who have been resurrected representatively with Christ must be resurrected from spiritual death by the Holy Spirit in the new birth, and will be resurrected physically at the Second Coming of Christ (Job 19:25-27). It is by virtue of this first resurrection that God's saints are made kings and priests unto God. 'And they shall never perish' (John 10:28)

6. The promise is to all who keep, or obey, the words of Christ

'Behold, I come quickly: blessed is he that keepeth the sayings of the prophecy of this book' (Rev. 22:7). 'The sayings of the prophecy of this book' are the commandments of the gospel issued to sinners in the book of Revelation. They are all matters of faith, acts of faith which grace alone can enable us to perform, but commandments which we are responsible to obey. Our Lord requires us, by an act of faith, to buy from him everlasting salvation (3:18; Isa. 55:1-3). He demands that any of his saints desiring communion with him open the door to him (3:20).Yet we know that if we open to him, it is because he put his hand to the door and opened it first (S. of S. 5:2-6). The Son of God also demands that all who follow him make a clean break from all false religion (18:4). And he calls whosoever will to come to him and drink of the water of life freely (22:17). All who obey his voice of grace have been blessed with grace from eternity (Eph. 1:3), and will be blessed with grace for ever.

7. The promise is to all who obey the commandments of God

'Blessed are they that do his commandments, that they may have right to the tree of life, and may enter in through the gates into the city' (Rev. 22:14). His commandments are very simple (1 John 3:23). Believing Christ, we offer to God perfect righteousness and the complete fulfilment of all his commandments (Rom. 3:28-31). All who believe on the Lord Jesus Christ have the right to live for ever. By the gift of God, the purchase of Christ and the imputation of righteousness to them, they are worthy to inherit eternal life (Col. 1:12).

63.

Four names for our Saviour

Revelation 22:16

'I Jesus have sent mine angel to testify unto you these things in the churches. I am the root and the offspring of David, and the bright and morning star' (Rev. 22:16).

Our Lord here uses four names to describe and identify himself. 'I Jesus have sent mine angel to testify unto you these things in the churches. I am the root and the offspring of David, and the bright and morning star.' In the Bible the names of Christ show us his personal character, covenant offices, mediatorial work and divine authority. In the Scriptures everything revolves around, is built upon, and points to, the name of our Lord Jesus Christ.

1. We are saved by faith in his name (Acts 4:12; 10:43).

2. We are baptized in the name of the Lord Jesus (Acts 2:38).

3. We pray in the name of Christ (John 14:13-14; 16:23-26).

4. We gather to worship in his name (Matt. 18:20).

5. We preach his name (Acts 9:15).

6. We suffer the afflictions of the gospel for his name's sake (Acts 5:41).

7. We are preserved, kept and accepted by God in his name (Rev. 22:4).

8. One day soon all the world will know his name
(Phil. 2:8-11).

The prophet Isaiah tells us, 'His name shall be called Wonderful, Counsellor, The mighty God, The everlasting Father,
The Prince of Peace' (Isa. 9:6). Our Lord's name tells us
who he is and what he does for us as our God and Saviour.
In this chapter we shall look at the meaning of the four
names used by our Saviour to describe himself in Revelation 22:16. As God the Holy Spirit gives understanding,
these names will yield to the believing heart both comfort
and strength.

'Jesus'

Though he is exalted in the glory of heaven, our Saviour
still wears the name of his humiliation to assure us that he
is the same now as he ever was. He says, 'I Jesus...' The
angel said to Joseph, 'Thou shalt call his name JESUS: for he
shall save his people from their sins' (Matt. 1:21). The name
of the incarnate Son of God is 'Jesus' — 'Deliverer'. It tells
us what he came into this world to do. This angelic messenger told Joseph, and us, three things about this 'Jesus'
who is the Christ of God.

1. He has a people in this world

Long before he came into the world, the Son of God had a
people in the world, chosen by him in eternal election and
given to him in the covenant of grace. There are many false
christs today called 'Jesus'. But the Jesus who is the Christ
of God is the Jesus of sovereign, electing grace (John 15:16;
Matt. 11:25-27). He has a people whom he must and will
save (John 10:16).

2. He came to save his people

This Jesus, who is the Christ, came into this world on an errand of mercy, with a mission to accomplish and a work to perform. The Son of God did not come into this world to start a new religion, to establish a Jewish kingdom, or to bring about a moral, social revolution. He came here to save his people from their sins. He did not come to provide salvation, but to save. He did not come to make salvation possible, but to save. He did not come to save all people in general, but his people in particular (John 6:37-40; Heb. 10:5-14).

3. He is an effectual, successful Saviour

He came to save his people from their sins, and save them he does. He saved all his people from the penalty of their sins by his obedience unto death (Heb. 9:12,26). He saves all his people from the power of their sins by his almighty power and sovereign grace in regeneration (John 17:2). He will save all his people from the presence of sin by bringing them home to heaven at last (Heb. 2:13). The Lord Jesus Christ is so glorious a Saviour that he saves his people from all sin, all the punishment of sin, all the consequences of sin and ultimately even from all the sorrow of sin. The Lord Jesus Christ, though he is exalted to heaven's glory, is still Jesus, the Friend of sinners. He says, 'I Jesus'. He is the same yesterday and today and for ever (Heb. 13:8).

'The Root of David'

This title simply means that Jesus Christ, the man, is himself Almighty God. He is the root, the source and cause of David's existence, faith, spiritual life and everlasting glory. David was what he was, did what he did and is what he is in heaven today, because of, and by the power of, Jesus

Christ, our eternal God. Let us never, for a moment, lose sight of this glorious truth: our blessed Saviour, Redeemer and King is himself God (John 1:1; 1 Tim. 3:16; Rom. 9:5; Acts 20:28; Col. 2:9-10).

'The Offspring of David'

That is to say, Christ Jesus is a man, born of the lineage of David and rightful heir to the throne of Israel, the Messiah. In Romans 1:1-5 the apostle Paul tells us that the gospel is 'of God ... promised ... by his prophets in the Holy Scriptures, concerning his Son ... made of the seed of David ... declared to be the Son of God ... by whom we have received grace' and faith. The gospel is the proclamation of the accomplishments of the Son of God in his incarnation.

God and man are for ever united in immutable and indissoluble union in the person of Jesus Christ. By means of his miraculous incarnation, the Son of God took manhood into union with himself. Every ransomed sinner ought constantly to give thanks to God for 'his unspeakable gift' (2 Cor. 9:15; Gal. 4:4-6). Only as man could he obey the law and suffer the penalty of the law for men (Heb. 2:10,17). But only as God could his obedience and death be effectual, meritorious and satisfying for the accomplishment of our salvation. Only a man in heaven could be touched with the feeling of our infirmities. But only God could effectually deliver us from those infirmities.

'The Bright and Morning Star'

He is the light by whom God is revealed and known to men. In his light we live now and will live for ever (John 1:5,9; 1 John 1:5-7; Rev. 21:23). The voice of prophecy announced Christ's coming as 'a Star out of Jacob' who should come (Num. 24:16-17). But here our Lord calls himself 'the bright and morning star'. The morning star does not merely give light. All the stars do that. The morning star announces and ushers in the day. That is what Christ is. He is the Bright and Morning Star who announces and ushers in the day.

His incarnation

When our Saviour first arose in this world, he dispelled the darkness of Judaism and ushered in the gospel day. Before he came, there were faint sparkles of light in the types and shadows of the law. But as soon as he began to preach the gospel, light shone into the world. The Pharisees obscured the law with their traditions in darkness. He gave light to the law. By his life, his death and his resurrection, our Lord fulfilled the dark shadows of the law. And by sending his Spirit and his gospel into the world, he dispelled the darkness of heathenism and brought the light of day. He appeared as 'the Dayspring from on high' (Luke 1:78), and 'the Sun of Righteousness with healing in his wings' (Mal. 4:2).

The experience of his people

In conversion Christ arises as the Day Star in the hearts of his people and drives away darkness (2 Peter 1:19). We see the glory of God in the face of Jesus Christ (2 Cor. 4:6). He enlightens our minds and instructs our hearts by his Spirit (1 Cor. 2:14-16). He gives hope of a brighter day (1 Cor. 13:12; Titus 2:11-14). Until Christ came to us in his saving grace, we groped about in darkness. Now we walk in the light, as he is in the light.

His second coming

When the Bright and Morning Star appears at the end of this world, he will introduce the great eternal day. In that great day, he will give his elect 'the morning star' and all that the morning star promises (Rev. 2:28). In that great day, our great Saviour will bring all things to light, and we shall see all things clearly. Then, but not until then, shall we understand all the purposes of God, all the dispensations of providence, all the work of redemption, all the fulness of the covenant, all the glory of grace — and why he saved us.

This is the name of our dear Saviour: 'Jesus' — our Saviour; 'the Root of David' — our God; 'the Offspring of David' — our mediator; 'The Bright and Morning Star' — our revelation.

64.

Come to the Saviour

Revelation 22:17

'And the Spirit and the bride say, Come. And let him that heareth say, Come. And let him that is athirst come. And whosoever will, let him take the water of life freely' (Rev. 22:17).

There is a vast difference between being religious and knowing the living God as he is revealed in his Son, the Lord Jesus Christ. We must never presume that people are saved, born again and truly know the Lord Jesus Christ simply because they attend church, participate in Bible studies, or even engage in a personal study of Holy Scripture. With that fact in mind, I want to persuade any reading these lines who have not yet come to Christ in faith to do so. I know of no better way to do so than to instruct you in the great and glorious truths of the gospel. As you read, pray that God the Holy Spirit will grant you life and faith in Christ. It is he who through the revelation of the gospel bids us come to the Saviour. Yet the most mature, well-taught and deeply experienced of God's saints will find the contents of this chapter comforting, edifying and delightful, as they are applied to their hearts by the Holy Spirit.

Five great gospel truths

1. God will save some

He has planned, purposed and predestinated the salvation
of a great multitude of sinners. He will save some. That is
certain (Rom. 8:29-30). He saves them by grace alone, without condition or qualification. If God has purposed to save
some, perhaps I am one, perhaps you are one. It may be
that he has kept you alive all this time so that he may be
gracious to you at this moment.

2. Christ has done it all

The Lord Jesus Christ has fully met and satisfied every requirement of God for the salvation of his elect. There is
nothing for us to do. Jesus Christ has done it all. All who
are saved are saved upon the basis of, and by the merits of,
Christ's obedience to God as the sinner's substitute (Rom.
5:19). He has finished the work of righteousness (John 17:4).
He has finished the work of redemption (John 19:30); that
is to say, he has both obeyed and satisfied all the demands
of God's holy law as the surety and representative of God's
elect.

3. Christ will save those for whom he died

God the Holy Spirit will effectually regenerate and call every
chosen, redeemed sinner to life and faith in Christ (Ps. 65:4;
John 6:63). Christ will save his sheep. Not one of God's
elect will perish. The Son of God will see of the travail of
his soul and be satisfied. Christ's blood was not shed in
vain. God's purpose will not be overturned. The grace of
God cannot be frustrated.

4. Every sinner who comes to Christ in faith is saved.

'He that believeth on the Son hath everlasting life' (John 3:36). Faith in Christ is the evidence of eternal election, effectual redemption and saving grace (Heb. 11:1). If you trust Christ, you have life. It really is as simple as that. Your faith is the fruit and result of God's predestination, Christ's redemption and the Spirit's call.

5. Sinners are urged to come to Christ

Every sinner who hears (or reads) the gospel is called, invited and urged to come to Christ and live (Rev. 22:17). You are invited, you are called, you are urged to come to Christ. The blessings held forth to you in the Word of life are rich beyond expression. The invitations given to you in the gospel are as free as sunshine. Throughout the Scriptures every encouragement is given to sinners to 'lay hold upon the hope that is set before you' in the gospel. Everything in the Bible is designed by God to encourage sinners to come to Christ and live. There is not a word in Scripture to discourage any sinner from trusting Christ. And here, at the close of the inspired volume, invitations are heaped upon invitations from every quarter, urging you to enter the door of mercy before it is closed: 'And the Spirit and the bride say, Come. And let him that heareth say, Come. And let him that is athirst come. And whosoever will, let him take of the water of life freely.'

If you come to the Lord Jesus Christ by faith you will have eternal life. If you come to Christ, you have already passed from death unto life, and will never, under any circumstances, come into condemnation (John 5:24). We do not believe on Christ in order to be born again; we believe on Christ because we have been born again. Faith is not our contribution to the work of grace; our faith is the fruit of grace already bestowed (Gal. 5:22; Eph. 2:8; Phil. 1:29; Col. 2:12).

A gospel invitation

'And the Spirit and the bride say, Come. And let him that heareth say, Come. And let him that is athirst come. And whosoever will, let him take the water of life freely.' I know that sinners are commanded to trust Christ. And I know that it is the responsibility of every sinner to do so. Yet the Lord Jesus, by his Spirit, in the gospel, also gently woos and invites needy sinners to come to him, and tenderly urges them to do so (Matt. 11:28-30; 23:37). The spirit of this passage is not so much that of an authoritative command as it is that of a tender, loving, urgent invitation. It is an invitation from three sources.

1. The Spirit says, 'Come'

It is the work of God the Holy Spirit to reveal Christ to men and effectually bring sinners to him in repentance and faith, causing them to look to him and be saved (Zech. 12:10; John 16:7-13). Whenever the Word comes in power, it comes in the power, not of men, but of the Holy Spirit, who alone can conquer the hearts of men and bring them effectually to Christ (1 Thess. 1:4-5). Only God the Holy Spirit can give life to the dead, faith to the faithless and grace to the graceless. The success of the gospel is not determined by the ability and ingenuity of preachers, but by the power of God the Holy Spirit. By the ministry of his servants preaching the gospel of Christ, the Holy Spirit pleads with and beseeches sinners to come to Christ (2 Cor. 5:18-21). By the voices of men the Spirit of God urges sinners to come to Christ. Yet, sincere as these gospel invitations are, they will be unheeded by those who hear them unless the Spirit of God graciously arrests them, compels them and forces them to come. It takes more than an invitation to get sinners to trust Christ. It takes a mighty operation of grace (Col. 2:12).

Man has neither the ability nor the will to come to Christ (John 6:44; 5:40). Only God the Holy Spirit can make you willing and give you the ability to come to Christ (Ps. 110:3).

2. The bride says, 'Come'

The bride is the church, the Lamb's wife. Because she has experienced the blessedness of salvation, she is anxious for all around her to know its delight. Those who have experienced grace are anxious to see others experience it too. In the Song of Solomon, the church cries, 'Draw me, we will run after thee' (1:4), as if to say, 'Draw me and I will not be content to come alone. I will do everything in my power to bring others with me.' This is the work of the church in every age. She is the pillar and ground of the truth. She supports the truth, proclaims the truth, publishes the truth and seeks to bring men and women into the knowledge of the truth. The church of God unites with the Spirit of God and says, 'Come. Come to the Saviour. See what a wonderful Saviour he is. See in us what Christ can do for you. You are far off, but Christ can bring you nigh. You are strangers, foreigners and aliens from the commonwealth of Israel, but Christ can make you heirs of God. You are dead, but Christ can give you life. You are lost, but Christ can save you. You are sinful, but Christ can make you holy. Come, and see!'

3. 'And let him that heareth say, Come'

All who have heard and believe the gospel are to be actively engaged in the furtherance of the gospel. Let us use every means at our disposal and every opportunity given to induce sinners to come to Christ. Each one is to be a preacher in his own circle (John 1:35-49).

This gracious invitation is both free and universal

It is an unconditional offer of grace to all who will but come to Christ. All who are thirsty are welcome to come. The invitation is to you: 'And let him that is athirst come.' Every mourning, broken, heavy-hearted sinner in the universe is bidden to come. Perhaps you think, 'I am not thirsty enough. I would come, but I do not really pant and thirst for Christ as I should, as the hart pants for the water-brooks. If I had greater thirst, then I could come to Christ.' If that is the case, answer this question: are you willing to come to Christ? If you are willing to come, you are welcome to come. The invitation reads, 'And whosoever will, let him take the water of life freely.' Are you inclined to come to Christ? Do you desire to come to Christ? Will you come to Christ? If you will come, you can come and may come. That is the rub: will you come to Christ? Will you be saved by grace alone? Will you be saved by the righteousness of another? Will you be saved by the blood of Jesus? If you are willing to come, the invitation is free and unconditional. 'Let him take,' by personal faith, 'the water of life,' Christ Jesus, 'freely', without cost, condition, or cause.

This invitation is easily obeyed

This is what must be done: 'Come.' This coming is not a physical act involving the body. It is a spiritual act of the heart and mind. Right where you sit, without moving a muscle, come to Jesus Christ now. To come to Christ is to trust him. Come like the leper — in submission (Matt. 8:2). Come like the woman with an issue of blood — in desperation (Matt. 9:20-21). Come like Bartimaeus — in earnest (Mark 10:46-52). Come like the Gadarene — naked and vile (Mark 5:1-15). Come like the tax collector — a sinner needing mercy (Luke 18:13). Come like the thief — to be remembered (Luke 23:42). Come like the adulterous woman — with all your accusers (John 8:1-12). But come to the Saviour!

Obedience to this invitation is richly rewarded

If you do come to Christ, you will be saved. Come to Christ any way you can, any way you will, believing on him, trusting him alone to save you. He promises, 'Him that cometh to me I will in no wise cast out' (John 6:37). Come to Christ in faith and eternal life is yours. The blessings of grace in Christ are called the 'water of life'. The source from which this water of life flows is the Lord Jesus Christ himself (Rev. 22:1). As the waters gushed out of the smitten rock in the wilderness to supply life to Israel, so our Lord Jesus Christ, smitten by the rod of God's law and justice, pours out the waters of salvation upon perishing sinners (1 Cor. 10:4).

Christ is the fountain of living waters, who gives life and grace to thirsty sinners (Rev. 21:6; John 4:10-14; 7:37-38). Pardon (Zech. 13:1; Isa. 1:18; 1 John 1:7), holiness (Ezek. 36:25-27) and everlasting life are found in this fountain of living waters (Ps. 36:8-9). The Lord Jesus Christ is a fountain opened to sinners. He is not a sealed fountain, but an opened fountain. He is not a secret fountain, hidden in the mists of religious confusion, but an opened fountain. This fountain was opened in the covenant, opened at the cross, and is opened by the faithful exposition of the gospel. None who drinks of this fountain shall be disappointed (John 7:37-39; 4:14). May God give you grace to come to the fountain and drink.

'And the Spirit and the bride say, Come. And let him that heareth say, Come. And let him that is athirst come. And whosoever will, let him take of the water of life freely.'

65.

The perfection and sanctity of the Scriptures

Revelation 22:18-19

'For I testify unto every man that heareth the words of the prophecy of this book, If any man shall add unto these things, God shall add unto him the plagues that are written in this book' (Rev. 22:18).

Revelation 22:18-19 stands as a flaming sword planted by God to guard the canon of Holy Scripture from profane hands. Similar passages are found in the Old Testament Scriptures. After the giving of the law, God gave a strict command forbidding anyone to add a single word to it or take a single word from it (Deut. 4:2). And when he gave his final word of prophecy in the Old Testament, the Lord placed the same prohibition upon the words of the prophets (Mal. 4:4; cf. Deut. 4:10). Here, as he concludes the volume of inspiration, in the most solemn manner possible, our Lord warns all men that none dare add anything to, or take anything away from, the holy Word of God. Any who dare to do so will suffer all the terrible wrath of God for ever in hell without mercy.

The person speaking in this text is the Lord Jesus Christ himself. He holds the volume of Holy Scripture before us, elevating it to the position of highest possible reverence. It is written in the Psalms: 'Thou hast magnified thy word above all thy name' (Ps. 138:2). The warnings given here indicate that God regards nothing as more sacred than his

Word and looks upon the contempt of his Word as the highest crime and most hideously evil thing in the world.

That book which God has so highly magnified is the inspired Word of God. Without question, there is a particular reference in this text to the book of the Revelation of Jesus Christ. This last book of the inspired volume is of equal value and authority with the other sixty-five. However, because this book, by the arrangement of divine providence, closes the sacred volume, it is reasonable for us to assume that the warnings of this text extend to and include the entire Bible, from the opening word 'In ...' in Genesis to the final 'Amen' in Revelation. The entire Bible is the Word of God, authoritative, complete, perfect and holy, a book to be reverenced, believed and obeyed.

The divine authority of the Scriptures

I cannot stress enough the importance of what I am about to write. It may seem trite and insignificant to some. But this is one of the most profound statements you will ever read or hear, and one of the most important: that book which we call the Holy Bible, the book you probably have open before you as you read these words, is the Word of God! Its every word is inspired, infallible and holy. It contains no errors, contradictions, or inaccurate statements. It was written by 'holy men of God [who] spake as they were moved by the Holy Ghost' (2 Peter 1:21).

A book with one message

The message of the Bible is redemption by the blood of Christ and salvation by his grace. The scarlet thread which runs through every page of the book and binds them all together is the message of blood atonement by Jesus Christ, the Son of God (Luke 24:27,44-47; John 1:45; 5:39; Acts 10:43; 13:29). The Word of God might be compared to the alabaster box that was brought into Simon's house in Bethany (Mark 14:1-9) containing 'ointment of spikenard very precious'. When the box was broken and the ointment poured out, the sweet fragrance filled the room. Gospel preachers are like the woman who brought the box and broke it open. They come to the house of God with the Word of God, break it open and, as they expound the Scriptures, the sweet fragrance of Christ crucified fills the house. Those who faithfully expound the Scriptures proclaim Christ crucified (1 Cor. 1:23; 2:2), for he is the theme of all the Scriptures. The Old Testament declares that the Redeemer is coming. The four Gospels and the epistles tell us that the Redeemer has come. The book of Revelation promises us that the Redeemer is coming again.

The Bible alone can make us wise unto salvation (2 Tim. 3:15)

The Bible raises and answers every question regarding life and death, and eternal life and eternal death. If we want to know where and how life began, we need only to read the Word of God (Gen. 1:1; 2:7; John 1:1-3; Heb. 1:1-3). The facts of creation given throughout the Scriptures, unlike the theories of speculative science and vain philosophy, are in total agreement with one another and cannot be refuted.

If anyone is interested in knowing how the human race came to be in such a mess, he needs only to read the Word of God. We got into the state we are in through the sin and fall of our father Adam (Gen. 3; Rom. 5:12). We all became sinners by his sin. He was our representative before God. In him, the whole human race died spiritually. From him we all inherit our sinful nature. All human beings are born, as the children of Adam, in spiritual death, with depraved hearts, and go forth from the womb speaking lies (Ps. 51:5; 58:3; Matt. 15:19; Eph. 2:1-3).

If anyone wants to know the way out of the mess we are in, he needs only to read the Word of God. God's remedy for man's ruin is his own dear Son, the Lord Jesus Christ, the sinner's substitute, the Last Adam (John 3:14-16; 1 Cor. 15:21-22). By his obedience to the law and will of God as their representative, Christ brought in everlasting righteousness for his people, which God the Father imputes to all who believe on him (Rom. 5:19; 2 Cor. 5:21). The Lord Jesus took upon himself the sins of his people, died in their place and, by his blood, took away the curse of the law and the wrath of God, having satisfied the justice of God for their sins (Gal. 3:13). Sinners must be born again by the grace and power of God the Holy Spirit. There is no other way of salvation and life (John 3:5-7; Eph. 2:8-9). This great salvation is freely given to every sinner who believes on the Lord Jesus Christ (Rom. 3:28). And even the faith by which we believe on Christ is the gift of God (Eph. 2:8). So the whole work of salvation is by the grace of God and for the glory of God (1Cor. 1:30-31).

All men know by nature that there is life after death. All are conscious of that fact. But should anyone want to know what awaits him in eternity, again, he needs only to read the Bible (Luke 16:19-31; 2 Cor. 5:1-11; Heb. 9:27; Rev. 20:11 – 21:8). We are all creatures with immortal souls. We shall spend eternity somewhere, either in the torments of the damned or in the bliss of the saved, either in the presence of the devil or in the presence of God, either in hell or in heaven. In the resurrection day our bodies and souls will be reunited, either to everlasting damnation or to everlasting righteousness and life with Christ (John 5:28-29).

The Bible meets our every need

The Bible is able to meet every moral, spiritual and emotional need of our lives (2 Tim. 3:16-17). Everything that is needed for the temporal and eternal welfare of our souls is revealed in the Word of God. As we have already seen, the Bible tells us how spiritual life is imparted to the soul by divine regeneration, through the preaching of the gospel, and preserved and carried on to perfection by divine grace. The Bible tells us how to behave in every relationship and circumstance of life. The path of life is plainly marked out for us in the Word of God. The Bible teaches us how to live in this world in patience, comfort and hope (Rom. 15:4), submitting to the will of God, trusting the providence of God, waiting for the promises of God (Hab. 2:3; 3:17-19).

The authority of the Scriptures

The Bible alone is authoritative in the church and kingdom of God. It is our only rule of faith and practice. We have no right to believe any doctrine that is not specifically taught in the Bible, and we have no right to reject any doctrine that is taught in the Bible. We have no right to practise any form of worship that is not specifically taught in the Bible, and we have no right to reject any form of worship that is taught in the Bible.

The perfection of the Scriptures

That to which nothing can be added and from which nothing can be taken away is perfect and complete. When John wrote, 'Amen', at the end of verse 21, the Scriptures were perfect, complete, lacking nothing. It is to this perfection that Paul refers in 1 Corinthians 13:8-10. As the revelation of God, the Scriptures are perfect. There are many things about God which are, for the present, hidden from us. Those secret things belong to the Lord. But everything needful and useful for our souls is revealed in this book, revealed fully and revealed perfectly. There is nothing to be known about God in this world which is not revealed in his written Word. It clearly reveals and teaches the perfections of his being (Exod. 33:18-19; Isa. 45:18-22; 1 John 5:7), the purpose of his grace (Eph. 1:3-14; Rom. 8:28-30; 9:11-23), the meaning of his providence (Rom. 8:28) and the fulness of his perfect will (Prov. 3:5-6).There is nothing lacking in the Word of God, nothing to be added to it, no additional visions, prophecies, or revelations are needed, and none are to be accepted.

The sanctity of the Scriptures

A very solemn warning is given by God regarding his Word. Any alteration of it is strictly forbidden, upon penalty of the most severe consequences. If any man adds to the inspired writings, God will add to that man all the plagues of eternal damnation. If any man takes away from the inspired writings, God will take away from that man all that he appears to have: all life, all grace and all hope. The denunciations of God's wrath are never so full and comprehensive as they are in these two verses. God will not allow any man to suppress or add a single word. This is the sanctity of the Scriptures. If we presume to suppress, or leave out, anything God has revealed, that would be a denial of God's wisdom. If we presume to add our words to the Word of God, that would be a claim of equality with God. We dare not modify God's law. We dare not modify God's gospel. We dare not modify God's ordinances. We must take the whole Word of God, just as it is given. To alter it in any way is to court eternal damnation. This is the sanctity God has placed

upon his Word. No man is to touch it — no preacher, no
church, no denomination! Our Lord demands our reverence for the Scriptures. The Bible is the Word of God. Let
us reverence it as the Word of God. It is to be read prayer-
fully, preached faithfully, heard believingly, submitted to
willingly and obeyed implicitly!

66.
Pictures of Christ in Revelation

Revelation 22:20

'Even so, come, Lord Jesus' (Rev. 22:20).

The book of Revelation reveals many things which must come to pass. The prophecies of this book are matters of absolute certainty. All that is revealed in these twenty-two chapters is fixed by God's immutable, unalterable decree. We look upon the promises and prophecies of Holy Scripture as matters of certainty because we know that they are matters of divine predestination. Were God not totally sovereign, both in predestination and in providence, no promise of God could be believed with confidence, and no prophecy of Scripture could be looked upon as that which must come to pass. But this book is the revelation of one who is sovereign in all things and over all things. Therefore the prophecies it contains are certain. The church of God will be triumphant at last. The gospel of Christ will be victorious. God's elect will all be saved. The enemies of Christ and his people will be put to open and endless shame. And the Lord Jesus Christ, the Lamb of God, into whose hands all things have been committed, will be glorified in all things.

The most prominent and glorious prophecy that is yet to be fulfilled is the Second Coming of our Lord Jesus Christ. That is the subject of Revelation 22:20: 'He which testifieth these things saith, Surely I come quickly. Amen. Even so, come, Lord Jesus.' With those words the Holy Spirit teaches us three things about the Second Coming of our Lord Jesus Christ.

The Second Coming of Christ is certain

It is the Lord Jesus himself who speaks first. He says, 'He which testifieth these things saith, Surely I come.' I make no effort to prove that Christ is coming a second time to this earth with power and great glory. Scoffers and infidels do not bother me, and I will not bother them. I refuse to mar the beauty of the gospel by lowering it to speculation, investigation and argument. We simply declare the naked truth of God and demand that all men believe that which God has revealed. Any who refuse to believe God's revelation on its own merits will perish for ever under the wrath of God.

However, in this text, the Lord Jesus Christ does emphasize the certainty of his second coming. He says, 'Surely,' in spite of all the mockery of scoffing infidels, 'I come.' In that declaration our Saviour is graciously assuring us of his glorious advent. Knowing the weakness of our flesh, knowing our tendency to forget his promise and see only our present trouble, our dear Saviour condescends to our need and gives this word to drive away doubt and unbelief: 'Surely I come!'

It has been almost two thousand years now since our Lord died for us and ascended back into heaven. Men everywhere say, 'Where is the promise of his coming?' God forbid that we should be among them. There is a day and an hour appointed by God from eternity when Jesus Christ our Lord will come again to bring in the fulness of that everlasting covenant of grace, ordered in all things and sure. Christ, who loved us and gave himself for us, will come to gather us unto himself. As he ransomed our souls from the curse of the law and delivered our hearts from the bondage of sin, the Son of God will yet retrieve our bodies from the power of the grave. 'He shall see of the travail of his soul and shall be satisfied.' The Second Coming of Christ is promised repeatedly throughout the Scriptures. In fact, the Bible is so full of promises regarding the Second Coming of our Lord that it cannot be denied without denouncing the Word of God as a mere religious myth that is full of lies.

The patriarchs of old, those fathers of the church who were examples of faith, spoke plainly of our Lord's second coming. I do not know how much those ancient believers knew, or how clear their knowledge was. But they knew more than most religious people in these 'enlightened' times. They knew that God would come in the flesh to redeem his elect by substitutionary atonement (Gen. 22:8). And they knew that this God-man Redeemer would come again in glory to reign for ever. Enoch, who lived before the flood, gave a full description of Christ's coming in power and great glory (Jude 14-15). Job, who probably lived in the days of Abraham, lived in hope and expectation of Christ's second coming (Job 19:25-29). And David, the sweet singer of Israel, spoke with joy of the Lord's coming to judge the world (Ps. 96:13; 98:9).

All the prophets, since the beginning of the world, spoke of Christ's second coming with precise language (Acts 3:21). To those men of God in the Old Testament, Christ's second coming was no more vague or uncertain than his first coming. They anticipated his coming in glory as much as they did his coming in humiliation (Dan. 7:13-14; 12:1-3; Zech. 14:3-9; Mal. 4:1-3).

Throughout the days of his earthly ministry, our Saviour taught his disciples to look for and anticipate his second advent. While our Lord plainly declared that no man could know the day or hour of his coming (Matt. 24:36;

25:13; Acts 1:7), he did speak frequently, plainly and posi-
tively of that day when he would personally come again
(Matt. 24:27,30,36-37; 25:1,5-6,10,31-46; John 14:1-3).

Even the angels of God have been employed by our Lord
to assure us of his glorious second advent (Acts 1:11).

Throughout the book of Acts the apostles went everywhere preaching the lordship of Christ and his second coming in glory. They constantly declared Christ's sovereign
dominion as Lord and the certainty of his coming again to
judgement (3:19-21; 17:30-31). The same is true of their
inspired writings in the epistles of the New Testament, in
which we are constantly taught to watch for our Lord's return (1 Thess. 4:13-18; Titus 2:10-14; 2 Peter 3:9-14; 1 John
3:1-3).

And, of course, the book of Revelation repeatedly declares the promise of our Lord's return (1:7; 3:11; 22:7,12,20).
We are never told to look for signs of his coming, or given
any hint as to when our Lord will come again, but we are
constantly urged to be on the watch for his return with
immediate hope and the expectation of faith. If the Bible is
truly the Word of God, if there is a God in heaven, if there
is any hope for fallen men, then it is certain that Jesus Christ
will come again. This is his testimony: 'Surely, I come!'

Christ will come quickly

Our Saviour says, 'Surely I come quickly.' And he means
quickly. Time, in our very limited view of things, seems to
be very, very long. But with God one day is as a thousand
years, and a thousand years is as one day. When our Lord
was upon the earth, he spoke of his second coming as being at hand. Paul wrote of Christ's coming in the language
of immediate anticipation. And we should look for our Lord
to return quickly.

The word 'quickly' means two things. First, our Lord Jesus Christ will soon appear. There are no signs to be given, or prophecies to be fulfilled. Christ Jesus may come at any moment. Second, Christ will come suddenly, without warning! Whether viewed from the standpoint of Christ's coming to call men away from this state of existence at the hour of death, or from the standpoint of his glorious second advent, the Lord's coming will be sudden and without warning. While it is true that he sometimes gives advance warning of death, even then the fatal disease or other forerunner of death overcomes the one to be taken so suddenly that death usually takes men by surprise and unprepared.

In the light of these facts, what manner of persons ought we to be? (See 2 Peter 3:9-15). We ought always to live in the immediate prospect of eternity. Like Paul, let us make it our hearts' desire and determination to be found in Christ, seeking to know him, possess him and be possessed by him (Phil. 3:8-14).

The Second Coming of Christ is greatly desired by his people (Titus 2:11-14)

'The Spirit and the Bride say, Come.' And when John heard the Saviour say, 'Surely I come quickly,' his heart's immediate response was, 'Amen. Even so, come, Lord Jesus.' He said, 'That's it. That's what I want! So be it. Come, my Lord and my Saviour.' How is it possible for sinful men and women, who know themselves to be sinners altogether fit for hell and unfit for heaven by nature, to love Christ's appearing and anxiously desire it? Let me give you three answers to that question:

   1. Because we look to Christ alone as our Saviour, we look for Christ anxiously. Christ alone is all our

hope before God (1 Cor. 1:30). His blood is our only atonement for sin, and his righteousness is our only righteousness before God. Believing him, we have all that God demands of us and are accepted in the Beloved (Rom. 3:28,31; Eph. 1:6).

2. Because we have the earnest of the Spirit, we groan for our heavenly inheritance (Eph. 1:14; 2 Cor. 5:5; Rom. 8:16-23). God the Holy Spirit, by giving us faith in Christ, has sealed to our hearts all the blessings and benefits of the covenant of grace, assuring us that we are indeed the sons and daughters of God.

3. Because we have a good hope through grace, we anxiously await the fulfilment of our hope (Rom. 8:24-25; 1 John 3:1-2). We who believe on the Lord Jesus Christ live in hope of all that he has purchased for us and promised to us (1 Cor. 15:51-58). When he comes, he will be satisfied with us (Isa. 53:11), and we shall be satisfied with him (Eph. 5:25-27). 'Amen. Even so, come, Lord Jesus.'

67.

The benediction

Revelation 22:21

'The grace of our Lord Jesus Christ be with you all' (Rev. 22:21).

The book of Revelation is identified in the first verse of the first chapter as 'the Revelation of Jesus Christ'. Setting forth the theme of the whole book, it rings out the precious name of our Lord Jesus Christ. The last verse of the last chapter repeats the heavenly sound. The Lord Jesus Christ is the sum, substance and glory of every vision seen by John on the island of Patmos. All that John saw and wrote in this book by the inspiration of God the Holy Spirit was about the glorious person and gracious work of our Lord Jesus Christ. And before he laid his pen aside to write no more, he penned his benediction in these words: 'The grace of our Lord Jesus Christ be with you all. Amen.' This was John's prayer for God's elect. It is an invocation of blessing upon all the saints of God in every place.

The words of the benediction

How often we read and hear these words without thought or attention! Most commentators either ignore them entirely, or give them only passing attention. Many have heard them recited as part of a religious ceremony, but have never had the words explained to them. That ought not to be the case. The words of this text are full of spiritual instruction, recorded here by God the Holy Spirit, 'for our learning, that we through patience and comfort of the scriptures might have hope' (Rom. 15:4). Read the text again, slowly, pausing between the words to meditate upon and enjoy this final word from God to man.

'Lord'

The grace we need, the grace John seeks here for God's people, is the grace of our Lord and Master. Grace comes from His Majesty. It is the benefit of his sovereign pleasure. It is the gift of his will. It is the blessing of his throne. Grace belongs to God. And God the Father has given it to his Son as our mediator, whom he has made Lord over all flesh, to give to whomsoever he will (John 17:2). He has mercy on whom he will have mercy. He has compassion on whom he will have compassion. And he is gracious to whom he will be gracious.

'Jesus'

He is the Lord; therefore he has the right to be gracious. And he is Jesus our Saviour; therefore we know that he will be gracious. His grace is redeeming, saving, preserving, forgiving, justifying, sanctifying, glorifying grace. All grace is in Christ, and if we are in Christ all grace is ours in him (Eph. 1:3).

'Christ'

He is the 'Anointed One'. As Aaron was anointed with holy oil, Christ our great High Priest is anointed with grace. As the oil ran down over Aaron's beard and his robe, so the grace of God runs down from Christ our Head to all the members of his body, the church, giving us both the knowledge of, and acceptance with, God himself.

'Our'

Did you notice that little word 'our'? What a precious word! What a word of boldness, confidence and faith! John calls the Lord Jesus Christ, the God of the universe, the Lord of glory, 'our Lord Jesus Christ'! He is ours because he has made himself to be ours. He is ours by covenant agreement. And he is ours by faith. But he is ours! And if the Lord Jesus Christ is ours, then all the grace that he possesses is surely ours too.

'... be with you'

Therefore John says, 'The grace of our Lord Jesus Christ be with you.' This was John's prayer and desire for all his brethren in his day, and for all who would read his book in the days to come. I want to draw your attention to three things about this benediction, given by the inspiration of God the Spirit.

The blessing of it

The one thing we need and must have is grace. And grace is the blessing upon which John focuses his own attention and ours. The word used here is *'charis'*. It is the word from which we get our English word, 'charismatic'. It signifies love, kindness and favour. The root of the word *'charis'* is joy. Wherever grace is known and experienced, joy is also found. John is saying, 'Oh, that you may have the grace, the love, kindness and favour, of our Lord Jesus Christ, and the joy it brings!'

The grace mentioned in this benediction is divine grace

It is 'the grace of our Lord'. The original source of grace is
the everlasting love of God for his people (Deut. 7:8). God
the Father, God the Son and God the Holy Spirit loved us
before the world began. And because God loved us, he is
gracious to us. It is written: 'I have loved thee with an everlasting love: therefore with loving kindness have I drawn
thee' (Jer. 31:3). All grace comes to us from God the Father,
through God the Son, by God the Holy Spirit.

The grace spoken of is 'the grace of our Lord'

It is divine grace. Yet, it is 'the grace of our Lord Jesus Christ'.
That is to say, it is also the grace of a man, the God-man,
our Saviour. This grace has the stamp of deity upon it, but
it also has the stamp of humanity upon it. It is the tender,
compassionate, brotherly grace of our near kinsman. As
Ruth possessed all the love of Boaz, God's elect always possess all the love, grace and mercy of their dear Kinsman's
heart, the grace of that wondrous, mysterious, complex,
delightful person who is both God and man, Immanuel,
our Lord Jesus Christ. Here are nine things revealed in the
Word of God about the grace of our Lord Jesus Christ.

It is sure, covenant grace (Jer. 31:31-34; 2 Sam.
23:5).
It is eternal, electing grace (Eph. 1:3-6).
It is redeeming, justifying grace (Rom. 3:24-26).
It is effectual, saving grace (Eph. 2:8-9).
It is sovereign, distinguishing grace (Rom. 9:11-23).
It is infinite, rich grace (Eph. 3:8; Rom. 5:21; see
1Cor. 1:26-31).
It is immutable, preserving grace (Mal. 3:6; John
10:28-30).

It is daily, providential grace (Rom. 8:28).
It is unconditional, free grace (Rom. 9:16).

This is my heart's prayer and desire for you who read these lines, as it was John's prayer and desire for all who read what he had written: 'The grace [all the grace] of our Lord Jesus Christ be with you all' — young and old, rich and poor, strong and weak. May you trust the grace of our Lord Jesus Christ. May you enjoy all the favours that flow to sinners in the boundless river of grace. May you know the sweet communion of grace. May the grace of our Lord Jesus Christ be with you always and for ever: when you pray, when you are tempted, when you are discouraged, when you are tired, when you are weak, when you are in danger, when your heart and flesh fail you, when you have fallen, when you die and when you stand before God. The blessing of this benediction is grace, 'the grace of our Lord Jesus Christ'.

The position of it

This benediction is at the end. Divine providence has made it the last word of the book of the Revelation, the last word of the Bible, the last word from God to man. It is as though John were saying, as though God through John were saying, 'Whatever else you may miss, be sure you do not miss this. You must have grace.' Let the preacher, while preaching grace to others, be sure he possesses grace. Let the deacon, as he serves the church, be sure he is in the church. Let the teacher, as he teaches about the Saviour, be sure he knows the Saviour. When you eat the Lord's Supper, be sure you have eaten his flesh and drunk his blood by faith. Have you been baptized in water, professing faith in Christ? Be sure you have been baptized into Jesus Christ. We must have 'the grace of our Lord Jesus Christ', or we shall perish, no matter what else we have.

As the children of God, those to whom Christ is revealed and by whom he is known, grace is the one thing we must have as long as we are in this world. Therefore John says, 'The grace of our Lord Jesus Christ be with you all.' We shall need it to the end to cleanse, teach, guide, protect, strengthen, restore, comfort and keep us. If we have 'the grace of our Lord Jesus Christ' we have all we need. He said, 'My grace is sufficient for thee.' The fact that this blessing has been placed at the end of the Bible indicates to me that grace is the one and only thing we shall want when the end comes. When our appointed end comes, we shall care for nothing but 'the grace of our Lord Jesus Christ'.

The certainty of it

Look at the last word in the benediction: 'Amen'. That word, given by divine inspiration, means, 'So shall it be!' And so it shall be! It is a matter of certainty! The grace of our Lord Jesus Christ will indeed be with all those to whom the book of Revelation is addressed. The grace of Christ will be with all the churches of Christ. The grace of Christ will be with all God's elect. The grace of Christ will be with all who trust Christ. Amen.